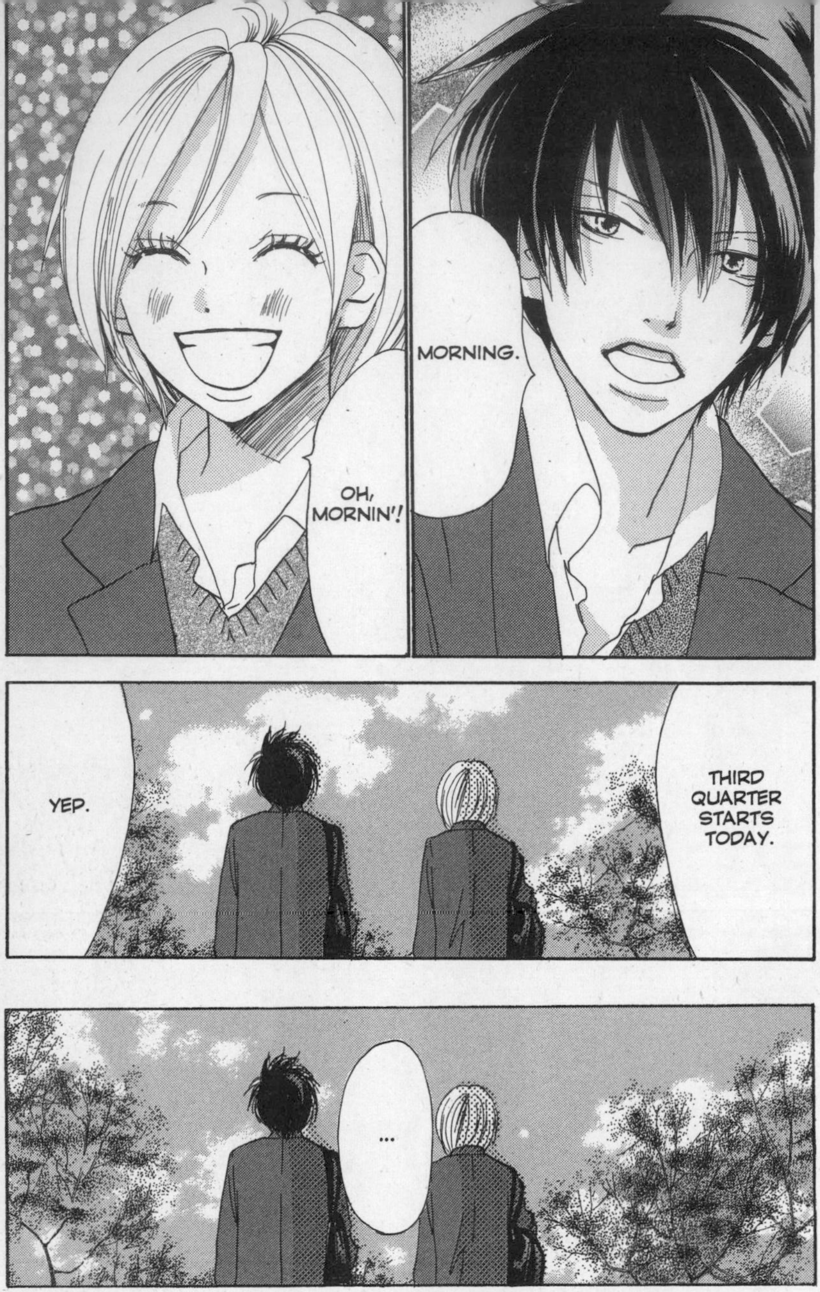
MORNING.
OH, MORNIN'!
THIRD QUARTER STARTS TODAY.
YEP.
...

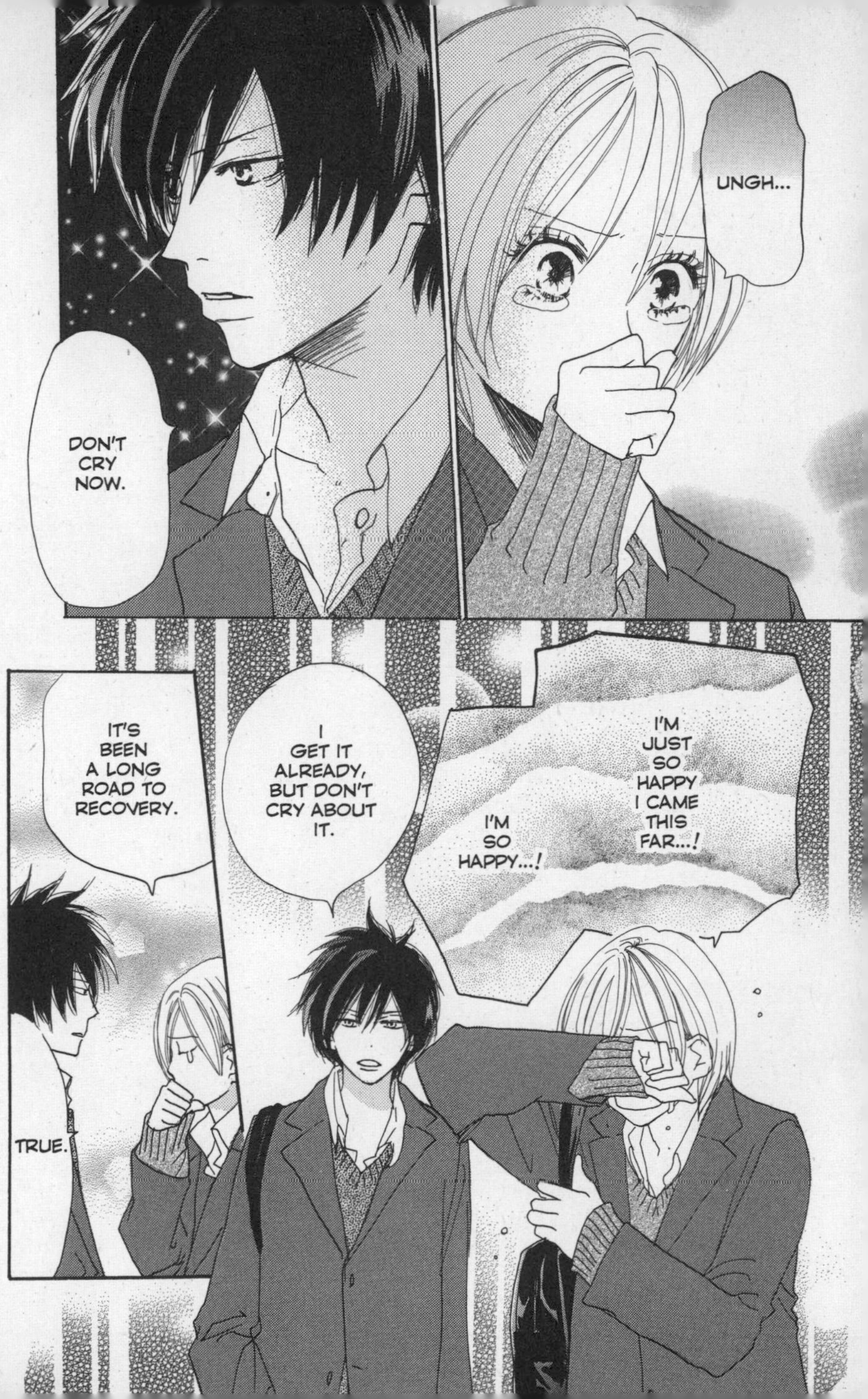
UNGH...
DON'T CRY NOW.
I'M JUST SO HAPPY I CAME THIS FAR...!
I'M SO HAPPY...!
I GET IT ALREADY, BUT DON'T CRY ABOUT IT.
IT'S BEEN A LONG ROAD TO RECOVERY.
TRUE.

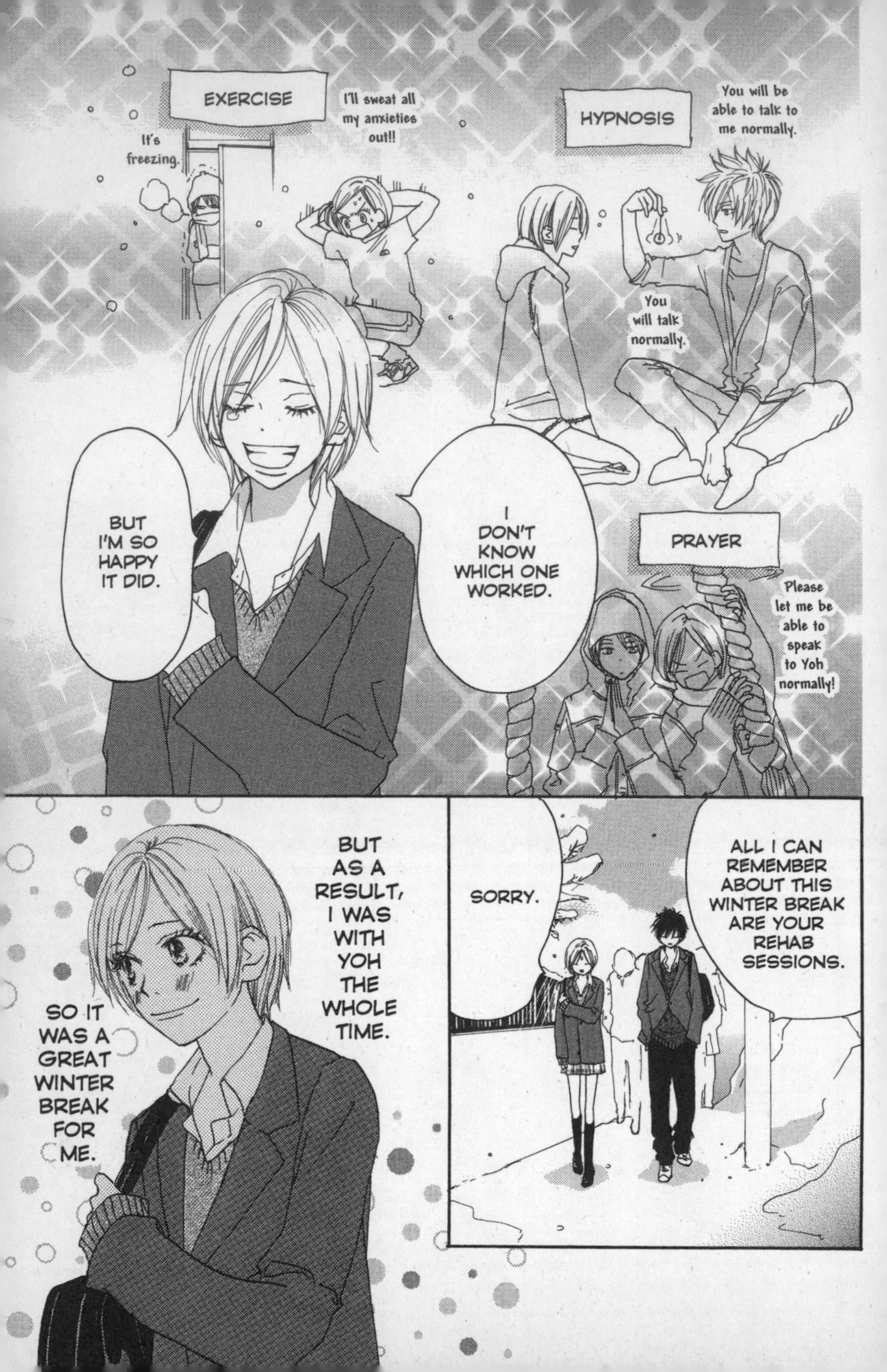
HYPNOSIS
You will be able to talk to me normally.
You will talk normally.
EXERCISE
I'll sweat all my anxieties out!!
It's freezing.
PRAYER
Please let me be able to speak to Yoh normally!
I DON'T KNOW WHICH ONE WORKED.
BUT I'M SO HAPPY IT DID.
ALL I CAN REMEMBER ABOUT THIS WINTER BREAK ARE YOUR REHAB SESSIONS.
SORRY.
BUT AS A RESULT, I WAS WITH YOH THE WHOLE TIME.
SO IT WAS A GREAT WINTER BREAK FOR ME.

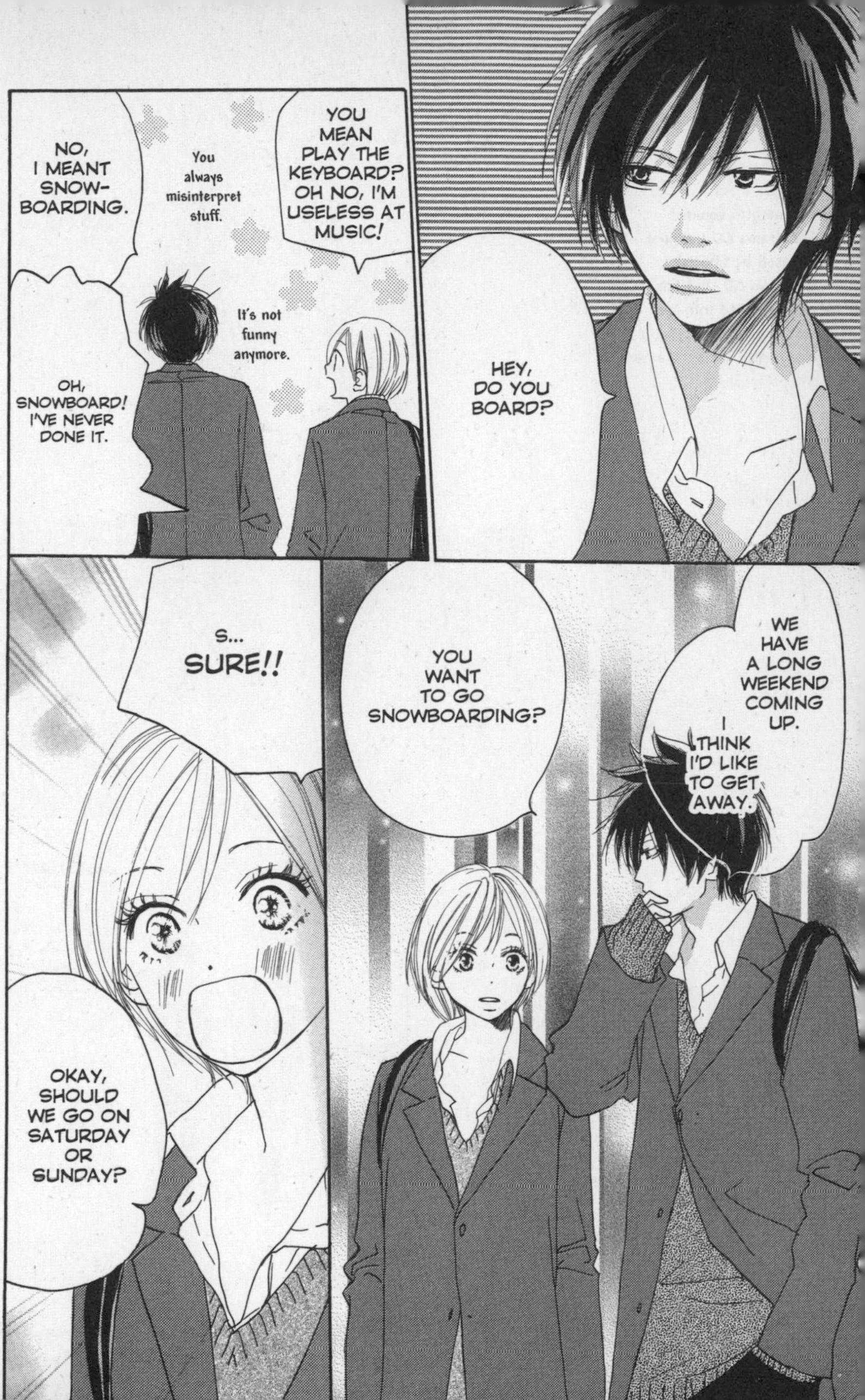
HEY, DO YOU BOARD?
YOU MEAN PLAY THE KEYBOARD? OH NO, I'M USELESS AT MUSIC!
You always misinterpret stuff.
NO, I MEANT SNOW-BOARDING.
It's not funny anymore.
OH, SNOWBOARD! I'VE NEVER DONE IT.
WE HAVE A LONG WEEKEND COMING UP.
I THINK I'D LIKE TO GET AWAY.
YOU WANT TO GO SNOWBOARDING?
S... SURE!!
OKAY, SHOULD WE GO ON SATURDAY OR SUNDAY?

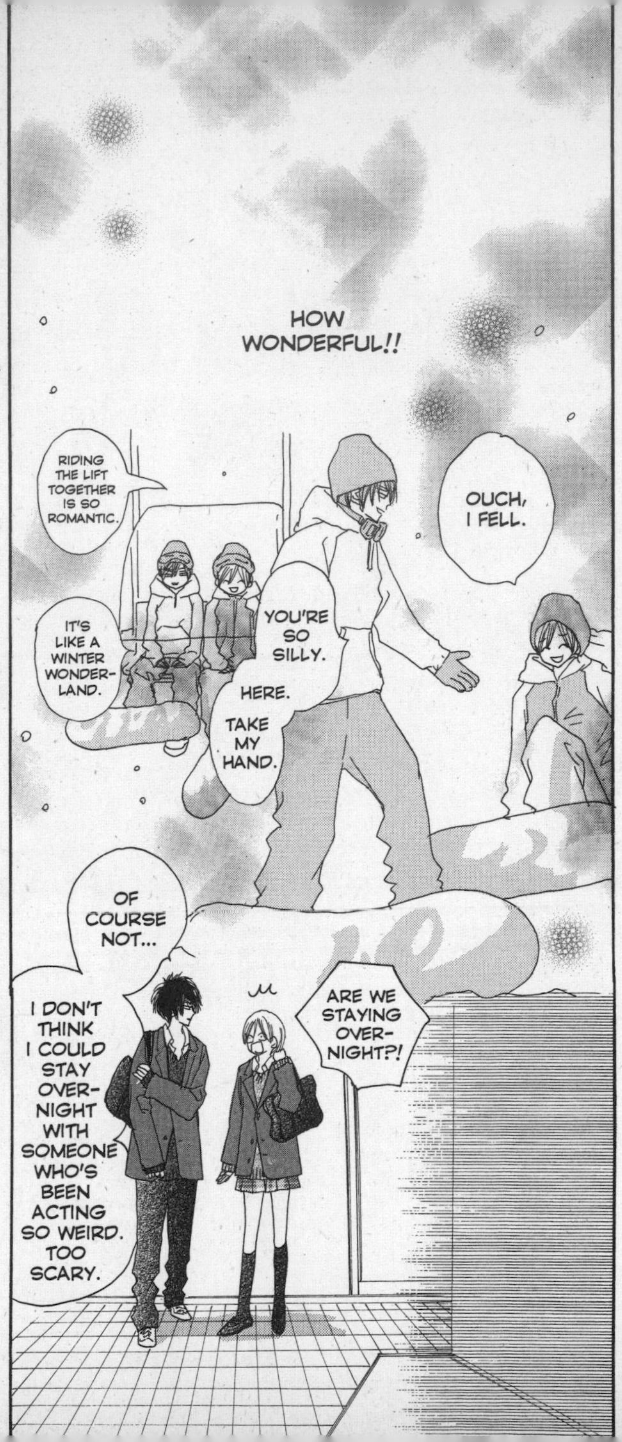
HOW WONDERFUL!!
OUCH, I FELL.
YOU'RE SO SILLY.
HERE.
TAKE MY HAND.
RIDING THE LIFT TOGETHER IS SO ROMANTIC.
IT'S LIKE A WINTER WONDER-LAND.
ARE WE STAYING OVER-NIGHT?!
OF COURSE NOT...
I DON'T THINK I COULD STAY OVER-NIGHT WITH SOMEONE WHO'S BEEN ACTING SO WEIRD. TOO SCARY.

1

Hello! Kawahara here! Thanks so much again! It's the fifth volume! The drama CD was just released by Shueisha. It's a fun CD, and I'm really pleased with the way it turned out. If you have some money to spare, I hope you'll listen to it. I don't think you'll be able to rent it... It's a CD, so it's a little expensive... Don't overstretch yourselves. End plug!

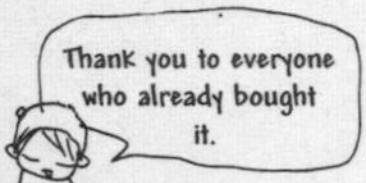
Thank you to everyone who already bought it.

I just adore all the members of the cast (voice actors?). If you don't like Asami, then you will after listening to the CD.

End plug!!

Some of my readers took part as voice actors. I was there at the recording and everyone was so cute. ♡ I felt like I was looking at my daughters. It'd be fun to do this kind of thing again!

That wasn't a plug, just some memories!

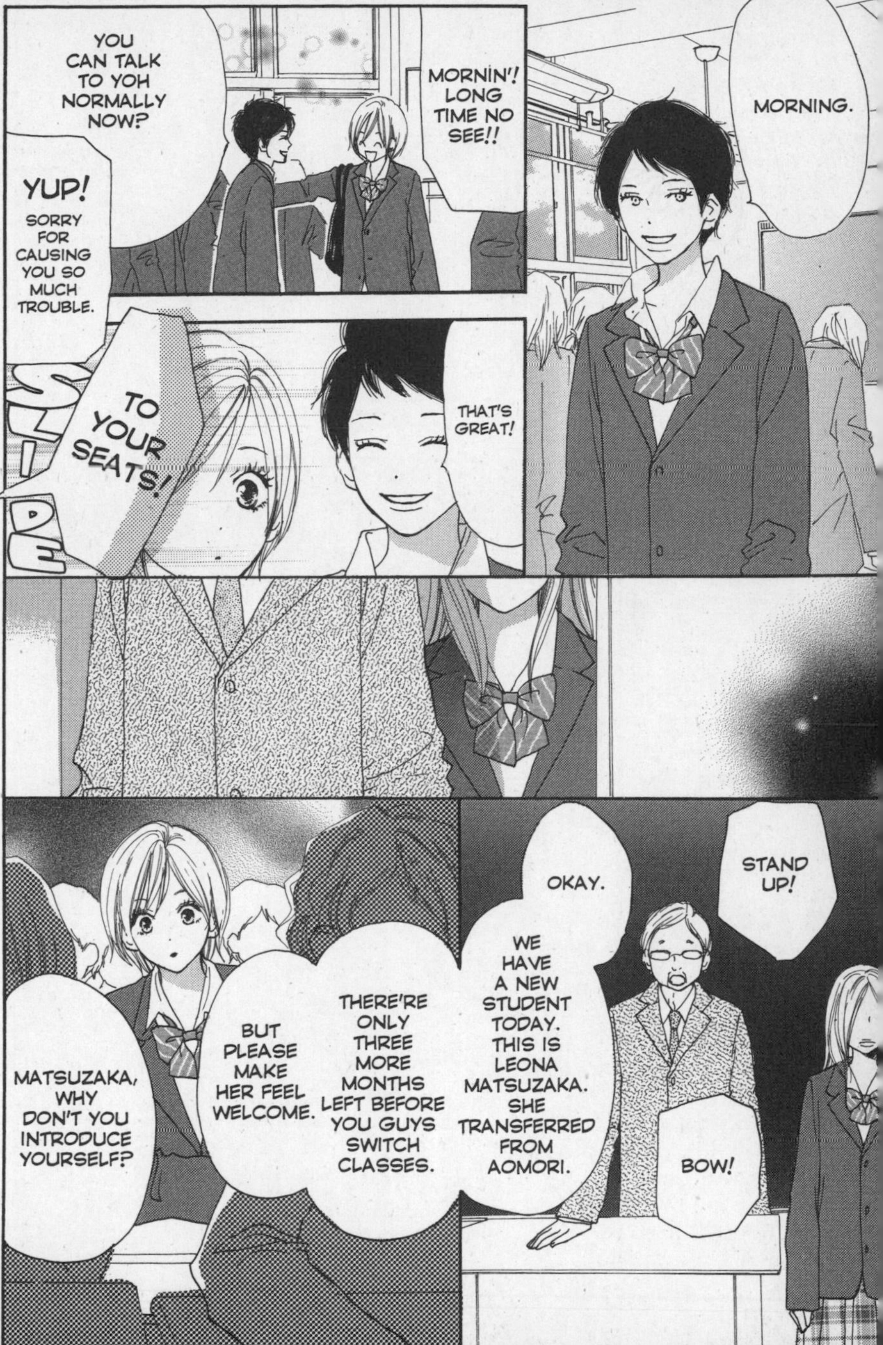
MORNING.
MORNIN'! LONG TIME NO SEE!!
YOU CAN TALK TO YOH NORMALLY NOW?
YUP! SORRY FOR CAUSING YOU SO MUCH TROUBLE.
THAT'S GREAT!
TO YOUR SEATS!
SLIDE
STAND UP!
BOW!
OKAY.
WE HAVE A NEW STUDENT TODAY. THIS IS LEONA MATSUZAKA. SHE TRANSFERRED FROM AOMORI.
THERE'RE ONLY THREE MORE MONTHS LEFT BEFORE YOU GUYS SWITCH CLASSES.
BUT PLEASE MAKE HER FEEL WELCOME.
MATSUZAKA, WHY DON'T YOU INTRODUCE YOURSELF?

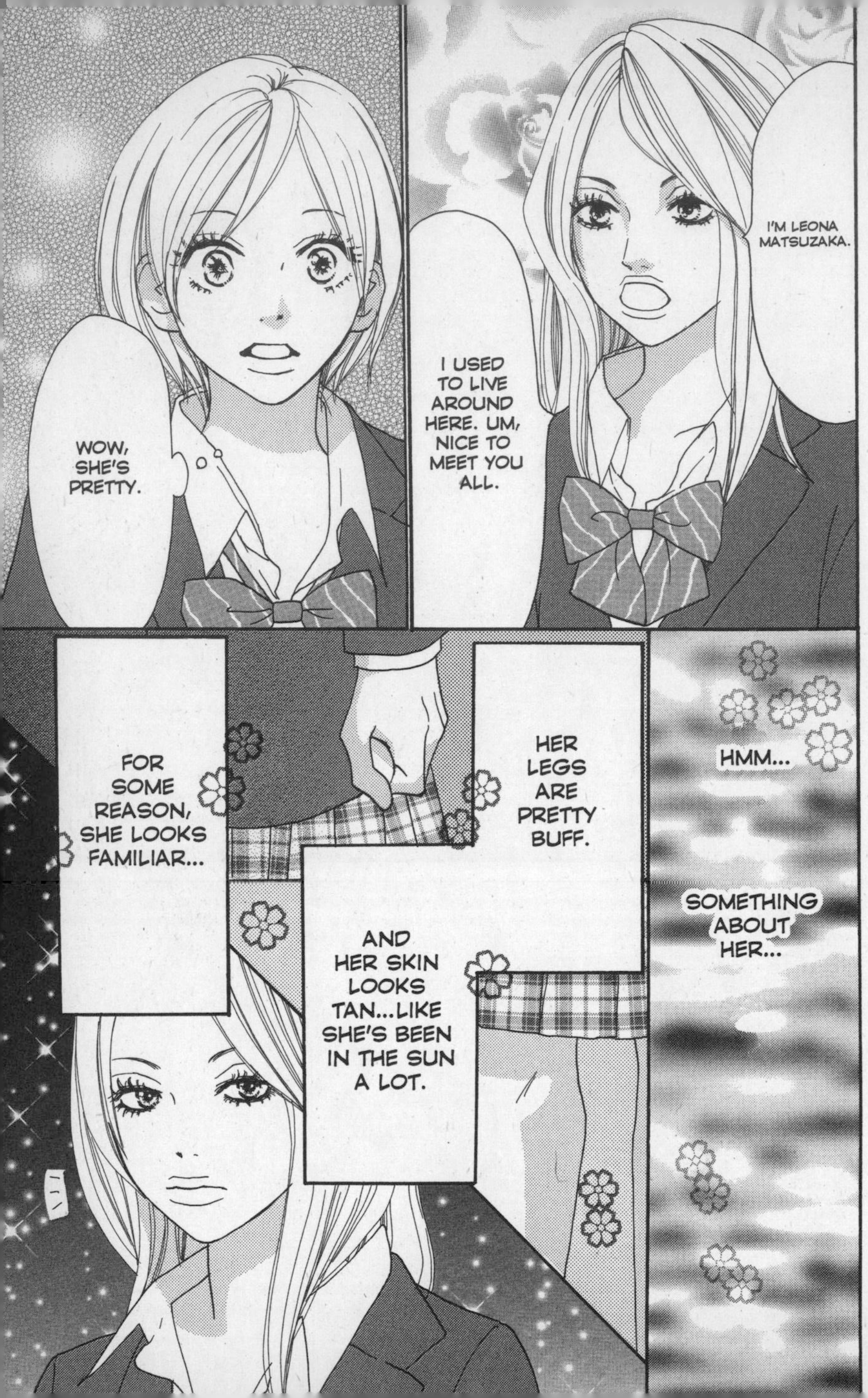
I'M LEONA MATSUZAKA.
I USED TO LIVE AROUND HERE. UM, NICE TO MEET YOU ALL.
WOW, SHE'S PRETTY.
HMM...
SOMETHING ABOUT HER...
HER LEGS ARE PRETTY BUFF.
FOR SOME REASON, SHE LOOKS FAMILIAR...
AND HER SKIN LOOKS TAN...LIKE SHE'S BEEN IN THE SUN A LOT.

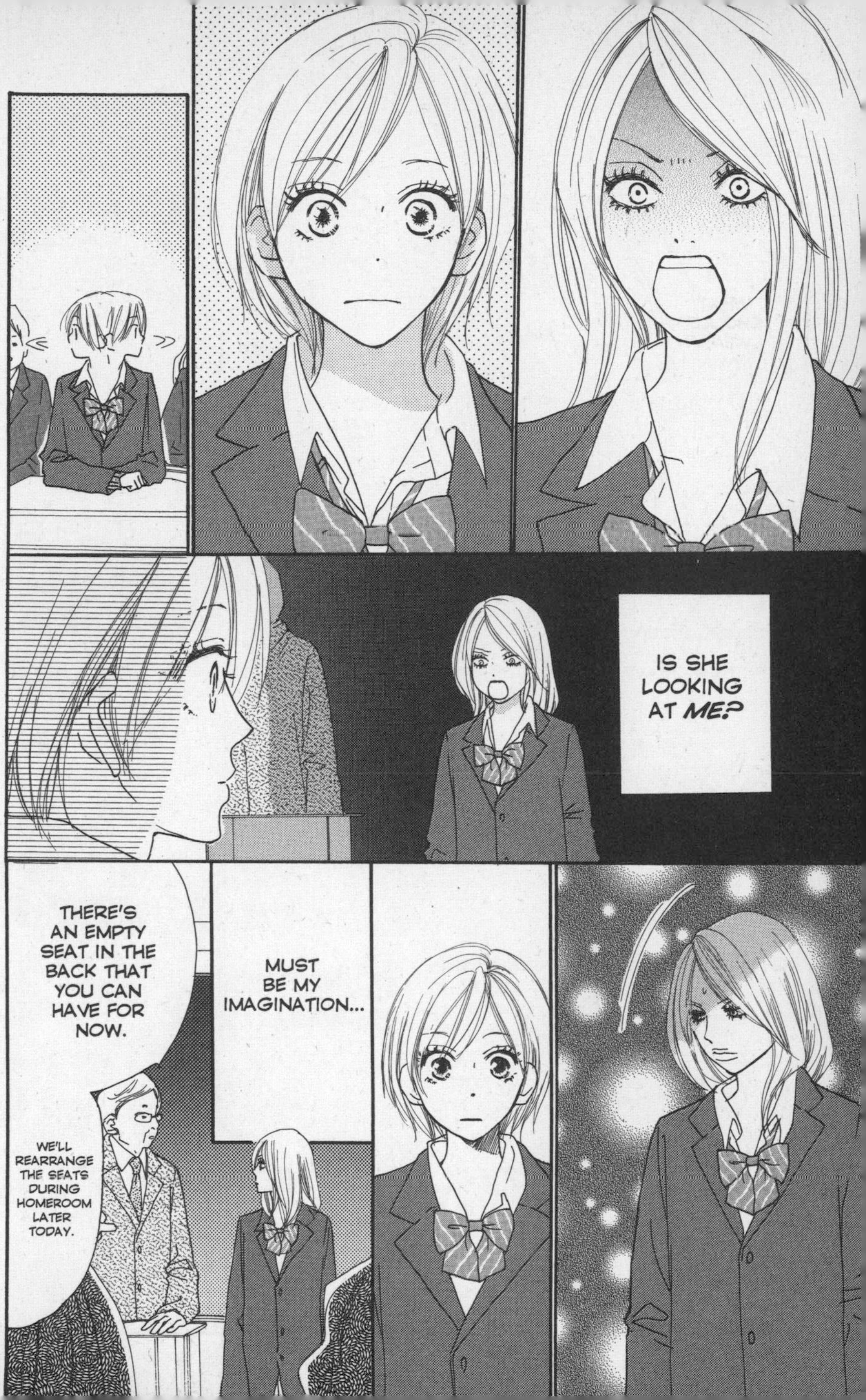
IS SHE LOOKING AT *ME?*
MUST BE MY IMAGINATION...
THERE'S AN EMPTY SEAT IN THE BACK THAT YOU CAN HAVE FOR NOW.
WE'LL REARRANGE THE SEATS DURING HOMEROOM LATER TODAY.

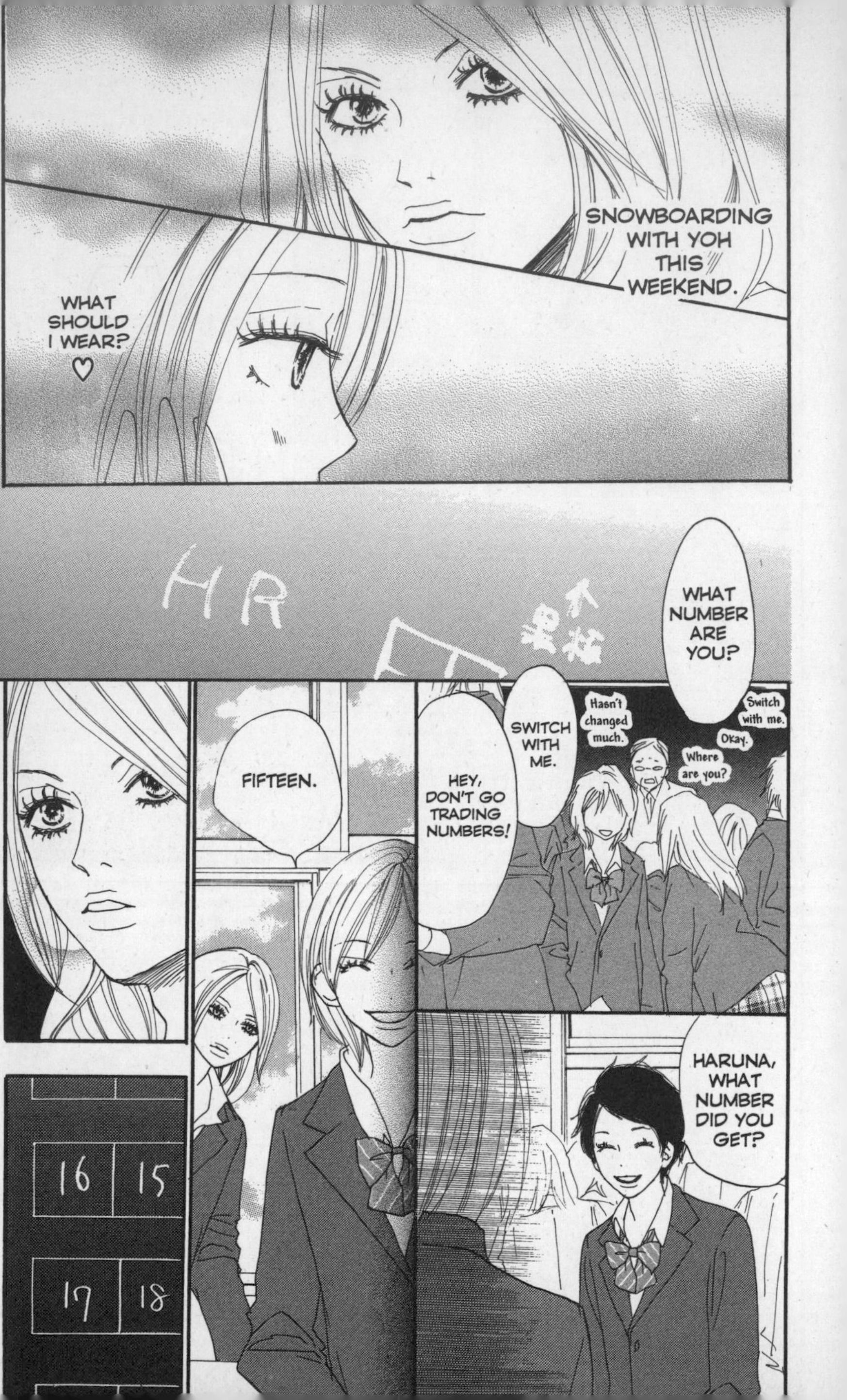
SNOWBOARDING WITH YOH THIS WEEKEND.
WHAT SHOULD I WEAR? ♡
HR
WHAT NUMBER ARE YOU?
Switch with me.
Okay.
Where are you?
Hasn't changed much.
SWITCH WITH ME.
HEY, DON'T GO TRADING NUMBERS!
FIFTEEN.
HARUNA, WHAT NUMBER DID YOU GET?
16 15
17 18

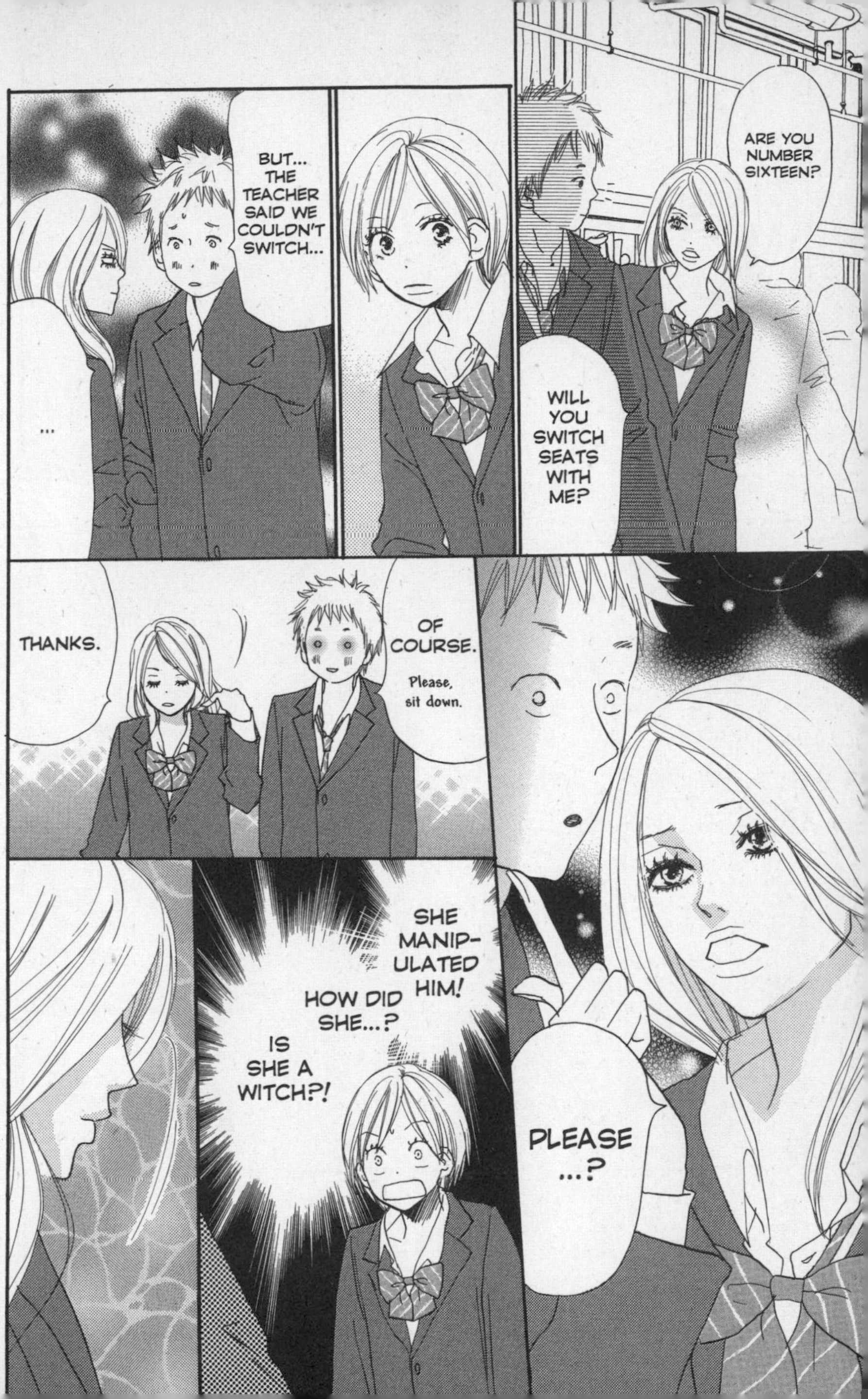
ARE YOU NUMBER SIXTEEN?
WILL YOU SWITCH SEATS WITH ME?
BUT... THE TEACHER SAID WE COULDN'T SWITCH...
...
PLEASE ...?
OF COURSE.
Please, sit down.
THANKS.
SHE MANIP-ULATED HIM!
HOW DID SHE...?
IS SHE A WITCH?!

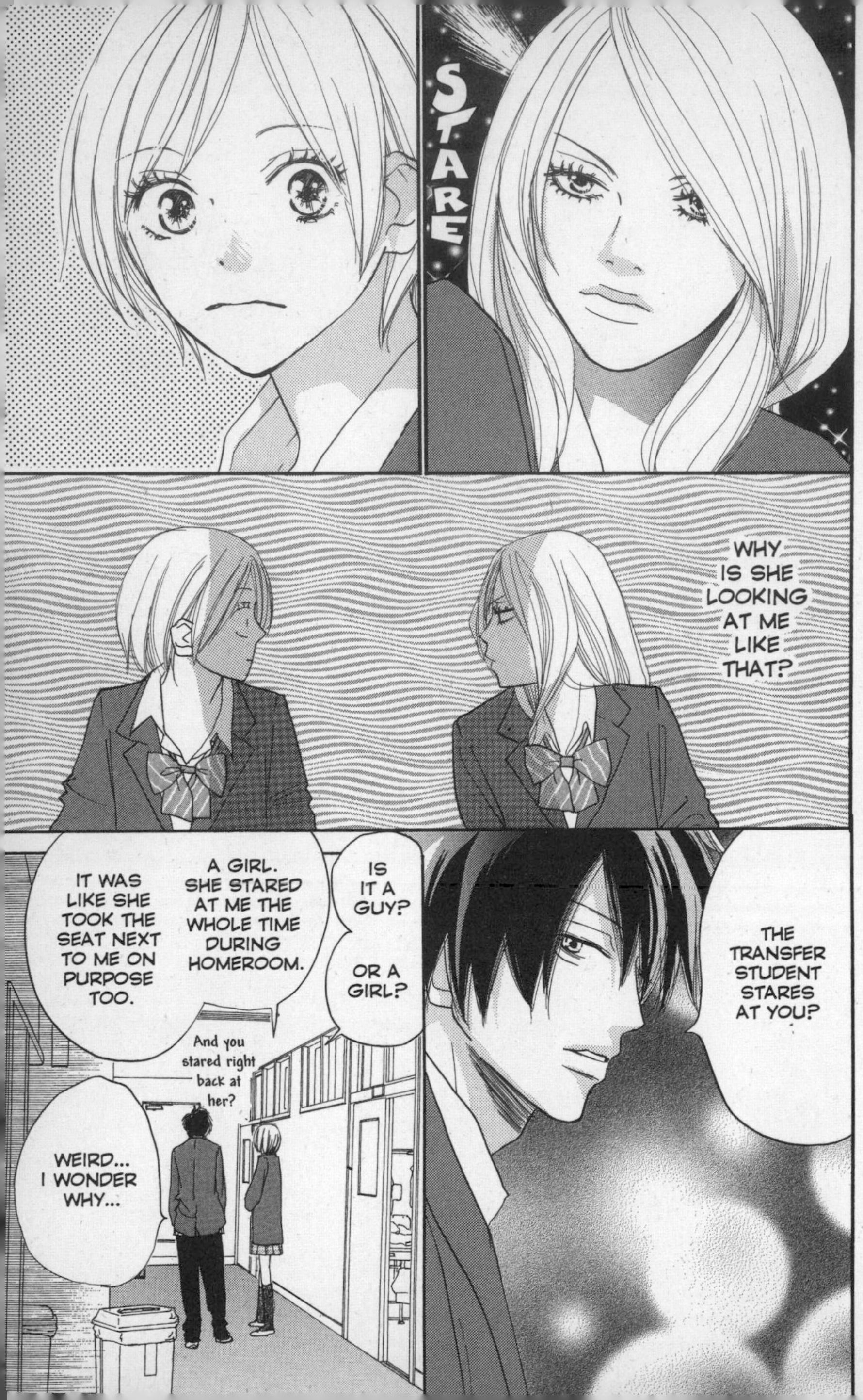
STARE
WHY IS SHE LOOKING AT ME LIKE THAT?
THE TRANSFER STUDENT STARES AT YOU?
IS IT A GUY?
OR A GIRL?
A GIRL. SHE STARED AT ME THE WHOLE TIME DURING HOMEROOM.
IT WAS LIKE SHE TOOK THE SEAT NEXT TO ME ON PURPOSE TOO.
And you stared right back at her?
WEIRD... I WONDER WHY...

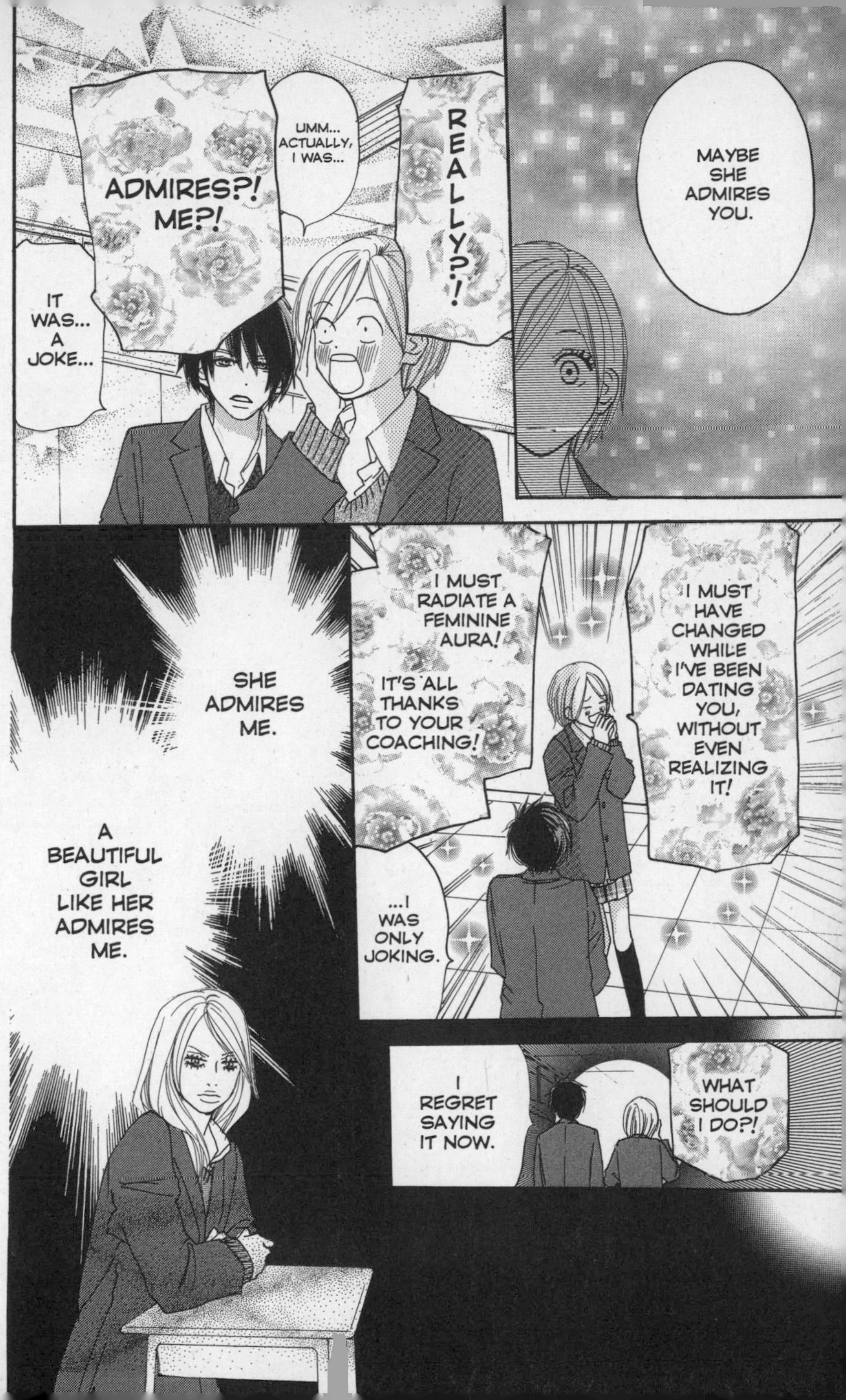
MAYBE SHE ADMIRES YOU.
REALLY?!
UMM... ACTUALLY, I WAS...
ADMIRES?! ME?!
IT WAS... A JOKE...
I MUST HAVE CHANGED WHILE I'VE BEEN DATING YOU, WITHOUT EVEN REALIZING IT!
I MUST RADIATE A FEMININE AURA!
IT'S ALL THANKS TO YOUR COACHING!
...I WAS ONLY JOKING.
WHAT SHOULD I DO?!
I REGRET SAYING IT NOW.
SHE ADMIRES ME.
A BEAUTIFUL GIRL LIKE HER ADMIRES ME.

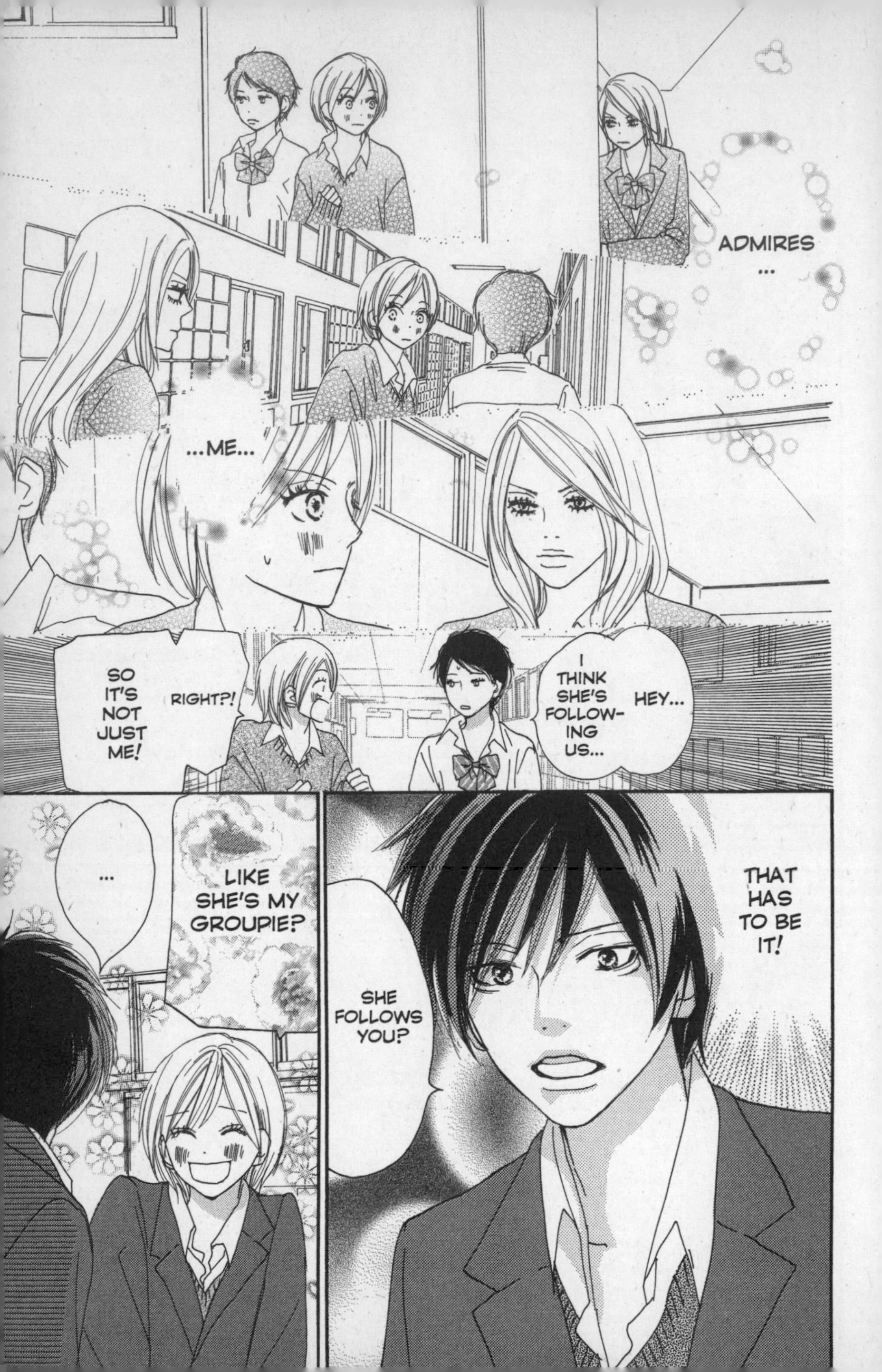
ADMIRES ...
...ME...
HEY...
I THINK SHE'S FOLLOW-ING US...
RIGHT?!
SO IT'S NOT JUST ME!
THAT HAS TO BE IT!
SHE FOLLOWS YOU?
LIKE SHE'S MY GROUPIE?
...

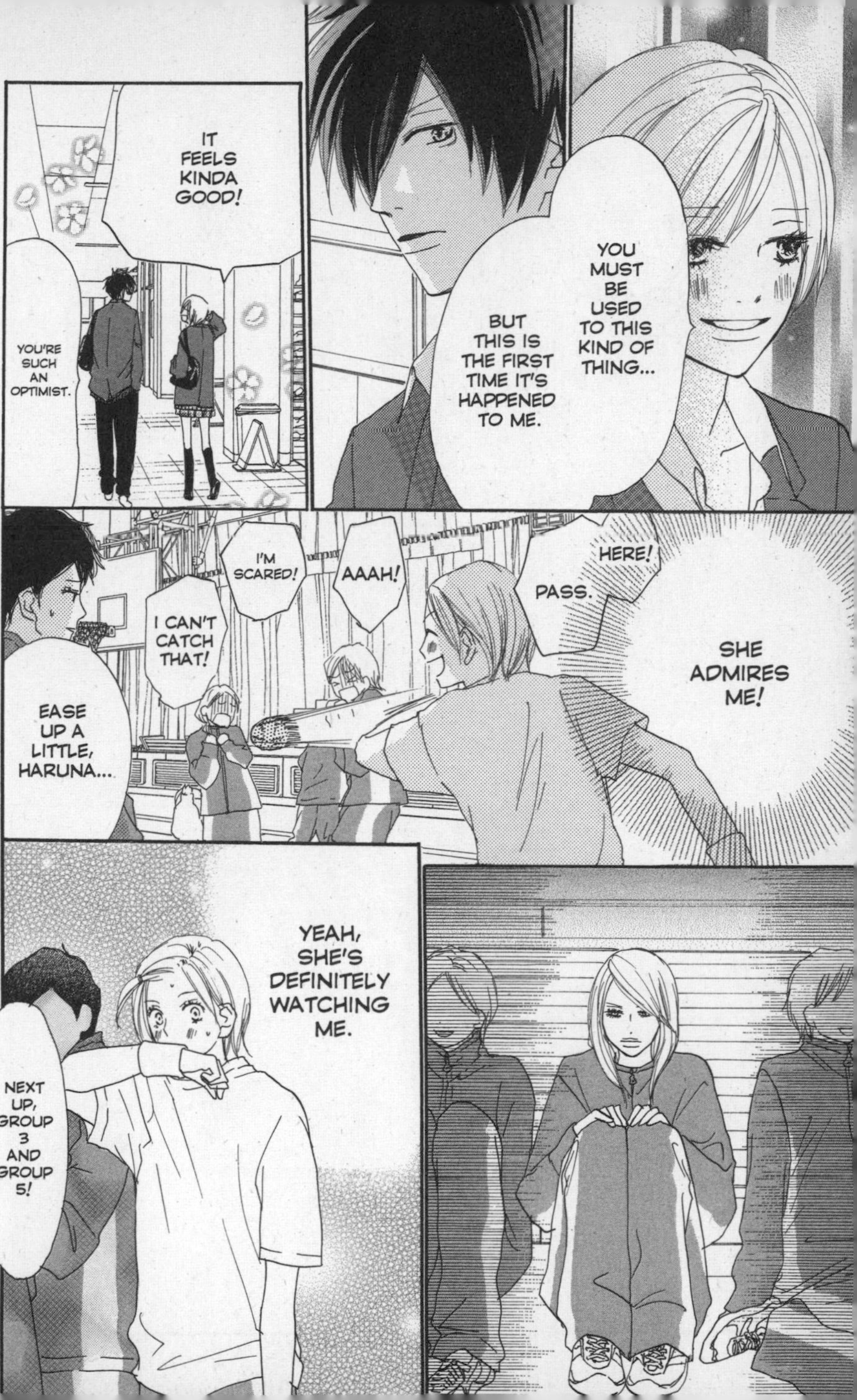
YOU MUST BE USED TO THIS KIND OF THING...
BUT THIS IS THE FIRST TIME IT'S HAPPENED TO ME.
IT FEELS KINDA GOOD!
YOU'RE SUCH AN OPTIMIST.
SHE ADMIRES ME!
HERE!
PASS.
AAAH!
I'M SCARED!
I CAN'T CATCH THAT!
EASE UP A LITTLE, HARUNA...
YEAH, SHE'S DEFINITELY WATCHING ME.
NEXT UP, GROUP 3 AND GROUP 5!

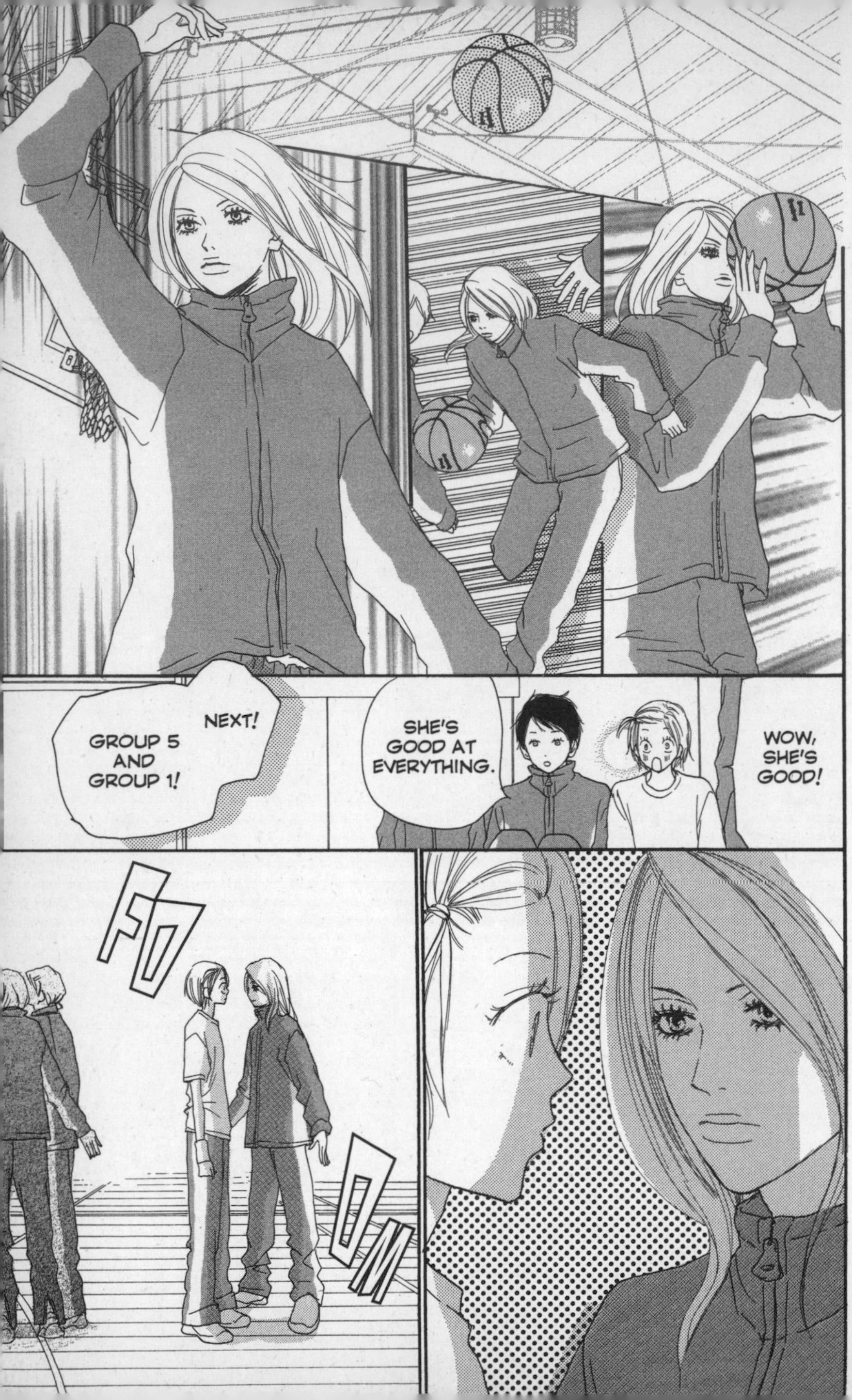
WOW, SHE'S GOOD!
SHE'S GOOD AT EVERYTHING.
NEXT! GROUP 5 AND GROUP 1!

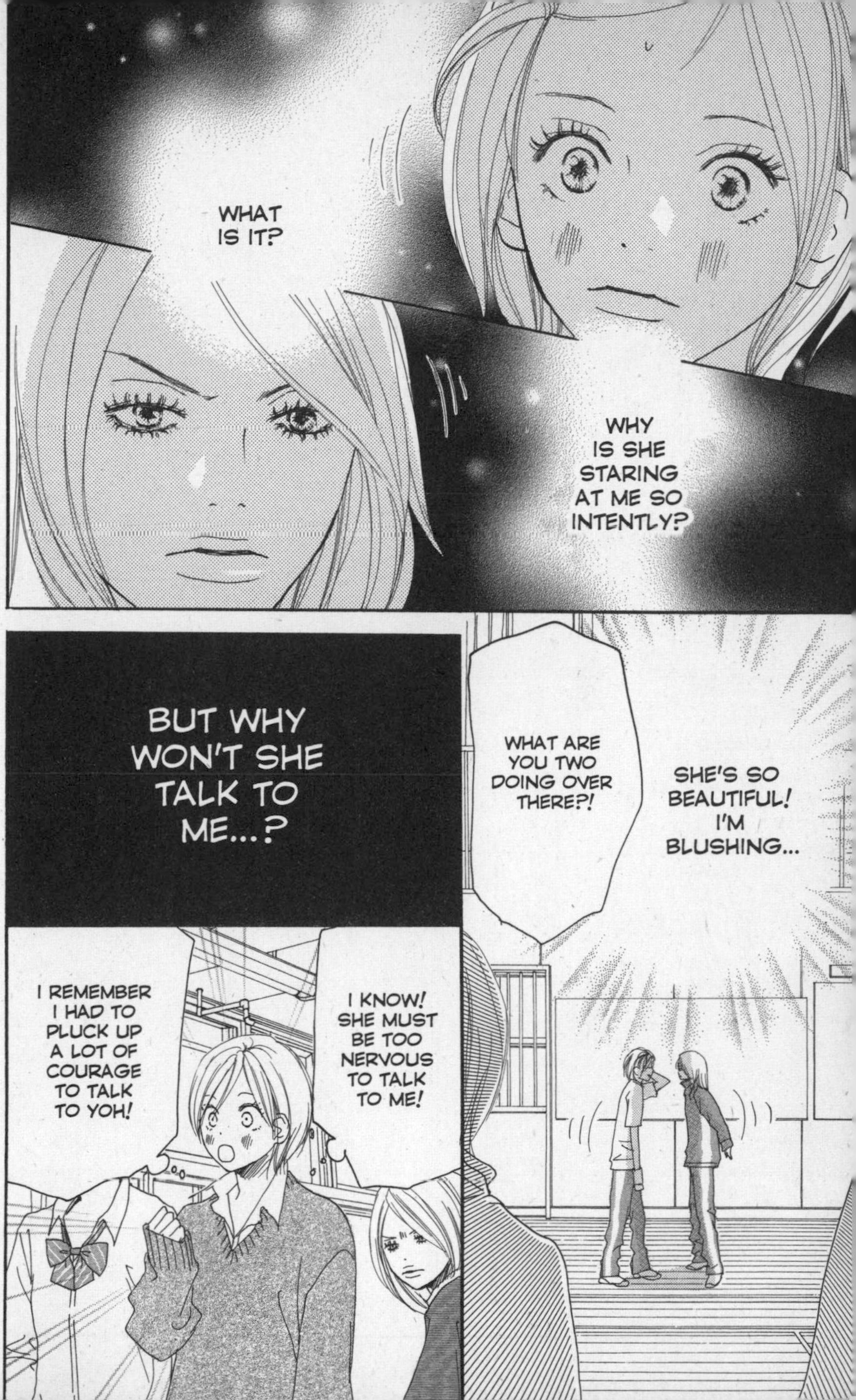
WHAT IS IT?
WHY IS SHE STARING AT ME SO INTENTLY?
SHE'S SO BEAUTIFUL! I'M BLUSHING...
WHAT ARE YOU TWO DOING OVER THERE?!
BUT WHY WON'T SHE TALK TO ME...?
I KNOW! SHE MUST BE TOO NERVOUS TO TALK TO ME!
I REMEMBER I HAD TO PLUCK UP A LOT OF COURAGE TO TALK TO YOH!

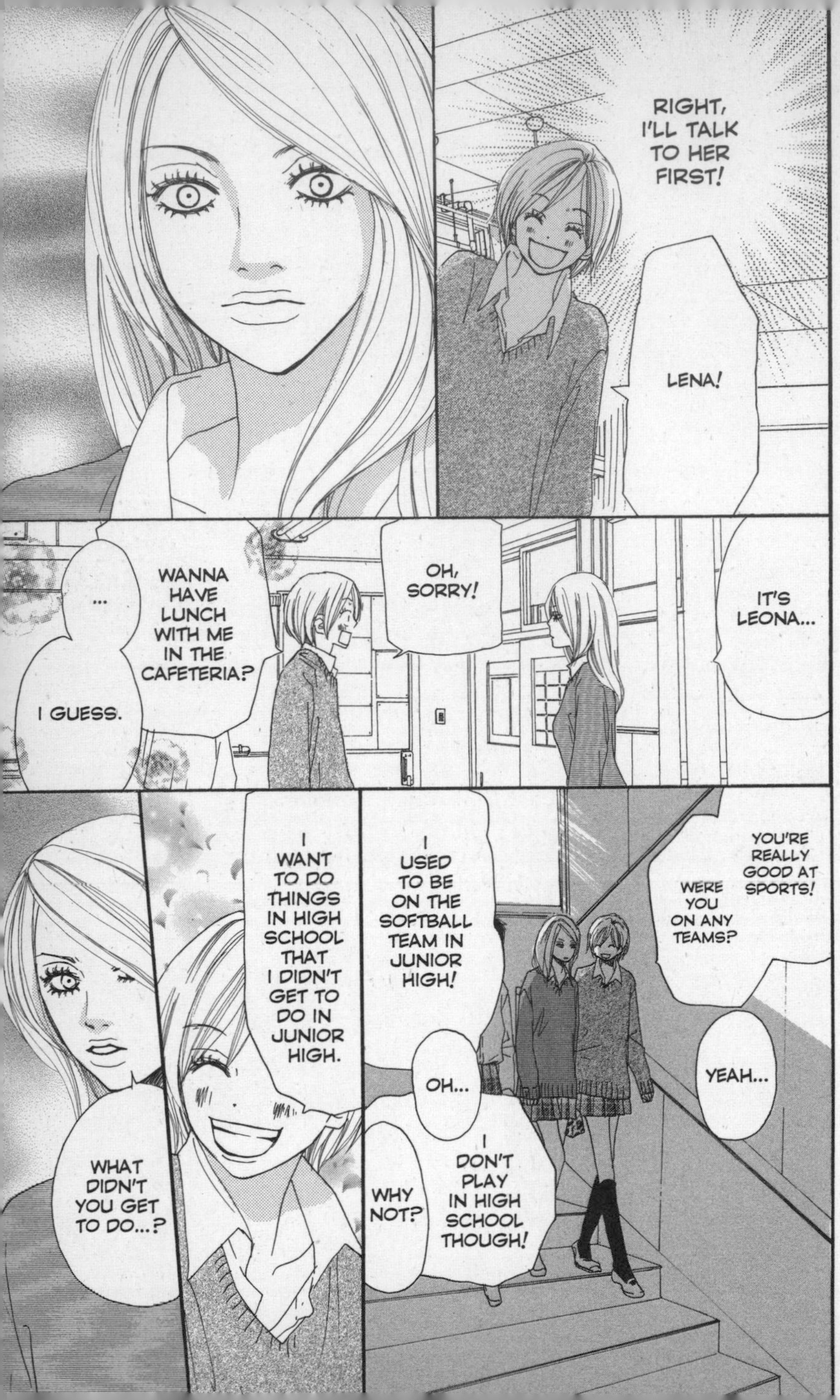
RIGHT, I'LL TALK TO HER FIRST!
LENA!
IT'S LEONA...
OH, SORRY!
WANNA HAVE LUNCH WITH ME IN THE CAFETERIA?
...
I GUESS.
YOU'RE REALLY GOOD AT SPORTS!
WERE YOU ON ANY TEAMS?
YEAH...
I USED TO BE ON THE SOFTBALL TEAM IN JUNIOR HIGH!
OH...
I DON'T PLAY IN HIGH SCHOOL THOUGH!
WHY NOT?
I WANT TO DO THINGS IN HIGH SCHOOL THAT I DIDN'T GET TO DO IN JUNIOR HIGH.
WHAT DIDN'T YOU GET TO DO...?

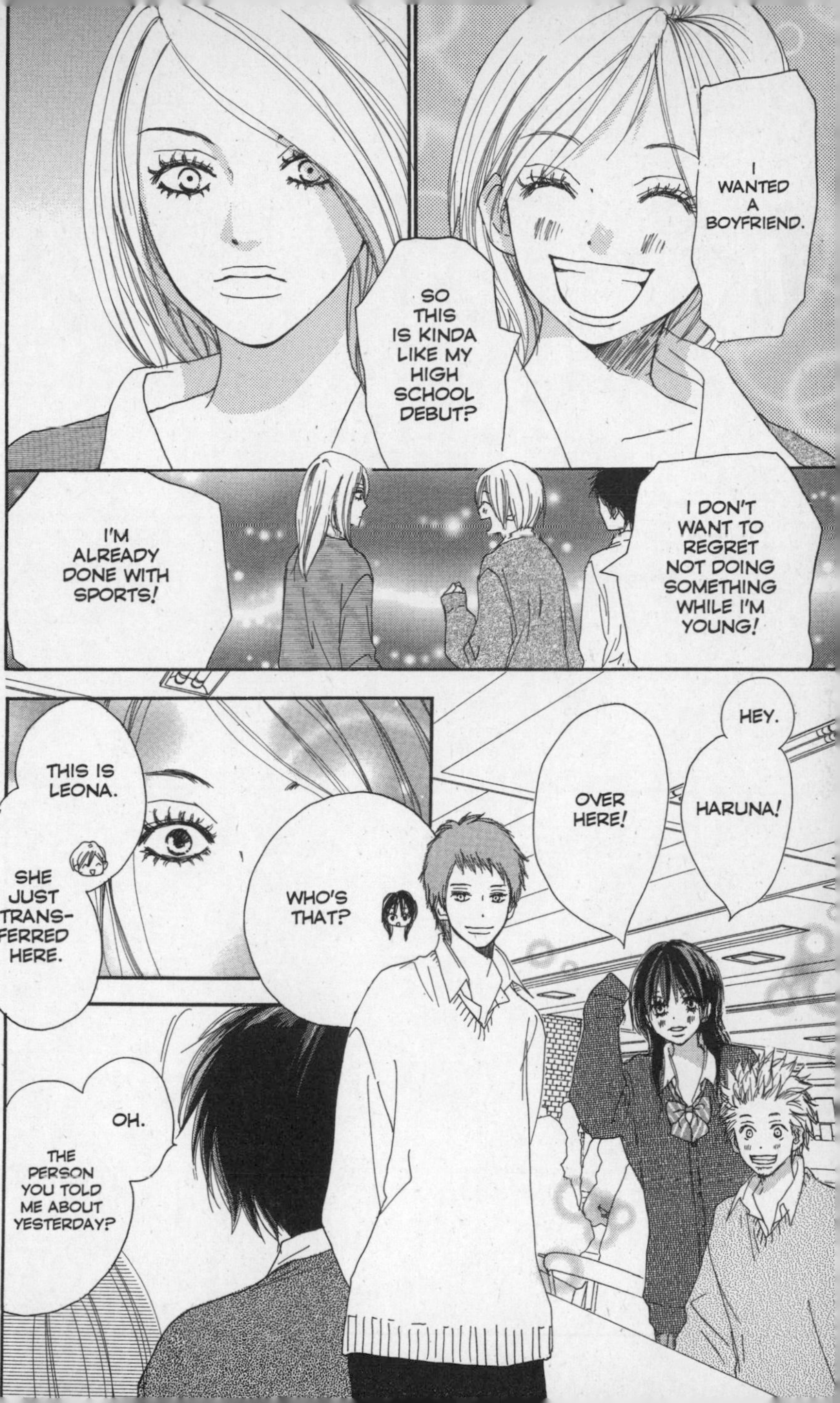
I WANTED A BOYFRIEND.
SO THIS IS KINDA LIKE MY HIGH SCHOOL DEBUT?
I DON'T WANT TO REGRET NOT DOING SOMETHING WHILE I'M YOUNG!
I'M ALREADY DONE WITH SPORTS!
HEY.
HARUNA!
OVER HERE!
WHO'S THAT?
THIS IS LEONA.
SHE JUST TRANS-FERRED HERE.
OH.
THE PERSON YOU TOLD ME ABOUT YESTERDAY?

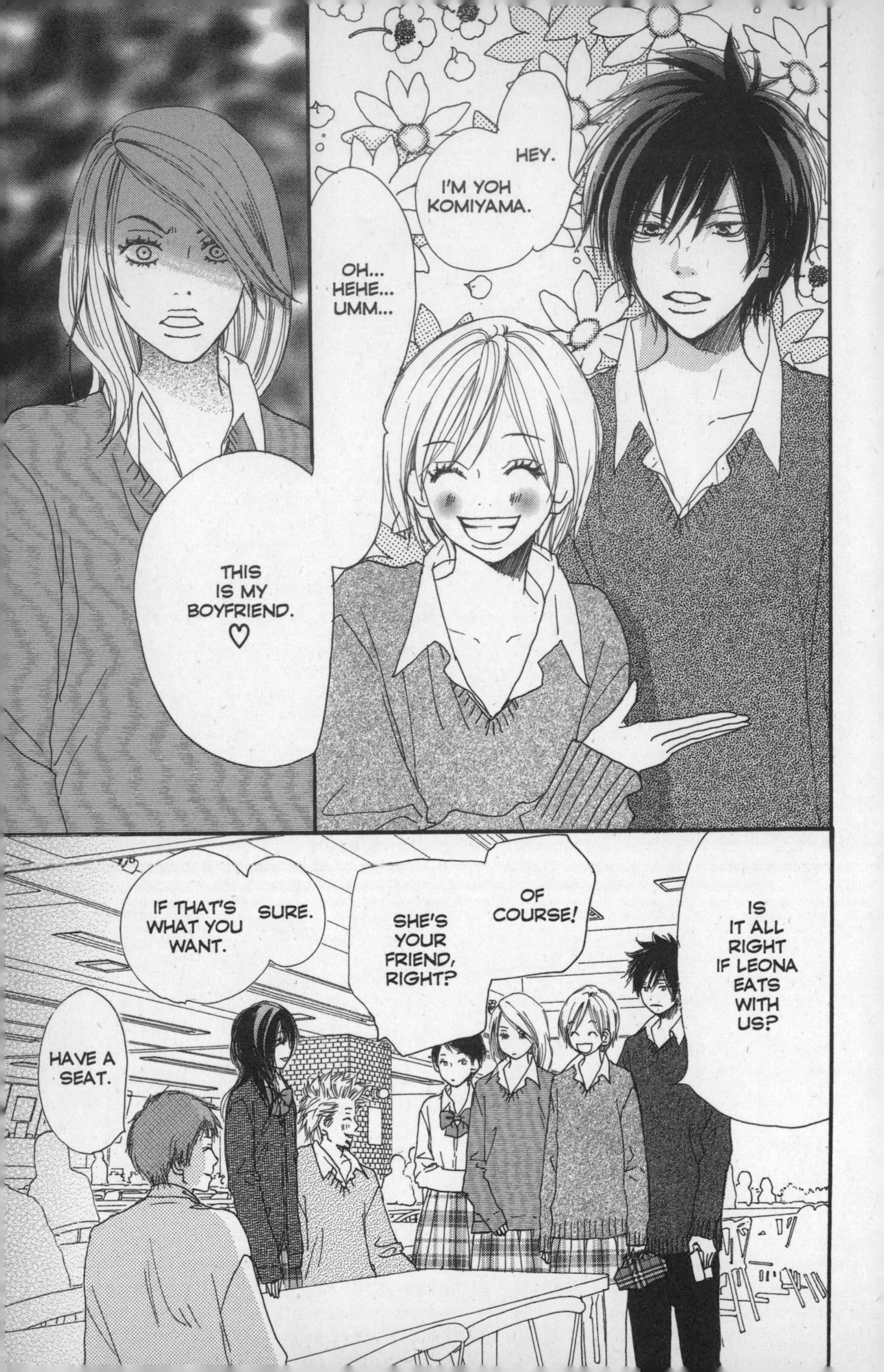
HEY.
I'M YOH KOMIYAMA.
OH... HEHE... UMM...
THIS IS MY BOYFRIEND. ♡
IS IT ALL RIGHT IF LEONA EATS WITH US?
OF COURSE!
SHE'S YOUR FRIEND, RIGHT?
SURE.
IF THAT'S WHAT YOU WANT.
HAVE A SEAT.

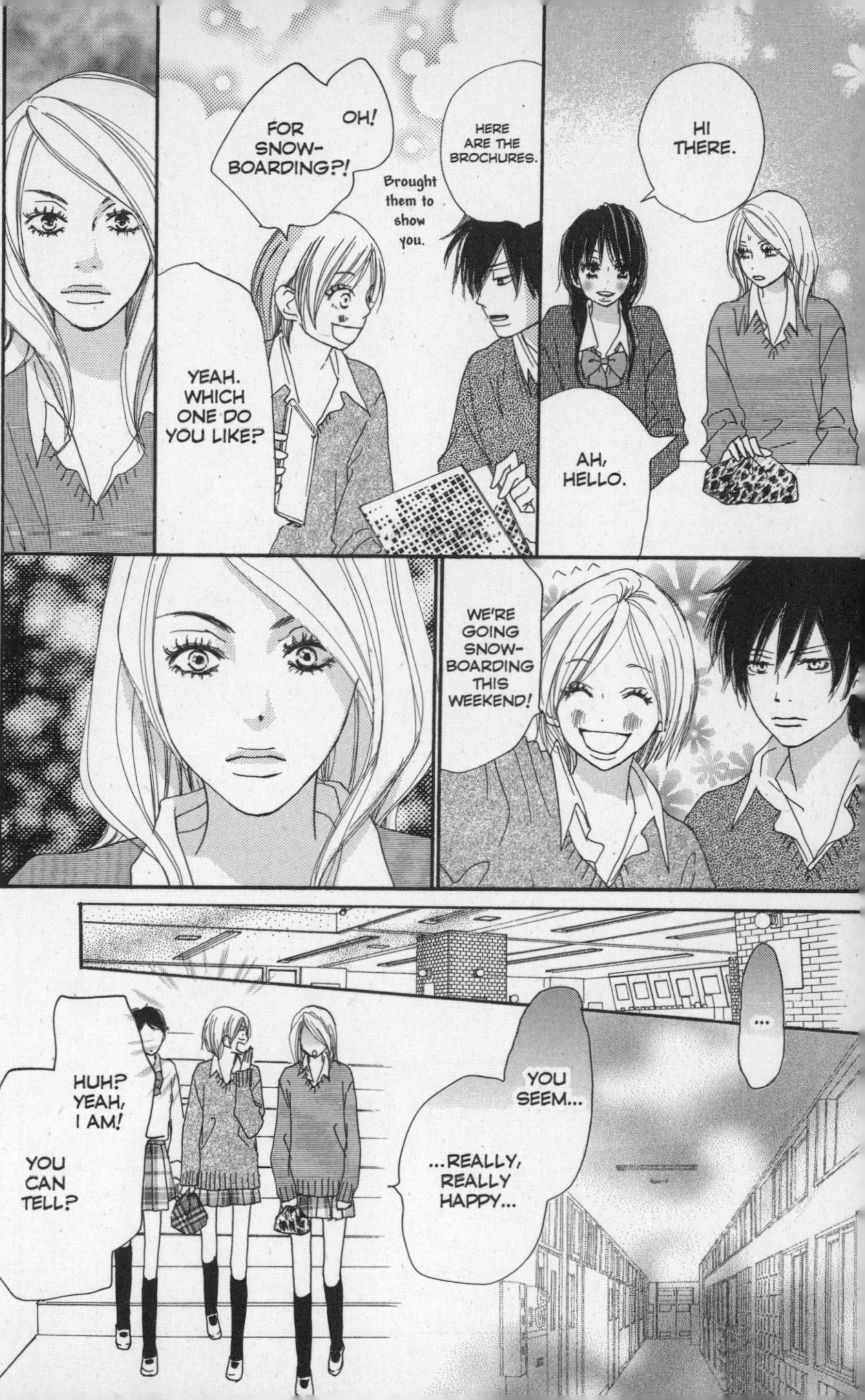
HI THERE.
AH, HELLO.
HERE ARE THE BROCHURES.
Brought them to show you.
OH! FOR SNOWBOARDING?!
YEAH. WHICH ONE DO YOU LIKE?
WE'RE GOING SNOWBOARDING THIS WEEKEND!
...
YOU SEEM...
...REALLY, REALLY HAPPY...
HUH? YEAH, I AM!
YOU CAN TELL?

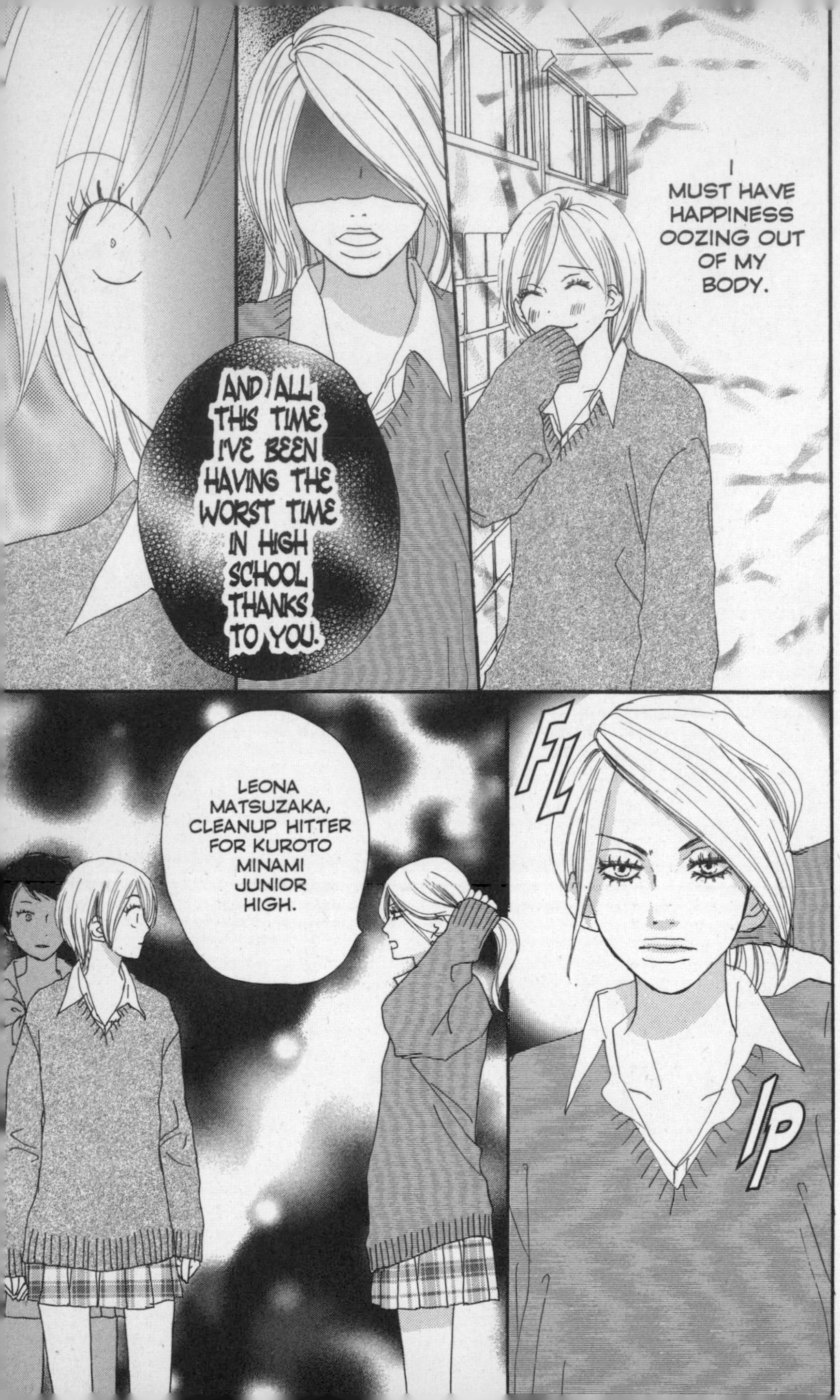
I MUST HAVE HAPPINESS OOZING OUT OF MY BODY.
AND ALL THIS TIME I'VE BEEN HAVING THE WORST TIME IN HIGH SCHOOL THANKS TO YOU.
FLIP
LEONA MATSUZAKA, CLEANUP HITTER FOR KUROTO MINAMI JUNIOR HIGH.

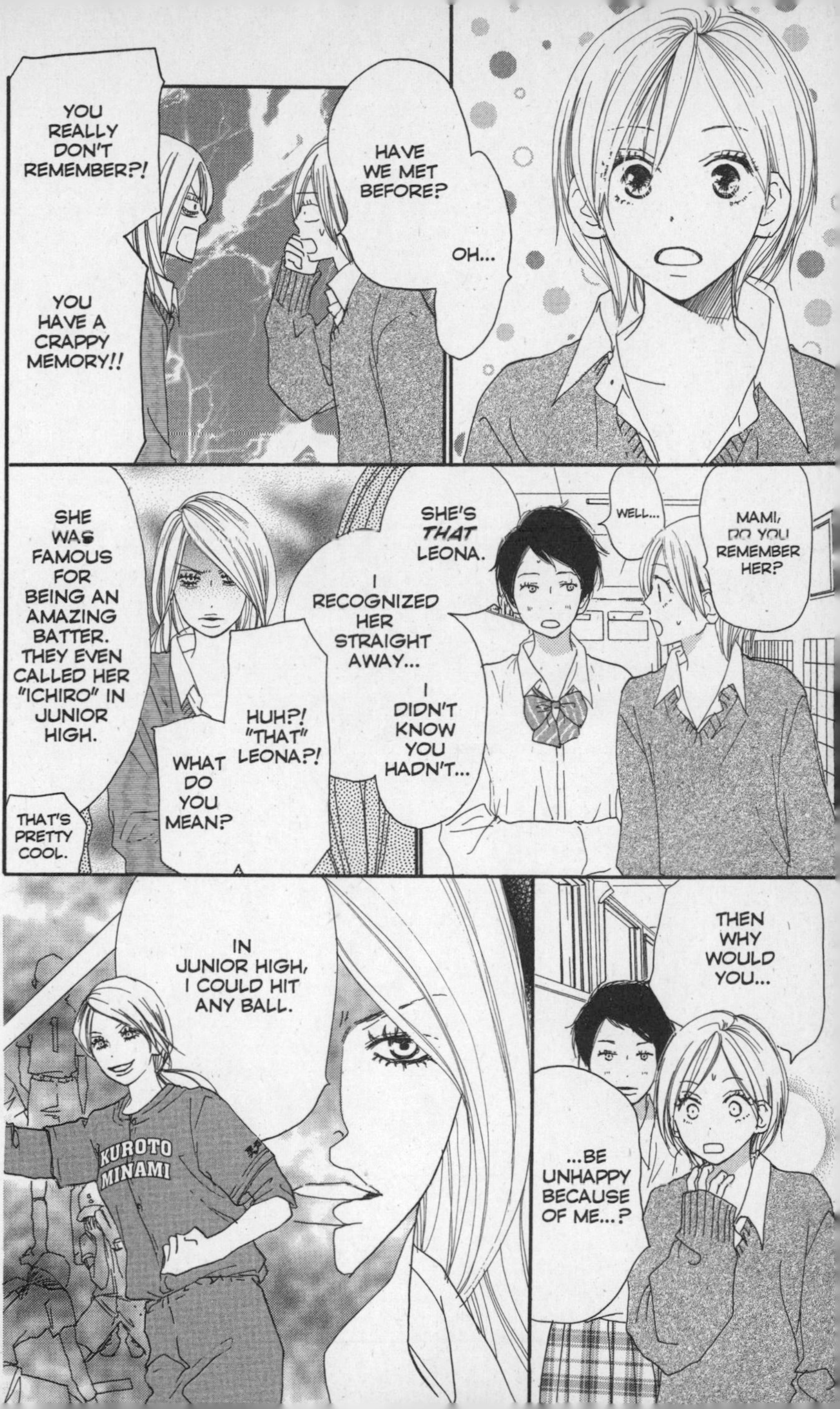
HAVE WE MET BEFORE?
OH...
YOU REALLY DON'T REMEMBER?!
YOU HAVE A CRAPPY MEMORY!!
MAMI, DO YOU REMEMBER HER?
WELL...
SHE'S *THAT* LEONA.
I RECOGNIZED HER STRAIGHT AWAY...
I DIDN'T KNOW YOU HADN'T...
HUH?! "THAT" LEONA?!
WHAT DO YOU MEAN?
SHE WAS FAMOUS FOR BEING AN AMAZING BATTER. THEY EVEN CALLED HER "ICHIRO" IN JUNIOR HIGH.
THAT'S PRETTY COOL.
THEN WHY WOULD YOU...
...BE UNHAPPY BECAUSE OF ME...?
IN JUNIOR HIGH, I COULD HIT ANY BALL.
KUROTO MINAMI

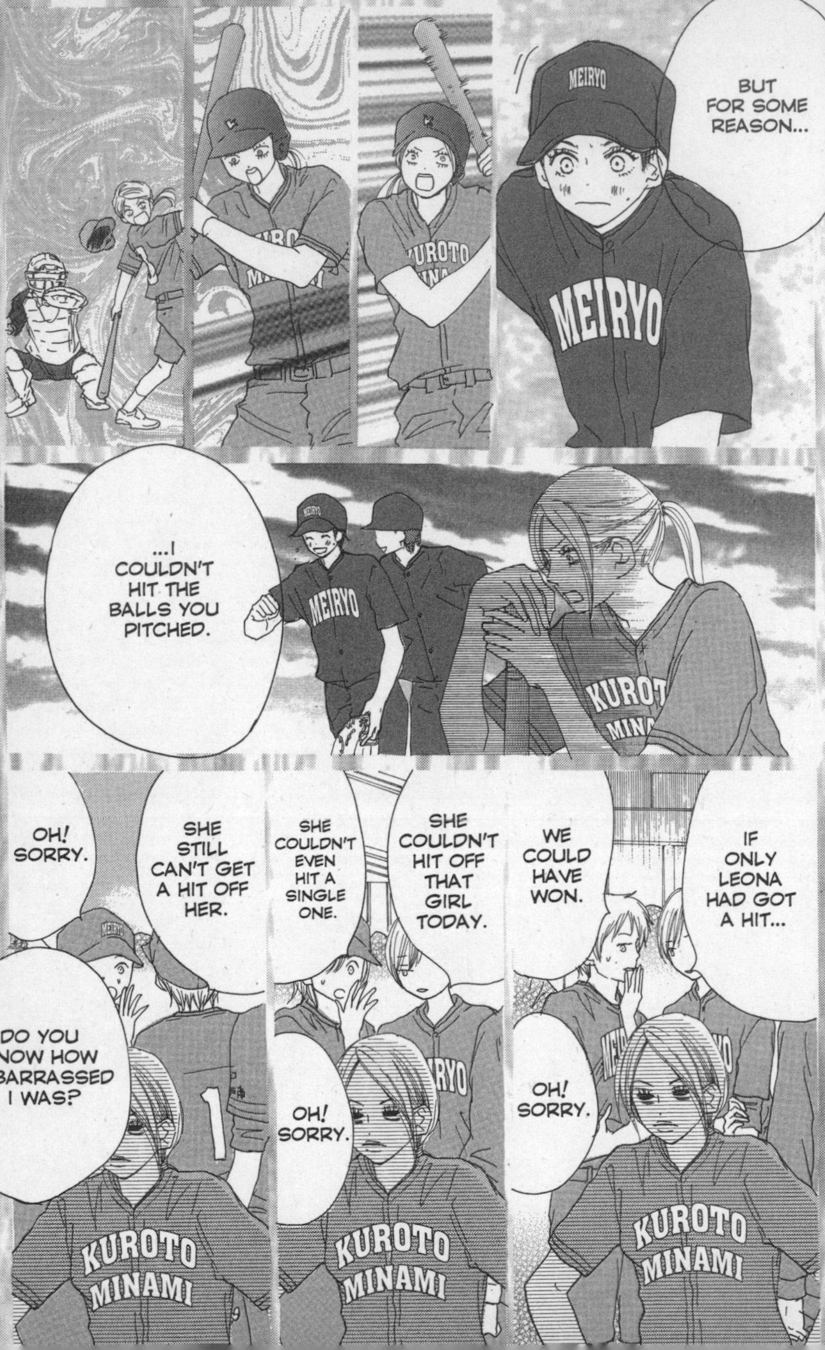
BUT FOR SOME REASON...
...I COULDN'T HIT THE BALLS YOU PITCHED.
IF ONLY LEONA HAD GOT A HIT...
WE COULD HAVE WON.
OH! SORRY.
SHE COULDN'T HIT OFF THAT GIRL TODAY.
SHE COULDN'T EVEN HIT A SINGLE ONE.
OH! SORRY.
SHE STILL CAN'T GET A HIT OFF HER.
OH! SORRY.
DO YOU KNOW HOW EMBARRASSED I WAS?

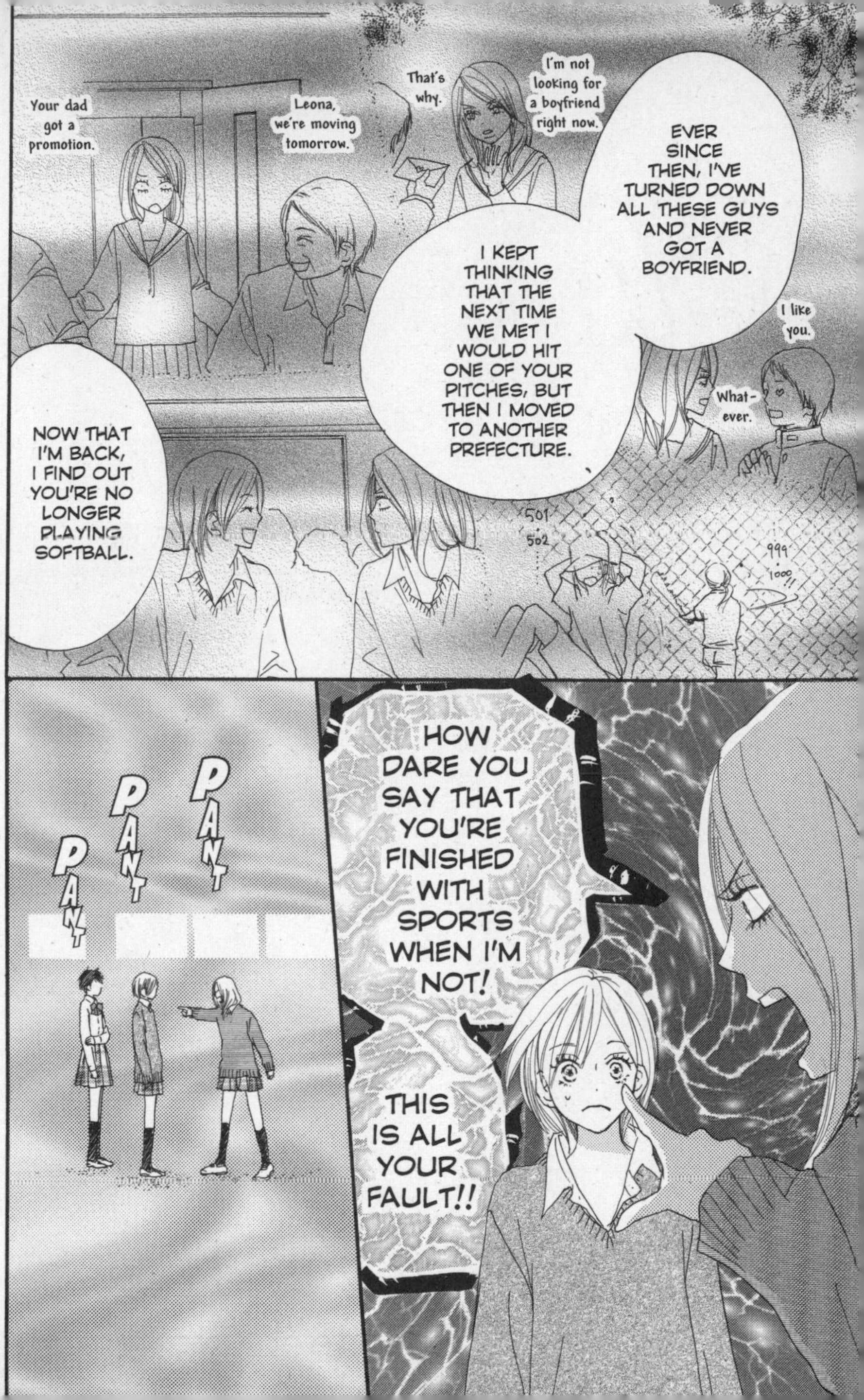
I'm not looking for a boyfriend right now.
That's why.
Leona, we're moving tomorrow.
Your dad got a promotion.
I KEPT THINKING THAT THE NEXT TIME WE MET I WOULD HIT ONE OF YOUR PITCHES, BUT THEN I MOVED TO ANOTHER PREFECTURE.
EVER SINCE THEN, I'VE TURNED DOWN ALL THESE GUYS AND NEVER GOT A BOYFRIEND.
I like you.
What-ever.
999
1000!!
501
502
NOW THAT I'M BACK, I FIND OUT YOU'RE NO LONGER PLAYING SOFTBALL.
HOW DARE YOU SAY THAT YOU'RE FINISHED WITH SPORTS WHEN I'M NOT!
THIS IS ALL YOUR FAULT!!
PANT
PANT
PANT

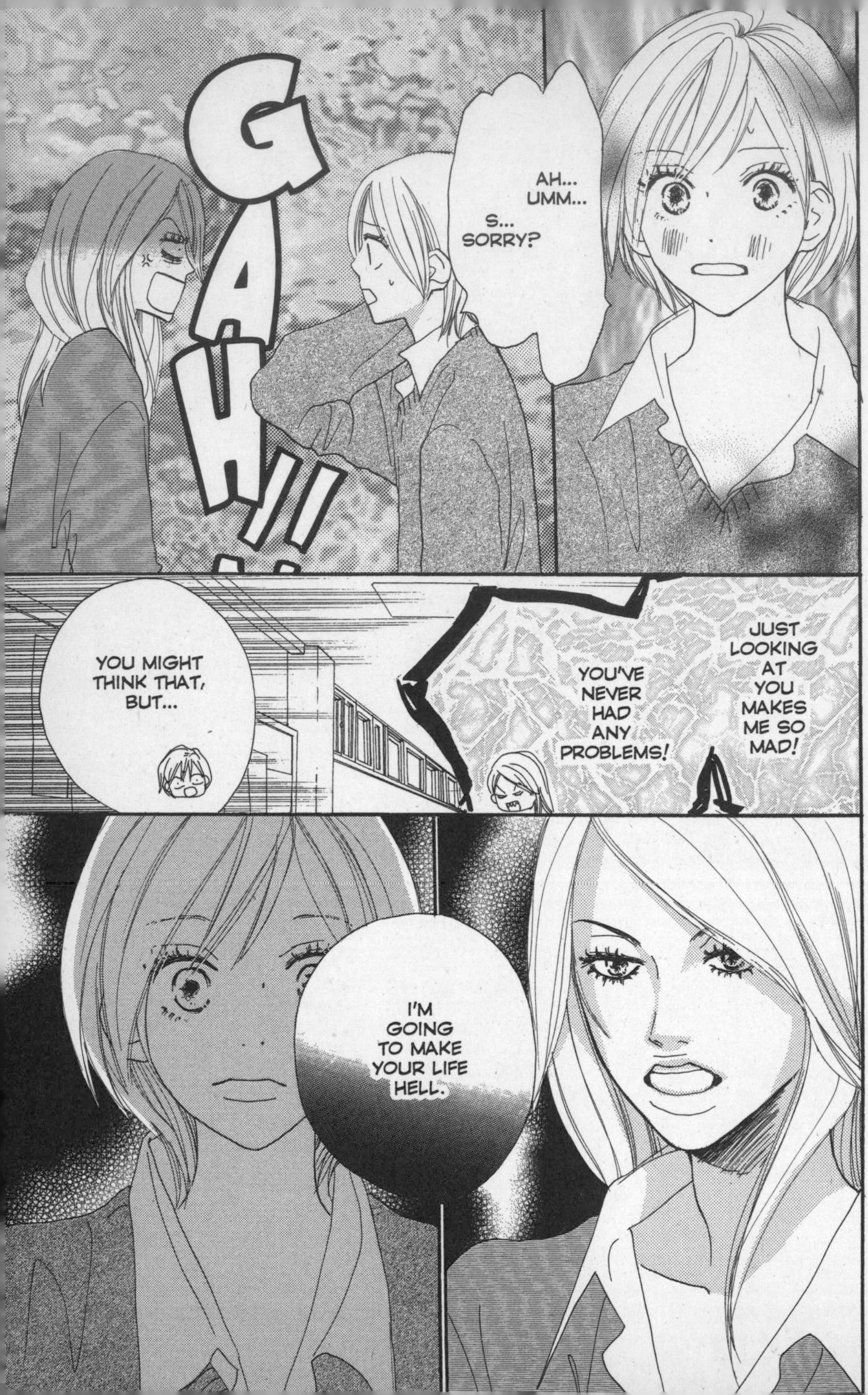
AH... UMM... S... SORRY?
GAH!!
JUST LOOKING AT YOU MAKES ME SO MAD!
YOU'VE NEVER HAD ANY PROBLEMS!
YOU MIGHT THINK THAT, BUT...
I'M GOING TO MAKE YOUR LIFE HELL.

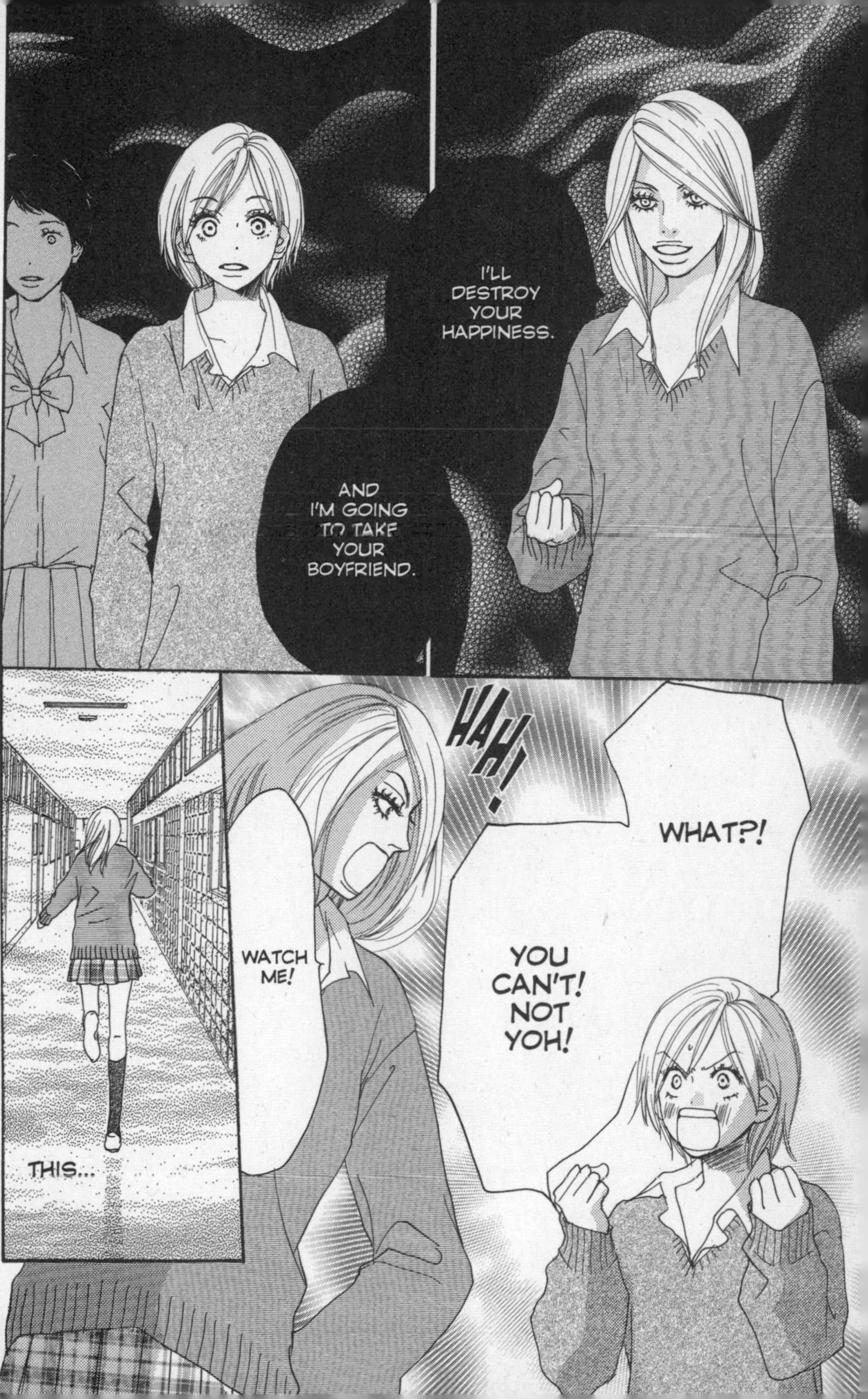
I'LL DESTROY YOUR HAPPINESS.
AND I'M GOING TO TAKE YOUR BOYFRIEND.
HAH!
WHAT?!
YOU CAN'T! NOT YOH!
WATCH ME!
THIS...

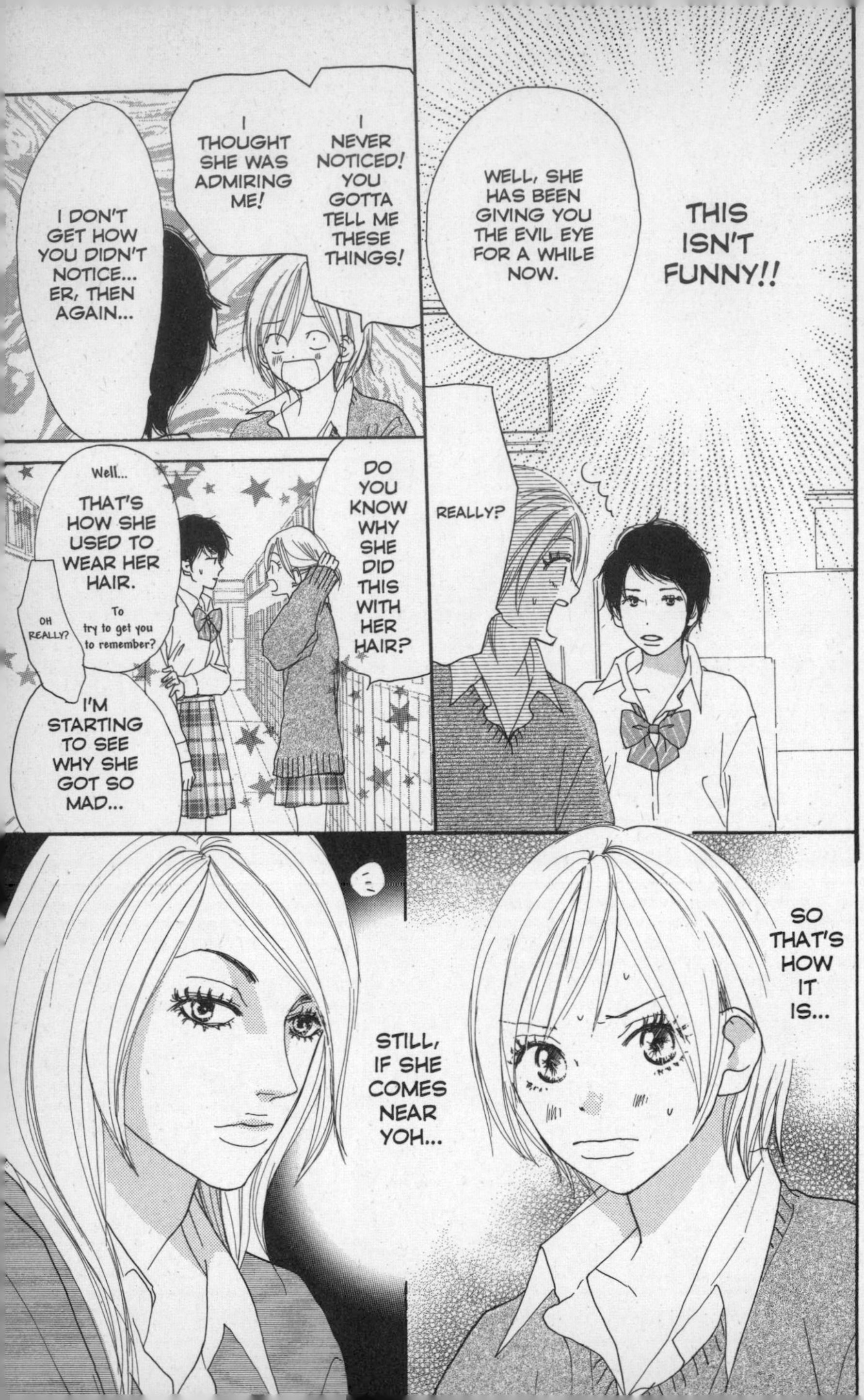
THIS ISN'T FUNNY!!
WELL, SHE HAS BEEN GIVING YOU THE EVIL EYE FOR A WHILE NOW.
REALLY?
I NEVER NOTICED! YOU GOTTA TELL ME THESE THINGS!
I THOUGHT SHE WAS ADMIRING ME!
I DON'T GET HOW YOU DIDN'T NOTICE... ER, THEN AGAIN...
DO YOU KNOW WHY SHE DID THIS WITH HER HAIR?
Well... THAT'S HOW SHE USED TO WEAR HER HAIR.
To try to get you to remember?
OH REALLY?
I'M STARTING TO SEE WHY SHE GOT SO MAD...
SO THAT'S HOW IT IS...
STILL, IF SHE COMES NEAR YOH...

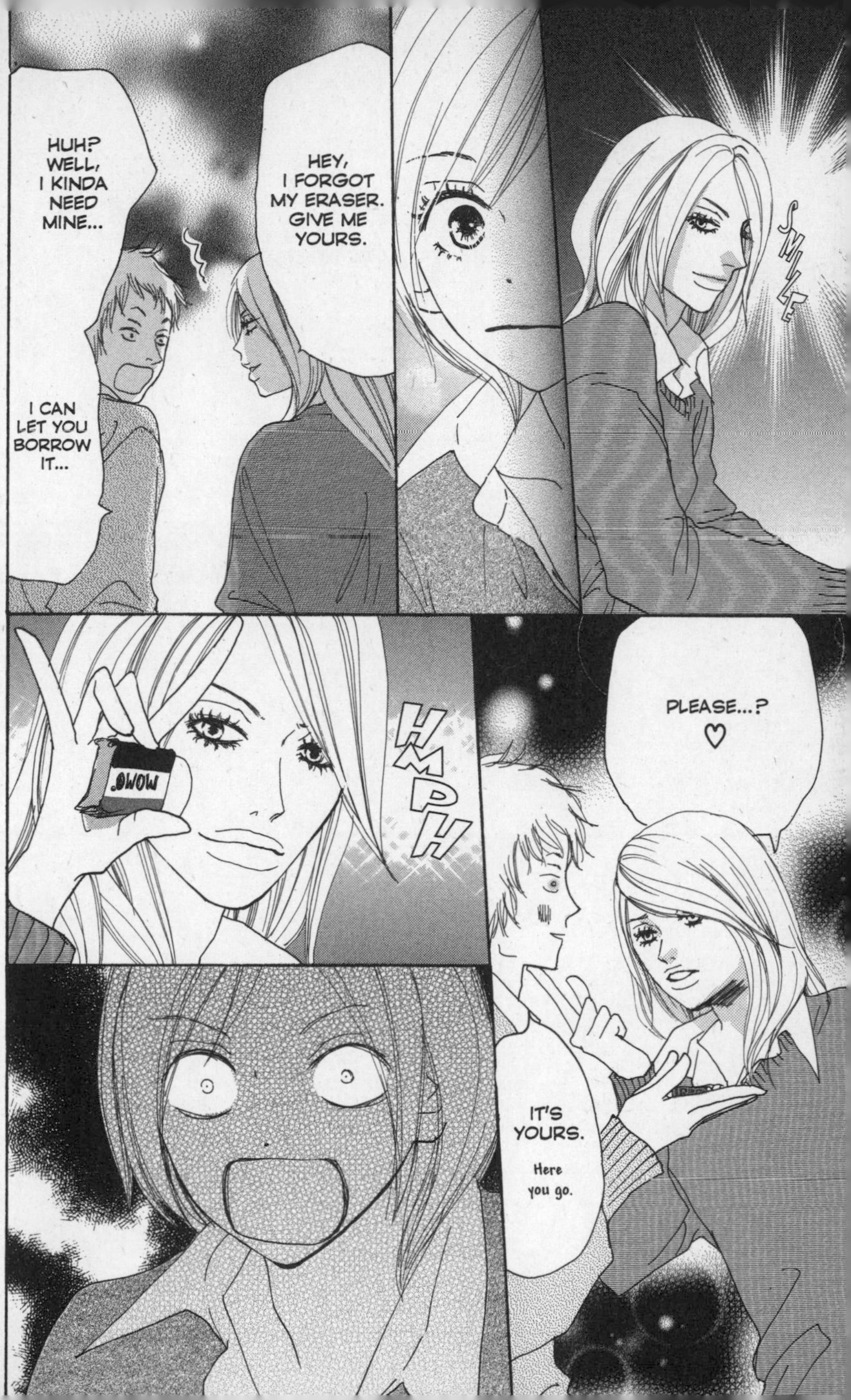
SMILE
HEY, I FORGOT MY ERASER. GIVE ME YOURS.
HUH? WELL, I KINDA NEED MINE...
I CAN LET YOU BORROW IT...
PLEASE...? ♡
IT'S YOURS.
Here you go.
HMPH

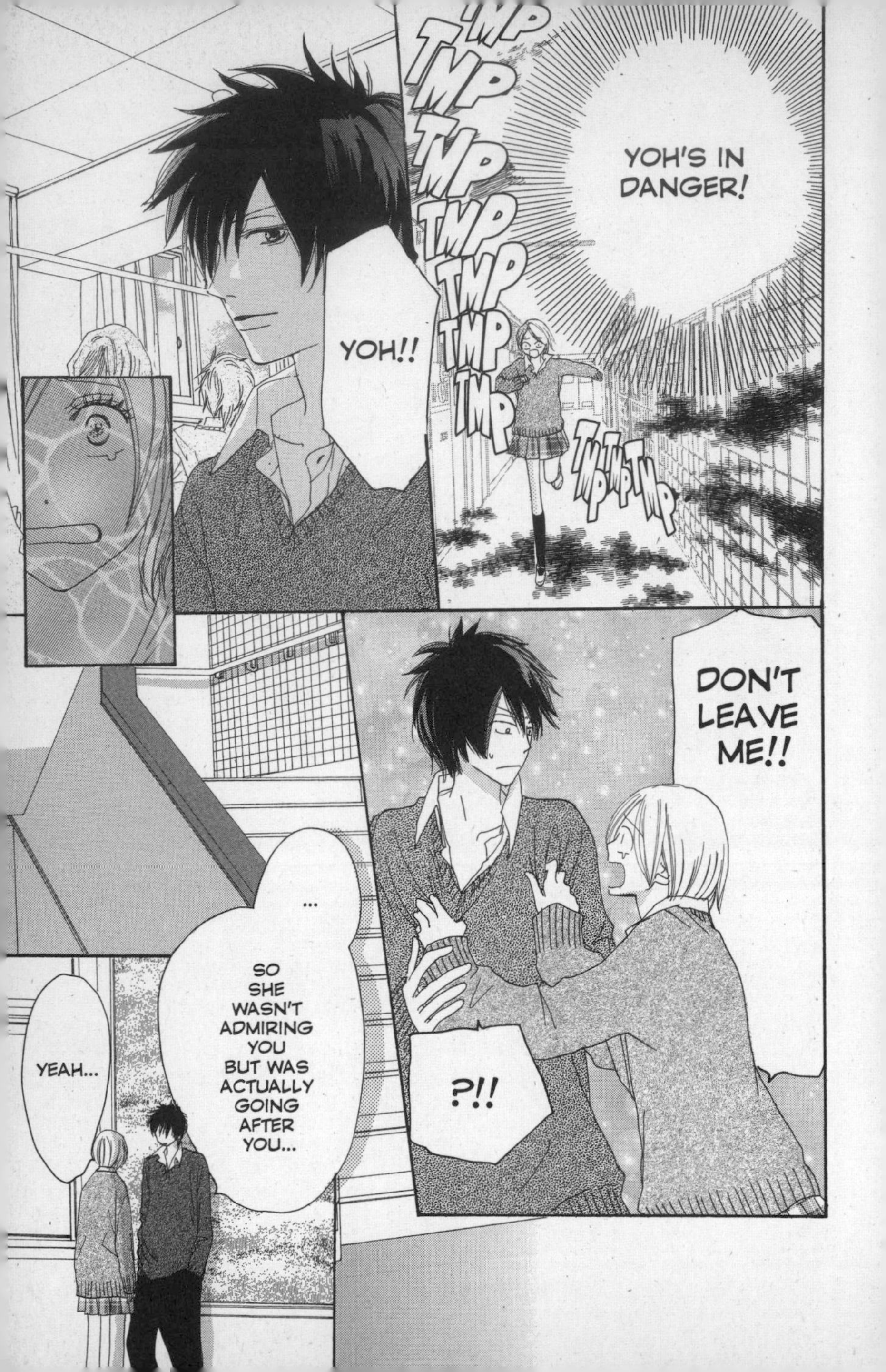
TMP TMP TMP TMP TMP TMP TMP
YOH'S IN DANGER!
TMP TMP TMP
YOH!!
DON'T LEAVE ME!!
?!!
...
SO SHE WASN'T ADMIRING YOU BUT WAS ACTUALLY GOING AFTER YOU...
YEAH...

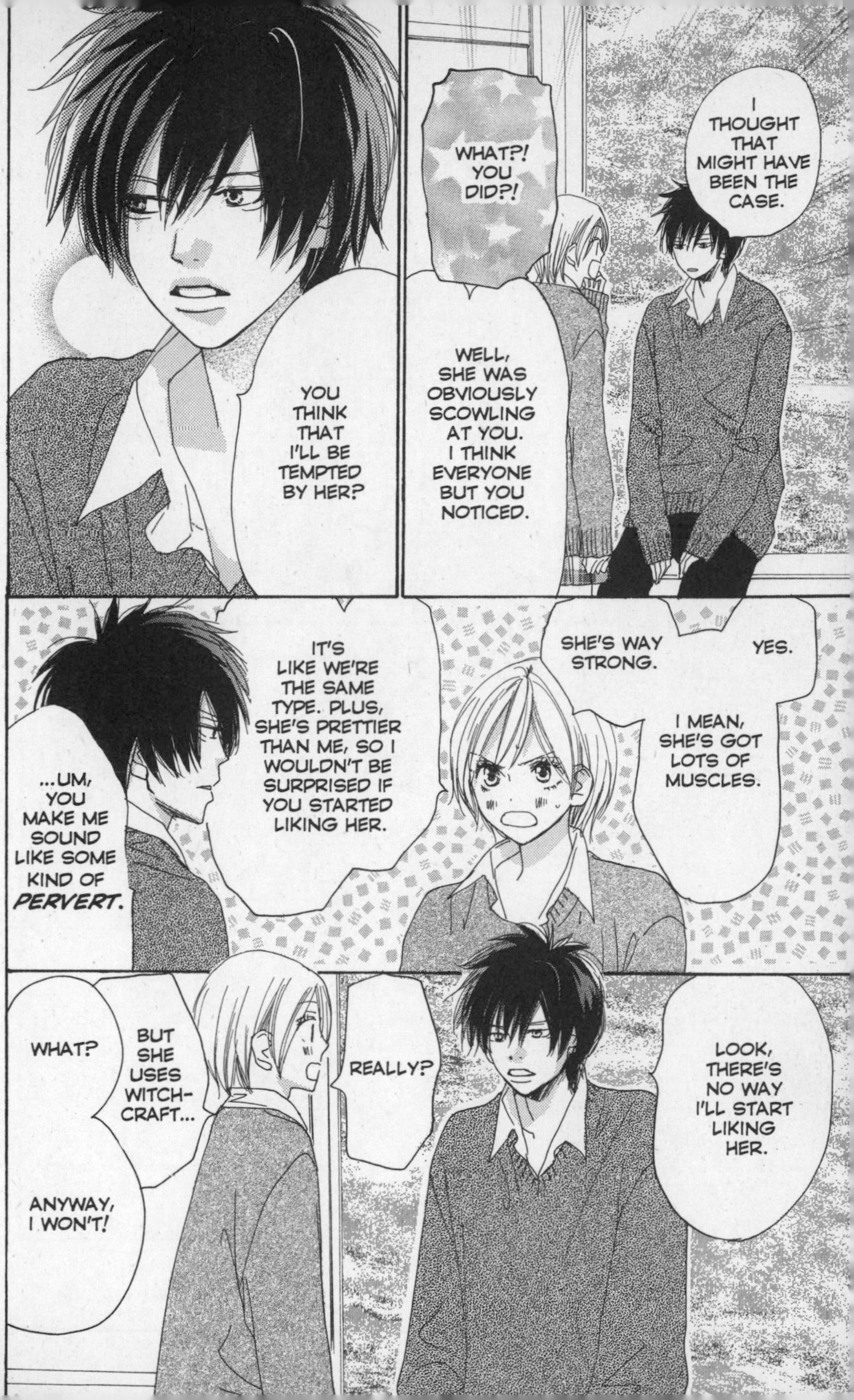
I THOUGHT THAT MIGHT HAVE BEEN THE CASE.
WHAT?! YOU DID?!
WELL, SHE WAS OBVIOUSLY SCOWLING AT YOU. I THINK EVERYONE BUT YOU NOTICED.
YOU THINK THAT I'LL BE TEMPTED BY HER?
YES.
SHE'S WAY STRONG.
I MEAN, SHE'S GOT LOTS OF MUSCLES.
IT'S LIKE WE'RE THE SAME TYPE. PLUS, SHE'S PRETTIER THAN ME, SO I WOULDN'T BE SURPRISED IF YOU STARTED LIKING HER.
...UM, YOU MAKE ME SOUND LIKE SOME KIND OF PERVERT.
LOOK, THERE'S NO WAY I'LL START LIKING HER.
REALLY?
BUT SHE USES WITCHCRAFT...
WHAT?
ANYWAY, I WON'T!

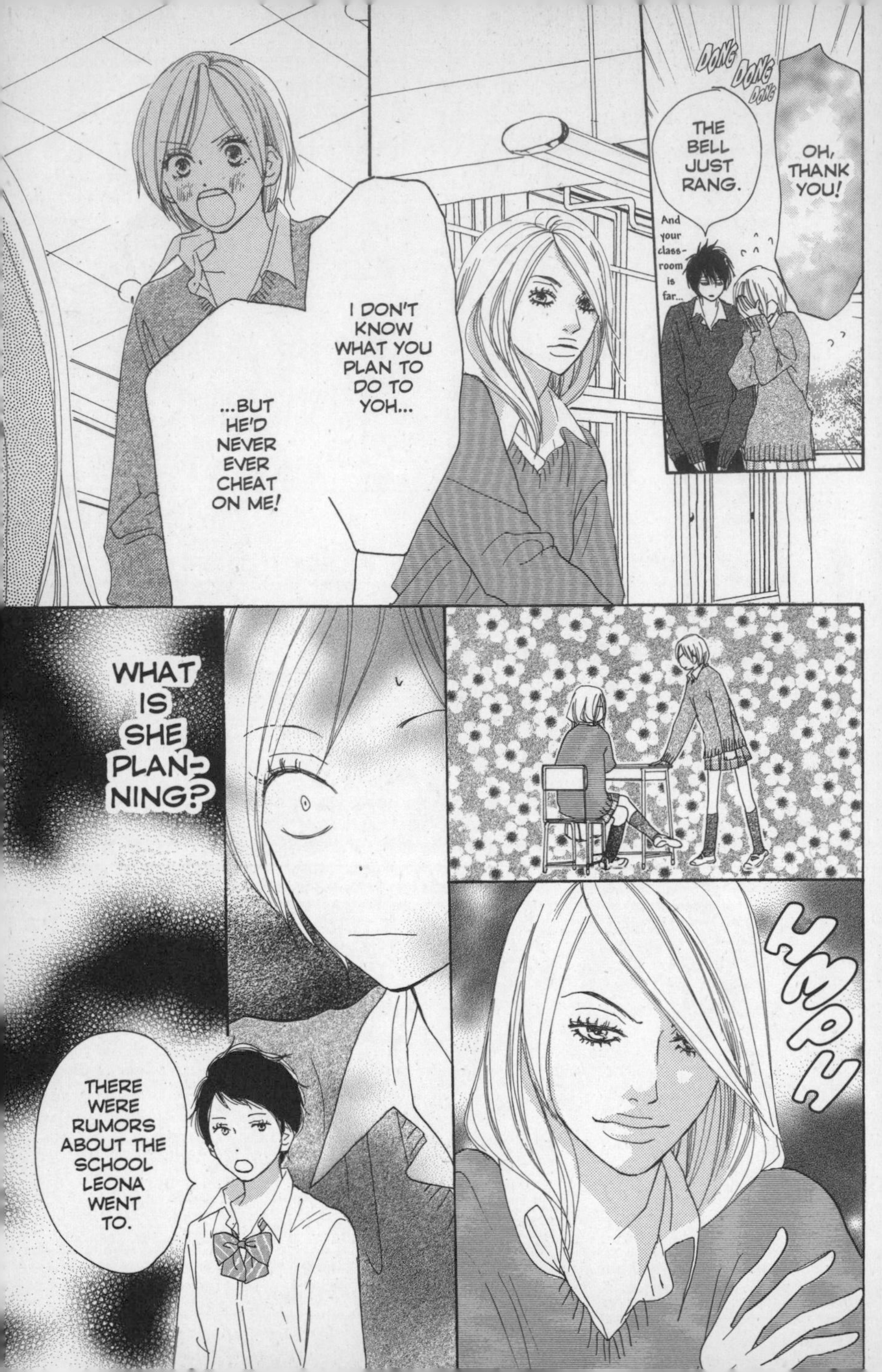
DONG DONG DONG
THE BELL JUST RANG.
And your class-room is far...
OH, THANK YOU!
I DON'T KNOW WHAT YOU PLAN TO DO TO YOH...
...BUT HE'D NEVER EVER CHEAT ON ME!
HMPH
WHAT IS SHE PLAN-NING?
THERE WERE RUMORS ABOUT THE SCHOOL LEONA WENT TO.

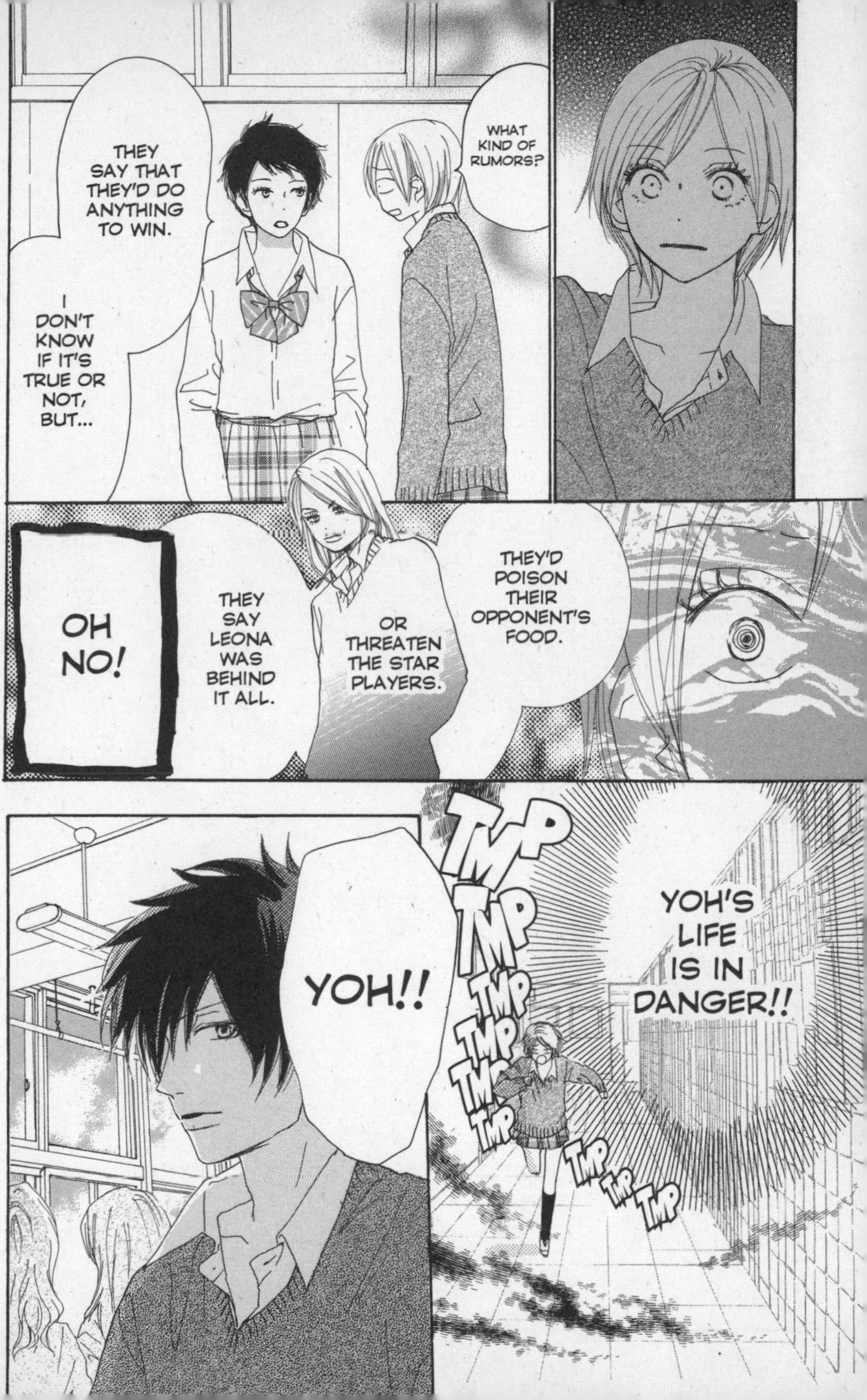
WHAT KIND OF RUMORS?
THEY SAY THAT THEY'D DO ANYTHING TO WIN.
I DON'T KNOW IF IT'S TRUE OR NOT, BUT...
THEY'D POISON THEIR OPPONENT'S FOOD.
OR THREATEN THE STAR PLAYERS.
THEY SAY LEONA WAS BEHIND IT ALL.
OH NO!
YOH'S LIFE IS IN DANGER!!
TMP TMP TMP TMP TMP TMP TMP
TMP TMP TMP
YOH!!

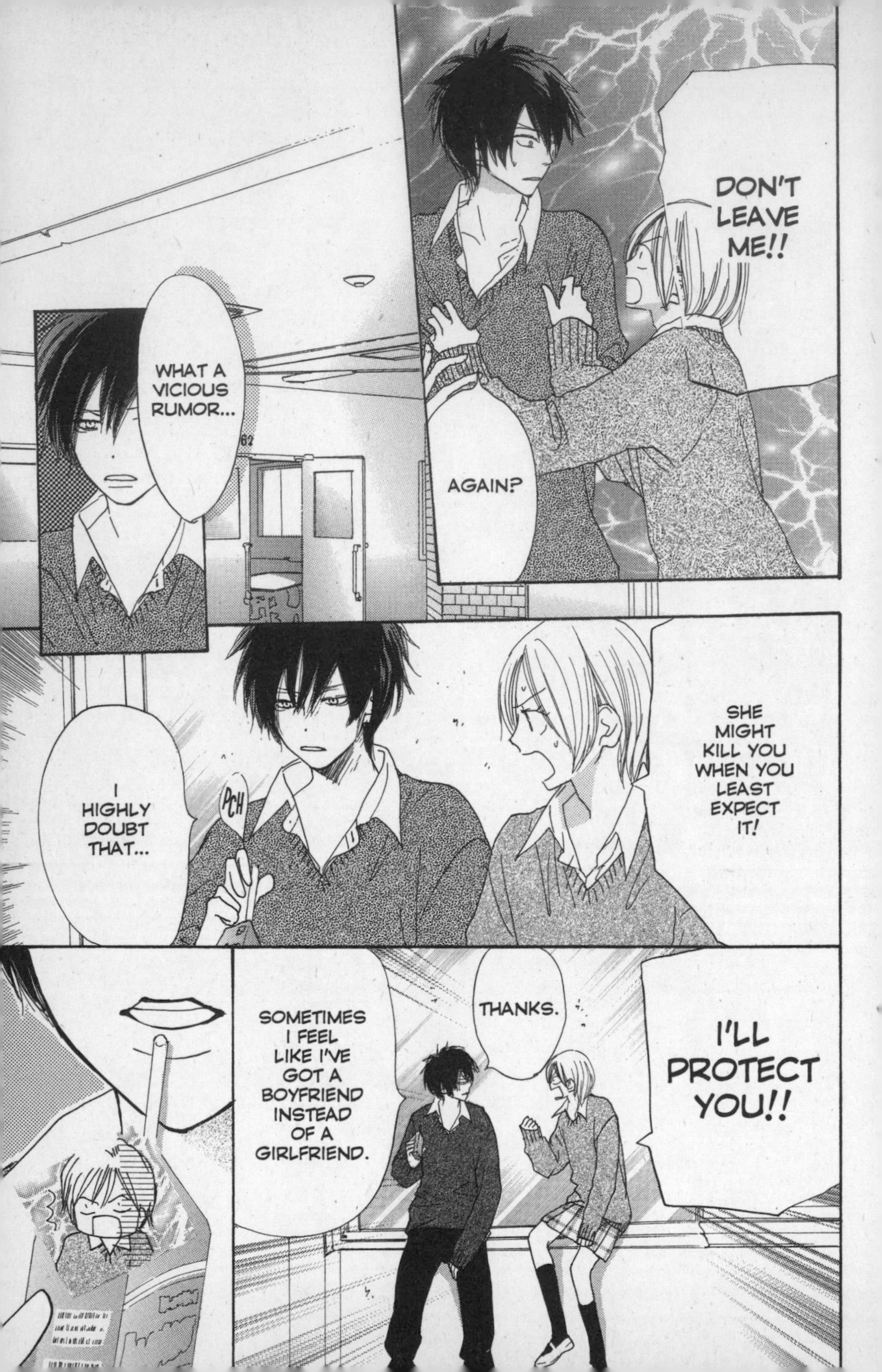
DON'T LEAVE ME!!
AGAIN?
WHAT A VICIOUS RUMOR...
SHE MIGHT KILL YOU WHEN YOU LEAST EXPECT IT!
PCH
I HIGHLY DOUBT THAT...
I'LL PROTECT YOU!!
THANKS.
SOMETIMES I FEEL LIKE I'VE GOT A BOYFRIEND INSTEAD OF A GIRLFRIEND.

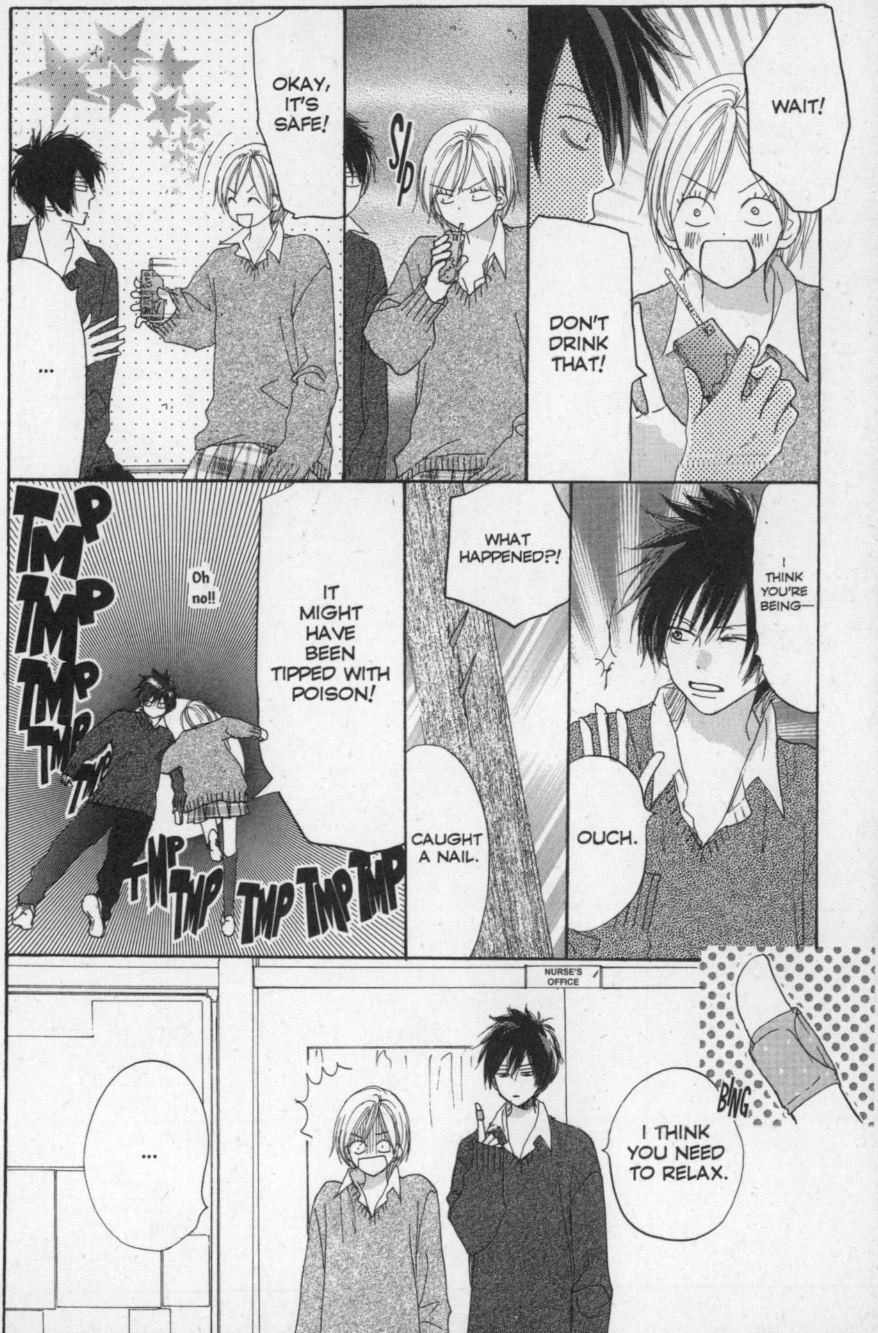
WAIT!
DON'T DRINK THAT!
SIP
OKAY, IT'S SAFE!
...
I THINK YOU'RE BEING—
OUCH.
WHAT HAPPENED?!
CAUGHT A NAIL.
IT MIGHT HAVE BEEN TIPPED WITH POISON!
Oh no!!
TMP TMP TMP TMP TMP TMP TMP TMP TMP TMP
BING
NURSE'S OFFICE
I THINK YOU NEED TO RELAX.
...

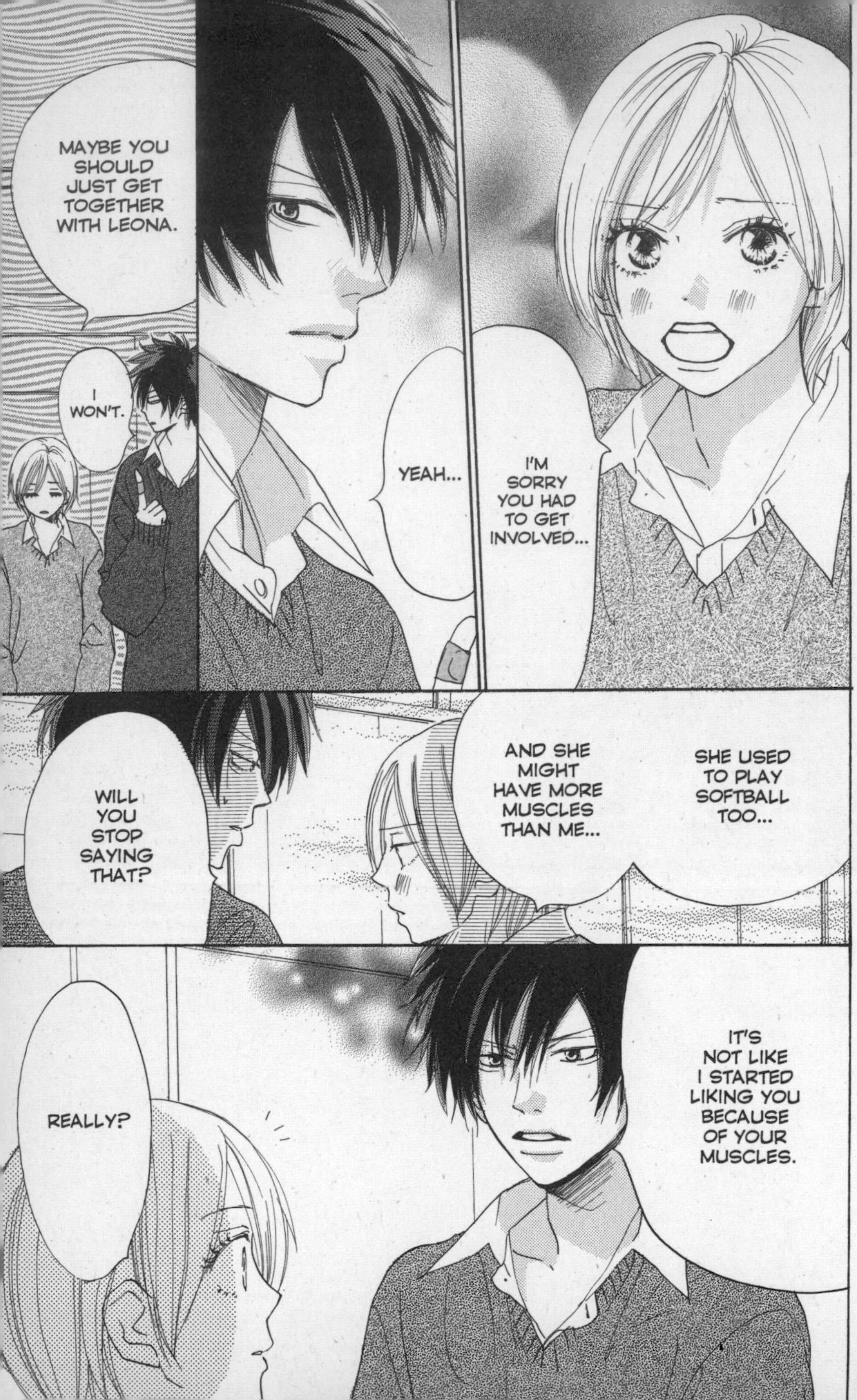
I'M SORRY YOU HAD TO GET INVOLVED...
YEAH...
MAYBE YOU SHOULD JUST GET TOGETHER WITH LEONA.
I WON'T.
SHE USED TO PLAY SOFTBALL TOO...
AND SHE MIGHT HAVE MORE MUSCLES THAN ME...
WILL YOU STOP SAYING THAT?
IT'S NOT LIKE I STARTED LIKING YOU BECAUSE OF YOUR MUSCLES.
REALLY?

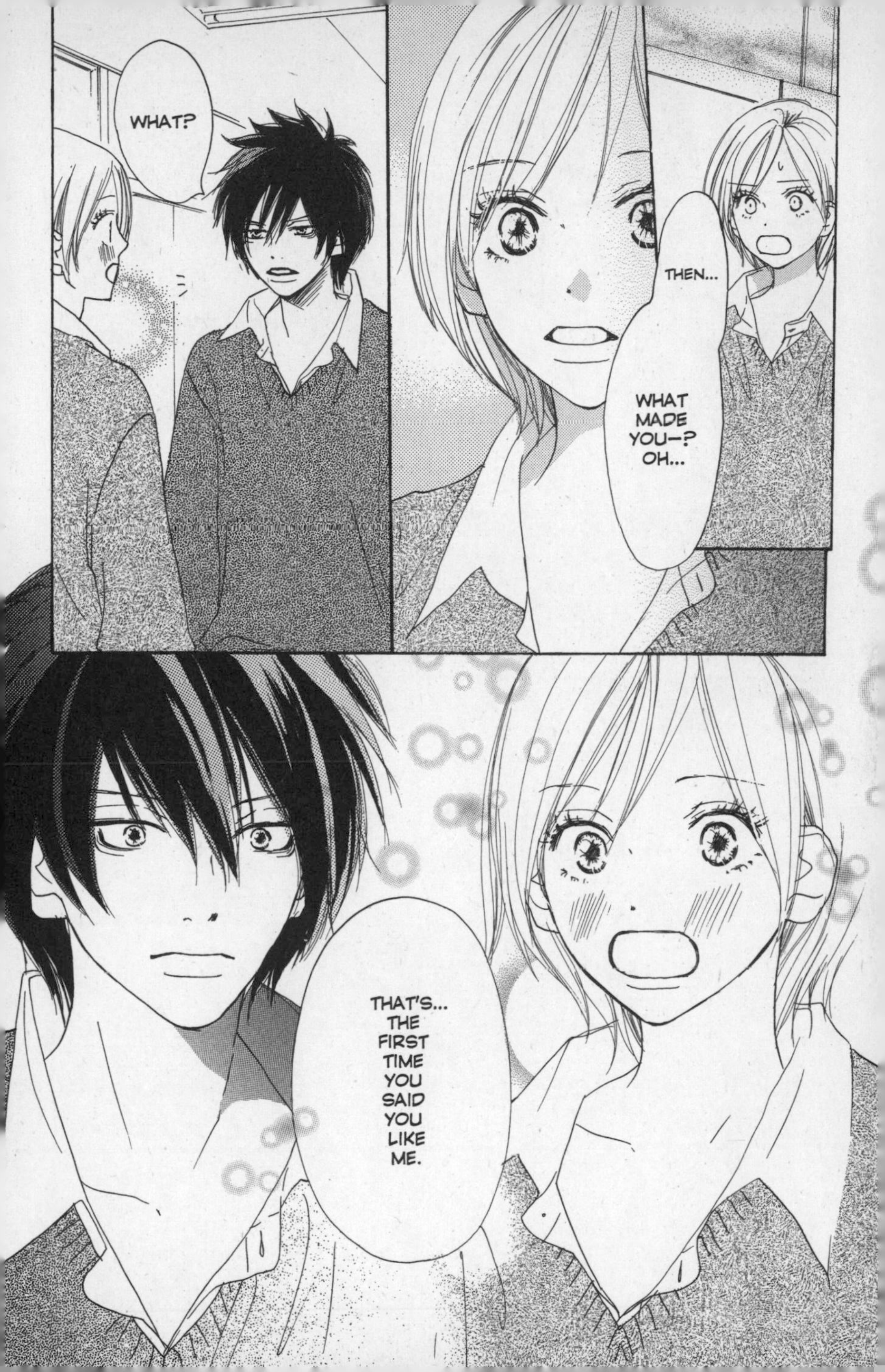
THEN...
WHAT MADE YOU—? OH...
WHAT?
THAT'S... THE FIRST TIME YOU SAID YOU LIKE ME.

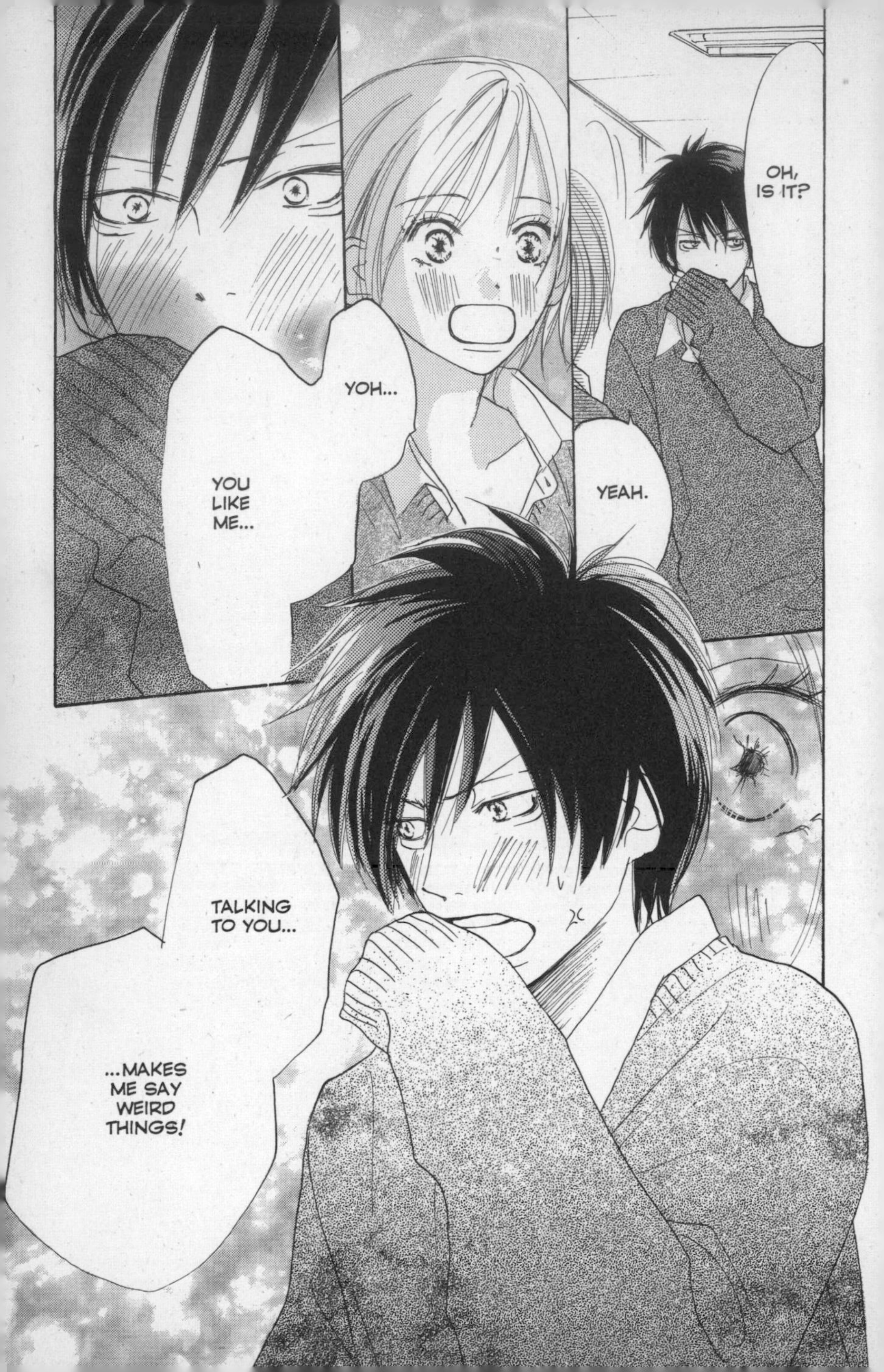
OH, IS IT?
YEAH.
YOH... YOU LIKE ME...
TALKING TO YOU...
...MAKES ME SAY WEIRD THINGS!

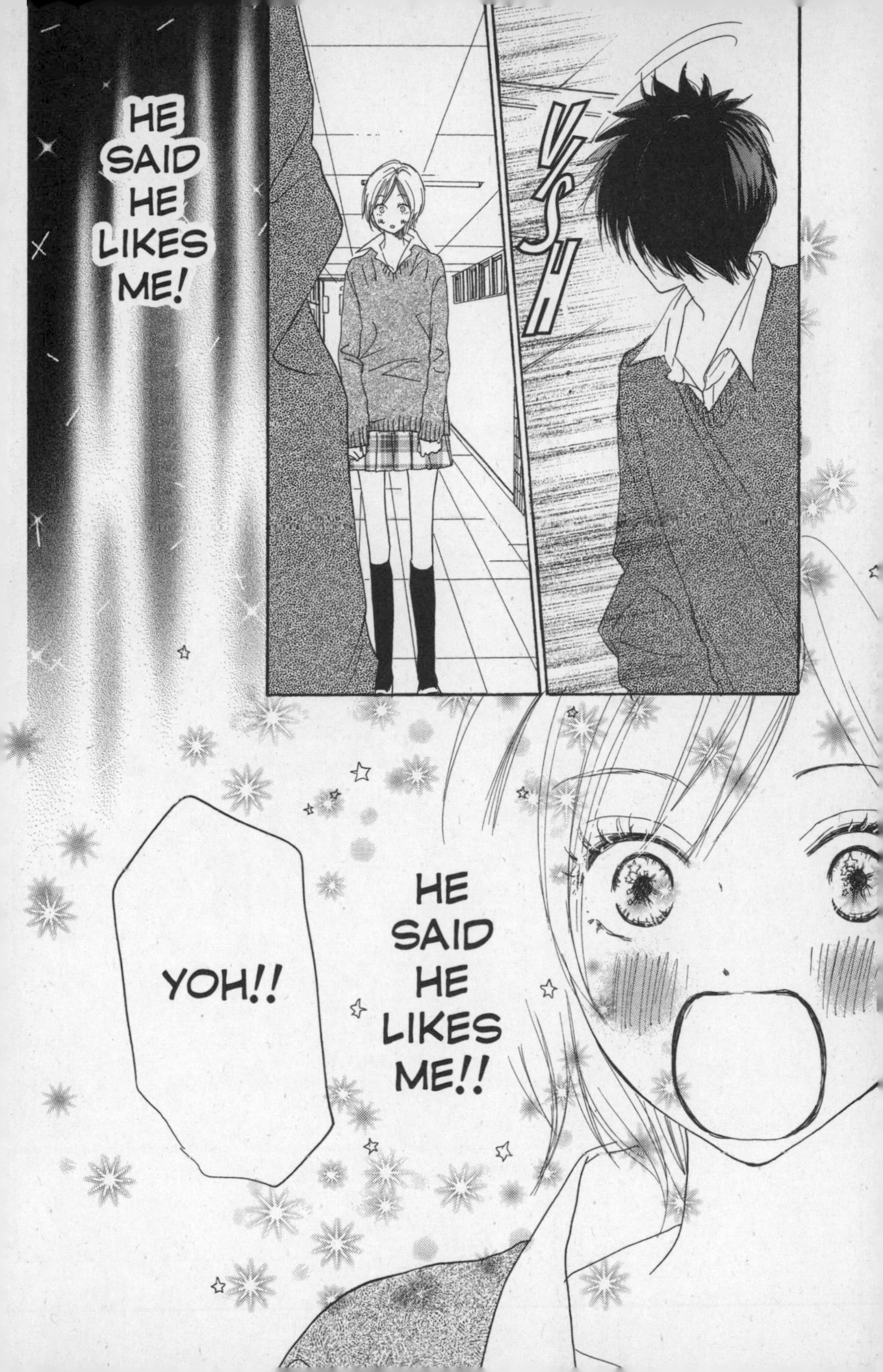
VWSH
HE SAID HE LIKES ME!
HE SAID HE LIKES ME!!
YOH!!

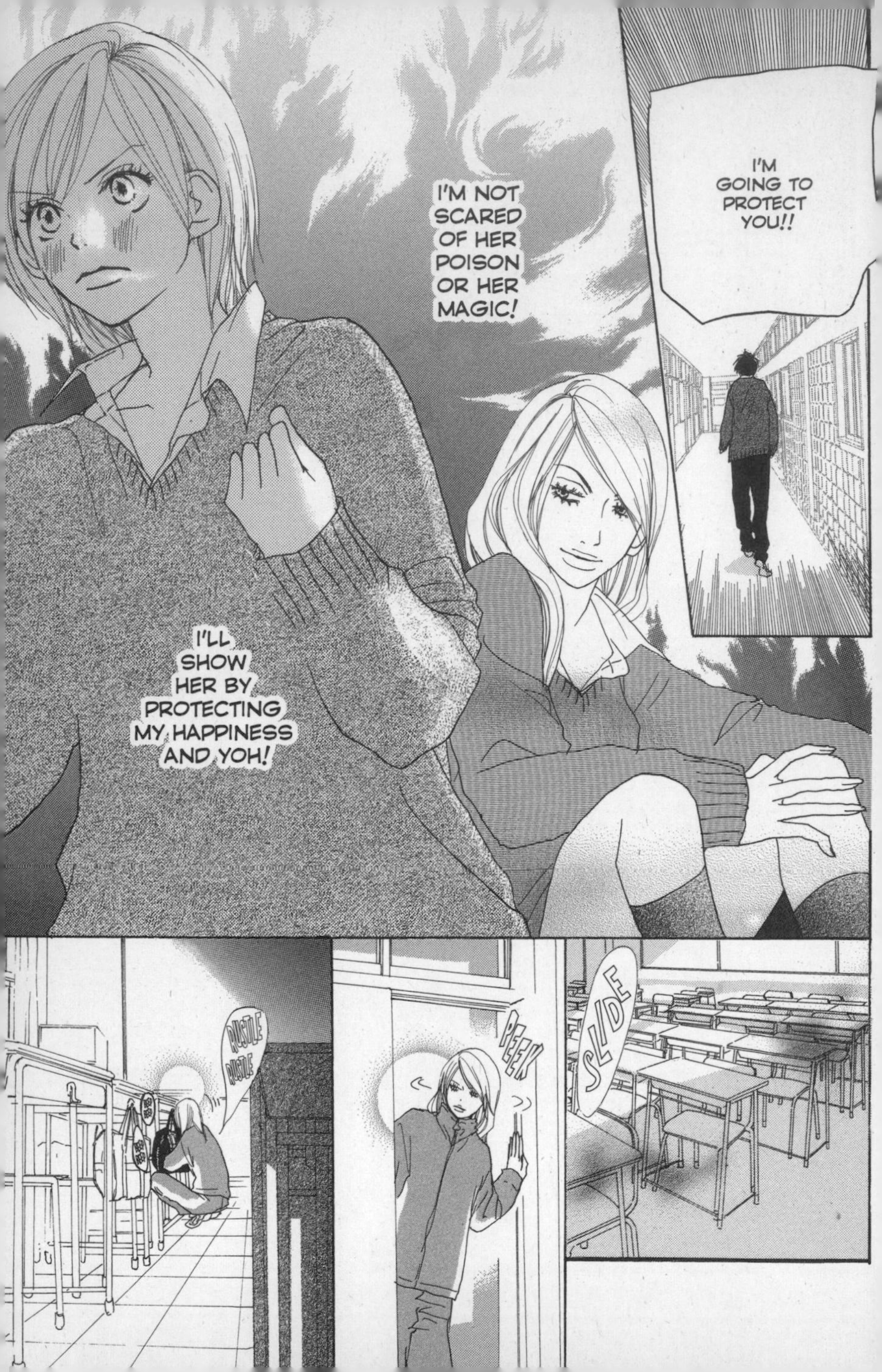
I'M GOING TO PROTECT YOU!!
I'M NOT SCARED OF HER POISON OR HER MAGIC!
I'LL SHOW HER BY PROTECTING MY HAPPINESS AND YOH!
SLIDE
PEEK
RUSTLE RUSTLE

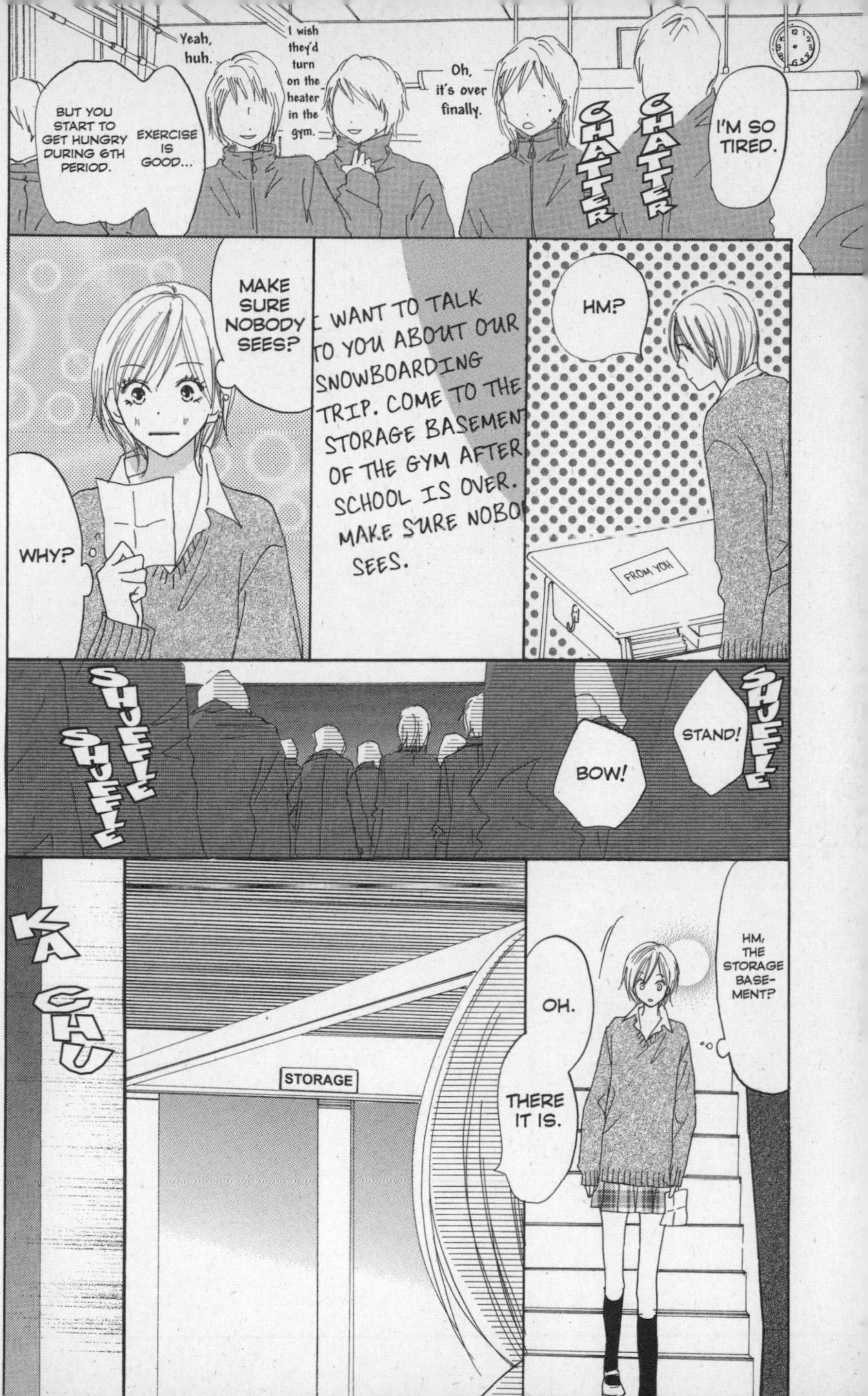
I'M SO TIRED.
CHATTER
CHATTER
Oh, it's over finally.
I wish they'd turn on the heater in the gym.
Yeah, huh.
EXERCISE IS GOOD...
BUT YOU START TO GET HUNGRY DURING 6TH PERIOD.
HM?
FROM YOH
I WANT TO TALK TO YOU ABOUT OUR SNOWBOARDING TRIP. COME TO THE STORAGE BASEMEN OF THE GYM AFTER SCHOOL IS OVER. MAKE SURE NOBO SEES.
MAKE SURE NOBODY SEES?
WHY?
SHUFFLE
STAND!
BOW!
SHUFFLE
SHUFFLE
HM, THE STORAGE BASE- MENT?
OH.
THERE IT IS.
STORAGE
KA CHU

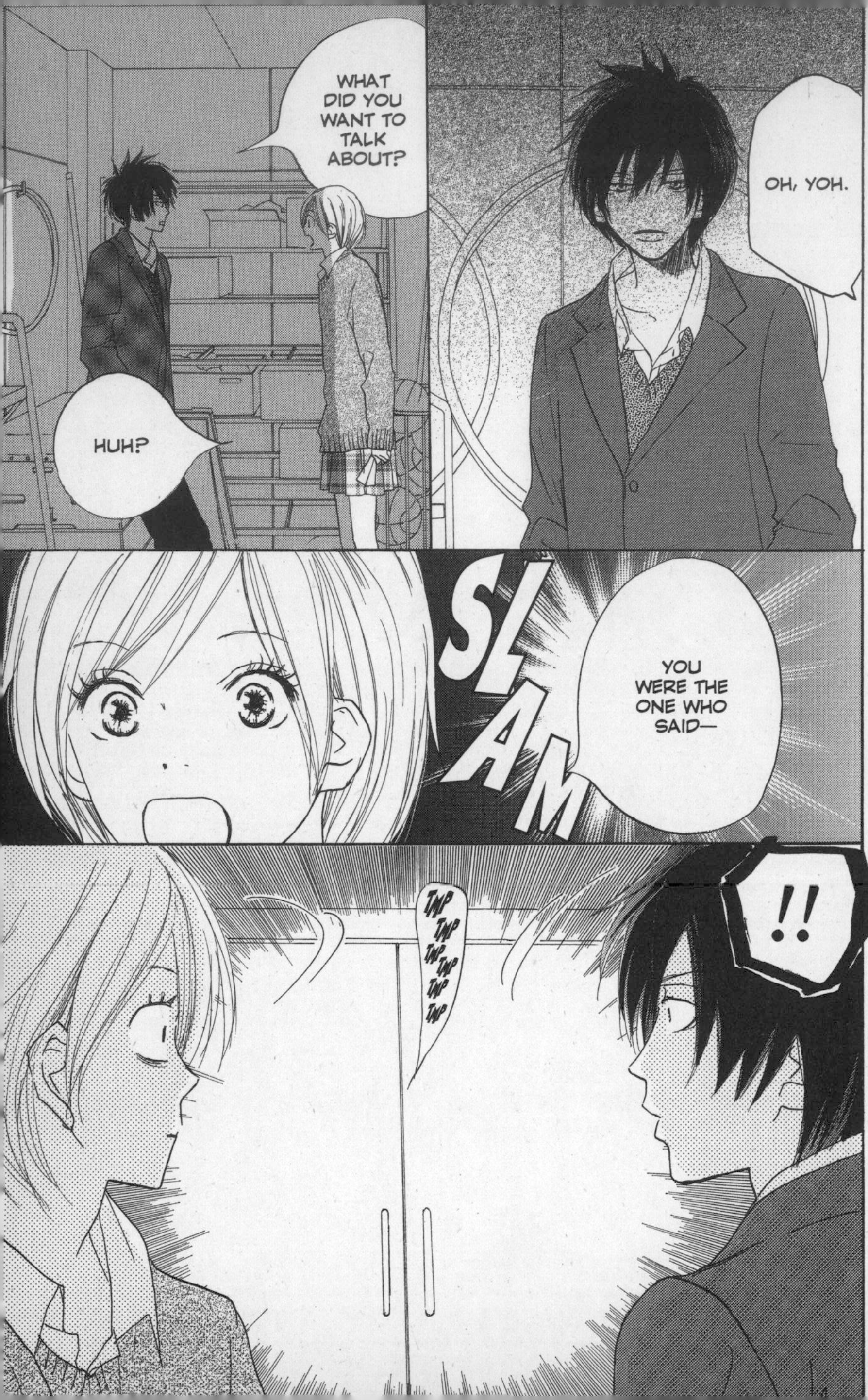
OH, YOH.
WHAT DID YOU WANT TO TALK ABOUT?
HUH?
YOU WERE THE ONE WHO SAID—
SLAM
!!
TMP TMP TMP TMP TMP TMP TMP

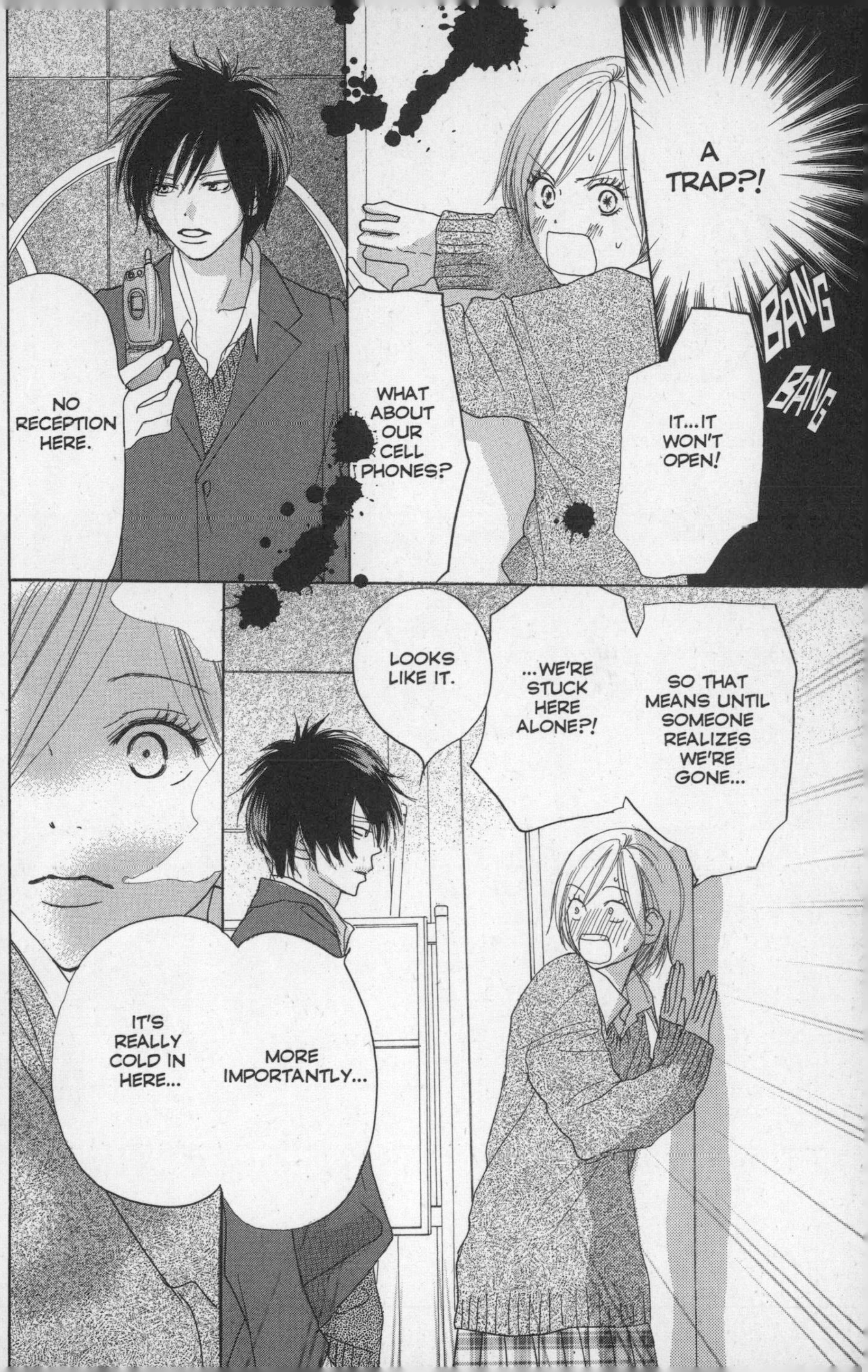
A TRAP?!
BANG
BANG
IT...IT WON'T OPEN!
WHAT ABOUT OUR CELL PHONES?
NO RECEPTION HERE.
SO THAT MEANS UNTIL SOMEONE REALIZES WE'RE GONE...
...WE'RE STUCK HERE ALONE?!
LOOKS LIKE IT.
MORE IMPORTANTLY...
IT'S REALLY COLD IN HERE...

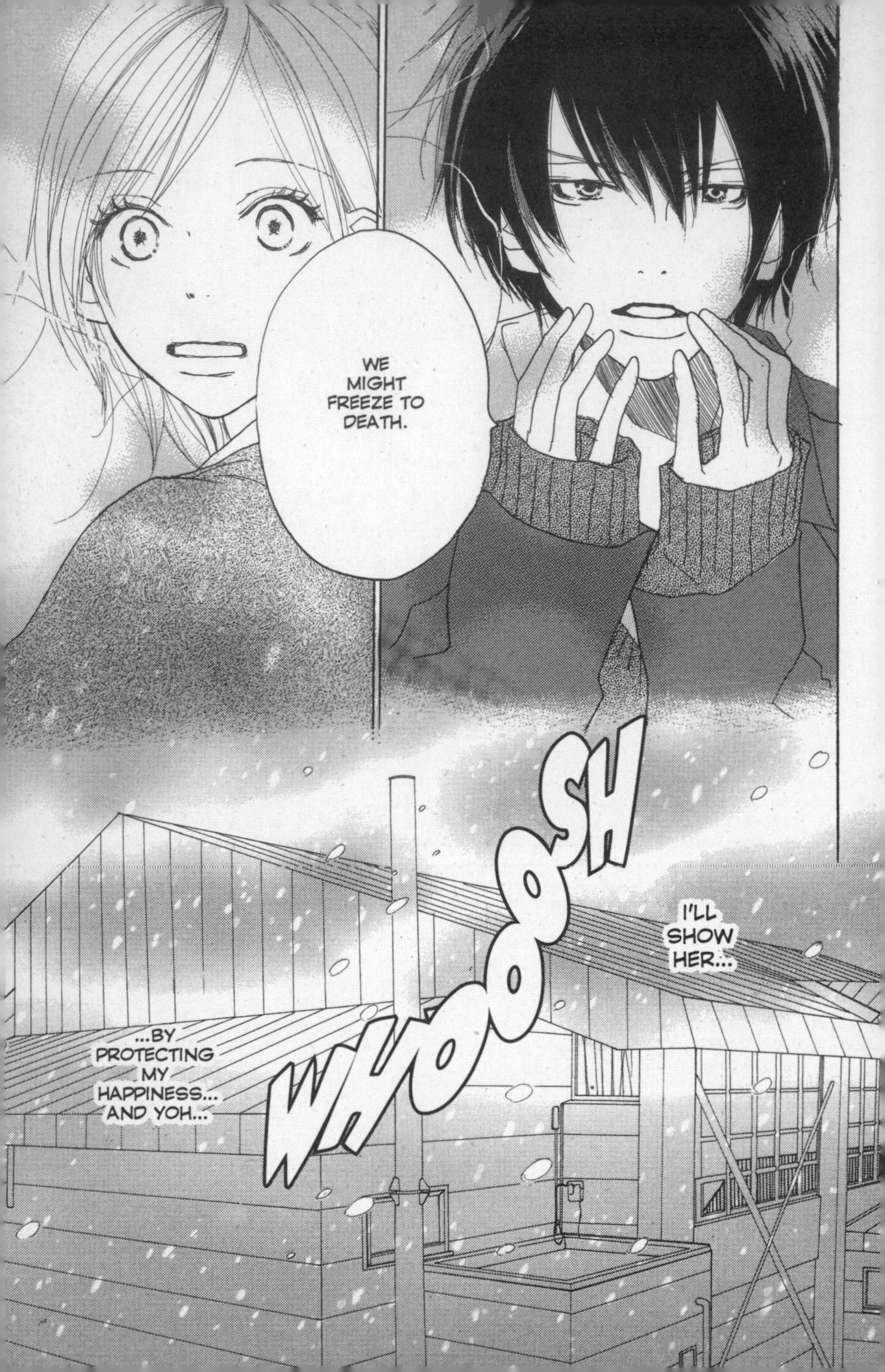
WE MIGHT FREEZE TO DEATH.
WHOOOOSH
I'LL SHOW HER...
...BY PROTECTING MY HAPPINESS... AND YOH...

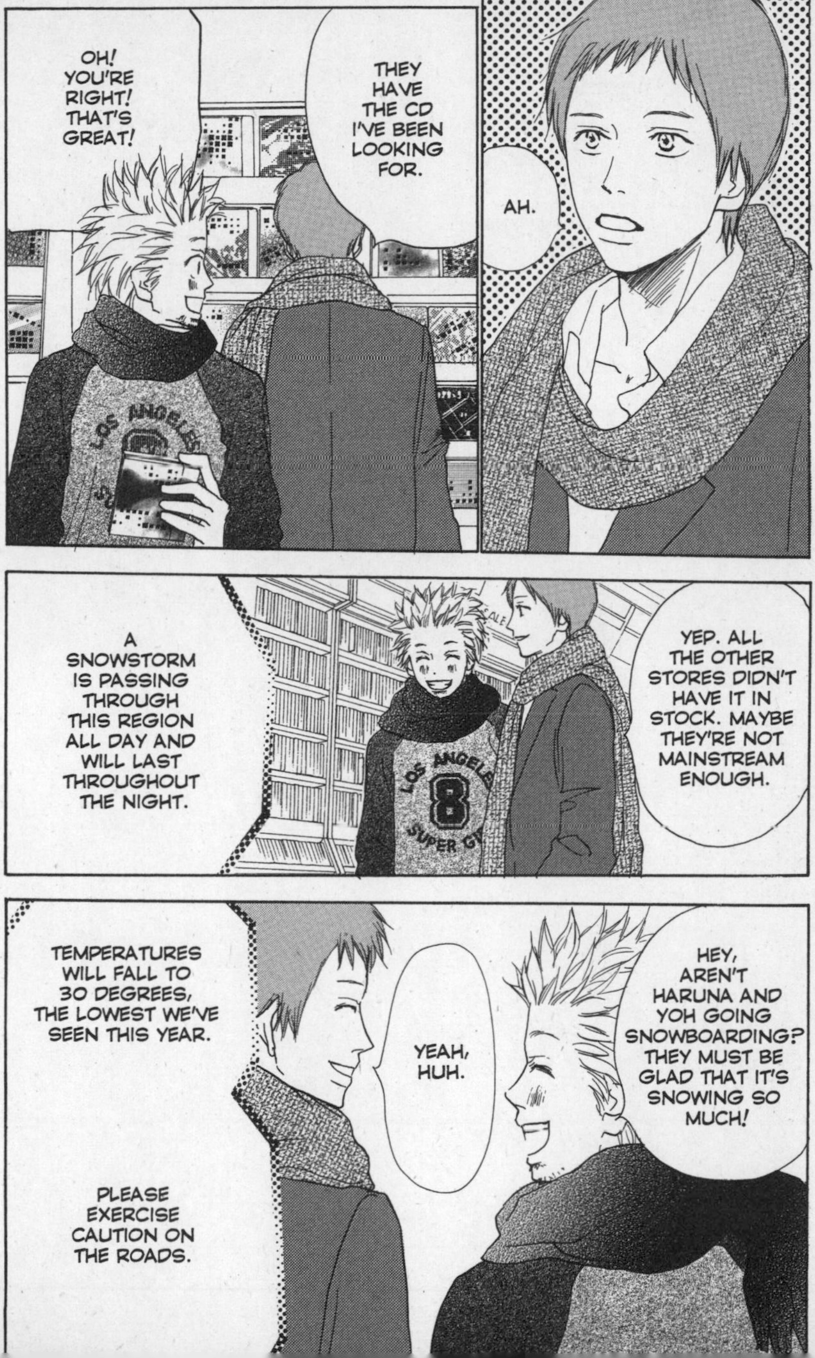
AH.
THEY HAVE THE CD I'VE BEEN LOOKING FOR.
OH! YOU'RE RIGHT! THAT'S GREAT!
YEP. ALL THE OTHER STORES DIDN'T HAVE IT IN STOCK. MAYBE THEY'RE NOT MAINSTREAM ENOUGH.
A SNOWSTORM IS PASSING THROUGH THIS REGION ALL DAY AND WILL LAST THROUGHOUT THE NIGHT.
HEY, AREN'T HARUNA AND YOH GOING SNOWBOARDING? THEY MUST BE GLAD THAT IT'S SNOWING SO MUCH!
YEAH, HUH.
TEMPERATURES WILL FALL TO 30 DEGREES, THE LOWEST WE'VE SEEN THIS YEAR.
PLEASE EXERCISE CAUTION ON THE ROADS.

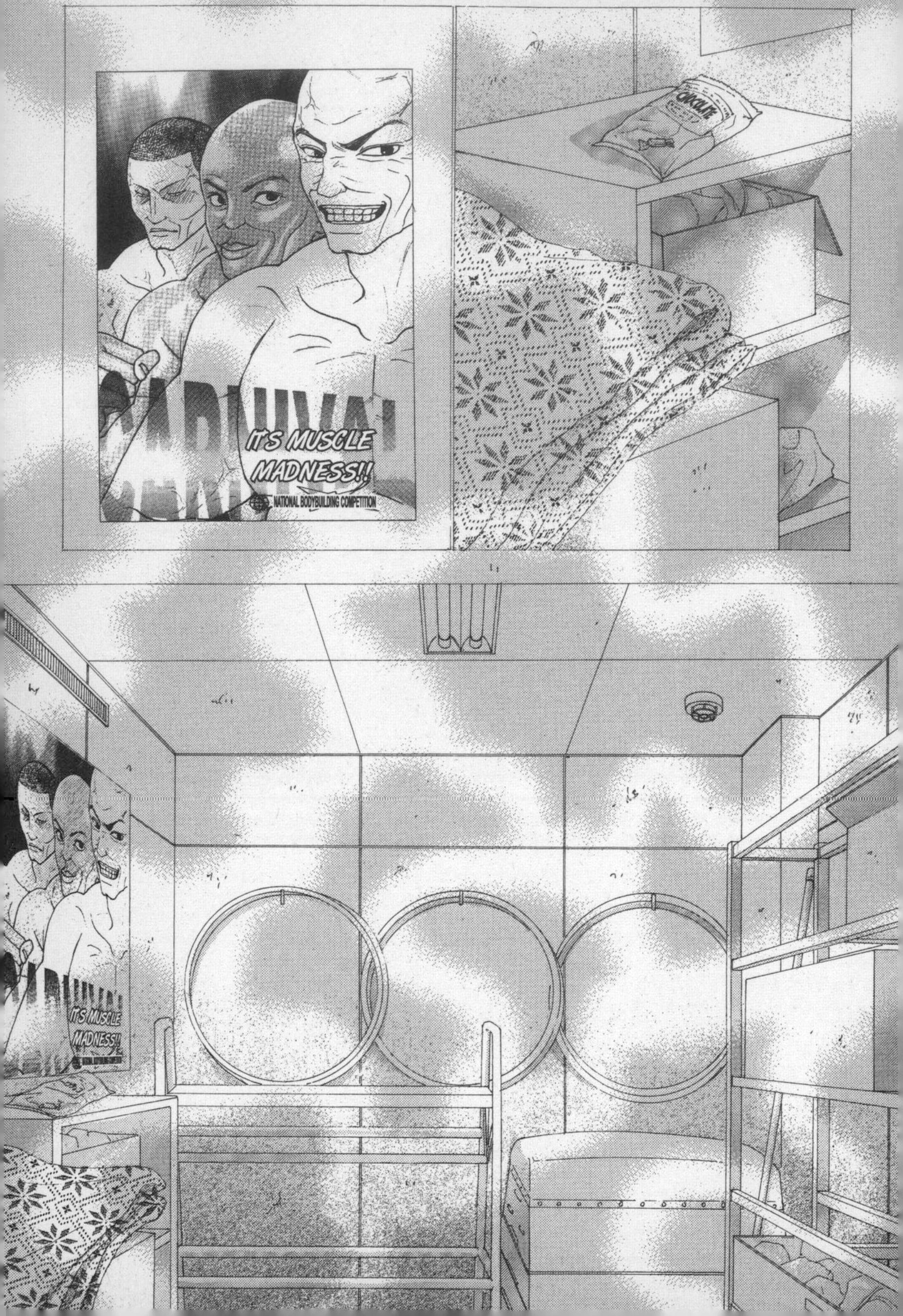
CHOCOLATE
IT'S MUSCLE MADNESS!!
NATIONAL BODYBUILDING COMPETITION
IT'S MUSCLE MADNESS!!

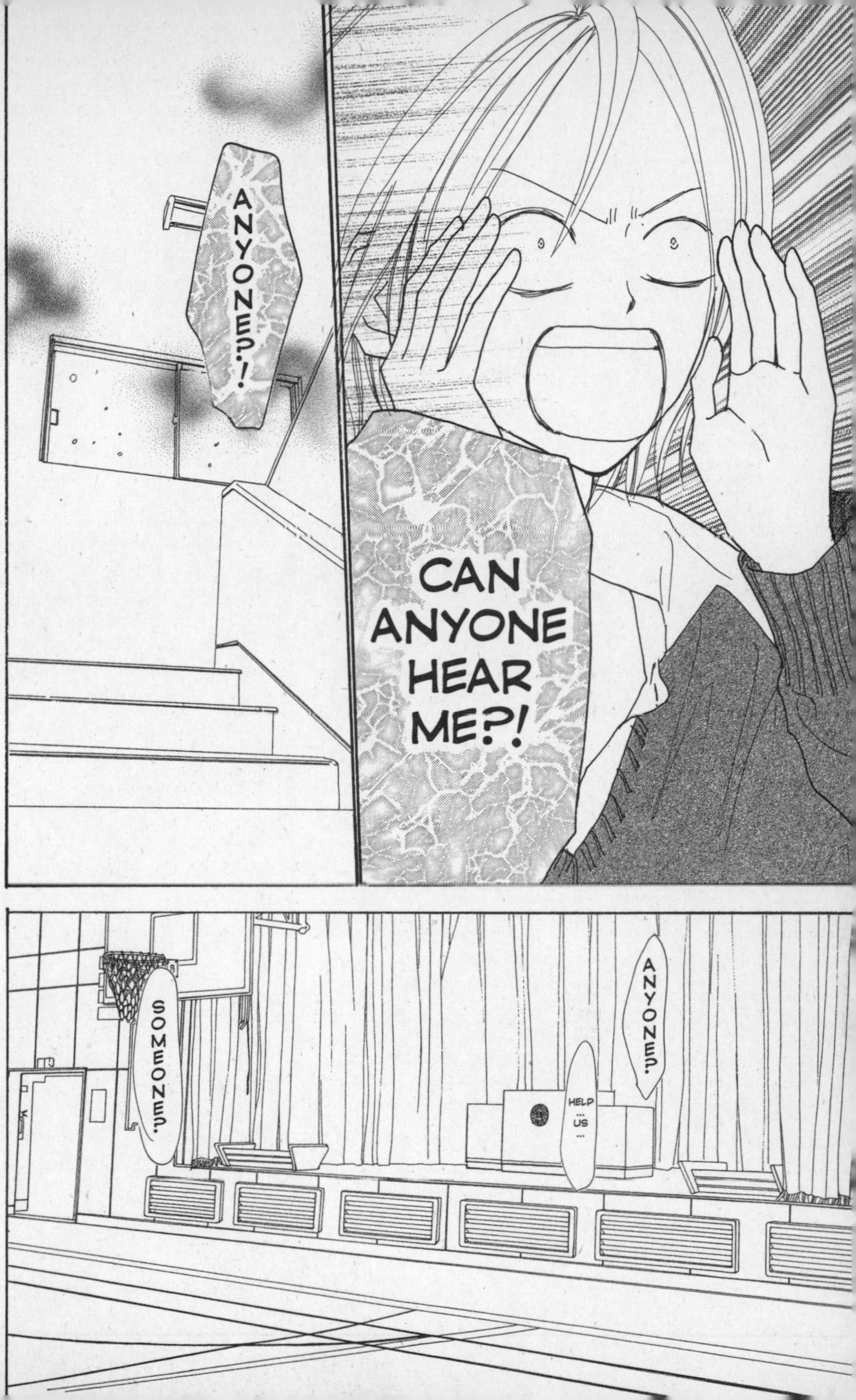
CAN ANYONE HEAR ME?!
ANYONE?!
ANYONE?
HELP ... US ...
SOMEONE?

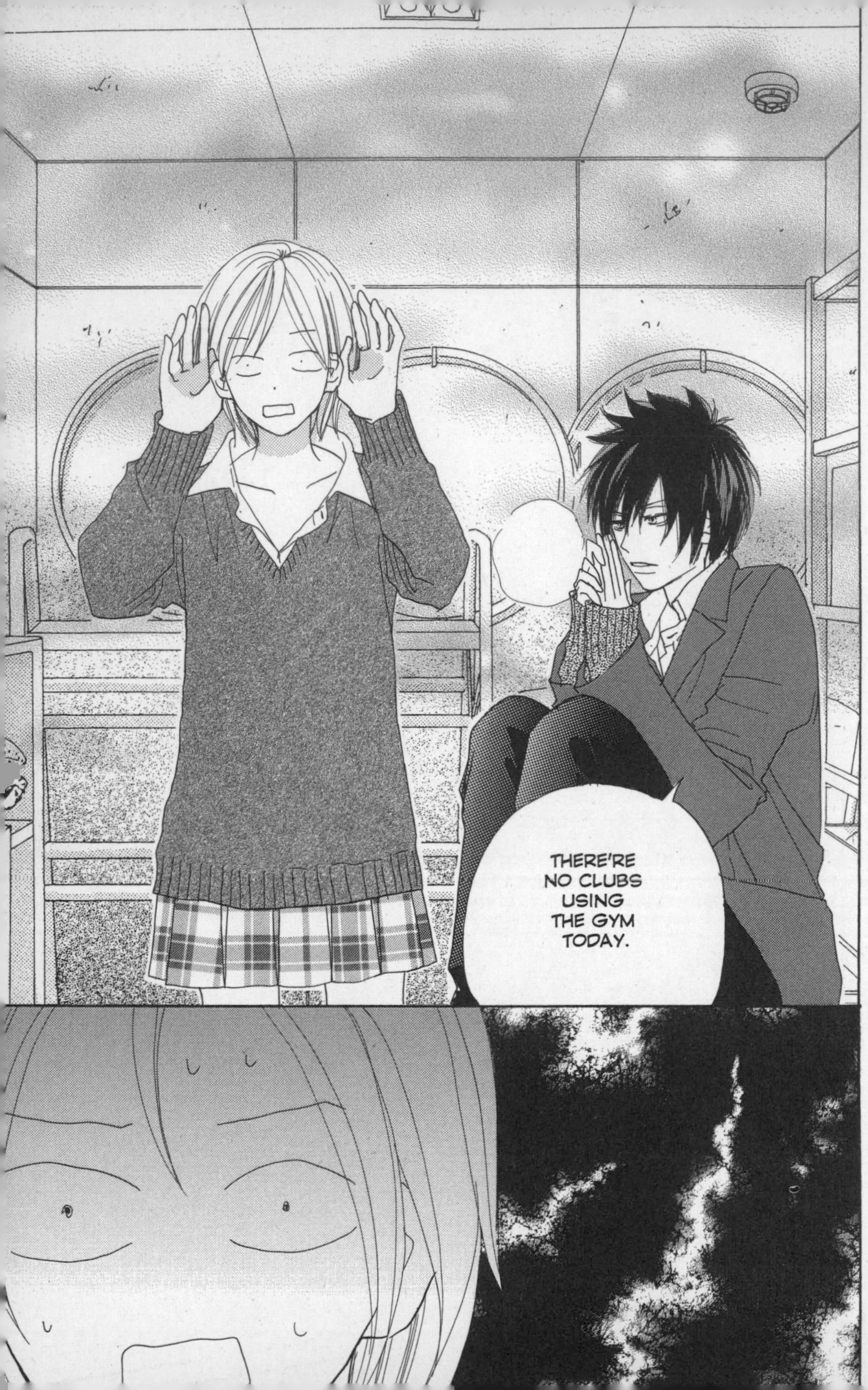
THERE'RE NO CLUBS USING THE GYM TODAY.

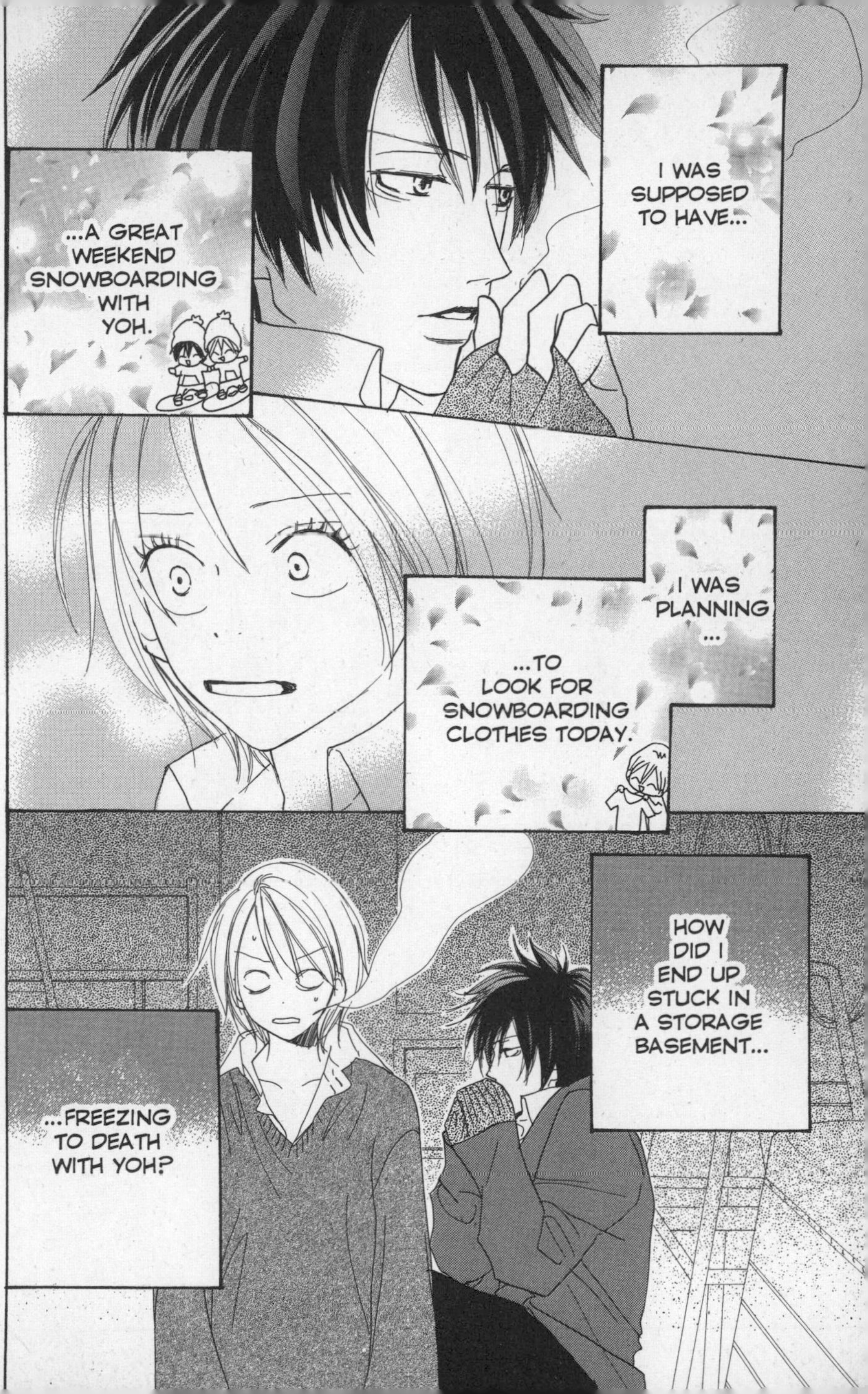
I WAS SUPPOSED TO HAVE...
...A GREAT WEEKEND SNOWBOARDING WITH YOH.
I WAS PLANNING...
...TO LOOK FOR SNOWBOARDING CLOTHES TODAY.
HOW DID I END UP STUCK IN A STORAGE BASEMENT...
...FREEZING TO DEATH WITH YOH?

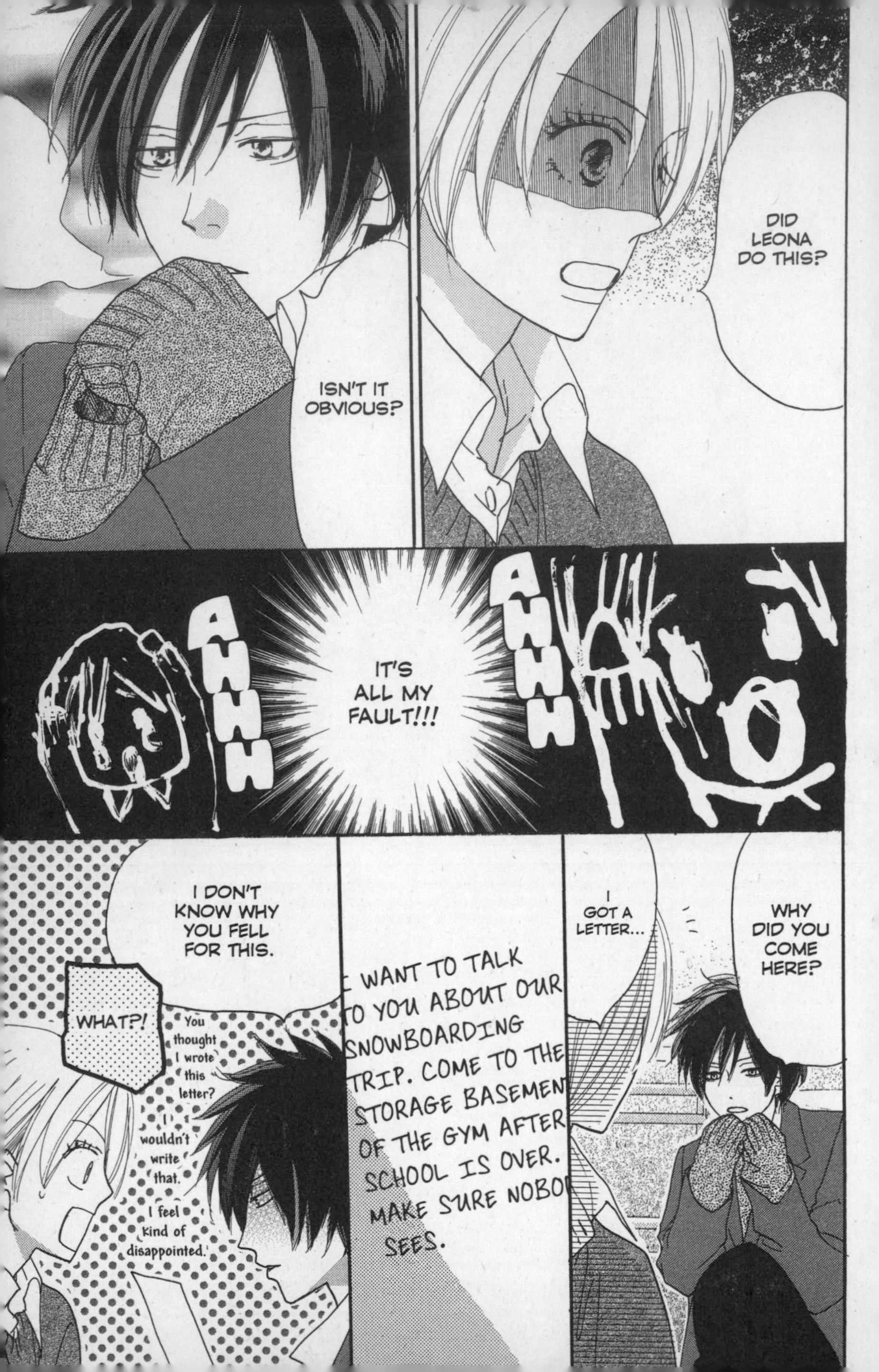
DID LEONA DO THIS?
ISN'T IT OBVIOUS?
AHHHH
IT'S ALL MY FAULT!!!
AHHHH
WHY DID YOU COME HERE?
I GOT A LETTER...
I WANT TO TALK TO YOU ABOUT OUR SNOWBOARDING TRIP. COME TO THE STORAGE BASEMEN OF THE GYM AFTER SCHOOL IS OVER. MAKE SURE NOBO SEES.
I DON'T KNOW WHY YOU FELL FOR THIS.
WHAT?!
You thought I wrote this letter? I wouldn't write that. I feel kind of disappointed.

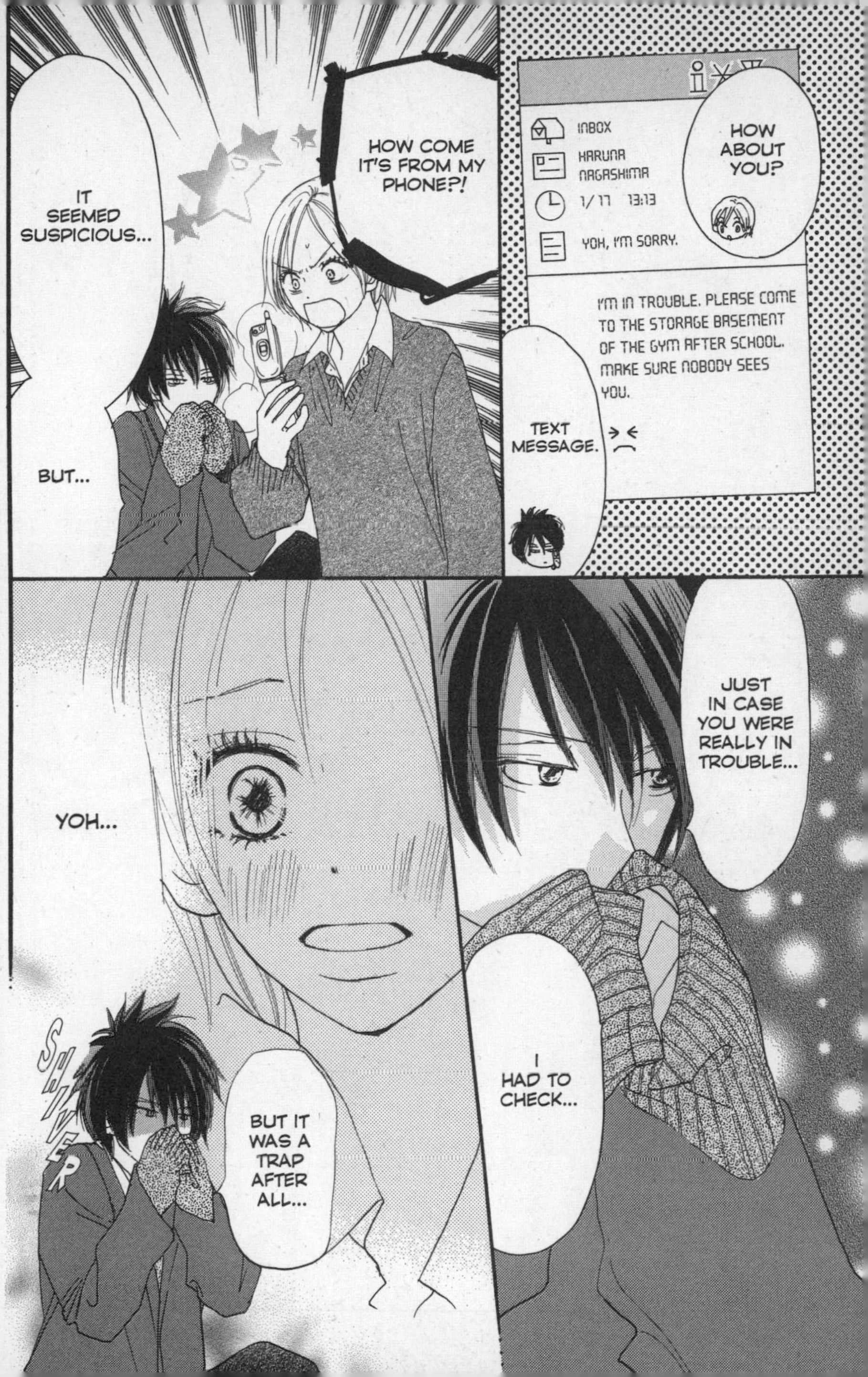
HOW ABOUT YOU?
INBOX
HARUNA NAGASHIMA
1/17 13:13
YOH, I'M SORRY.
I'M IN TROUBLE. PLEASE COME TO THE STORAGE BASEMENT OF THE GYM AFTER SCHOOL. MAKE SURE NOBODY SEES YOU.
>_<
TEXT MESSAGE.
HOW COME IT'S FROM MY PHONE?!
IT SEEMED SUSPICIOUS...
BUT...
JUST IN CASE YOU WERE REALLY IN TROUBLE...
I HAD TO CHECK...
YOH...
BUT IT WAS A TRAP AFTER ALL...
SHIVER

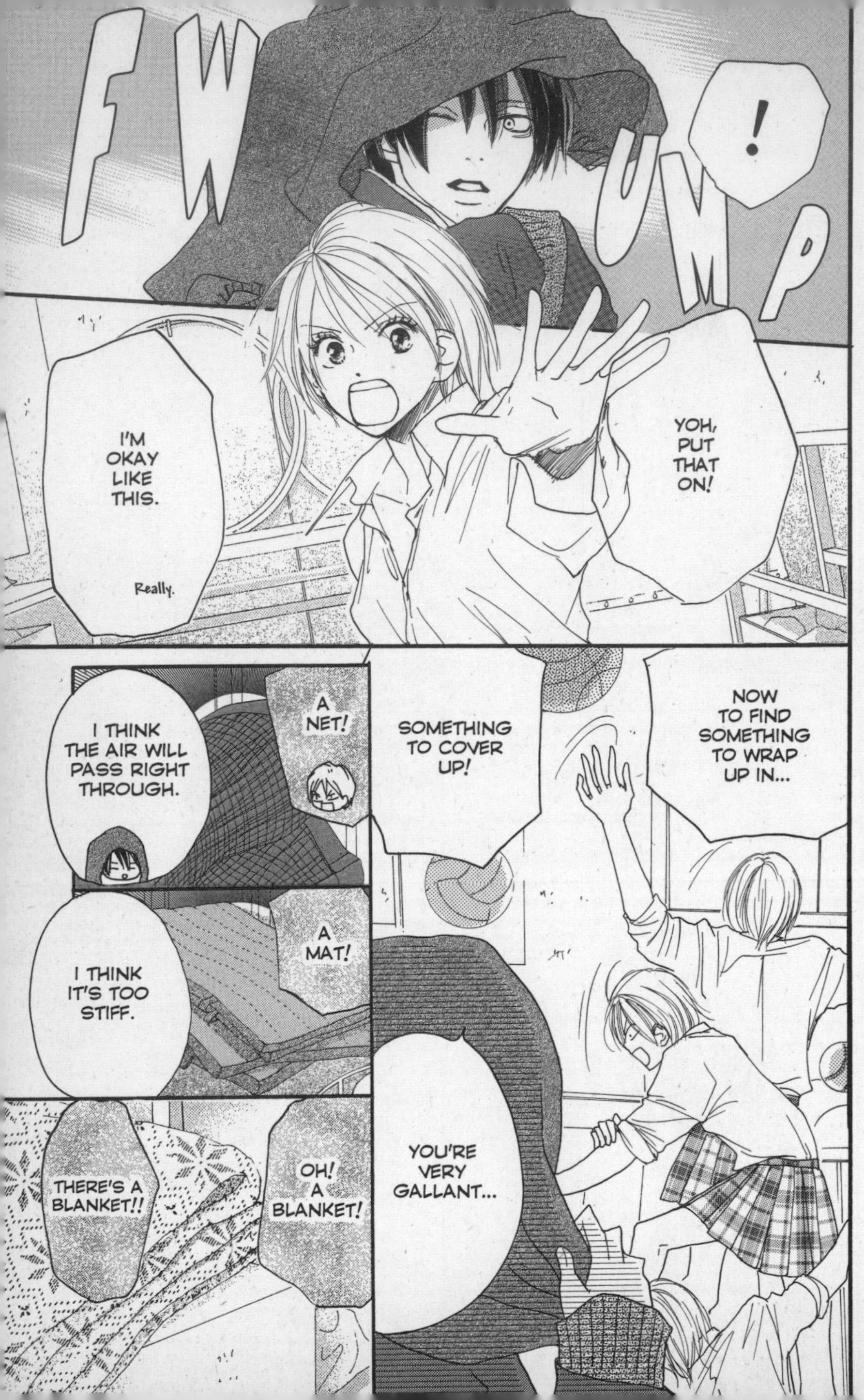
FWUMP!
YOH, PUT THAT ON!
I'M OKAY LIKE THIS.
Really.
NOW TO FIND SOMETHING TO WRAP UP IN...
SOMETHING TO COVER UP!
YOU'RE VERY GALLANT...
A NET!
I THINK THE AIR WILL PASS RIGHT THROUGH.
A MAT!
I THINK IT'S TOO STIFF.
OH! A BLANKET!
THERE'S A BLANKET!!

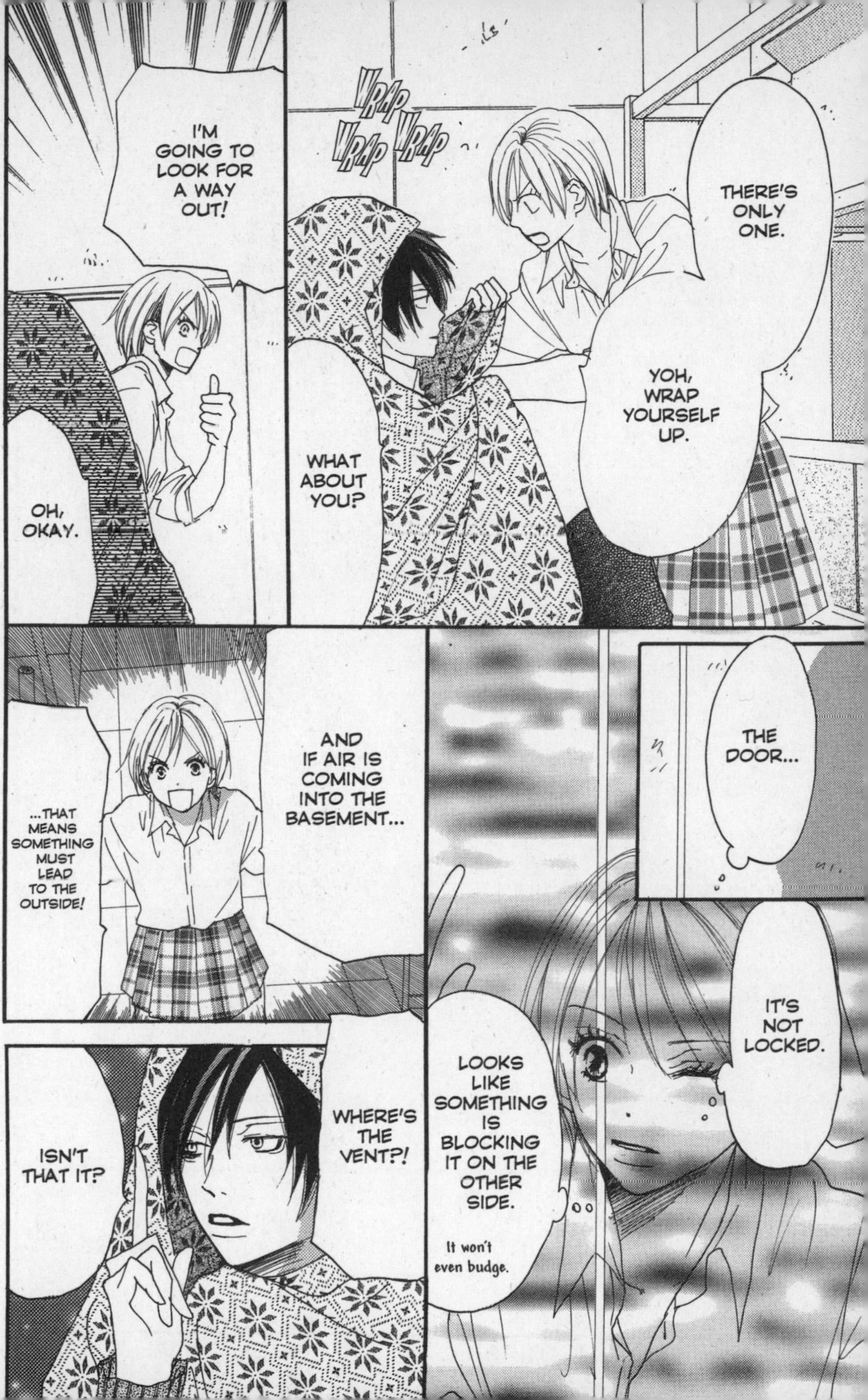
THERE'S ONLY ONE.
YOH, WRAP YOURSELF UP.
WRAP WRAP WRAP WRAP
WHAT ABOUT YOU?
I'M GOING TO LOOK FOR A WAY OUT!
OH, OKAY.
THE DOOR...
IT'S NOT LOCKED.
LOOKS LIKE SOMETHING IS BLOCKING IT ON THE OTHER SIDE.
It won't even budge.
AND IF AIR IS COMING INTO THE BASEMENT...
...THAT MEANS SOMETHING MUST LEAD TO THE OUTSIDE!
WHERE'S THE VENT?!
ISN'T THAT IT?

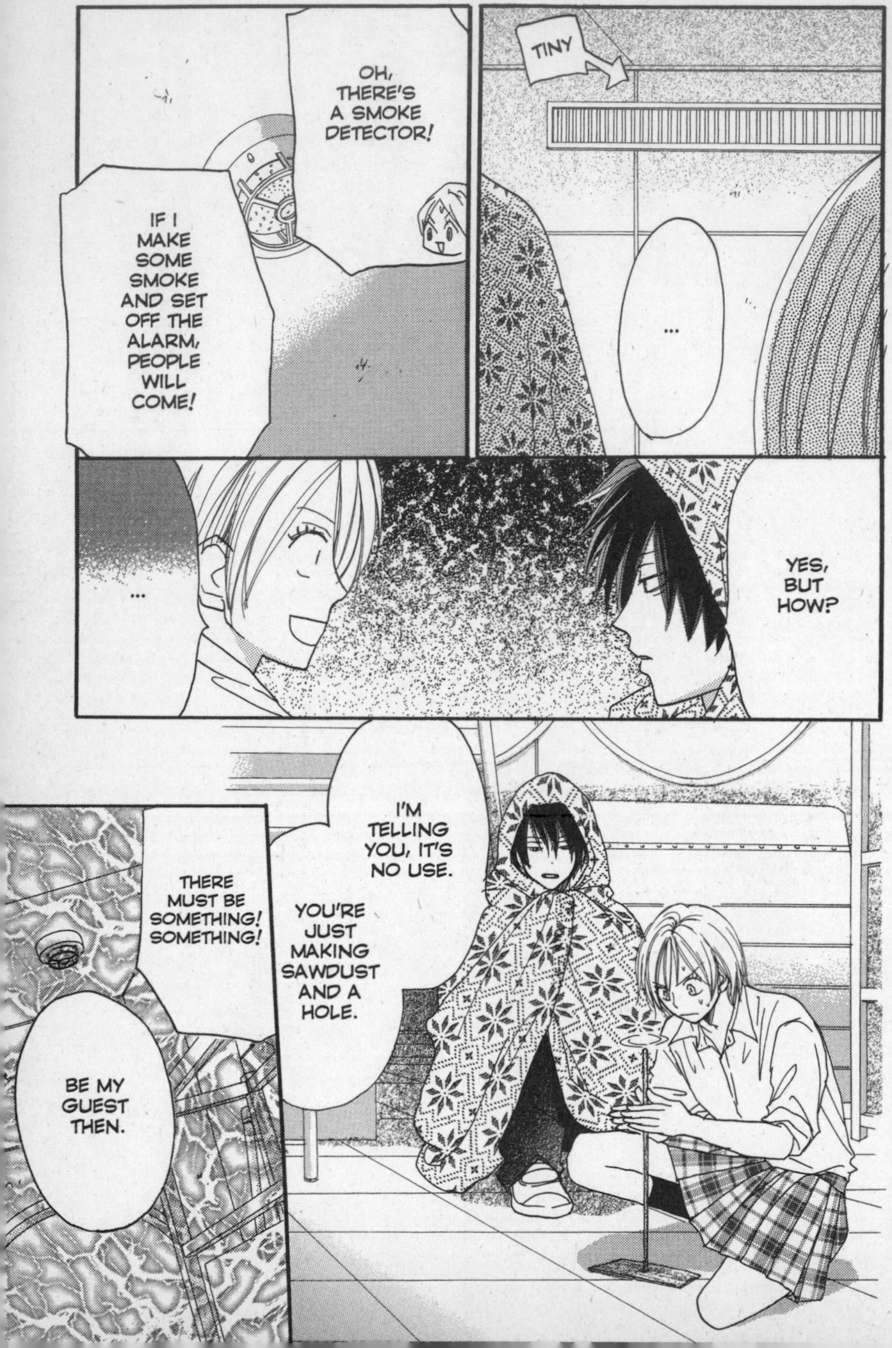
TINY
...
OH, THERE'S A SMOKE DETECTOR!
IF I MAKE SOME SMOKE AND SET OFF THE ALARM, PEOPLE WILL COME!
YES, BUT HOW?
...
I'M TELLING YOU, IT'S NO USE.
YOU'RE JUST MAKING SAWDUST AND A HOLE.
THERE MUST BE SOMETHING! SOMETHING!
BE MY GUEST THEN.

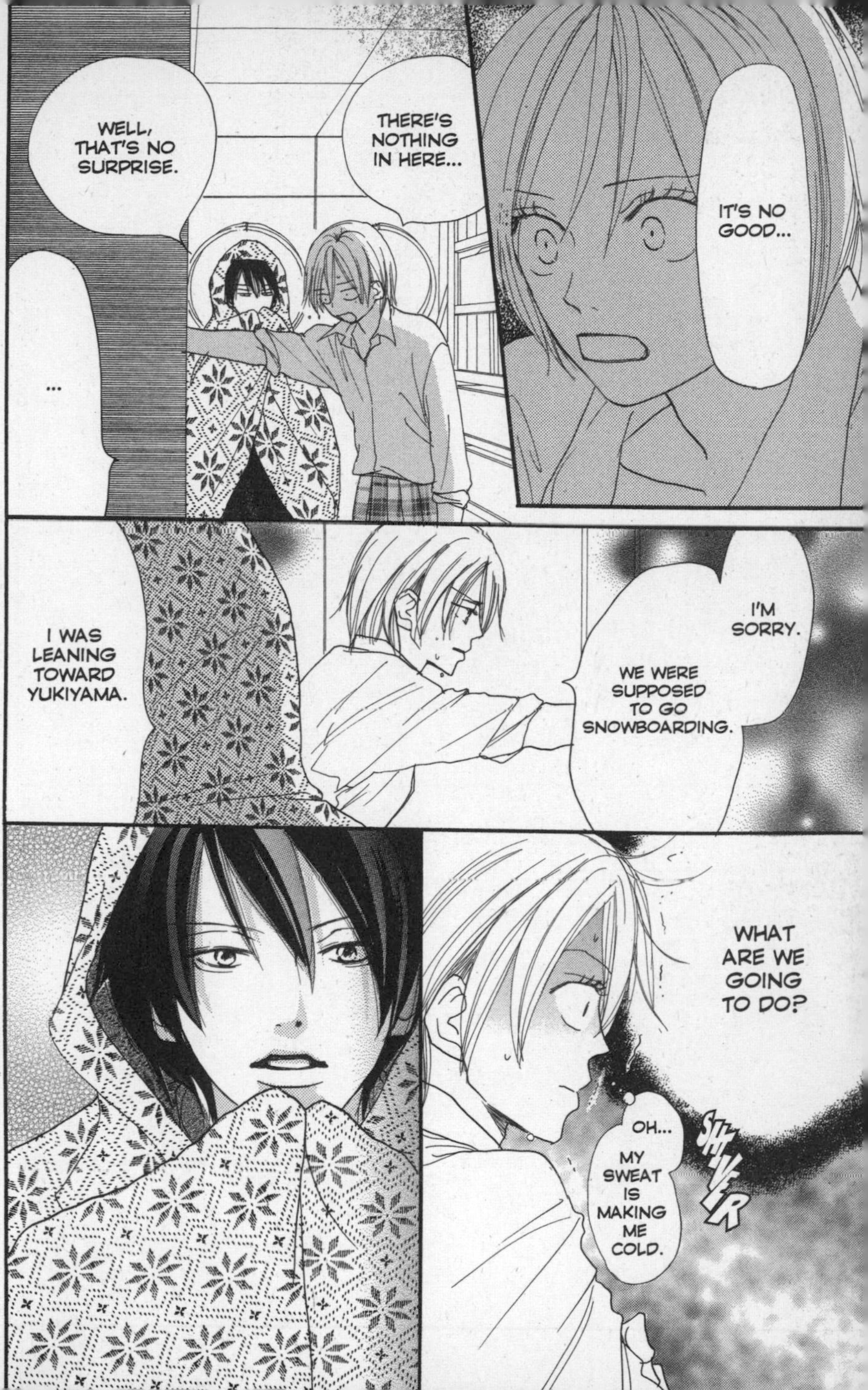
IT'S NO GOOD...
THERE'S NOTHING IN HERE...
WELL, THAT'S NO SURPRISE.
...
I'M SORRY.
WE WERE SUPPOSED TO GO SNOWBOARDING.
I WAS LEANING TOWARD YUKIYAMA.
WHAT ARE WE GOING TO DO?
SHIVER
OH... MY SWEAT IS MAKING ME COLD.

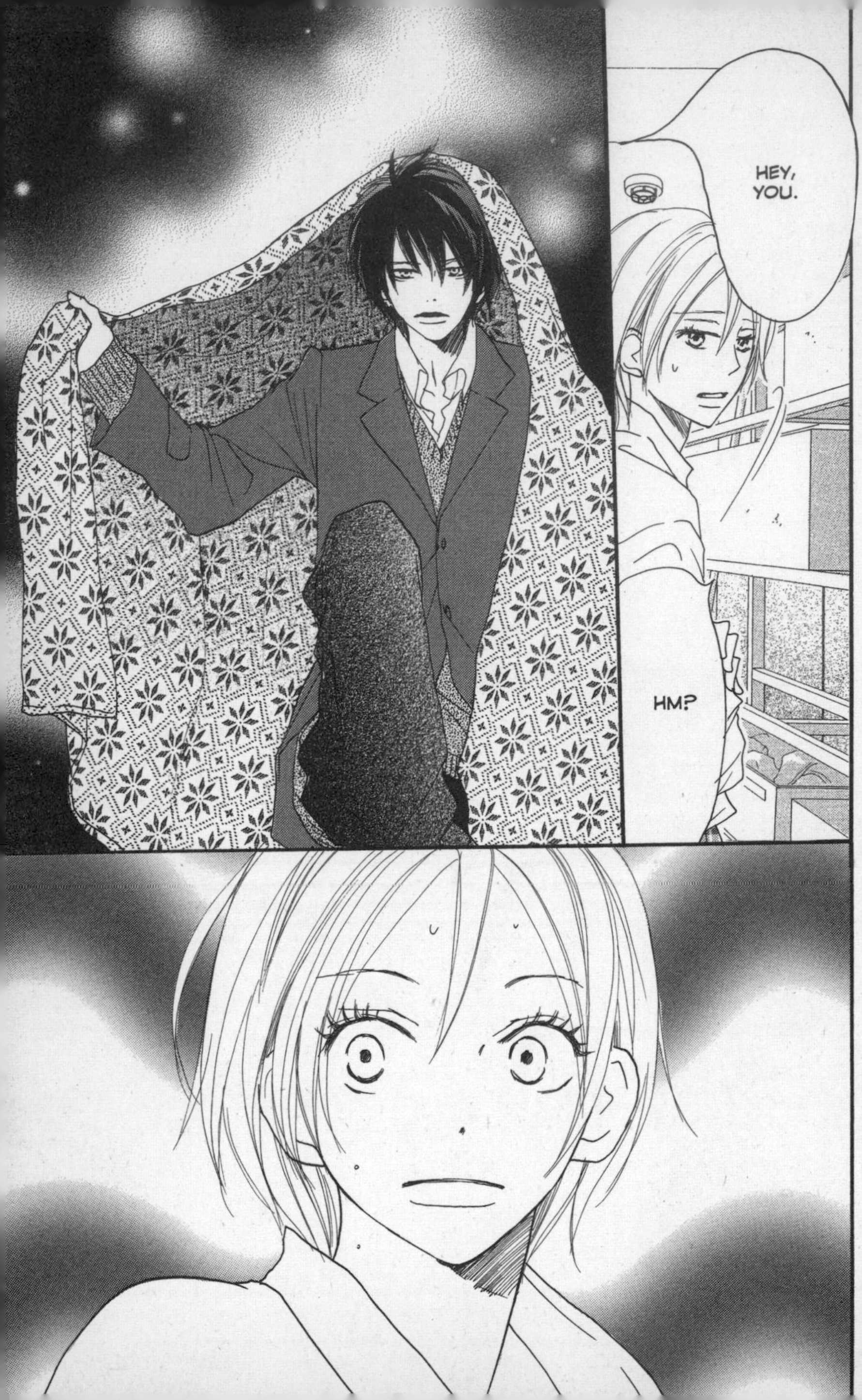
HEY, YOU.
HM?

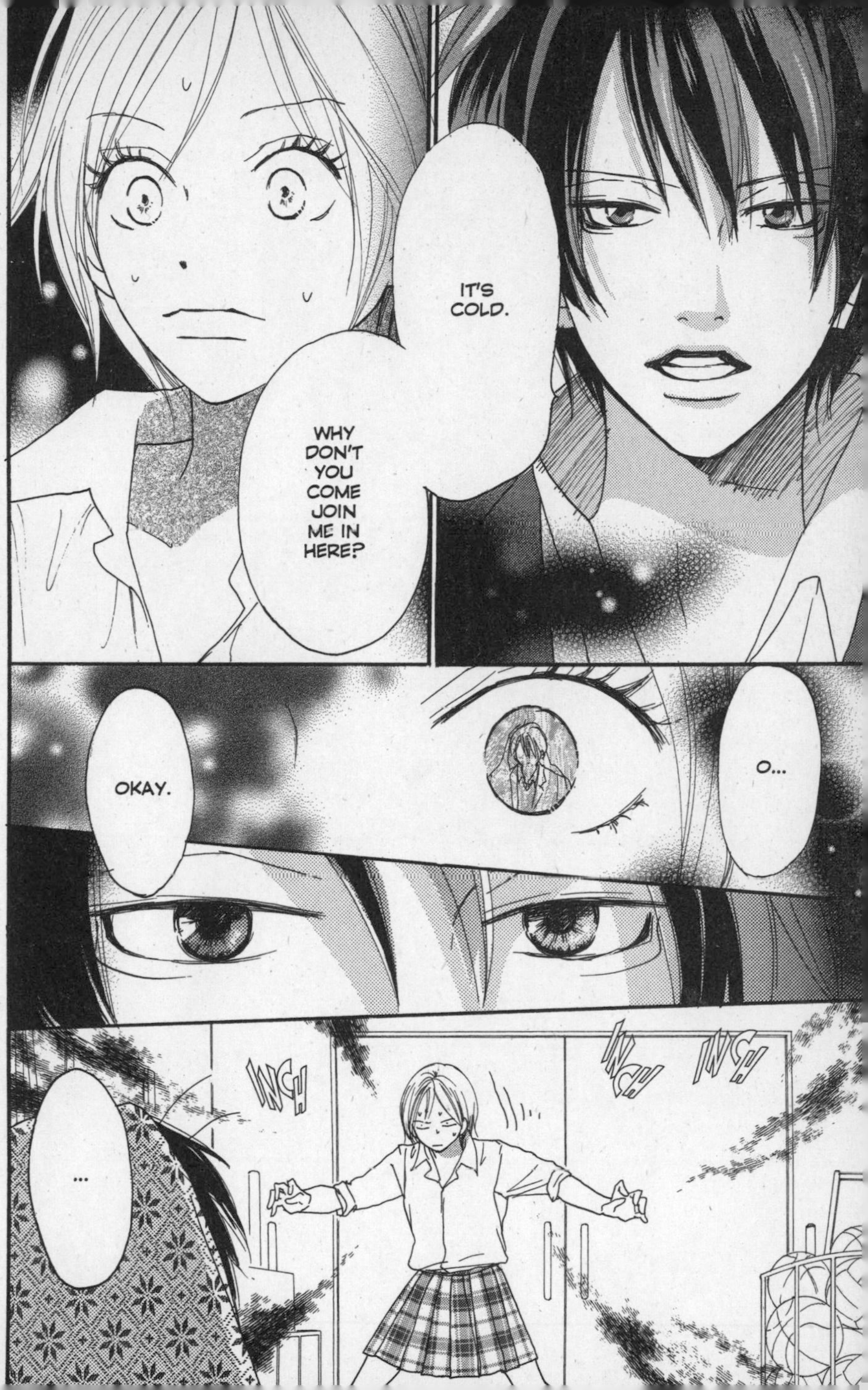
IT'S COLD.
WHY DON'T YOU COME JOIN ME IN HERE?
O...
OKAY.
INCH
INCH
INCH
...

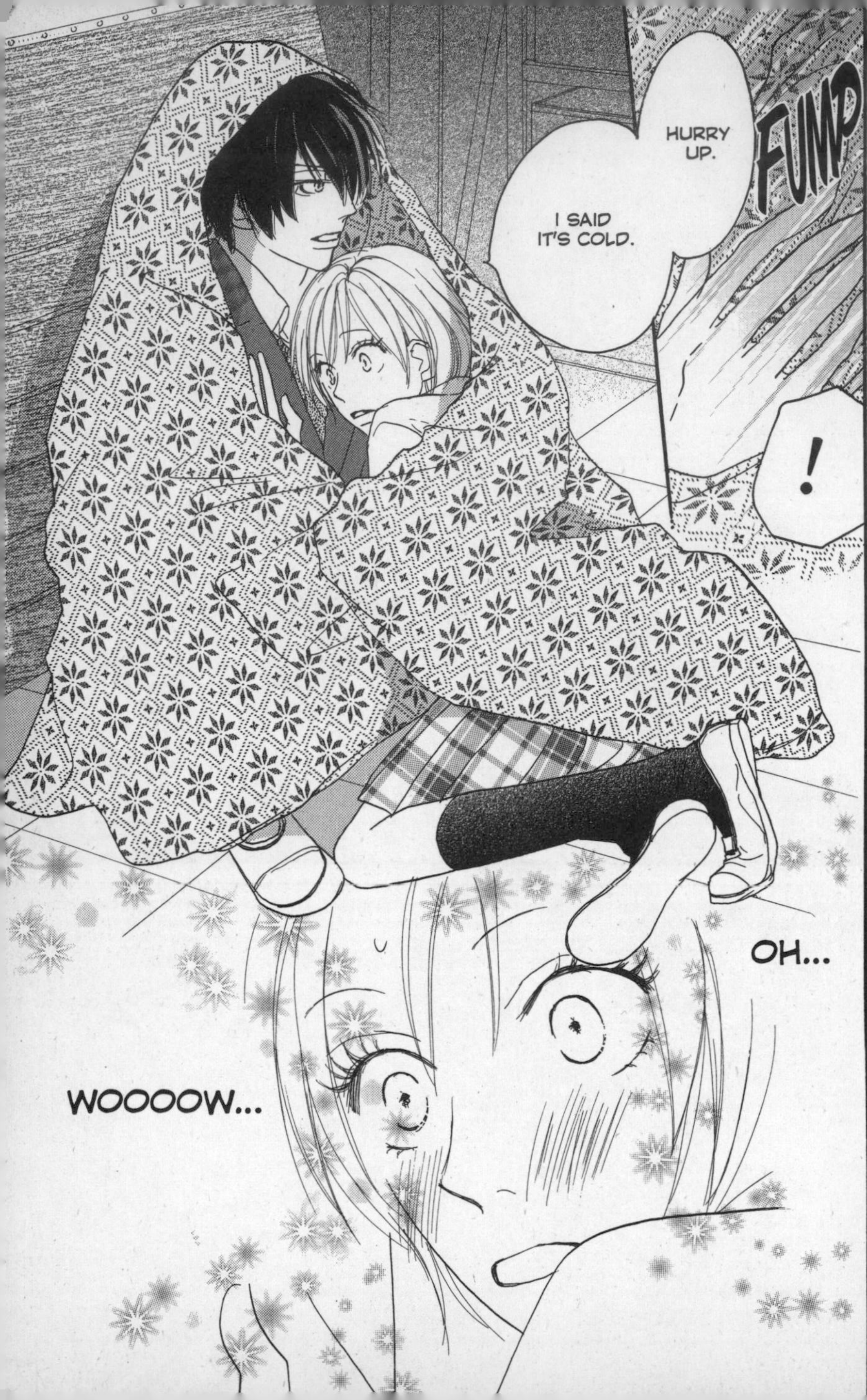
FUMP
HURRY UP.
I SAID IT'S COLD.
!
OH...
WOOOOW...

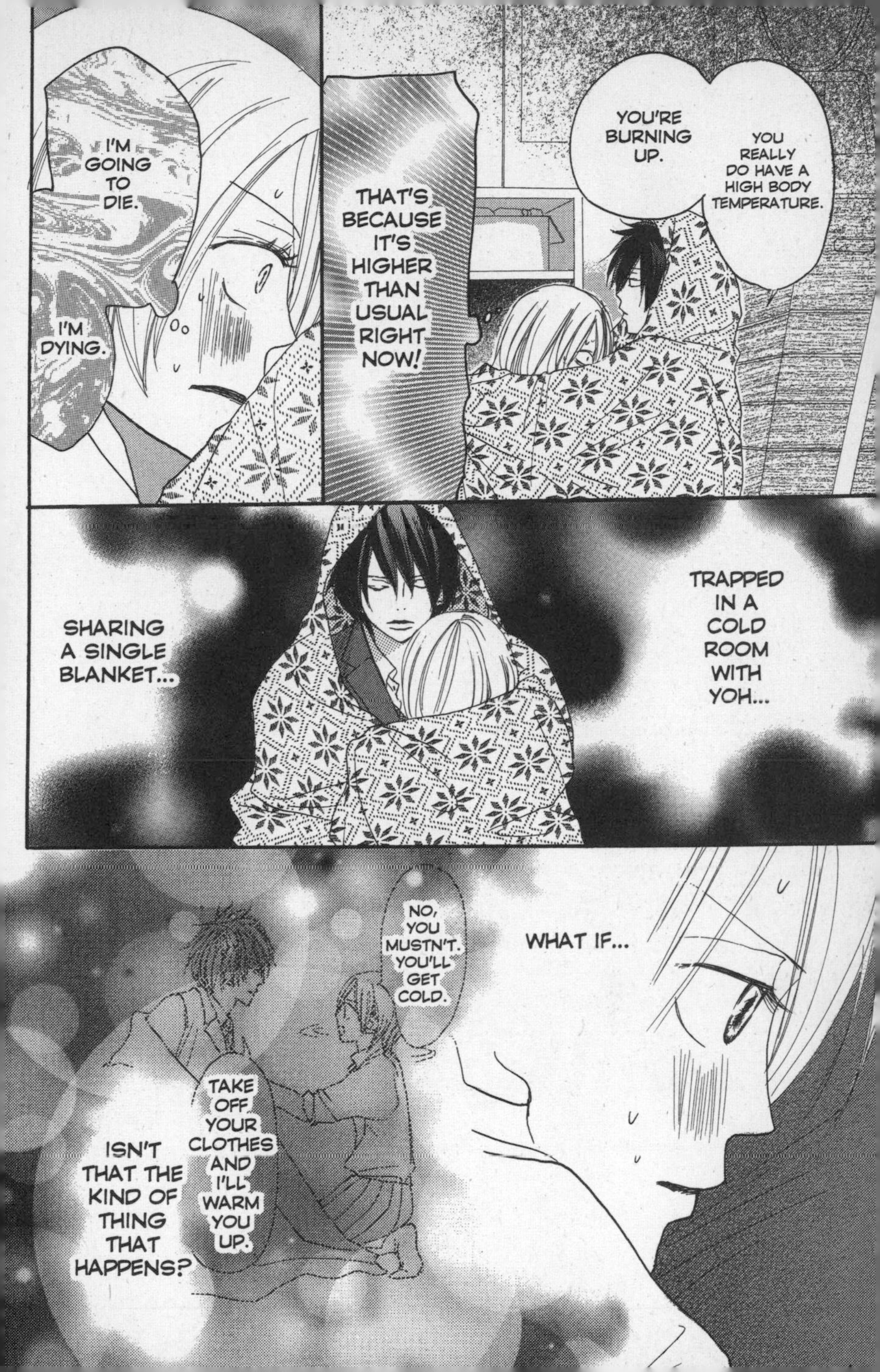
YOU'RE BURNING UP.
YOU REALLY DO HAVE A HIGH BODY TEMPERATURE.
THAT'S BECAUSE IT'S HIGHER THAN USUAL RIGHT NOW!
I'M GOING TO DIE.
I'M DYING.
TRAPPED IN A COLD ROOM WITH YOH...
SHARING A SINGLE BLANKET...
WHAT IF...
NO, YOU MUSTN'T. YOU'LL GET COLD.
TAKE OFF YOUR CLOTHES AND I'LL WARM YOU UP.
ISN'T THAT THE KIND OF THING THAT HAPPENS?

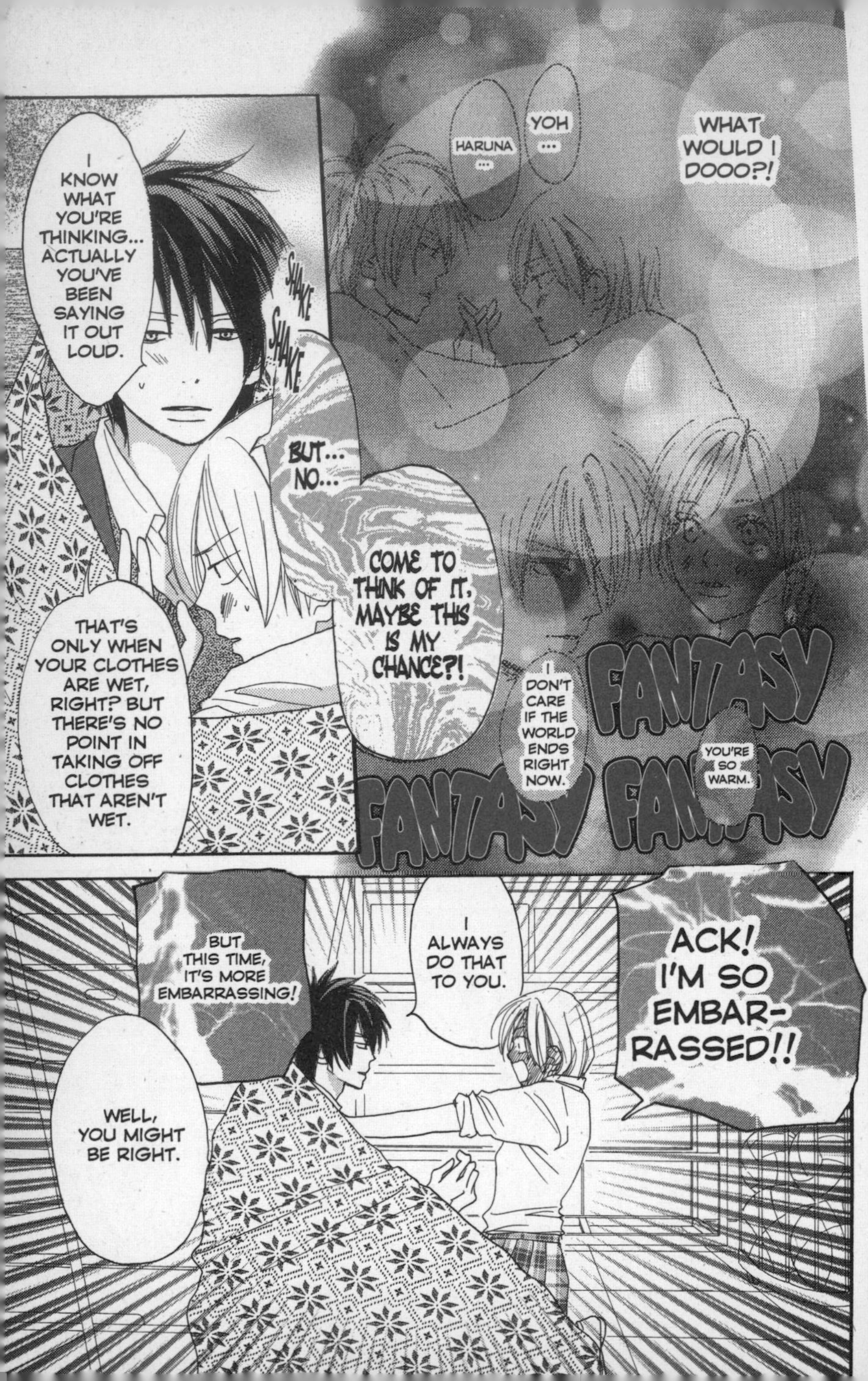
WHAT WOULD I DOOO?!
YOH...
HARUNA...
I DON'T CARE IF THE WORLD ENDS RIGHT NOW.
YOU'RE SO WARM.
FANTASY FANTASY FANTASY
COME TO THINK OF IT, MAYBE THIS IS MY CHANCE?!
BUT... NO...
SHAKE SHAKE
I KNOW WHAT YOU'RE THINKING... ACTUALLY YOU'VE BEEN SAYING IT OUT LOUD.
THAT'S ONLY WHEN YOUR CLOTHES ARE WET, RIGHT? BUT THERE'S NO POINT IN TAKING OFF CLOTHES THAT AREN'T WET.
ACK! I'M SO EMBAR-RASSED!!
I ALWAYS DO THAT TO YOU.
BUT THIS TIME, IT'S MORE EMBARRASSING!
WELL, YOU MIGHT BE RIGHT.

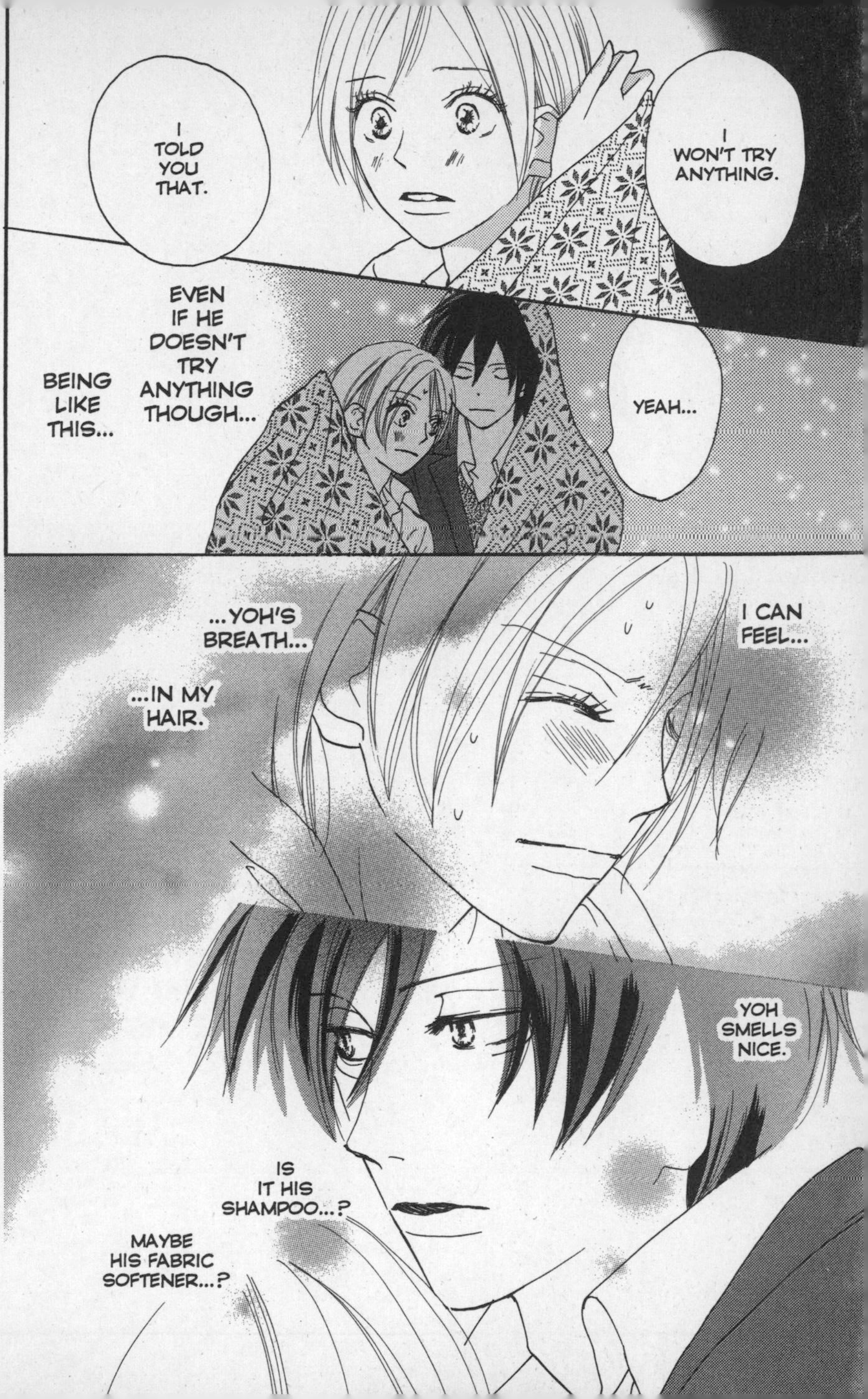
I WON'T TRY ANYTHING.
I TOLD YOU THAT.
YEAH...
EVEN IF HE DOESN'T TRY ANYTHING THOUGH...
BEING LIKE THIS...
I CAN FEEL...
...YOH'S BREATH...
...IN MY HAIR.
YOH SMELLS NICE.
IS IT HIS SHAMPOO...?
MAYBE HIS FABRIC SOFTENER...?

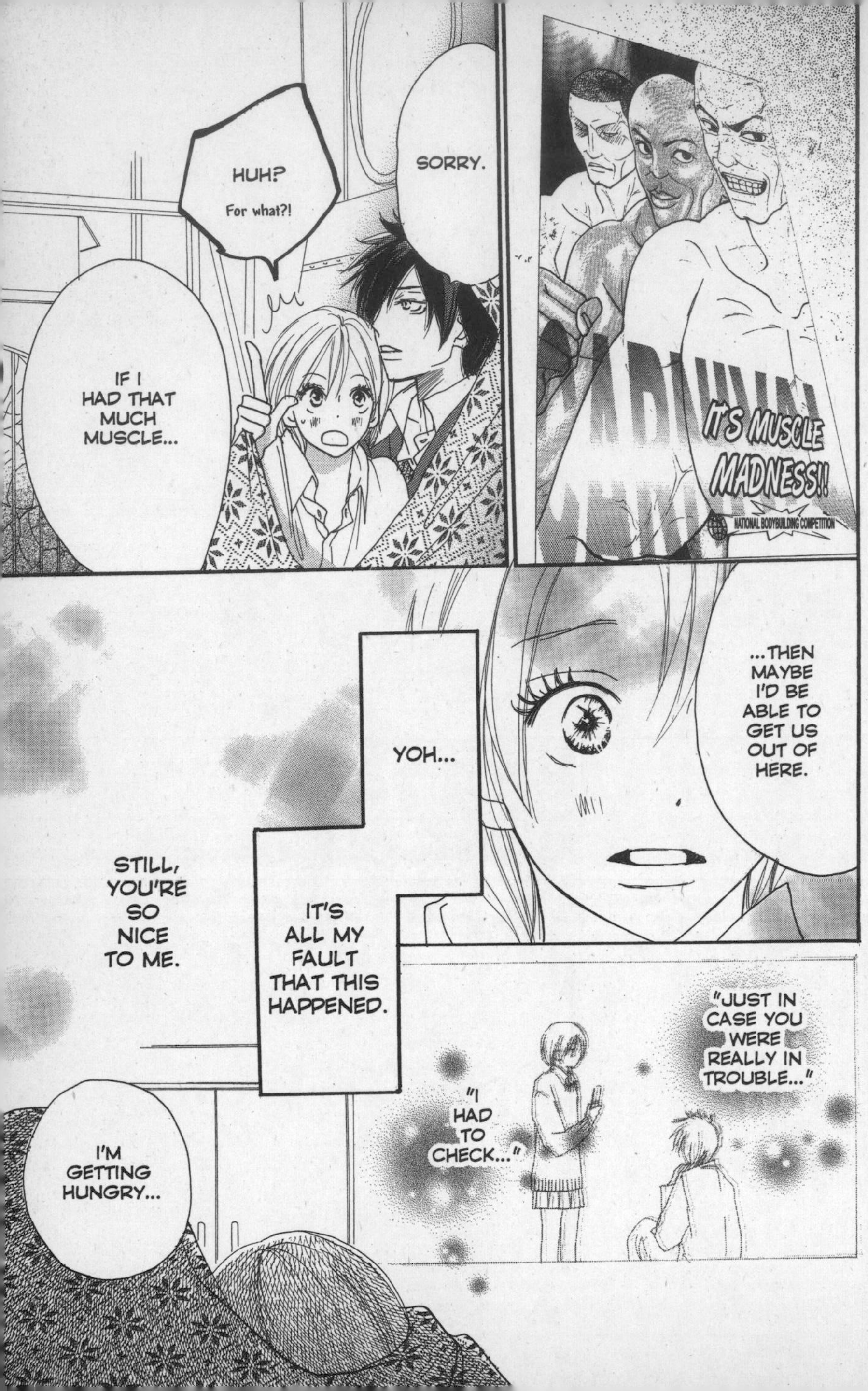
IT'S MUSCLE MADNESS!!
NATIONAL BODYBUILDING COMPETITION
SORRY.
HUH? For what?!
IF I HAD THAT MUCH MUSCLE...
...THEN MAYBE I'D BE ABLE TO GET US OUT OF HERE.
YOH...
IT'S ALL MY FAULT THAT THIS HAPPENED.
STILL, YOU'RE SO NICE TO ME.
"JUST IN CASE YOU WERE REALLY IN TROUBLE..."
"I HAD TO CHECK..."
I'M GETTING HUNGRY...

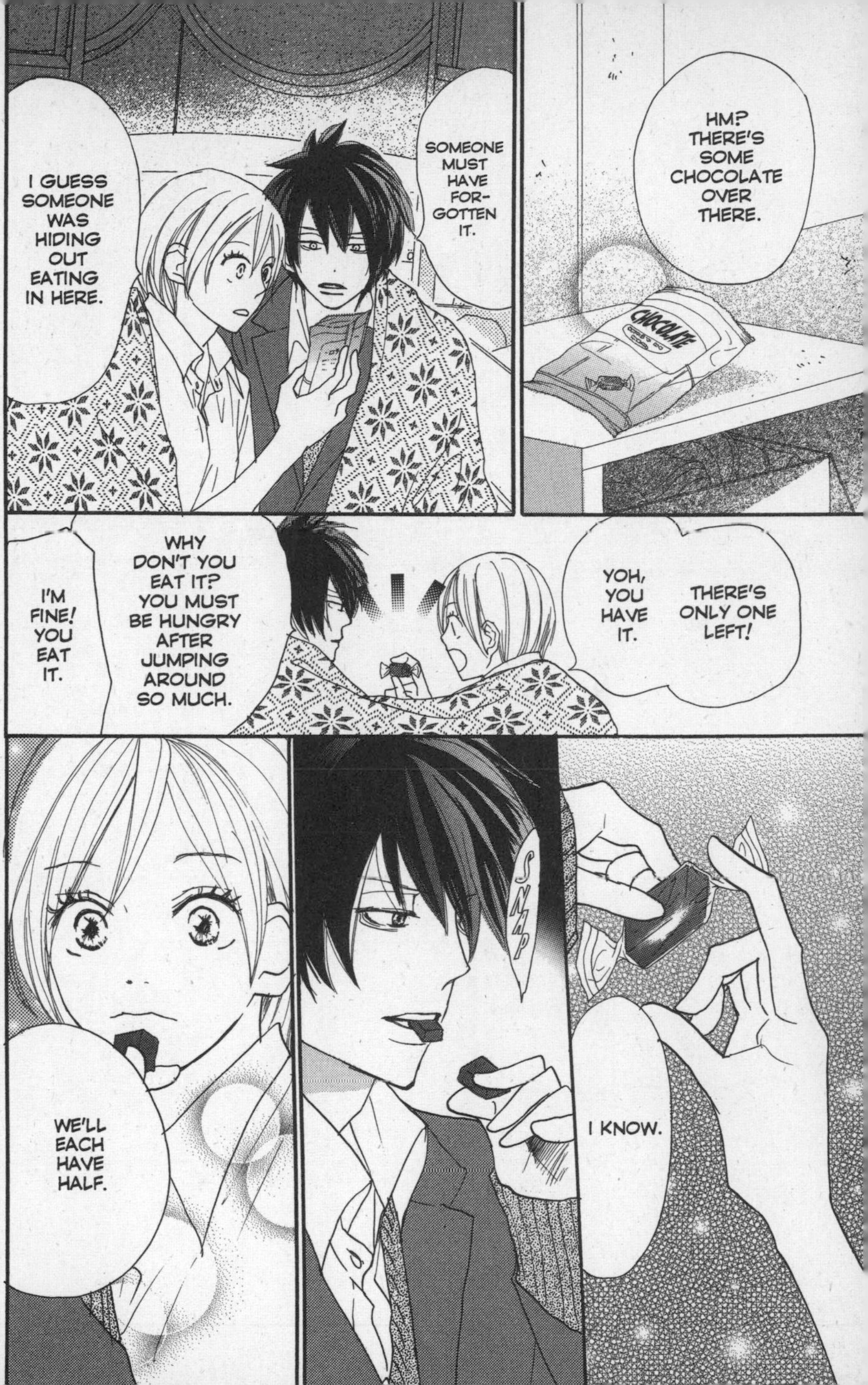
HM? THERE'S SOME CHOCOLATE OVER THERE.
CHOCOLATE
SOMEONE MUST HAVE FOR-GOTTEN IT.
I GUESS SOMEONE WAS HIDING OUT EATING IN HERE.
THERE'S ONLY ONE LEFT!
YOH, YOU HAVE IT.
WHY DON'T YOU EAT IT? YOU MUST BE HUNGRY AFTER JUMPING AROUND SO MUCH.
I'M FINE! YOU EAT IT.
I KNOW.
SNAP
WE'LL EACH HAVE HALF.

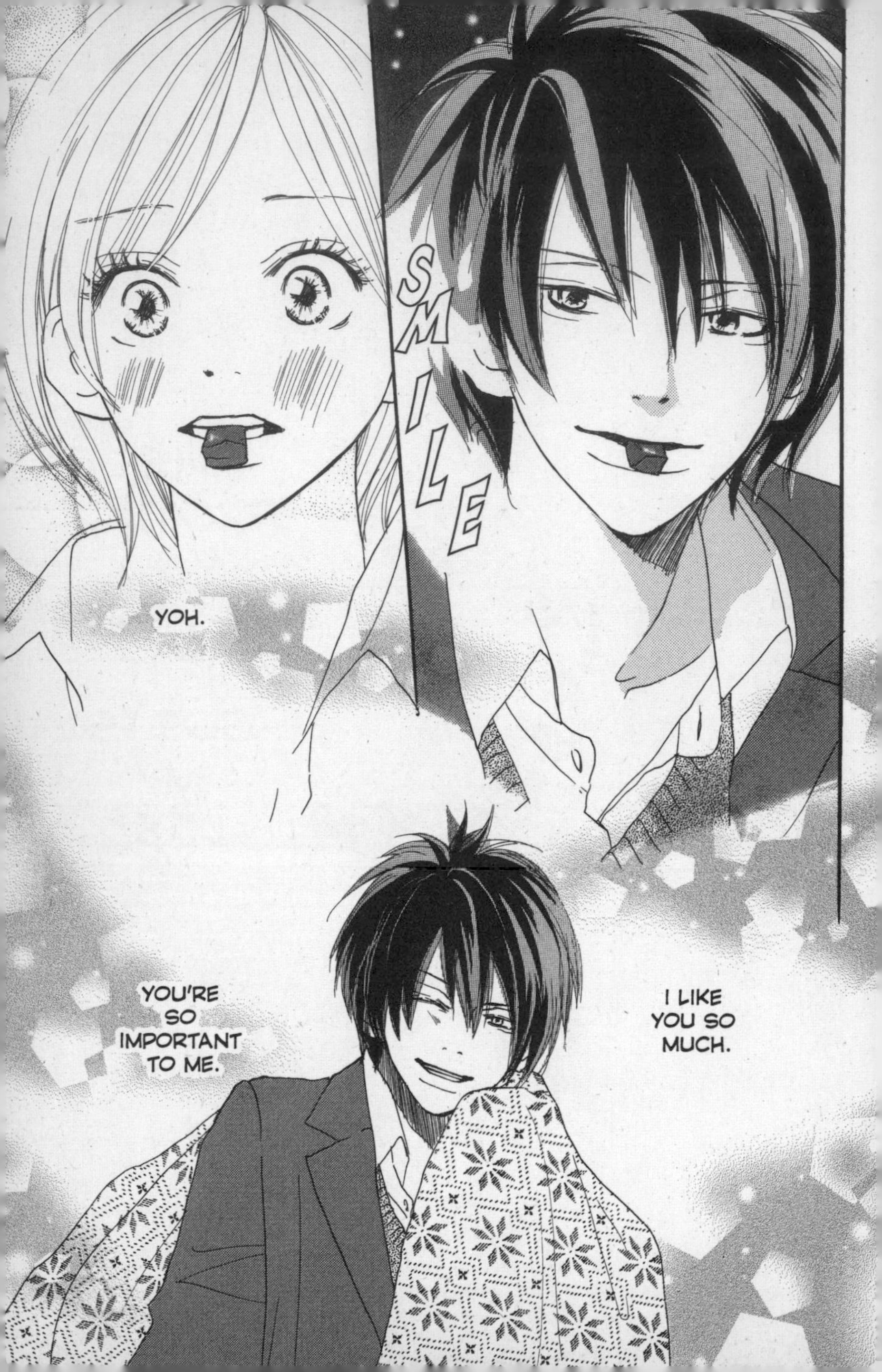
SMILE
YOH.
I LIKE YOU SO MUCH.
YOU'RE SO IMPORTANT TO ME.

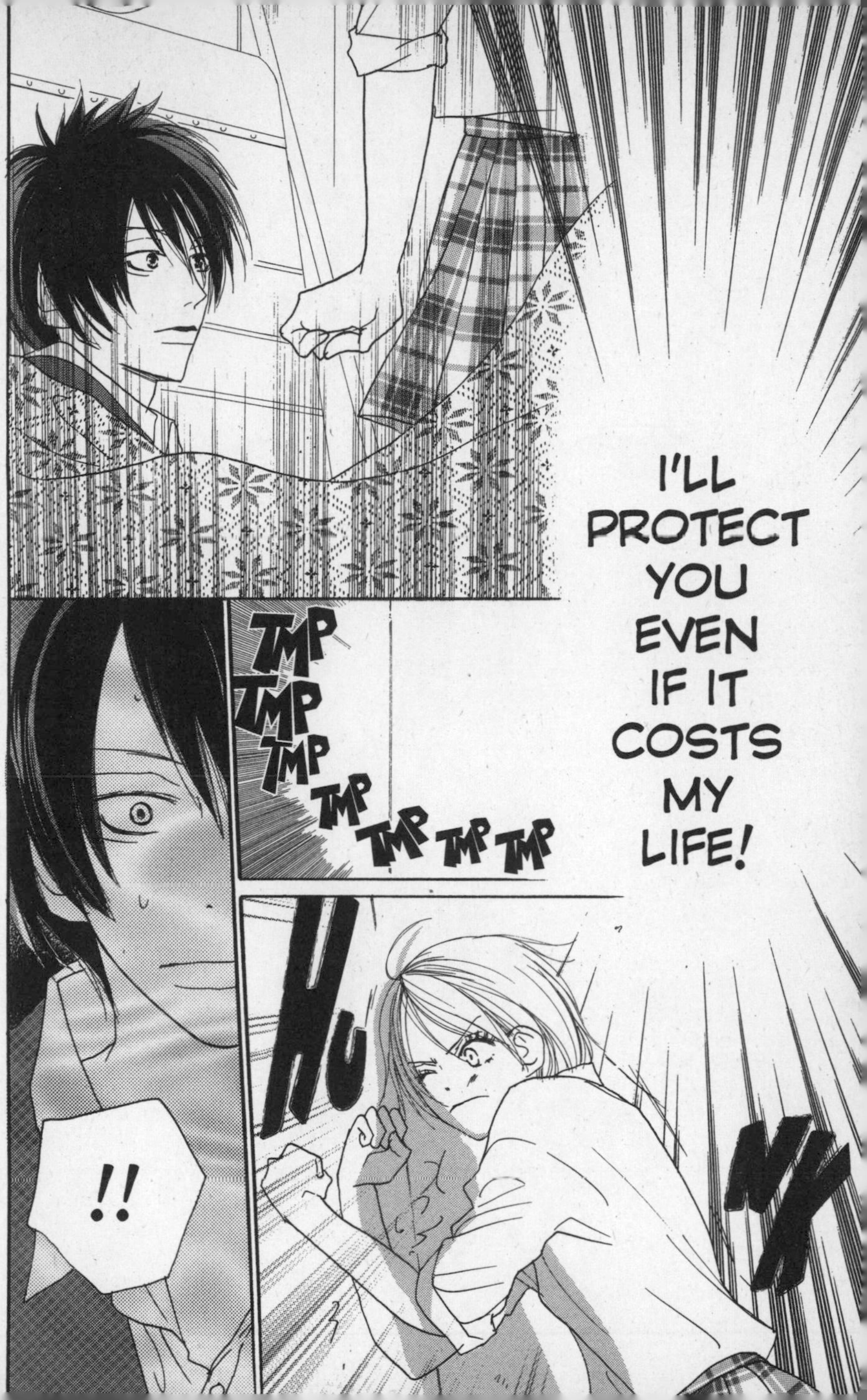
I'LL PROTECT YOU EVEN IF IT COSTS MY LIFE!
TMP TMP TMP TMP TMP TMP TMP
HU
NK
!!

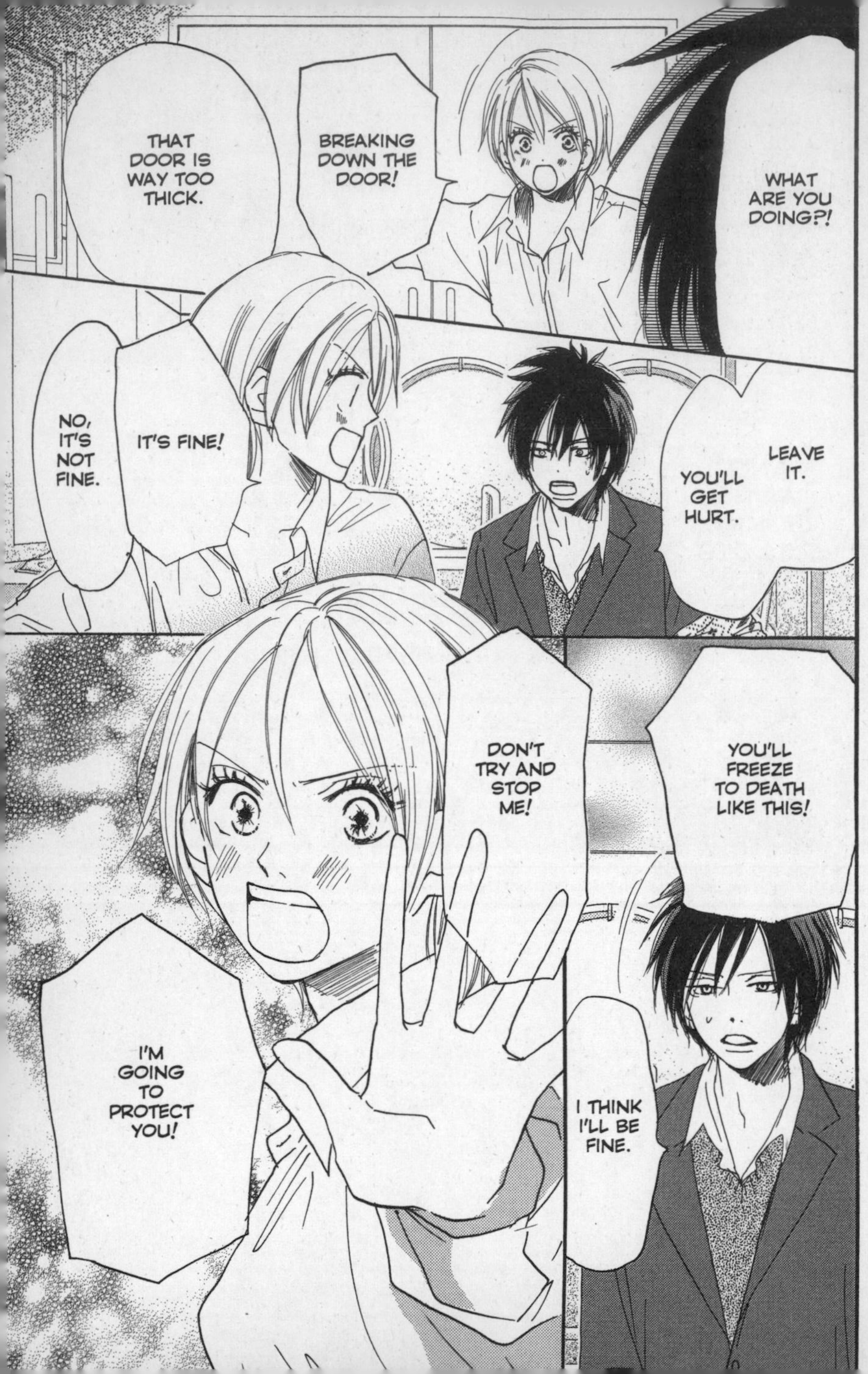
WHAT ARE YOU DOING?!
BREAKING DOWN THE DOOR!
THAT DOOR IS WAY TOO THICK.
LEAVE IT.
YOU'LL GET HURT.
IT'S FINE!
NO, IT'S NOT FINE.
YOU'LL FREEZE TO DEATH LIKE THIS!
I THINK I'LL BE FINE.
DON'T TRY AND STOP ME!
I'M GOING TO PROTECT YOU!

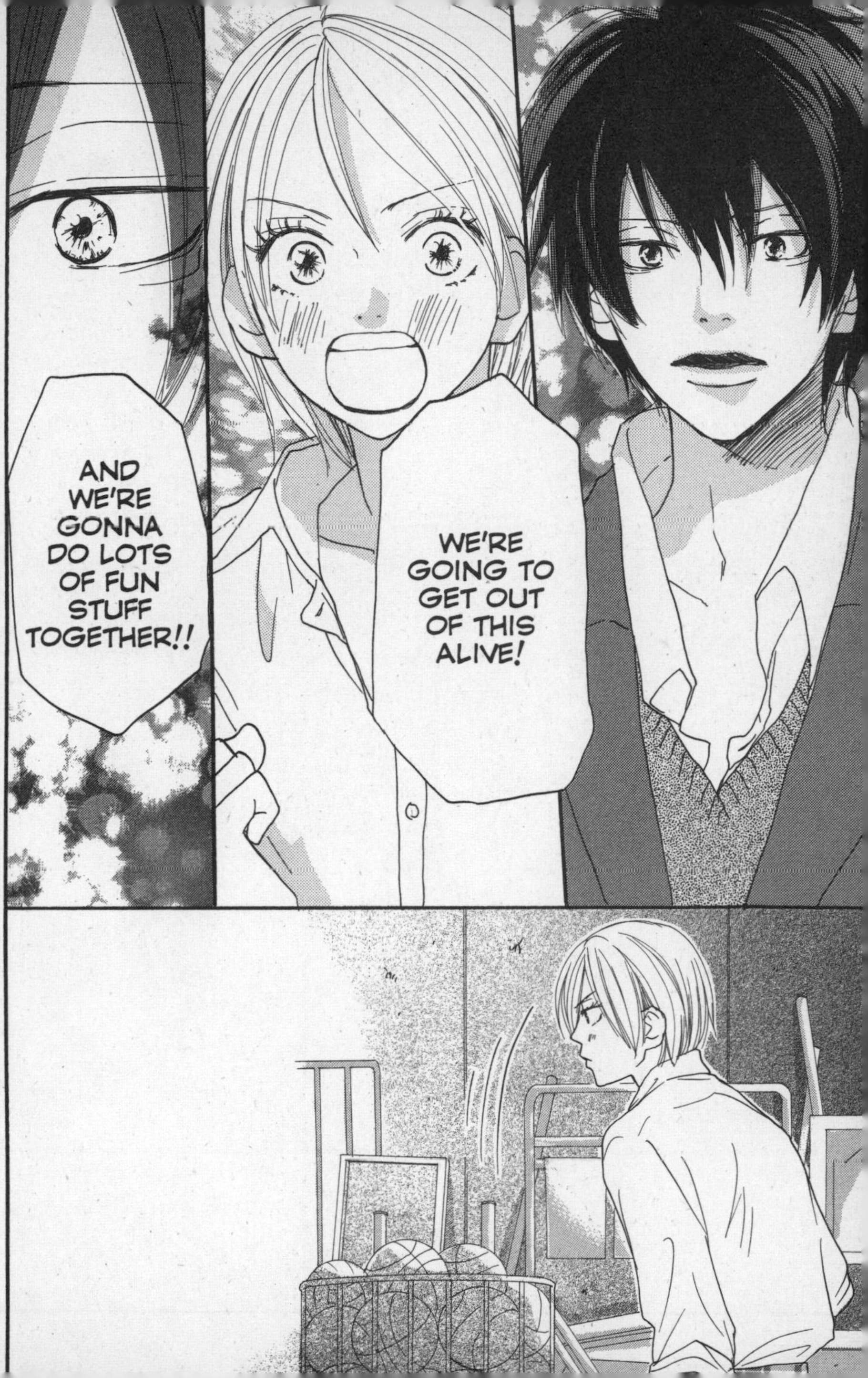
WE'RE GOING TO GET OUT OF THIS ALIVE!
AND WE'RE GONNA DO LOTS OF FUN STUFF TOGETHER!!

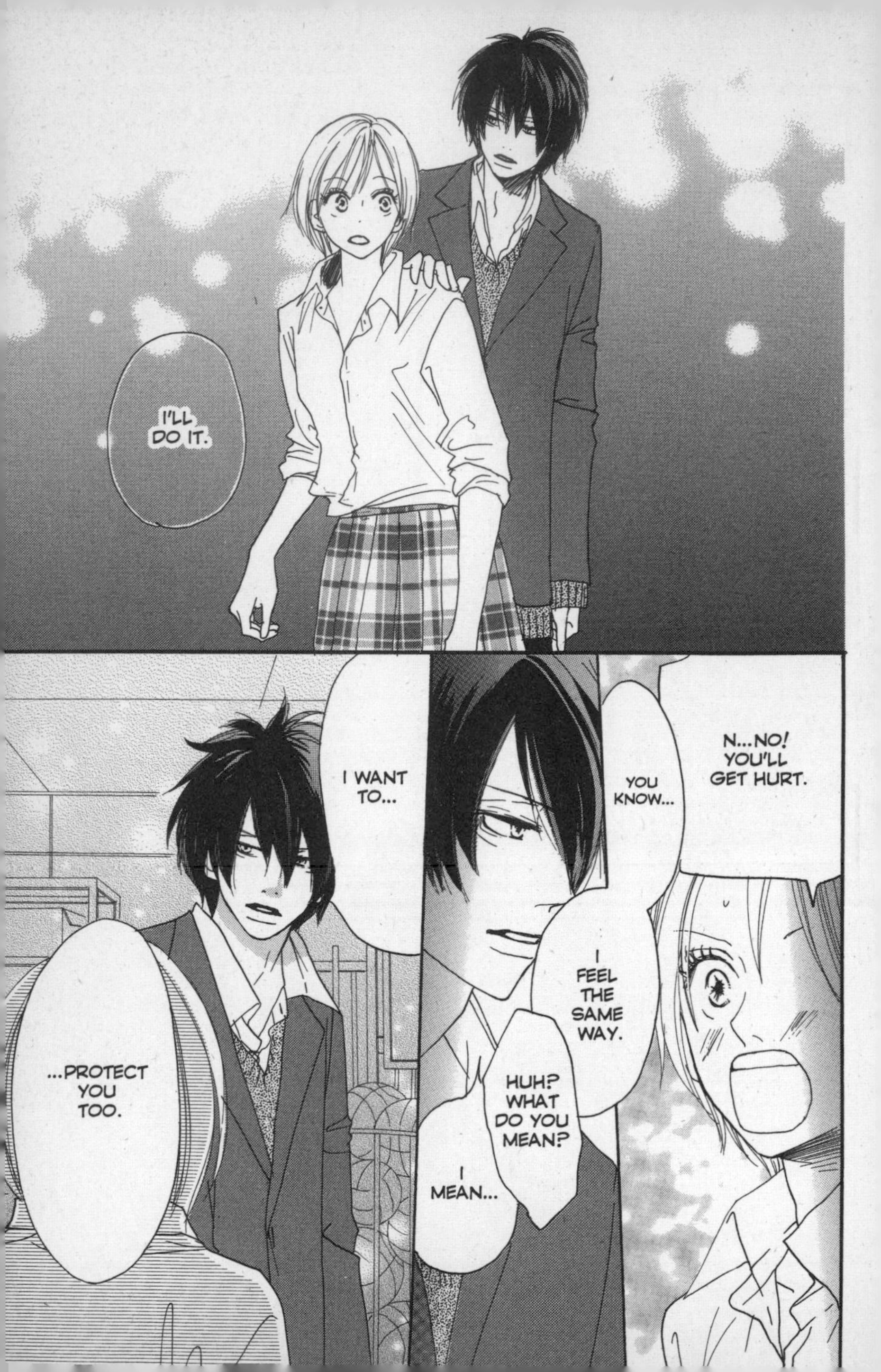
I'LL DO IT.
N...NO! YOU'LL GET HURT.
YOU KNOW...
I FEEL THE SAME WAY.
HUH? WHAT DO YOU MEAN?
I MEAN...
I WANT TO...
...PROTECT YOU TOO.

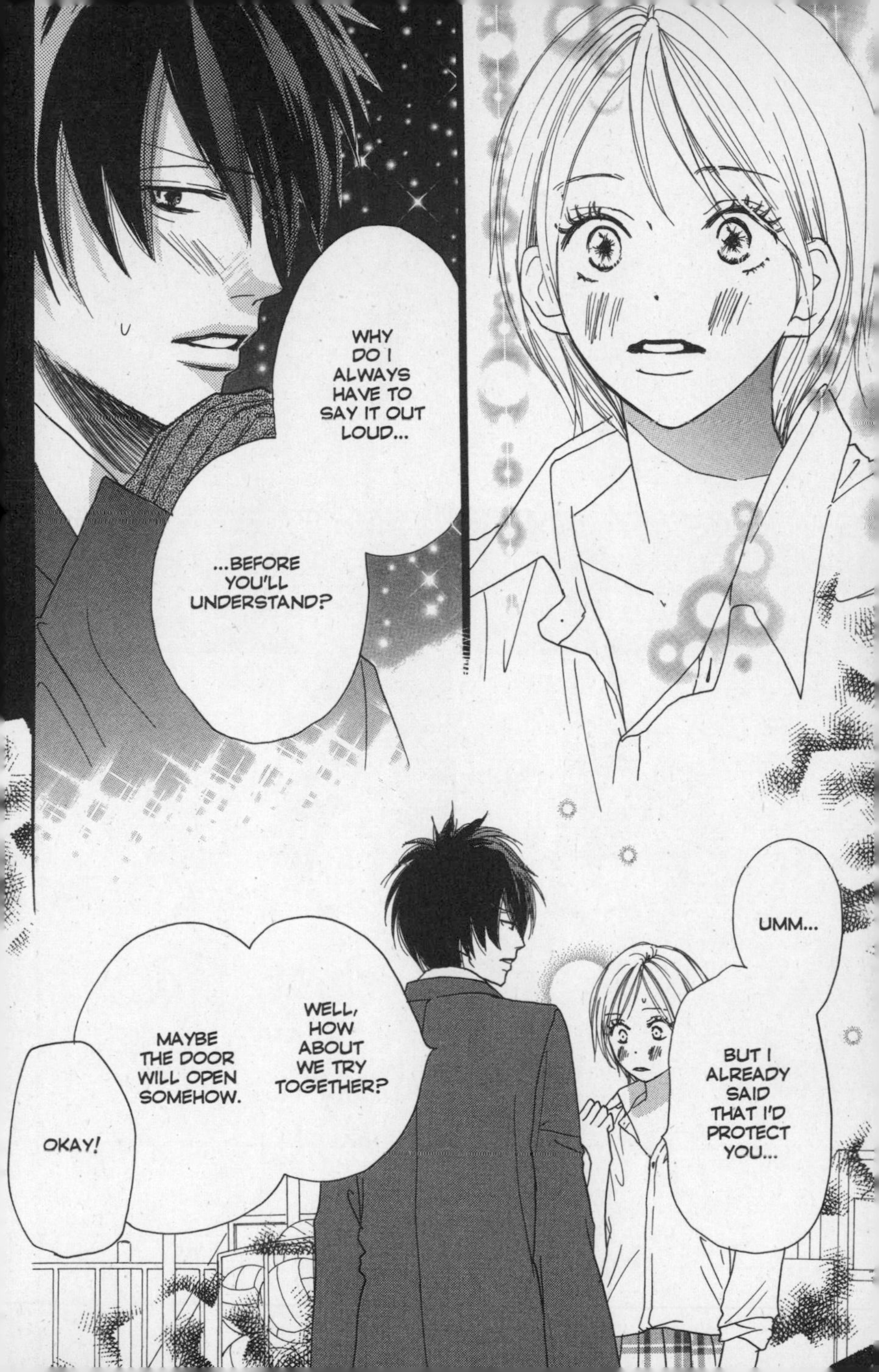
WHY DO I ALWAYS HAVE TO SAY IT OUT LOUD...
...BEFORE YOU'LL UNDERSTAND?
UMM...
BUT I ALREADY SAID THAT I'D PROTECT YOU...
WELL, HOW ABOUT WE TRY TOGETHER?
MAYBE THE DOOR WILL OPEN SOMEHOW.
OKAY!

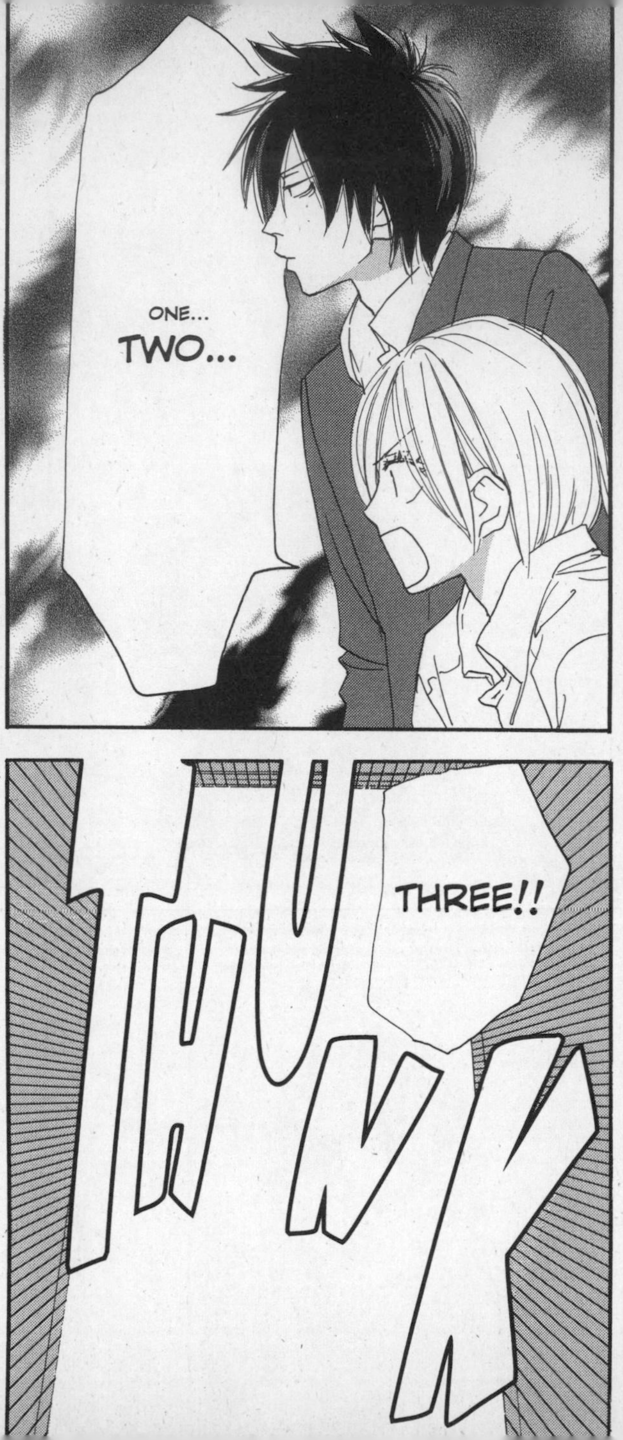
ONE... TWO...
THREE!!
THUNK

2

I tried vegetable juice for the first time. The [redacted] one. It looked greener than all the other brands, and I didn't think that I would be able to drink it at first. But once I got used to it, the other drinks seemed to be lacking and I ended up getting it. It's good! And my body is feeling healthy!

It's been my lifelong dream to have a good body, but even though I've been buying lots of healthy things, I don't seem to lose weight. Maybe I'm already healthy...? My meals are all so good, I'm getting rounder and I'm getting heavy... Time for some sports!

So I tried yoga with a friend. Now I do it every night before bed. I wonder how long I'll keep it up? By the time this volume comes out, I'll probably have quit... I've quit loads of exercise regimes before...but I think I'll still be drinking the vegetable juice! It's so good!

Tastes like grass...

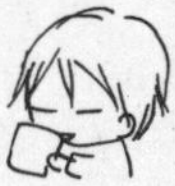

Well then, see you in the next volume.

From Kawahara!

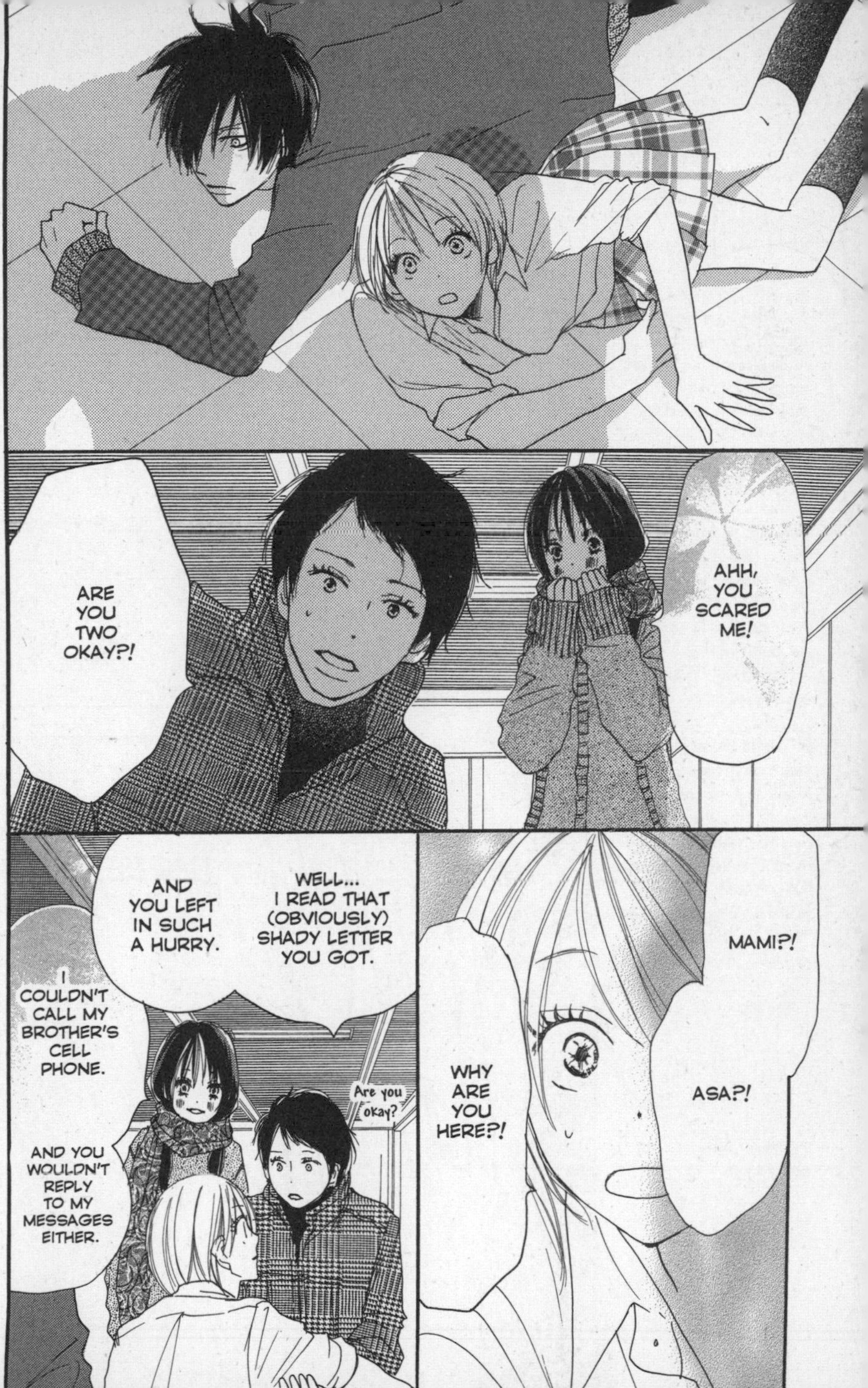
AHH, YOU SCARED ME!
ARE YOU TWO OKAY?!
MAMI?!
ASA?!
WHY ARE YOU HERE?!
WELL... I READ THAT (OBVIOUSLY) SHADY LETTER YOU GOT.
AND YOU LEFT IN SUCH A HURRY.
Are you okay?
I COULDN'T CALL MY BROTHER'S CELL PHONE.
AND YOU WOULDN'T REPLY TO MY MESSAGES EITHER.

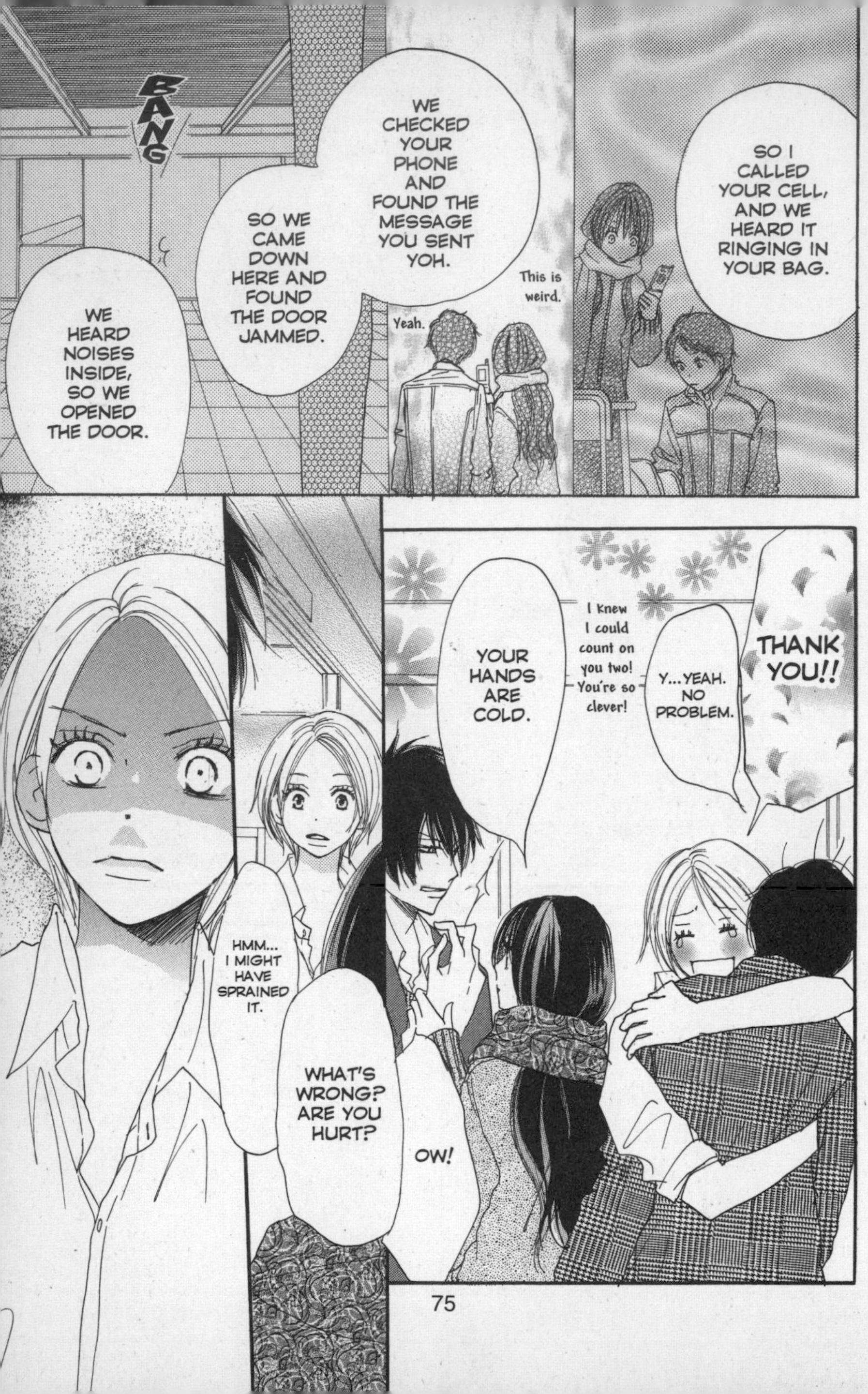
SO I CALLED YOUR CELL, AND WE HEARD IT RINGING IN YOUR BAG.
This is weird.
Yeah.
WE CHECKED YOUR PHONE AND FOUND THE MESSAGE YOU SENT YOH.
SO WE CAME DOWN HERE AND FOUND THE DOOR JAMMED.
BANG
WE HEARD NOISES INSIDE, SO WE OPENED THE DOOR.
THANK YOU!!
Y...YEAH. NO PROBLEM.
I knew I could count on you two! You're so clever!
YOUR HANDS ARE COLD.
OW!
WHAT'S WRONG? ARE YOU HURT?
HMM... I MIGHT HAVE SPRAINED IT.

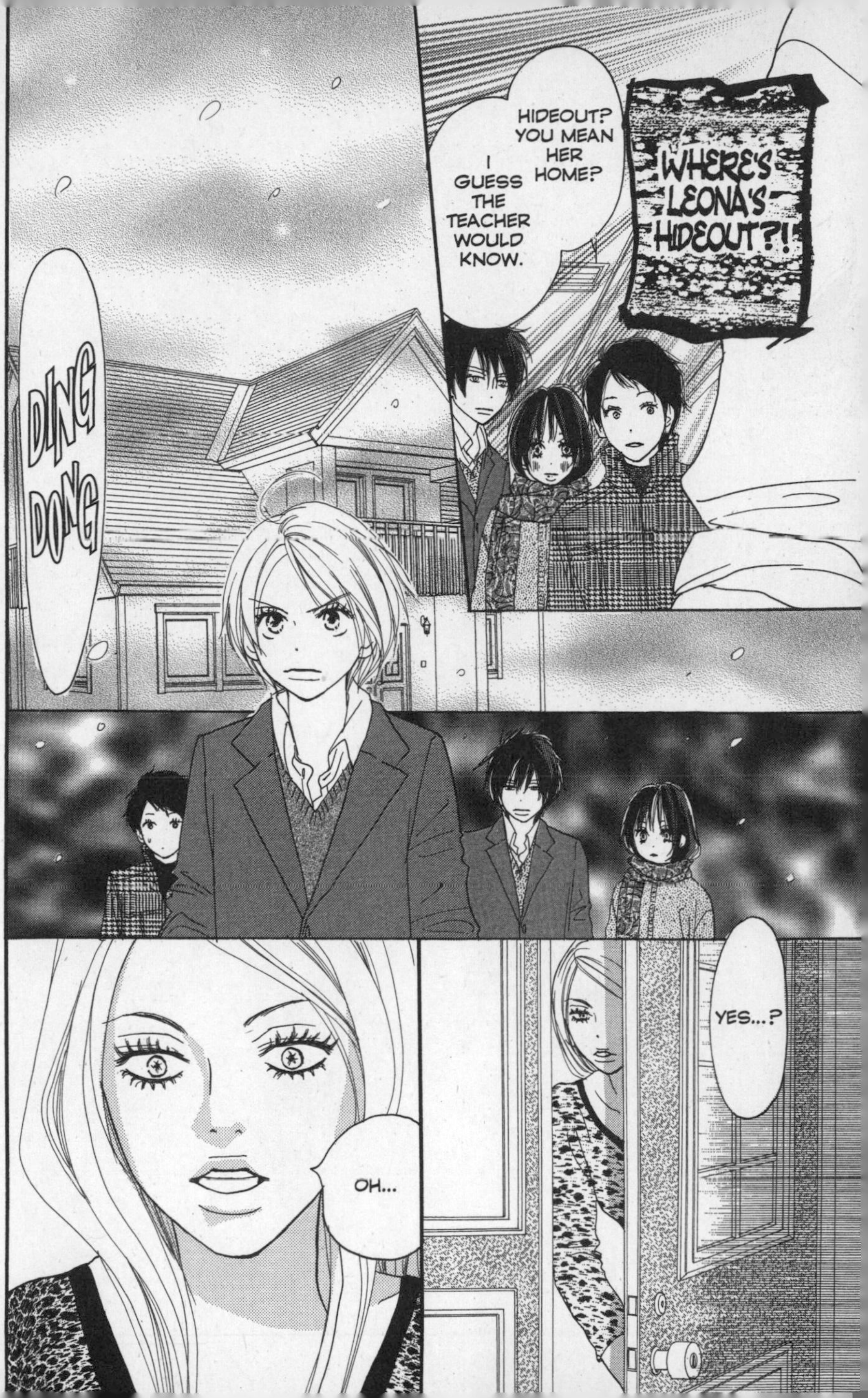
WHERE'S LEONA'S HIDEOUT?!
HIDEOUT? YOU MEAN HER HOME?
I GUESS THE TEACHER WOULD KNOW.
DING DONG
YES...?
OH...

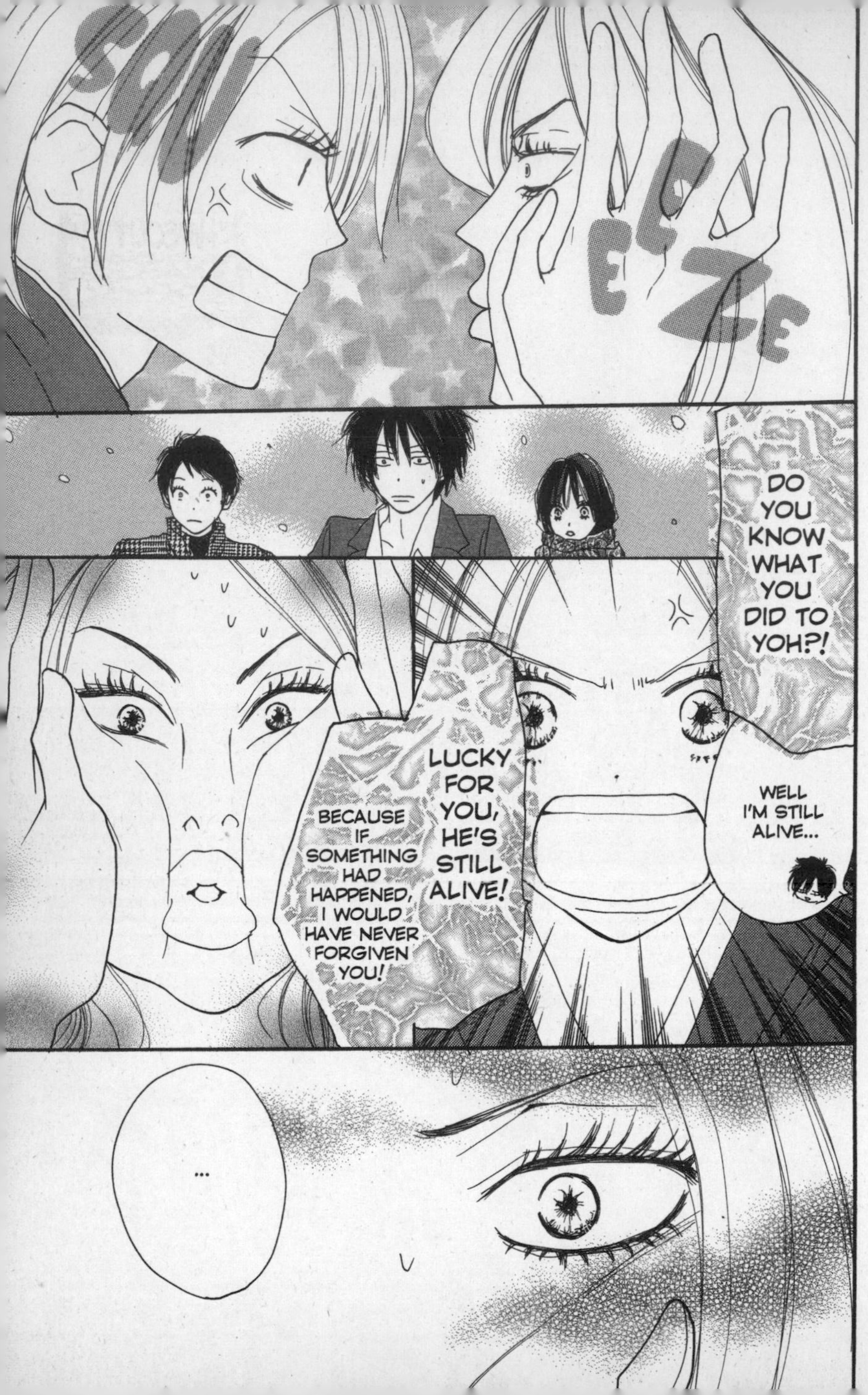
DO YOU KNOW WHAT YOU DID TO YOH?!
LUCKY FOR YOU, HE'S STILL ALIVE!
BECAUSE IF SOMETHING HAD HAPPENED, I WOULD HAVE NEVER FORGIVEN YOU!
WELL I'M STILL ALIVE...
...

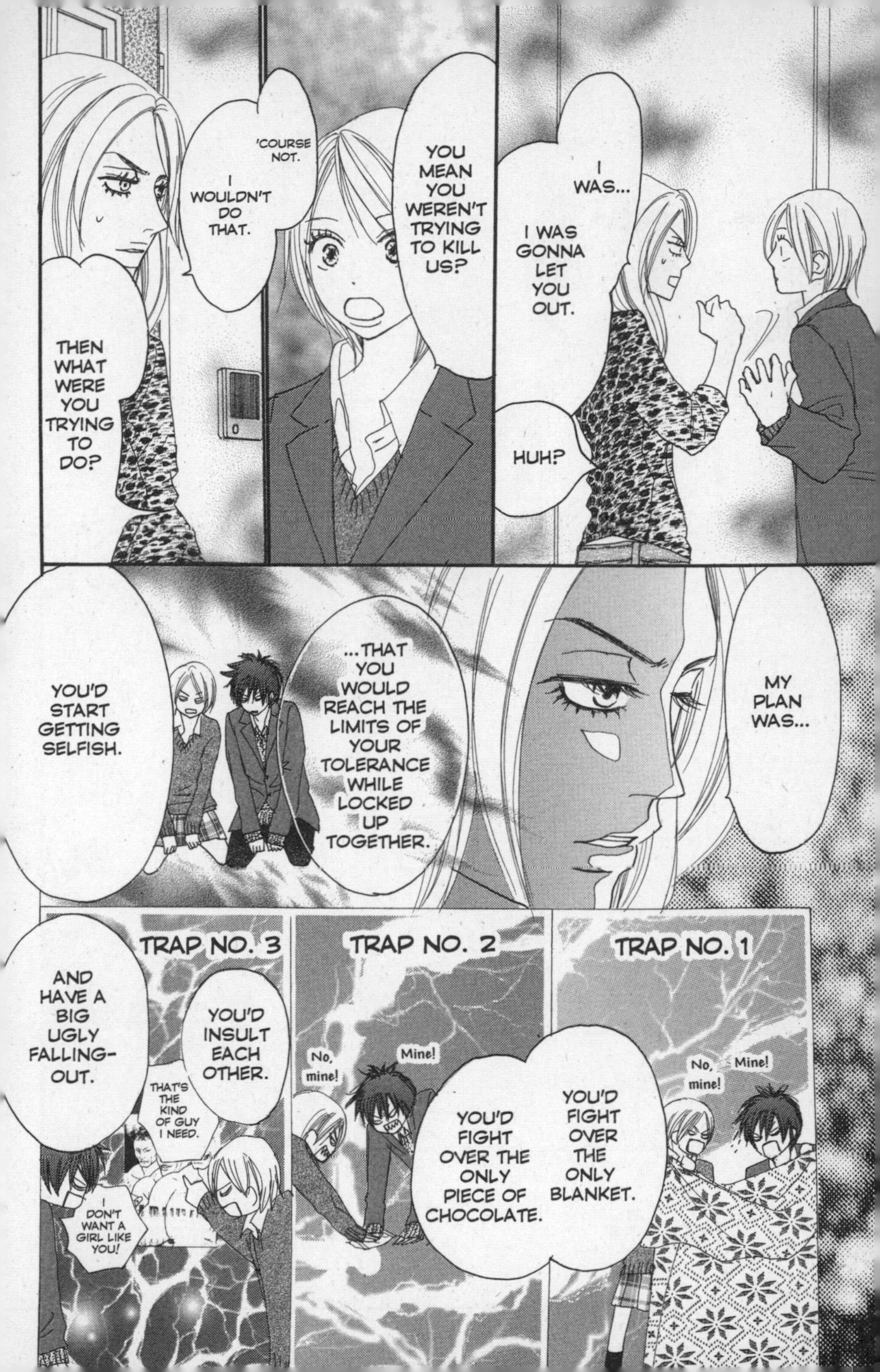
I WAS...
I WAS GONNA LET YOU OUT.
HUH?
YOU MEAN YOU WEREN'T TRYING TO KILL US?
'COURSE NOT.
I WOULDN'T DO THAT.
THEN WHAT WERE YOU TRYING TO DO?
MY PLAN WAS...
...THAT YOU WOULD REACH THE LIMITS OF YOUR TOLERANCE WHILE LOCKED UP TOGETHER.
YOU'D START GETTING SELFISH.
TRAP NO. 1
Mine!
No, mine!
YOU'D FIGHT OVER THE ONLY BLANKET.
TRAP NO. 2
YOU'D FIGHT OVER THE ONLY PIECE OF CHOCOLATE.
Mine!
No, mine!
TRAP NO. 3
YOU'D INSULT EACH OTHER.
AND HAVE A BIG UGLY FALLING-OUT.
THAT'S THE KIND OF GUY I NEED.
I DON'T WANT A GIRL LIKE YOU!

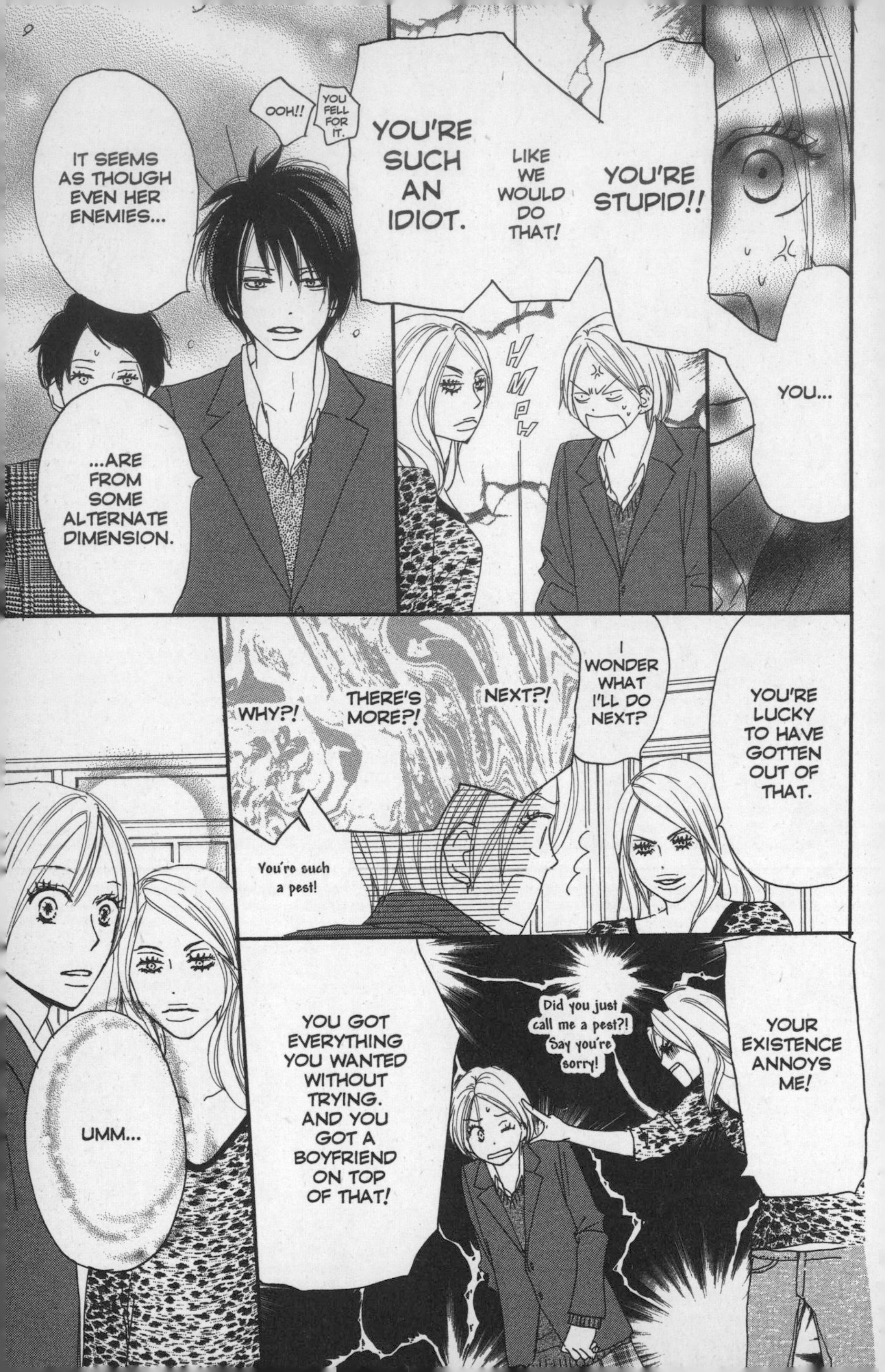
YOU...
YOU'RE STUPID!!
LIKE WE WOULD DO THAT!
YOU'RE SUCH AN IDIOT.
YOU FELL FOR IT.
OOH!!
HMPH
IT SEEMS AS THOUGH EVEN HER ENEMIES...
...ARE FROM SOME ALTERNATE DIMENSION.
YOU'RE LUCKY TO HAVE GOTTEN OUT OF THAT.
I WONDER WHAT I'LL DO NEXT?
NEXT?!
THERE'S MORE?!
WHY?!
You're such a pest!
YOUR EXISTENCE ANNOYS ME!
Did you just call me a pest?! Say you're sorry!
YOU GOT EVERYTHING YOU WANTED WITHOUT TRYING. AND YOU GOT A BOYFRIEND ON TOP OF THAT!
UMM...

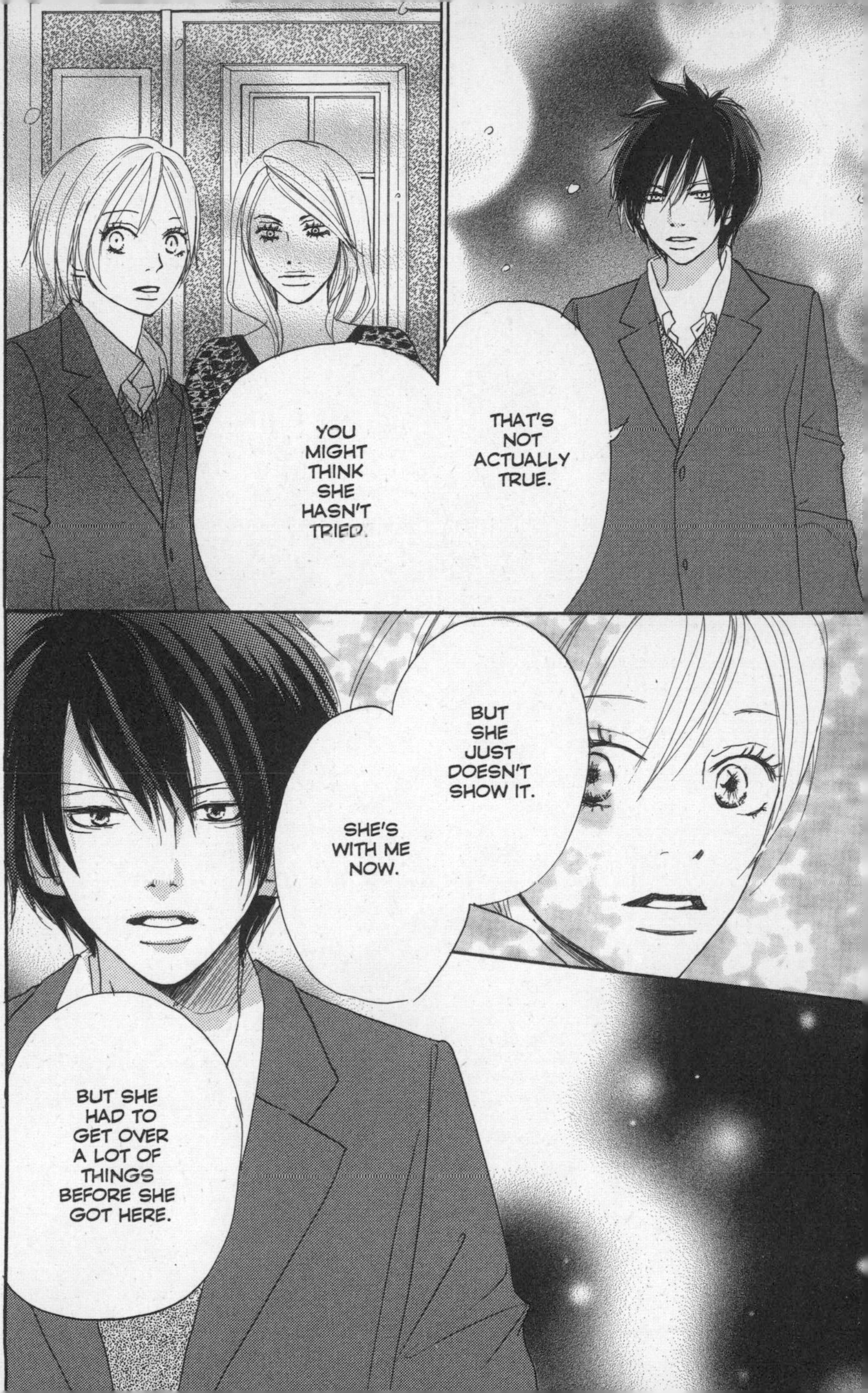
YOU MIGHT THINK SHE HASN'T TRIED.
THAT'S NOT ACTUALLY TRUE.
BUT SHE JUST DOESN'T SHOW IT.
SHE'S WITH ME NOW.
BUT SHE HAD TO GET OVER A LOT OF THINGS BEFORE SHE GOT HERE.

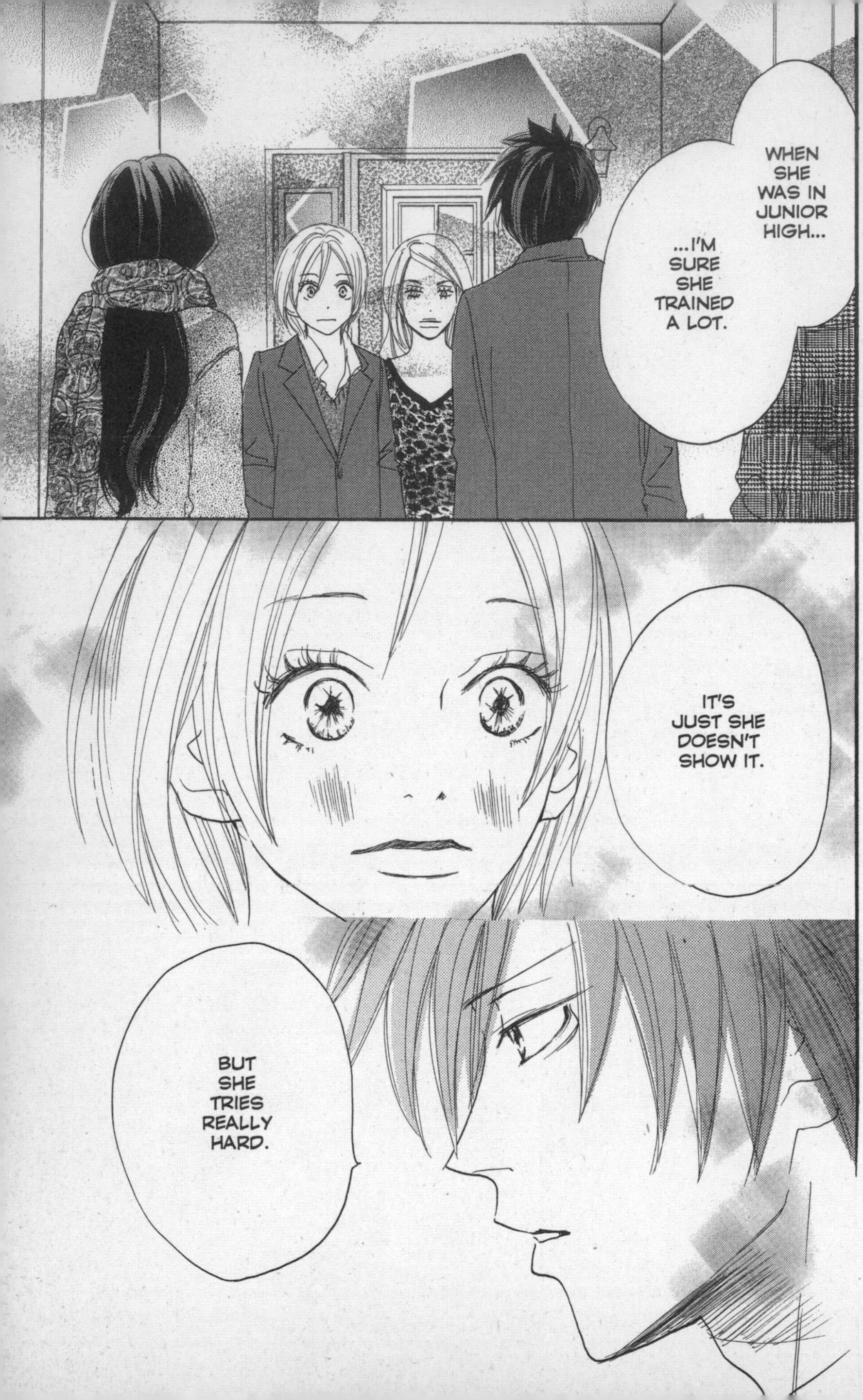
WHEN SHE WAS IN JUNIOR HIGH...
...I'M SURE SHE TRAINED A LOT.
IT'S JUST SHE DOESN'T SHOW IT.
BUT SHE TRIES REALLY HARD.

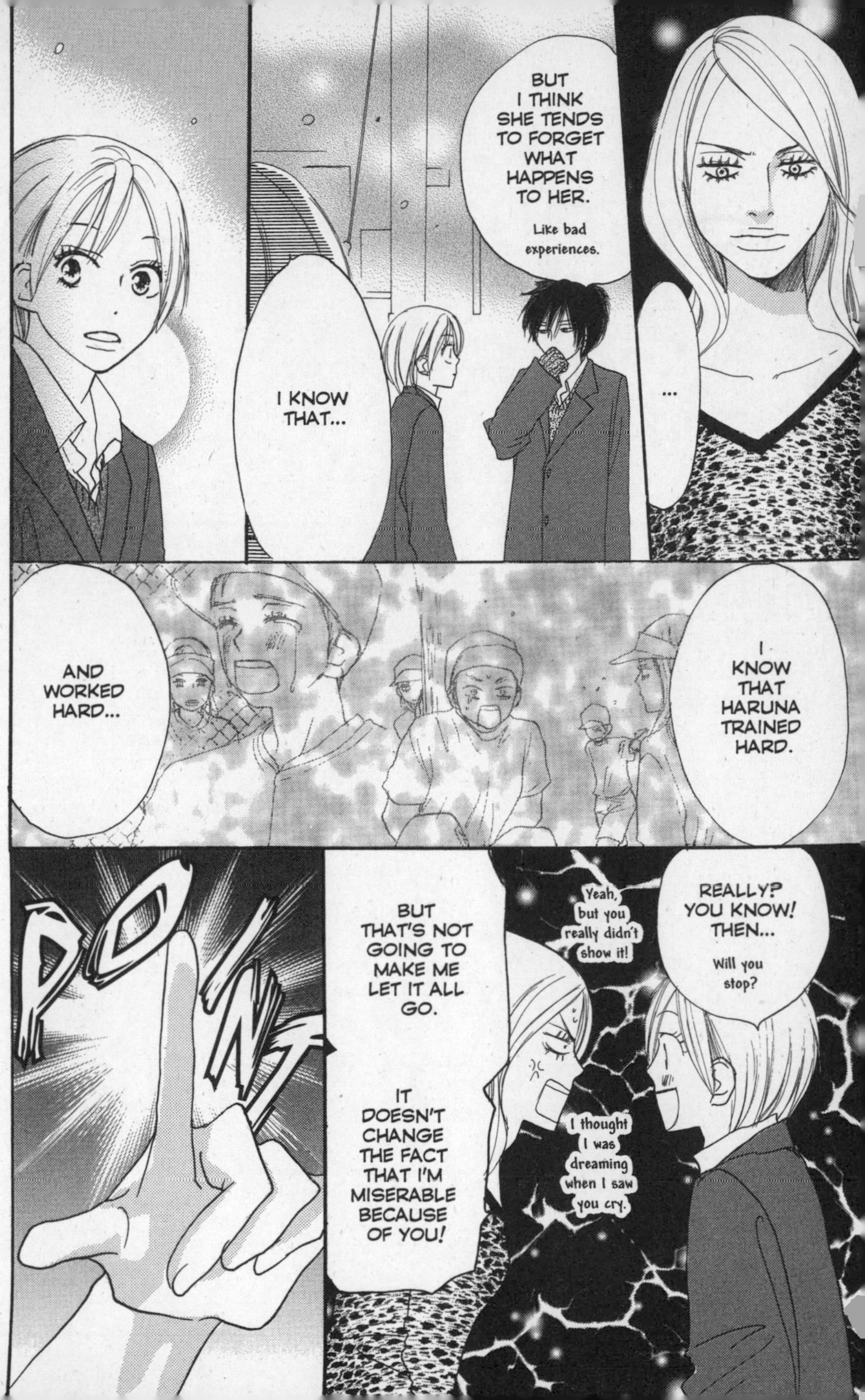
BUT I THINK SHE TENDS TO FORGET WHAT HAPPENS TO HER.
Like bad experiences.
...
I KNOW THAT...
I KNOW THAT HARUNA TRAINED HARD.
AND WORKED HARD...
REALLY? YOU KNOW! THEN...
Will you stop?
Yeah, but you really didn't show it!
BUT THAT'S NOT GOING TO MAKE ME LET IT ALL GO.
I thought I was dreaming when I saw you cry.
IT DOESN'T CHANGE THE FACT THAT I'M MISERABLE BECAUSE OF YOU!
POINT

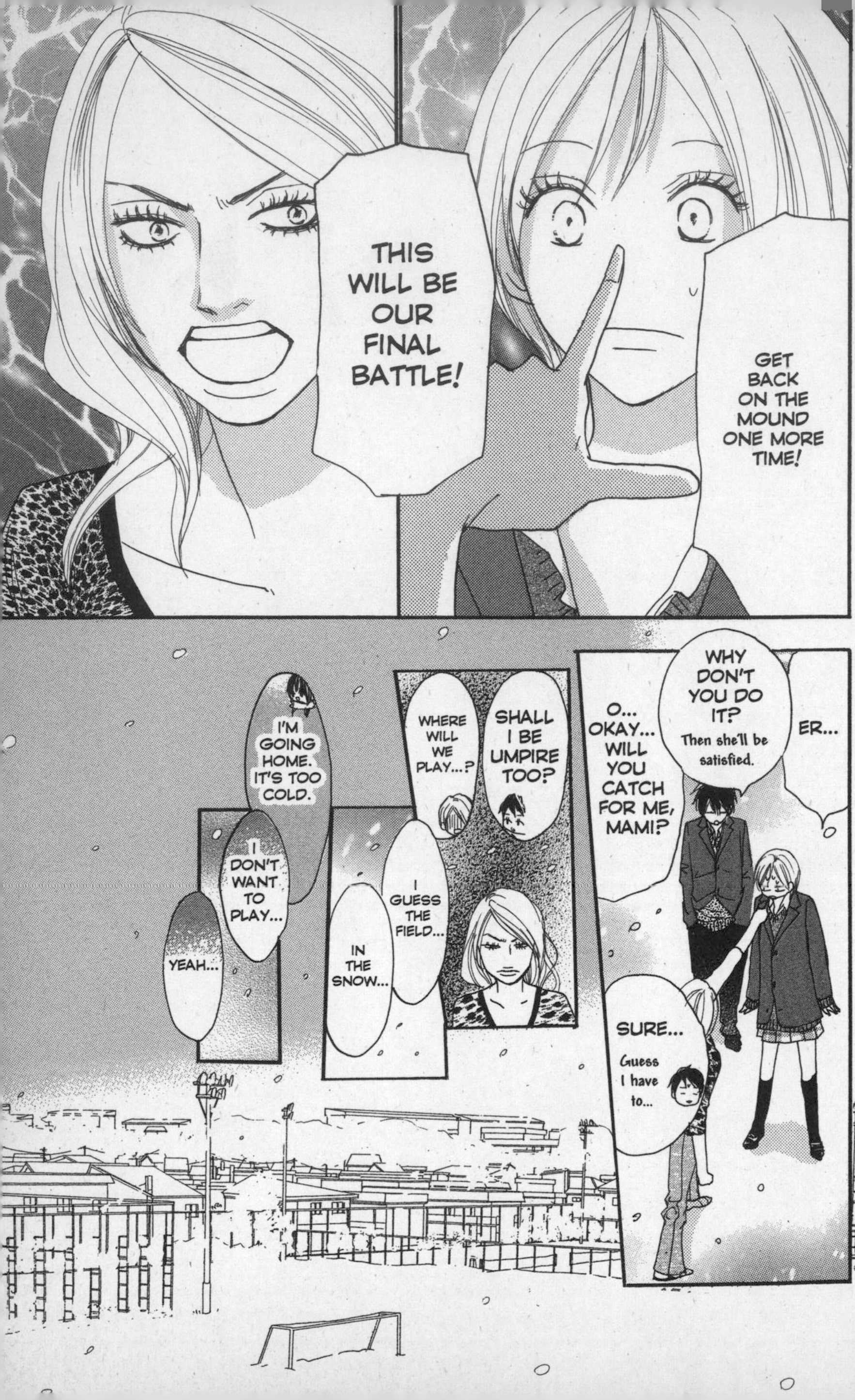
GET BACK ON THE MOUND ONE MORE TIME!
THIS WILL BE OUR FINAL BATTLE!
ER...
WHY DON'T YOU DO IT? Then she'll be satisfied.
O... OKAY... WILL YOU CATCH FOR ME, MAMI?
SURE... Guess I have to...
SHALL I BE UMPIRE TOO?
WHERE WILL WE PLAY...?
I GUESS THE FIELD...
IN THE SNOW...
I'M GOING HOME. IT'S TOO COLD.
I DON'T WANT TO PLAY...
YEAH...

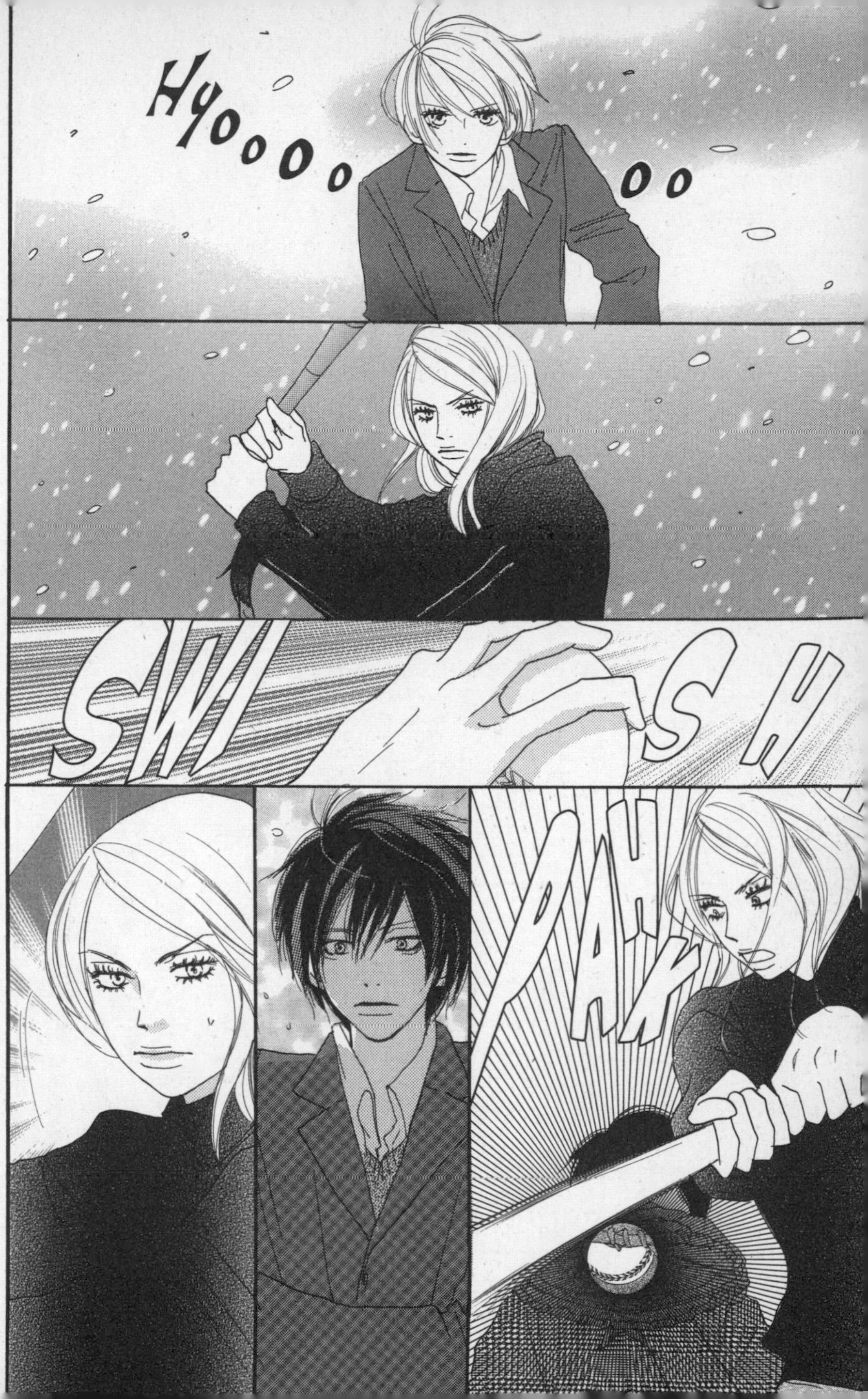
HYOOOOO
OO
SWI
SH
PAK

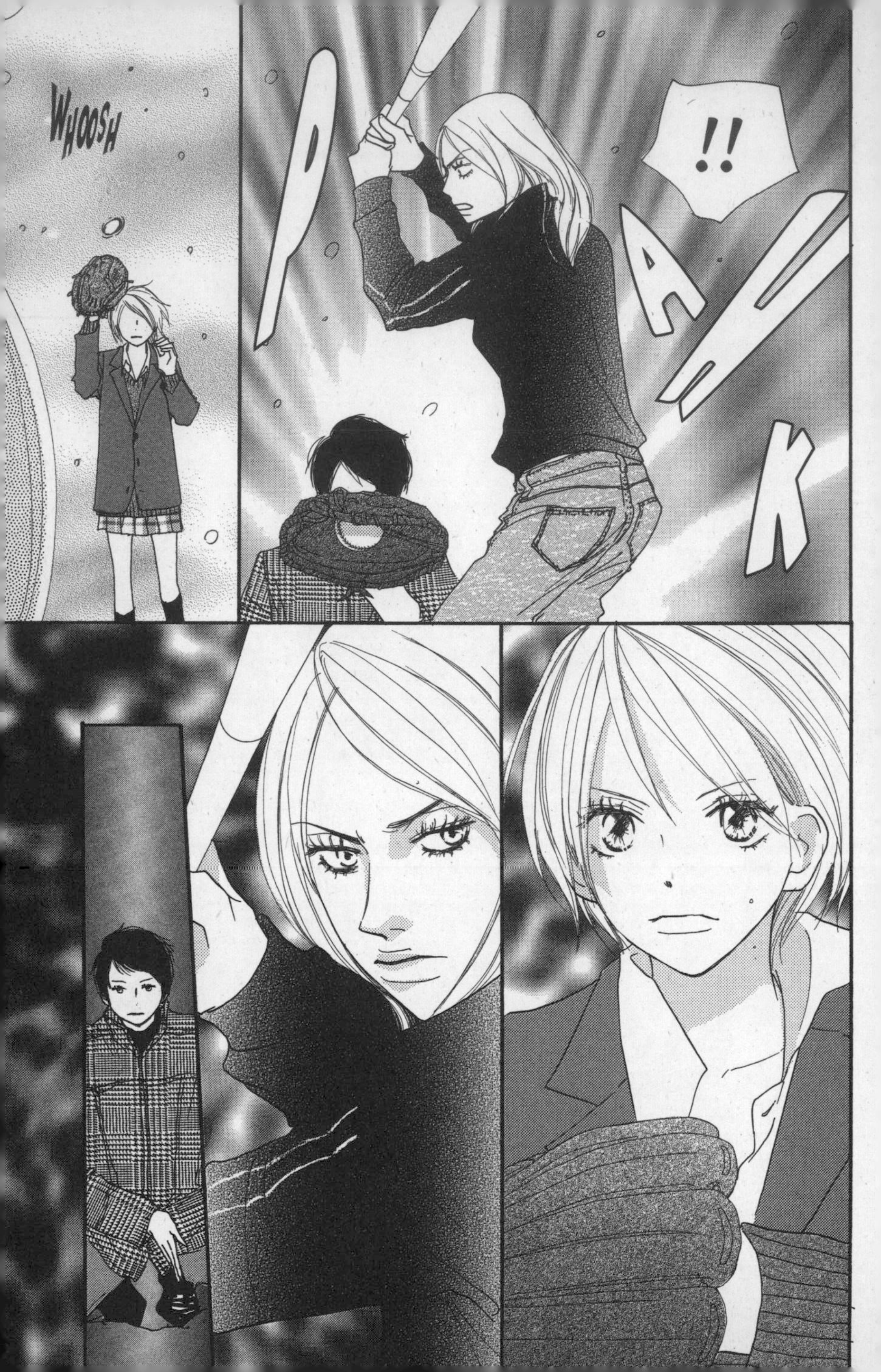
!!
PAKK
WHOOSH

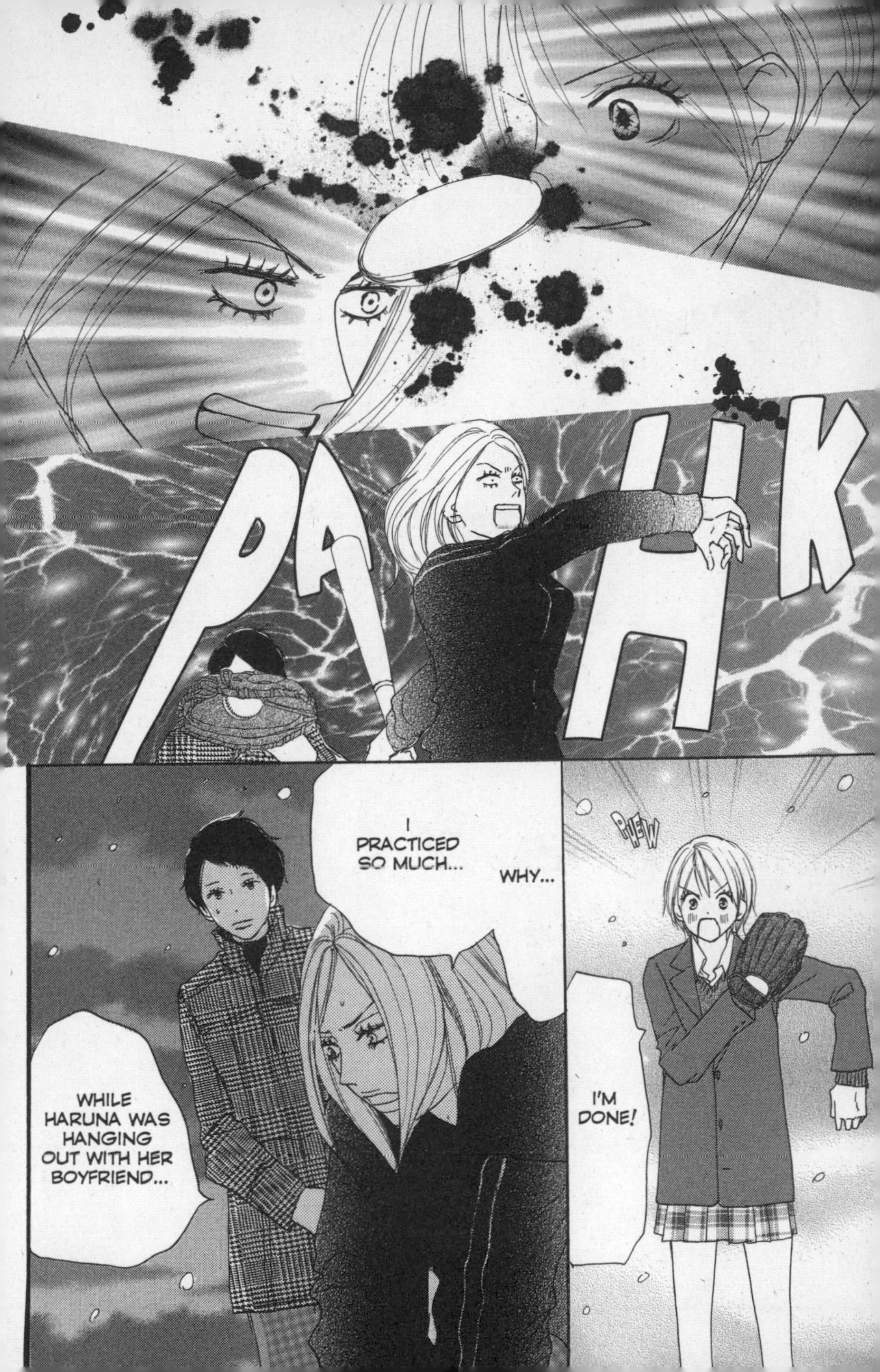
PAHIK
PHEW
I'M DONE!
WHY...
I PRACTICED SO MUCH...
WHILE HARUNA WAS HANGING OUT WITH HER BOYFRIEND...

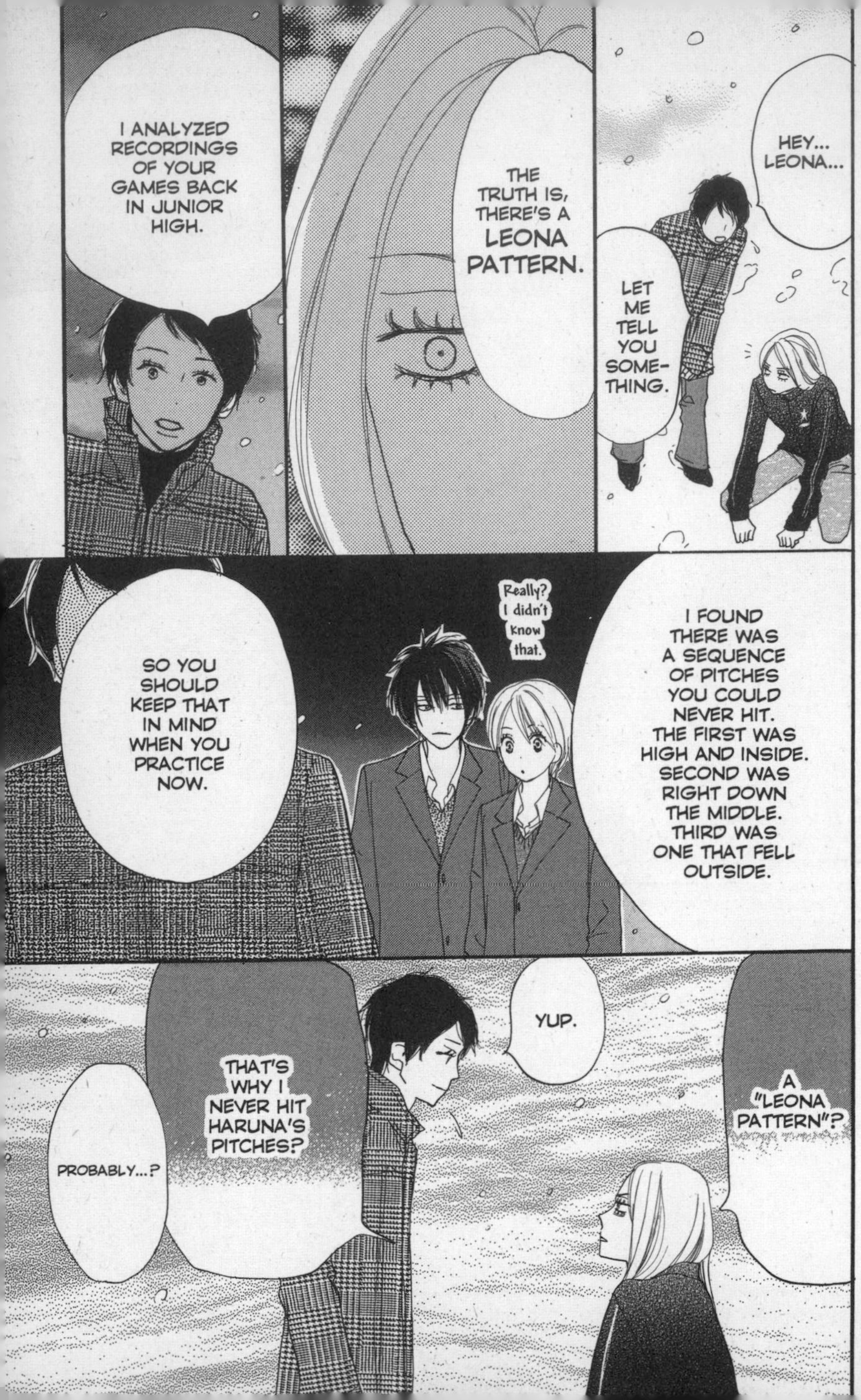
HEY... LEONA...
LET ME TELL YOU SOME-THING.
THE TRUTH IS, THERE'S A LEONA PATTERN.
I ANALYZED RECORDINGS OF YOUR GAMES BACK IN JUNIOR HIGH.
I FOUND THERE WAS A SEQUENCE OF PITCHES YOU COULD NEVER HIT. THE FIRST WAS HIGH AND INSIDE. SECOND WAS RIGHT DOWN THE MIDDLE. THIRD WAS ONE THAT FELL OUTSIDE.
Really? I didn't know that.
SO YOU SHOULD KEEP THAT IN MIND WHEN YOU PRACTICE NOW.
A "LEONA PATTERN"?
YUP.
THAT'S WHY I NEVER HIT HARUNA'S PITCHES?
PROBABLY...?

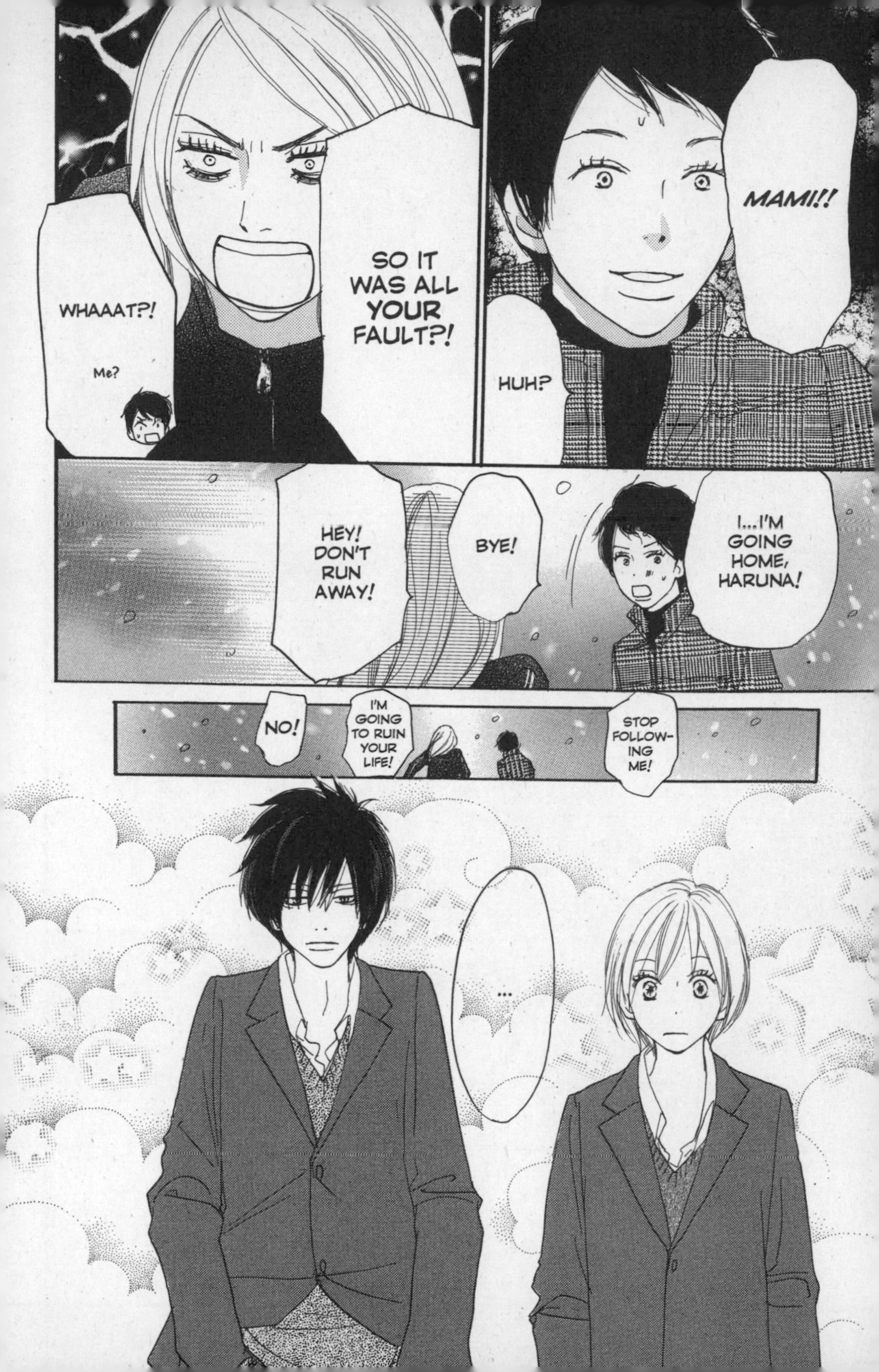
MAMI!!
HUH?
SO IT WAS ALL YOUR FAULT?!
WHAAAT?!
Me?
I...I'M GOING HOME, HARUNA!
BYE!
HEY! DON'T RUN AWAY!
STOP FOLLOW-ING ME!
I'M GOING TO RUIN YOUR LIFE!
NO!
...

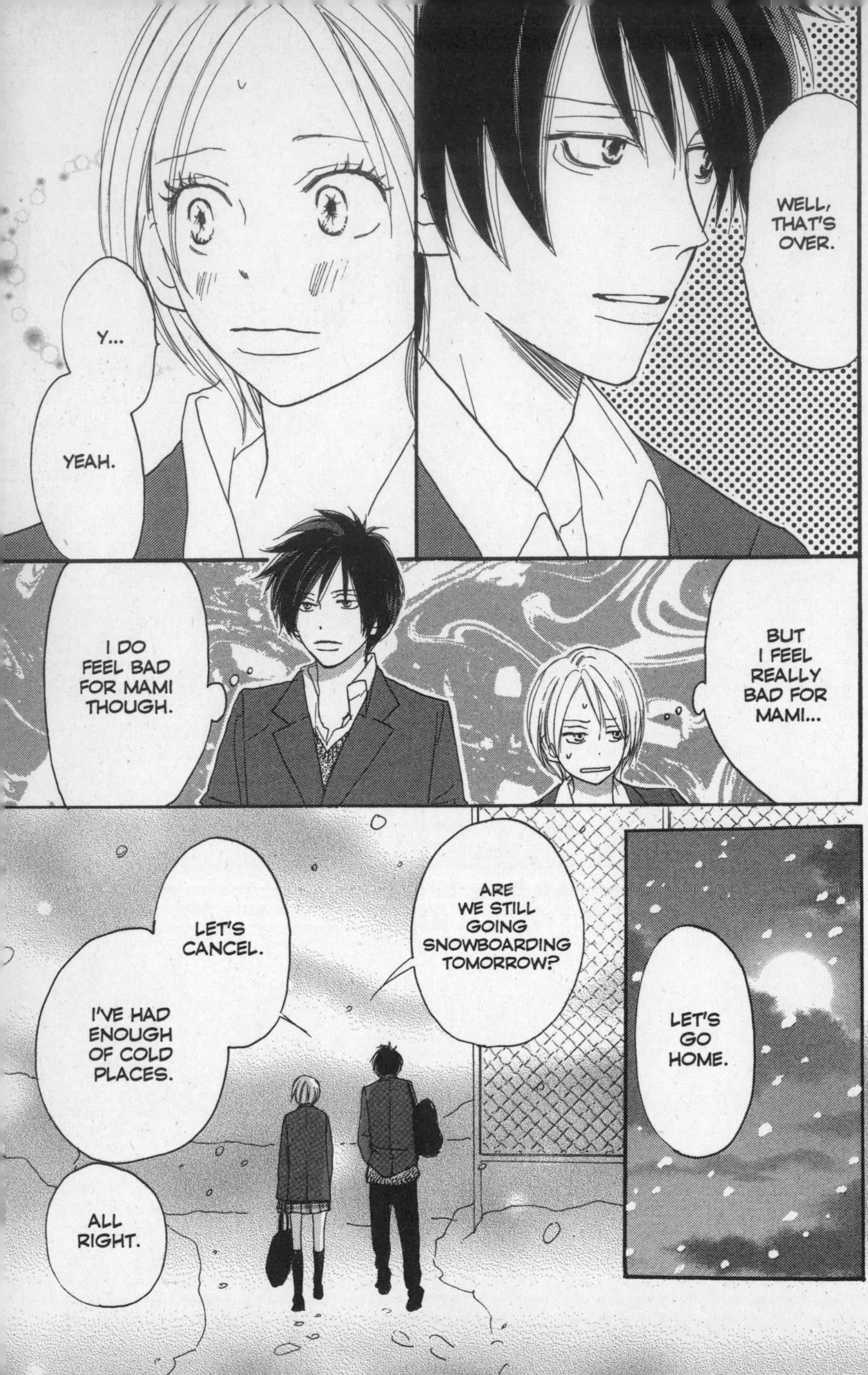
WELL, THAT'S OVER.
Y...
YEAH.
BUT I FEEL REALLY BAD FOR MAMI...
I DO FEEL BAD FOR MAMI THOUGH.
LET'S GO HOME.
ARE WE STILL GOING SNOWBOARDING TOMORROW?
LET'S CANCEL.
I'VE HAD ENOUGH OF COLD PLACES.
ALL RIGHT.

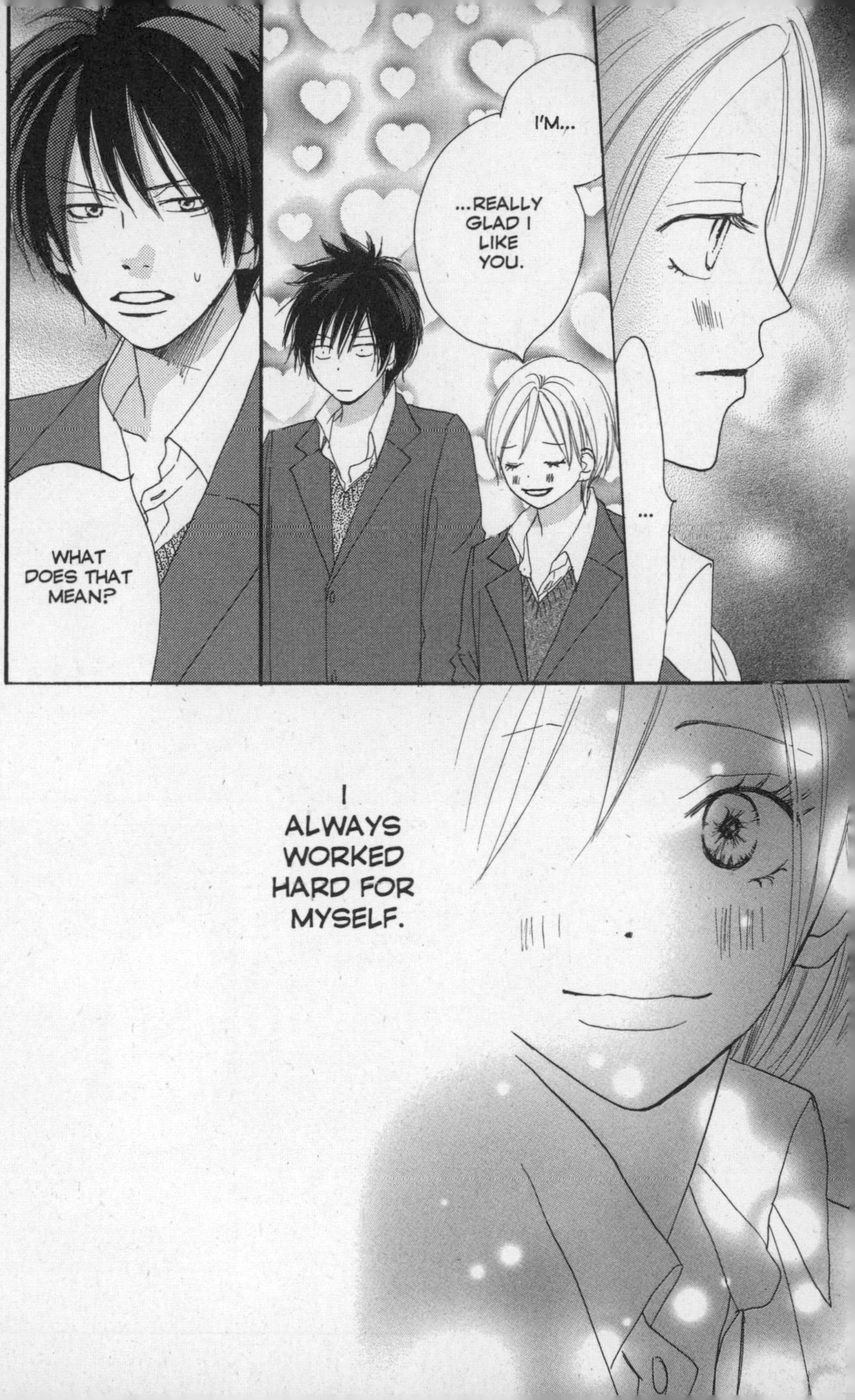
...
I'M...
...REALLY GLAD I LIKE YOU.
WHAT DOES THAT MEAN?
I ALWAYS WORKED HARD FOR MYSELF.

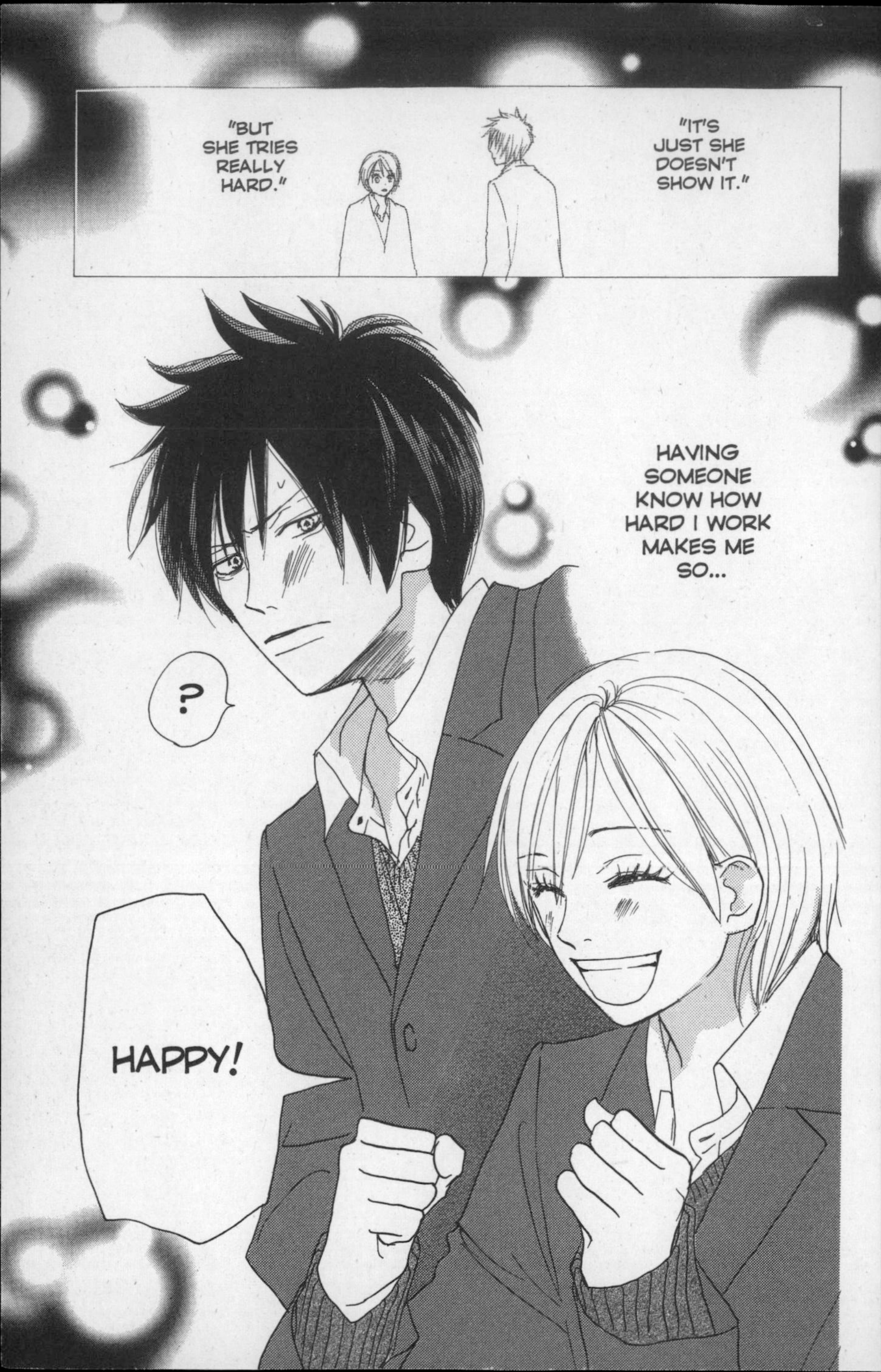
"IT'S JUST SHE DOESN'T SHOW IT."
"BUT SHE TRIES REALLY HARD."
HAVING SOMEONE KNOW HOW HARD I WORK MAKES ME SO...
?
HAPPY!

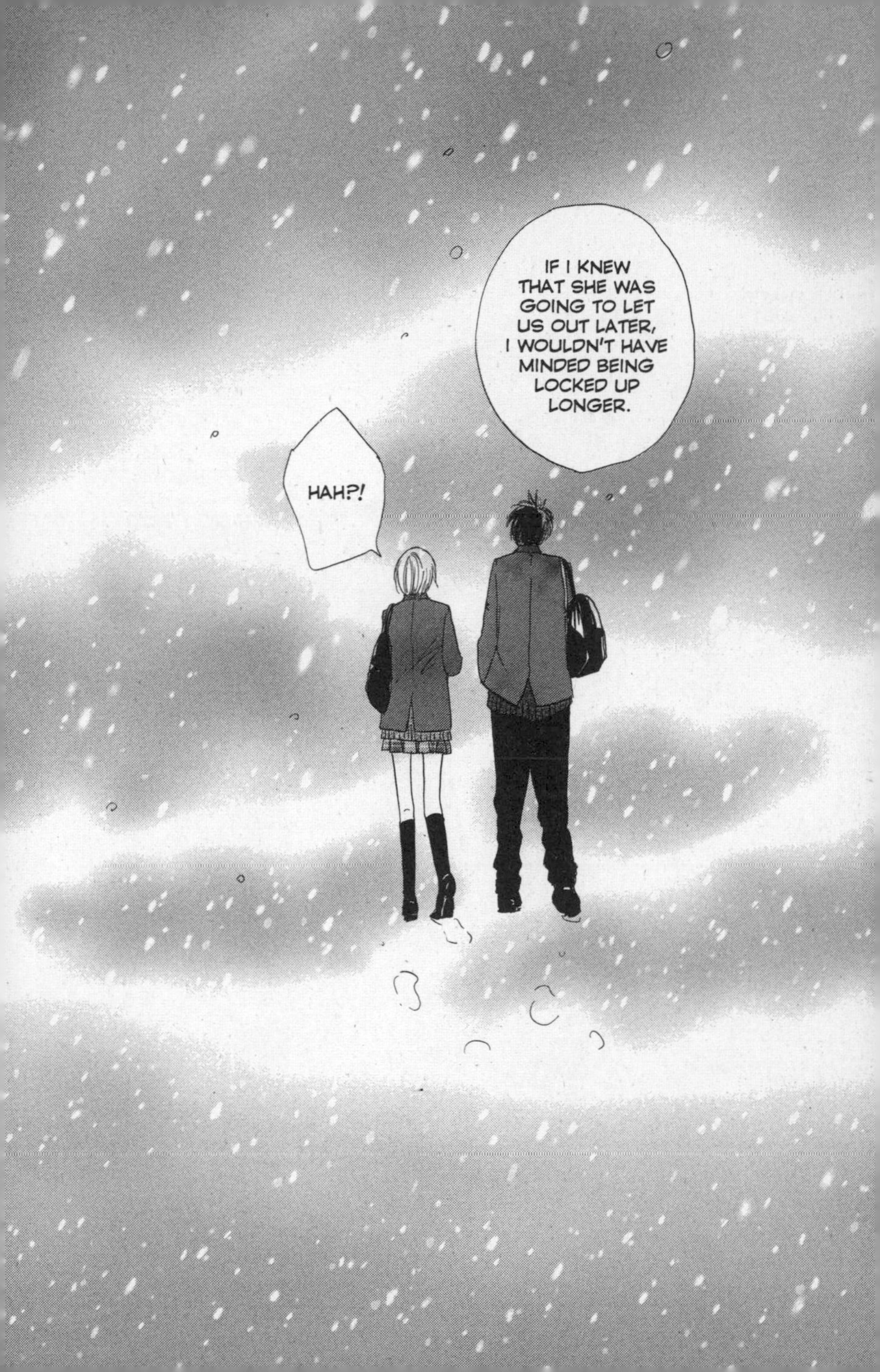
IF I KNEW THAT SHE WAS GOING TO LET US OUT LATER, I WOULDN'T HAVE MINDED BEING LOCKED UP LONGER.
HAH?!

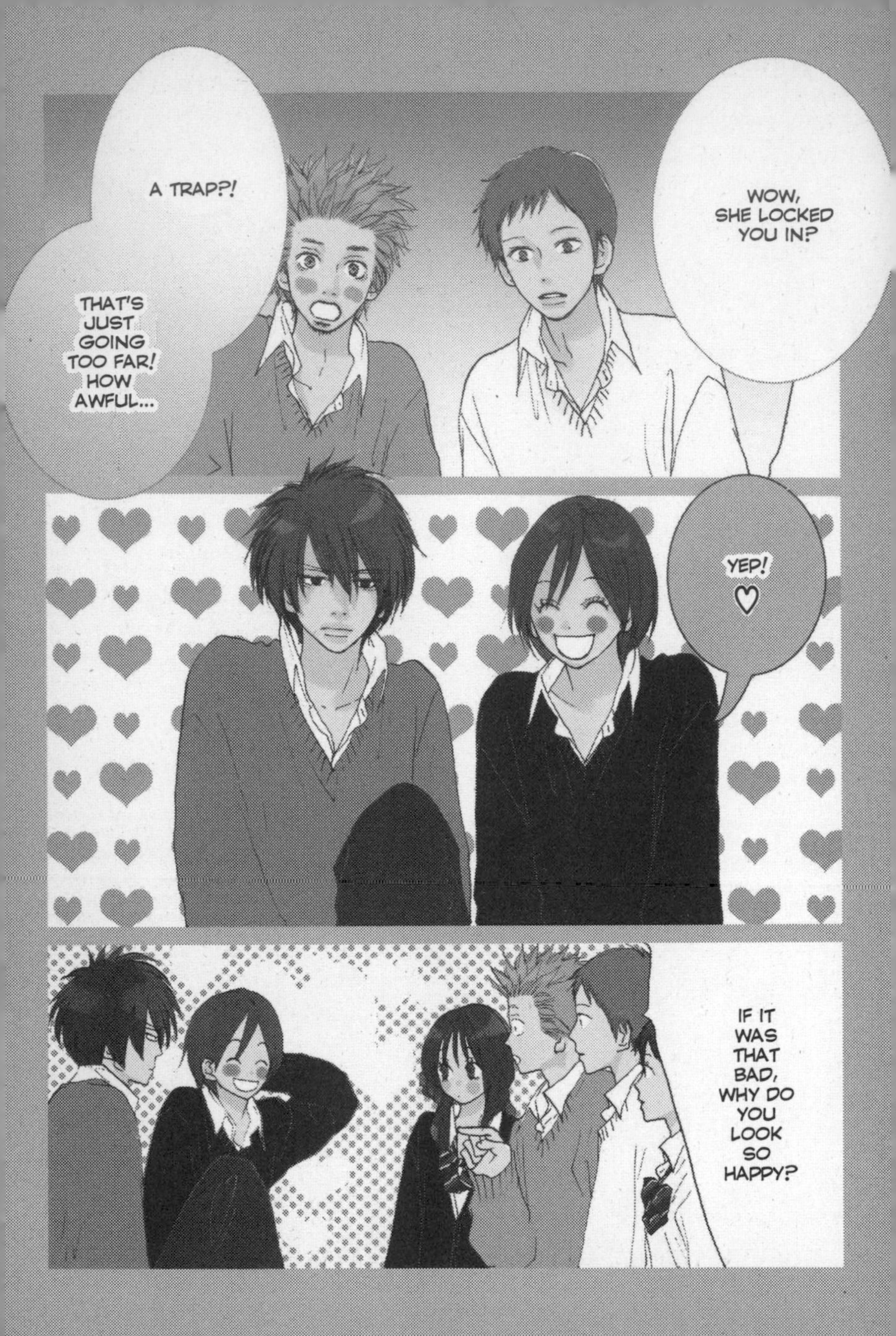
WOW, SHE LOCKED YOU IN?
A TRAP?!
THAT'S JUST GOING TOO FAR! HOW AWFUL...
YEP! ♡
IF IT WAS THAT BAD, WHY DO YOU LOOK SO HAPPY?

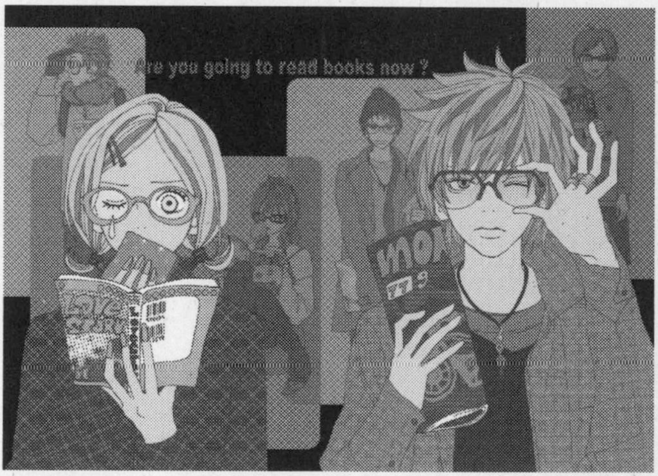
Are you going to read books now ?

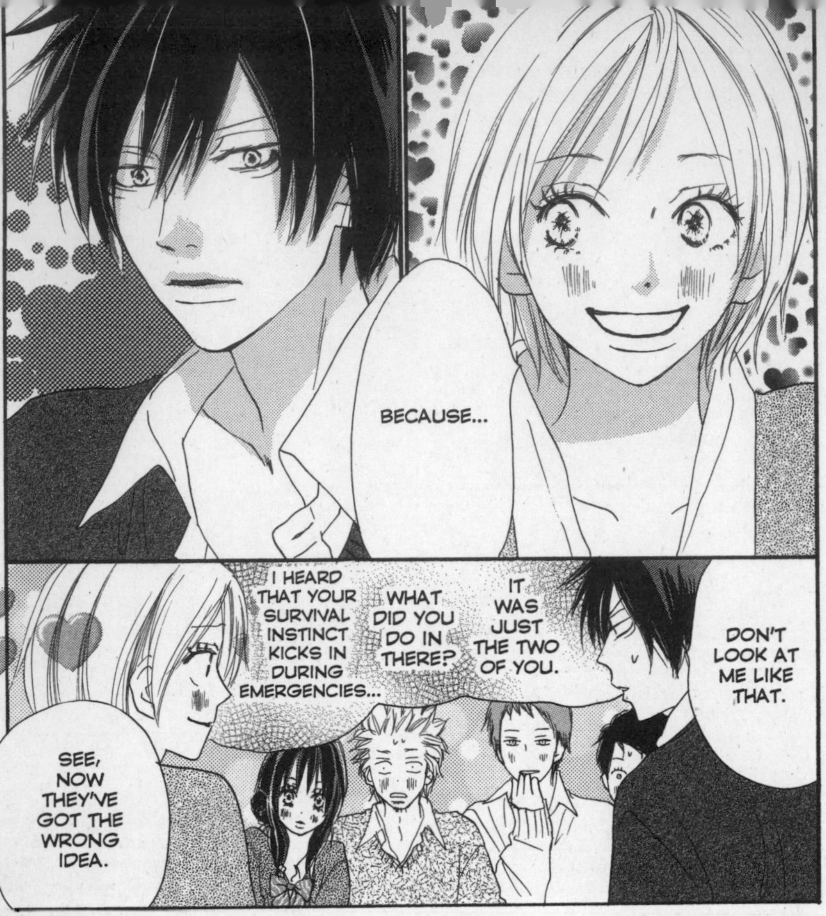
BECAUSE...
DON'T LOOK AT ME LIKE THAT.
IT WAS JUST THE TWO OF YOU.
WHAT DID YOU DO IN THERE?
I HEARD THAT YOUR SURVIVAL INSTINCT KICKS IN DURING EMERGENCIES...
SEE, NOW THEY'VE GOT THE WRONG IDEA.

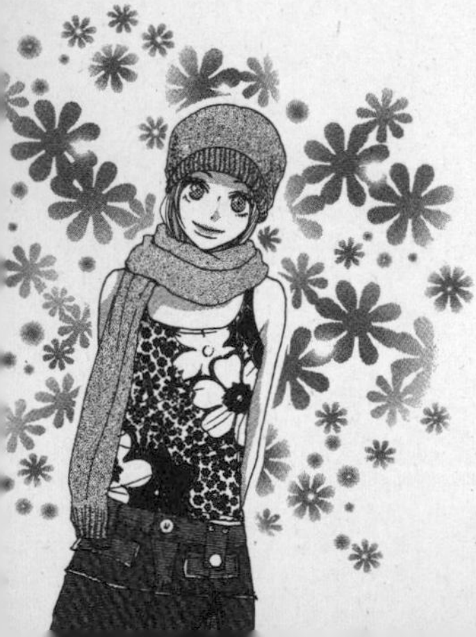

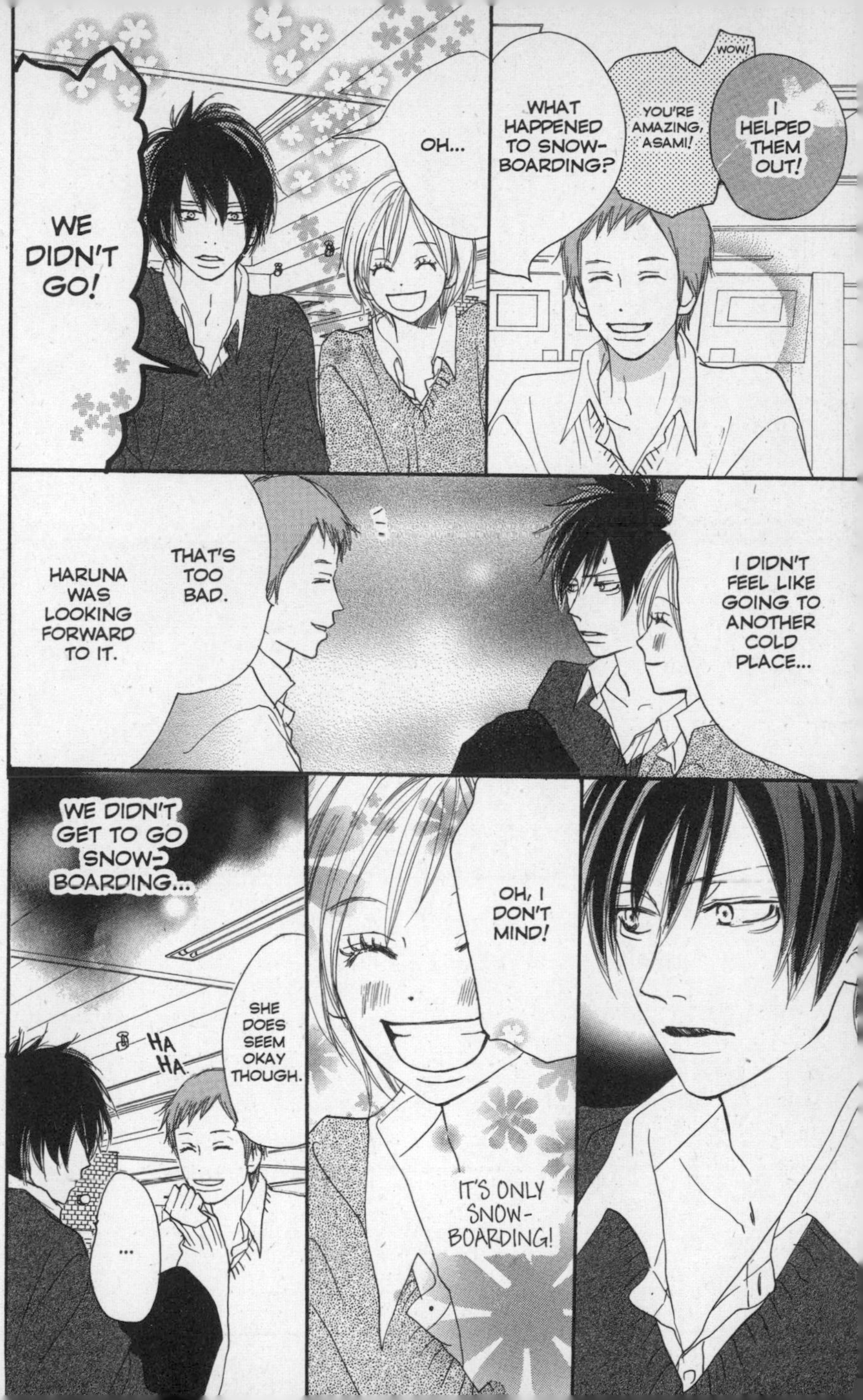
WOW!
I HELPED THEM OUT!
YOU'RE AMAZING, ASAMI!
WHAT HAPPENED TO SNOW-BOARDING?
OH...
WE DIDN'T GO!
I DIDN'T FEEL LIKE GOING TO ANOTHER COLD PLACE...
THAT'S TOO BAD.
HARUNA WAS LOOKING FORWARD TO IT.
OH, I DON'T MIND!
IT'S ONLY SNOW-BOARDING!
WE DIDN'T GET TO GO SNOW-BOARDING...
SHE DOES SEEM OKAY THOUGH.
HA HA
...

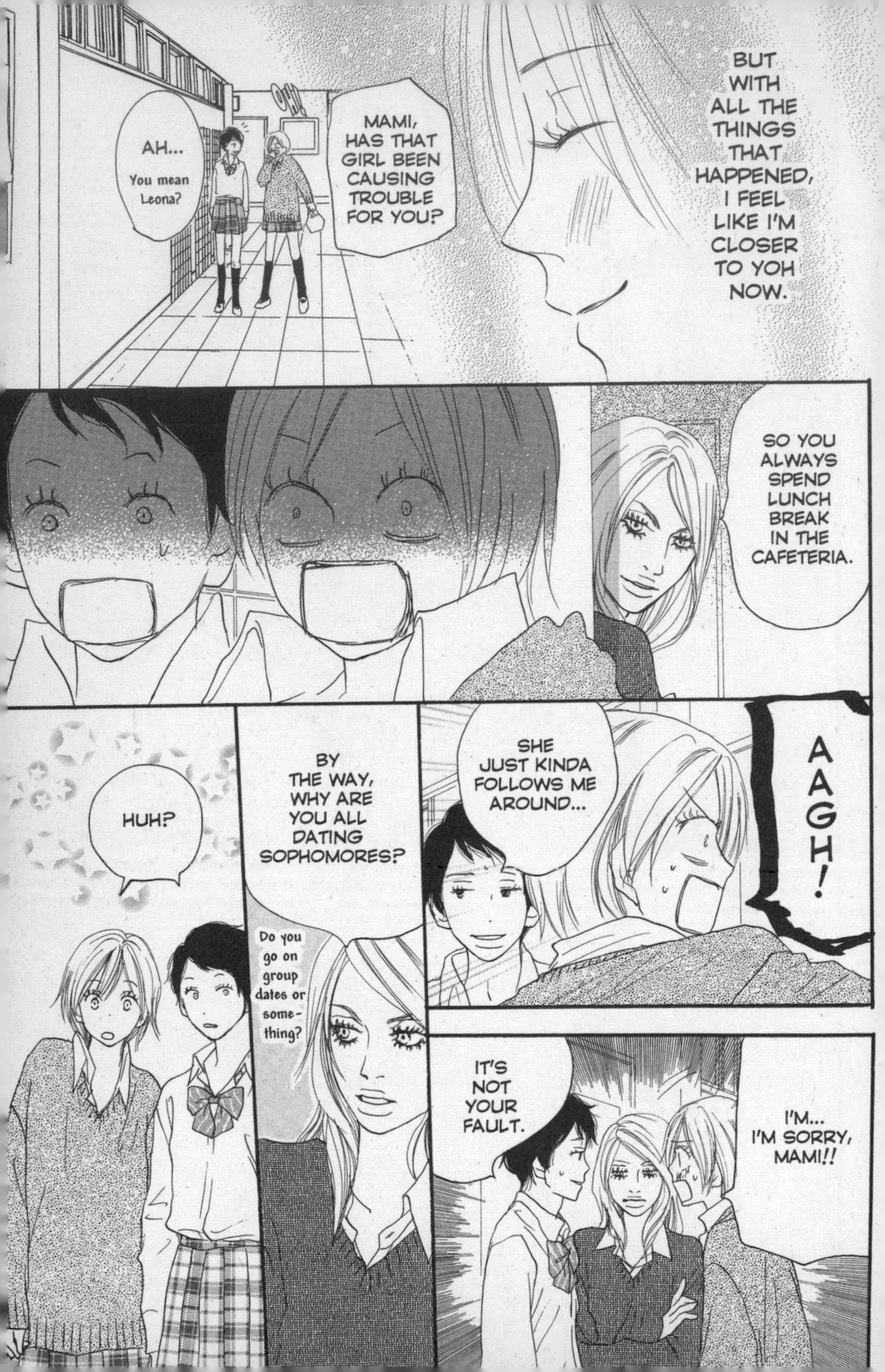
BUT WITH ALL THE THINGS THAT HAPPENED, I FEEL LIKE I'M CLOSER TO YOH NOW.
MAMI, HAS THAT GIRL BEEN CAUSING TROUBLE FOR YOU?
AH... You mean Leona?
SO YOU ALWAYS SPEND LUNCH BREAK IN THE CAFETERIA.
AAGH!
SHE JUST KINDA FOLLOWS ME AROUND...
I'M... I'M SORRY, MAMI!!
IT'S NOT YOUR FAULT.
BY THE WAY, WHY ARE YOU ALL DATING SOPHOMORES?
Do you go on group dates or some-thing?
HUH?

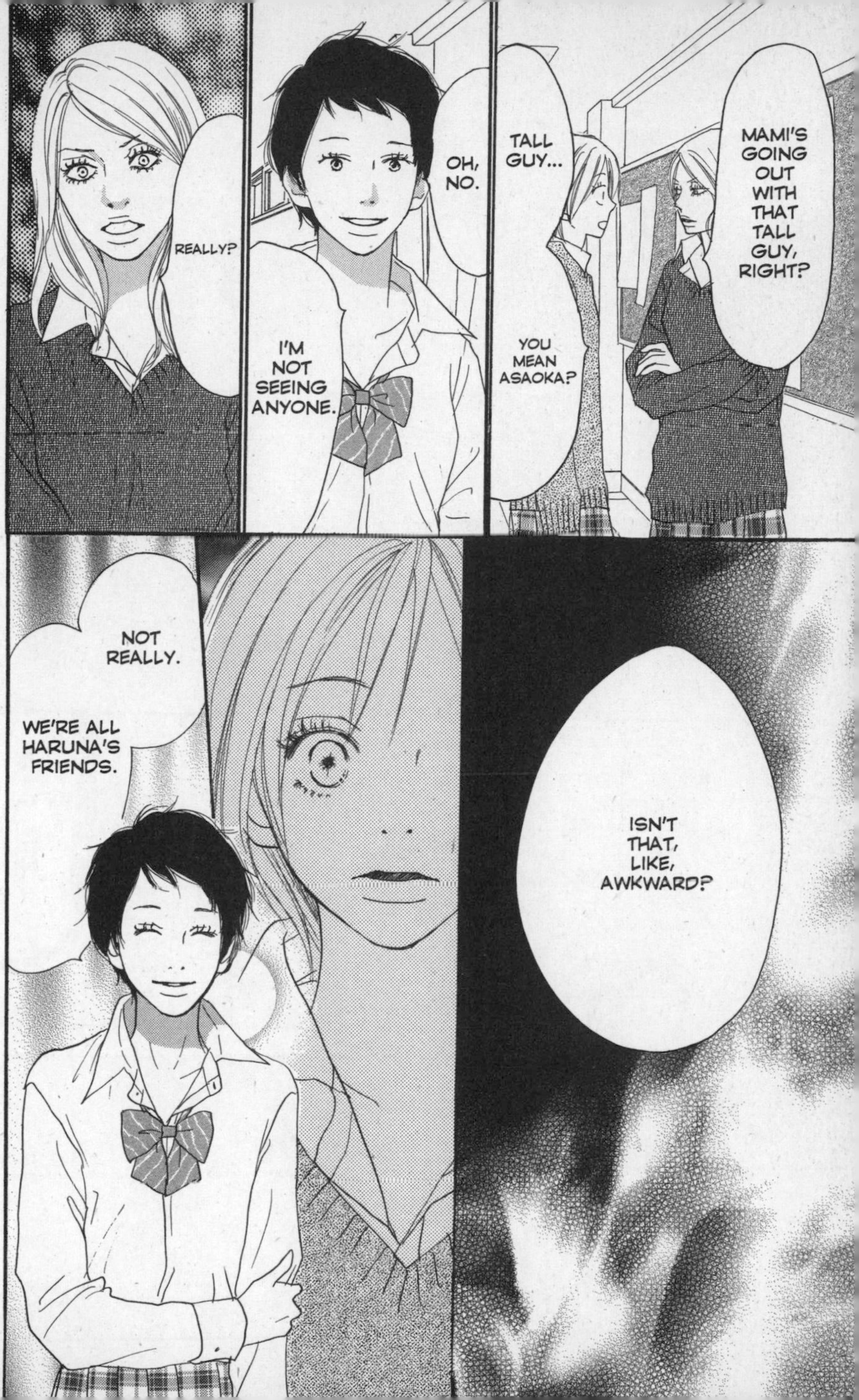
MAMI'S GOING OUT WITH THAT TALL GUY, RIGHT?
TALL GUY...
YOU MEAN ASAOKA?
OH, NO.
I'M NOT SEEING ANYONE.
REALLY?
ISN'T THAT, LIKE, AWKWARD?
NOT REALLY.
WE'RE ALL HARUNA'S FRIENDS.

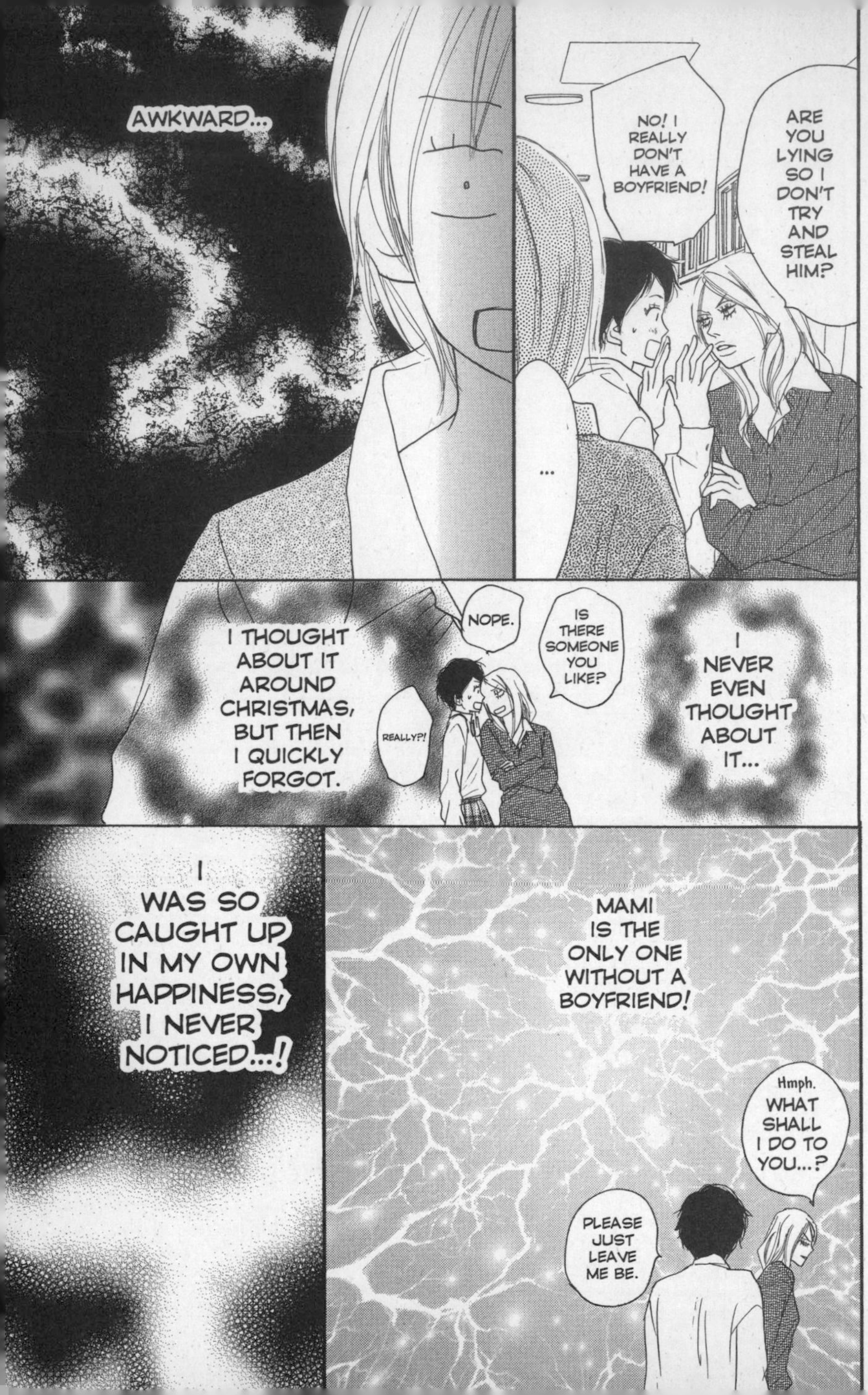
ARE YOU LYING SO I DON'T TRY AND STEAL HIM?
NO! I REALLY DON'T HAVE A BOYFRIEND!
...
AWKWARD...
I NEVER EVEN THOUGHT ABOUT IT...
IS THERE SOMEONE YOU LIKE?
NOPE.
REALLY?!
I THOUGHT ABOUT IT AROUND CHRISTMAS, BUT THEN I QUICKLY FORGOT.
MAMI IS THE ONLY ONE WITHOUT A BOYFRIEND!
Hmph. WHAT SHALL I DO TO YOU...?
PLEASE JUST LEAVE ME BE.
I WAS SO CAUGHT UP IN MY OWN HAPPINESS, I NEVER NOTICED...!

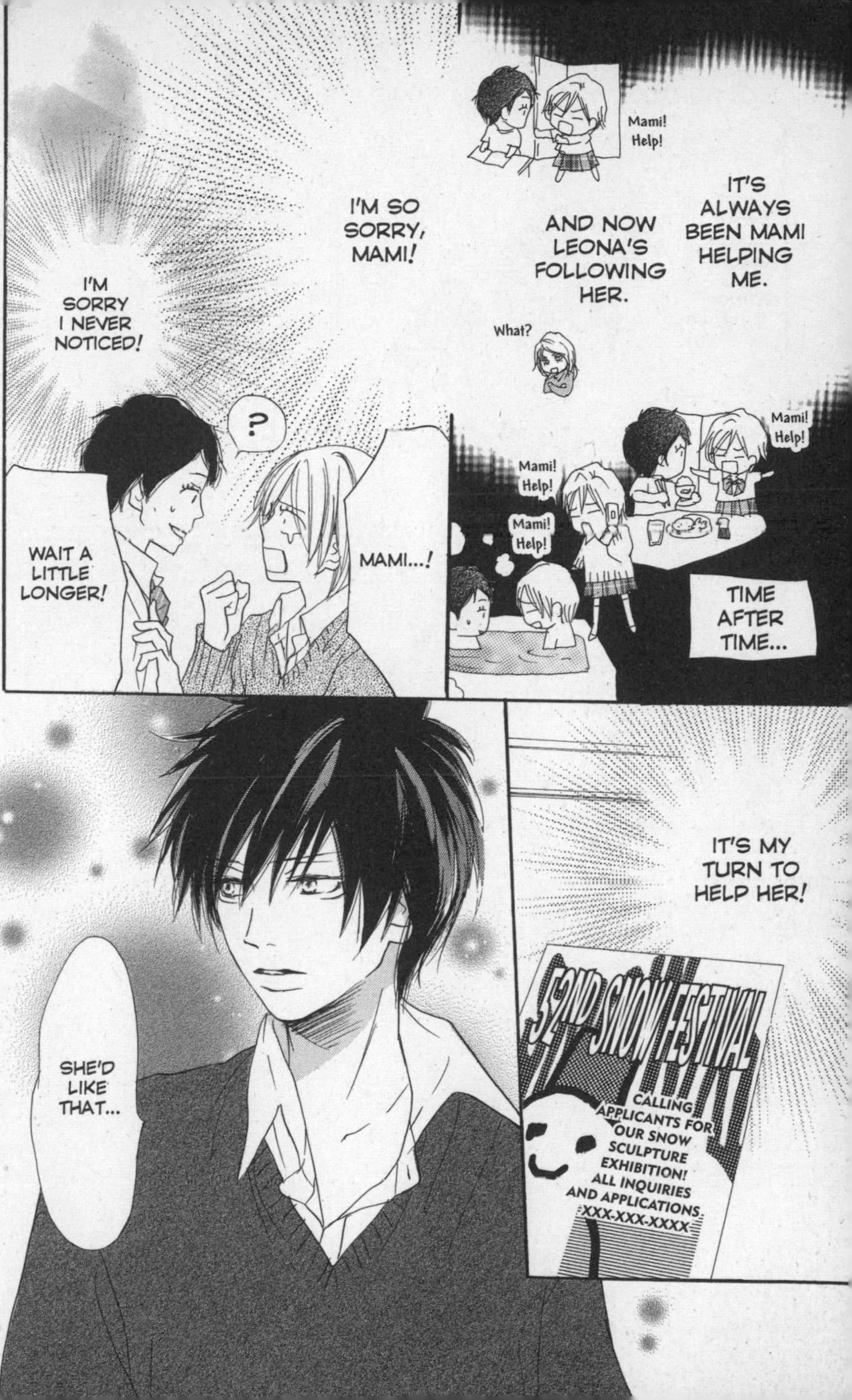
IT'S ALWAYS BEEN MAMI HELPING ME.
Mami! Help!
AND NOW LEONA'S FOLLOWING HER.
What?
Mami! Help!
Mami! Help!
Mami! Help!
TIME AFTER TIME...
I'M SO SORRY, MAMI!
I'M SORRY I NEVER NOTICED!
?
MAMI...!
WAIT A LITTLE LONGER!
IT'S MY TURN TO HELP HER!
52ND SNOW FESTIVAL
CALLING APPLICANTS FOR OUR SNOW SCULPTURE EXHIBITION! ALL INQUIRIES AND APPLICATIONS
XXX-XXX-XXXX
SHE'D LIKE THAT...

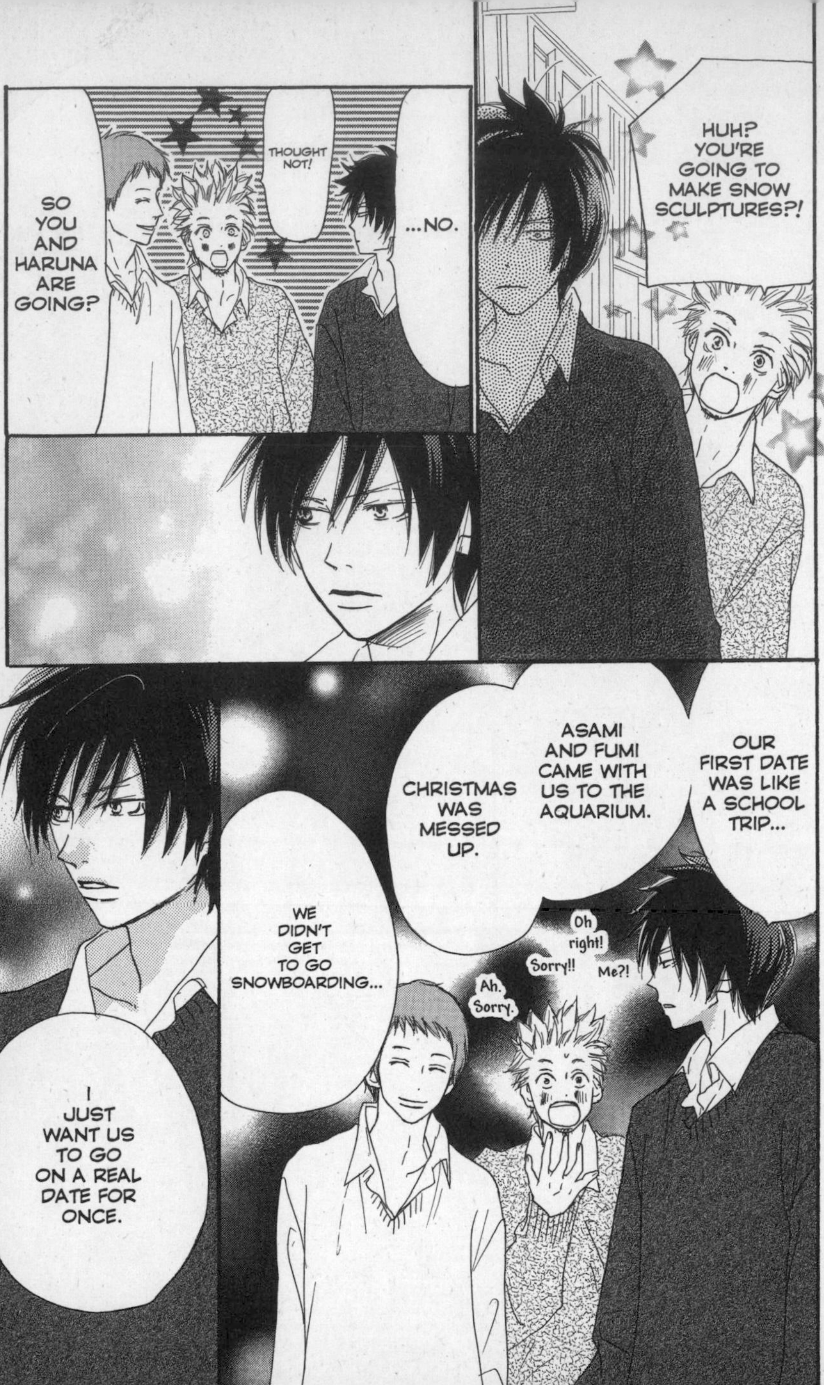
HUH? YOU'RE GOING TO MAKE SNOW SCULPTURES?!
...NO.
THOUGHT NOT!
SO YOU AND HARUNA ARE GOING?
OUR FIRST DATE WAS LIKE A SCHOOL TRIP...
ASAMI AND FUMI CAME WITH US TO THE AQUARIUM.
CHRISTMAS WAS MESSED UP.
WE DIDN'T GET TO GO SNOWBOARDING...
Me?!
Oh right!
Sorry!!
Ah. Sorry.
I JUST WANT US TO GO ON A REAL DATE FOR ONCE.

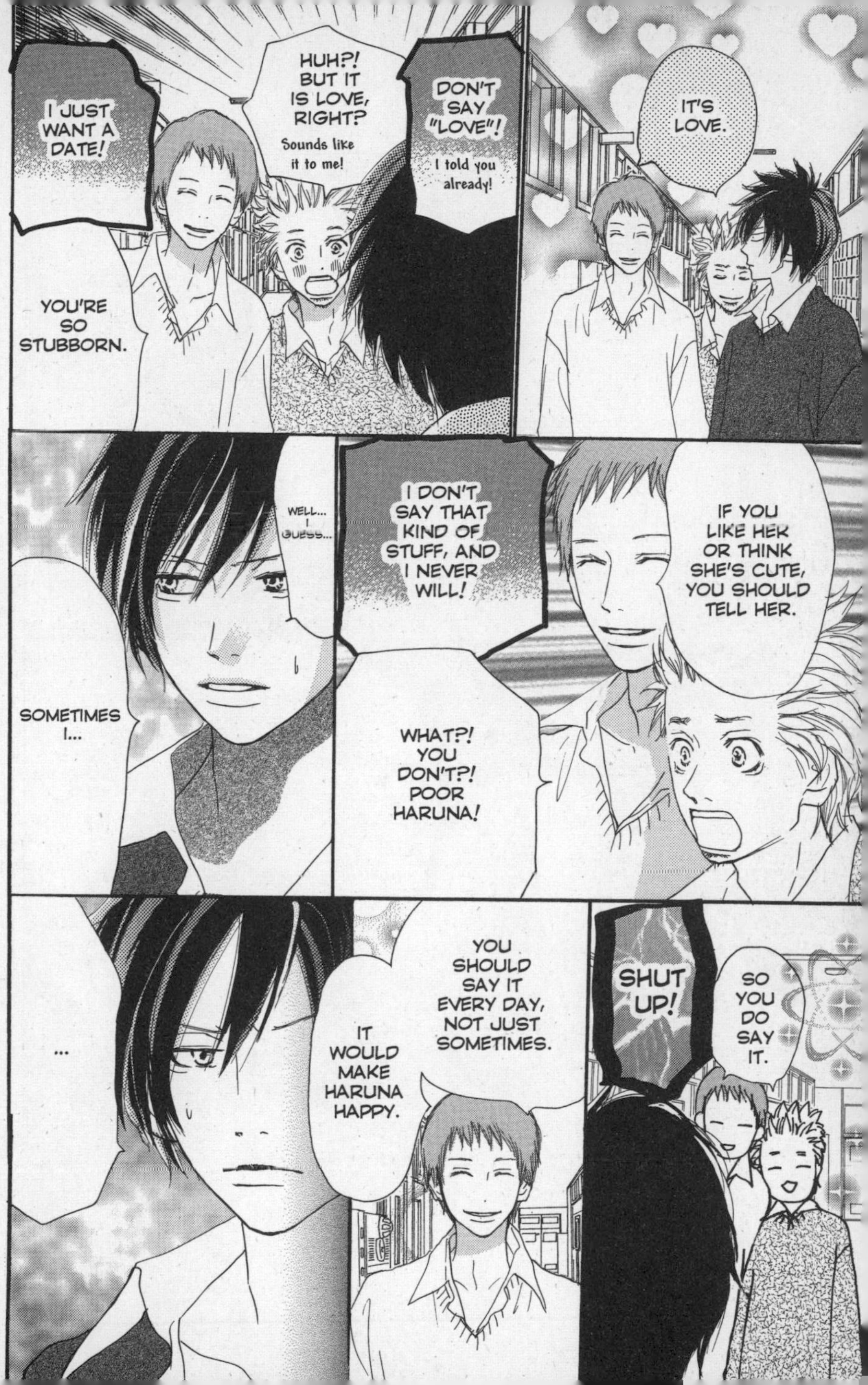

IT'S LOVE.
DON'T SAY "LOVE"! I told you already!
HUH?! BUT IT IS LOVE, RIGHT? Sounds like it to me!
I JUST WANT A DATE!
YOU'RE SO STUBBORN.
IF YOU LIKE HER OR THINK SHE'S CUTE, YOU SHOULD TELL HER.
I DON'T SAY THAT KIND OF STUFF, AND I NEVER WILL!
WHAT?! YOU DON'T?! POOR HARUNA!
WELL... I GUESS...
SOMETIMES I...
SO YOU DO SAY IT.
SHUT UP!
YOU SHOULD SAY IT EVERY DAY, NOT JUST SOMETIMES.
IT WOULD MAKE HARUNA HAPPY.
...

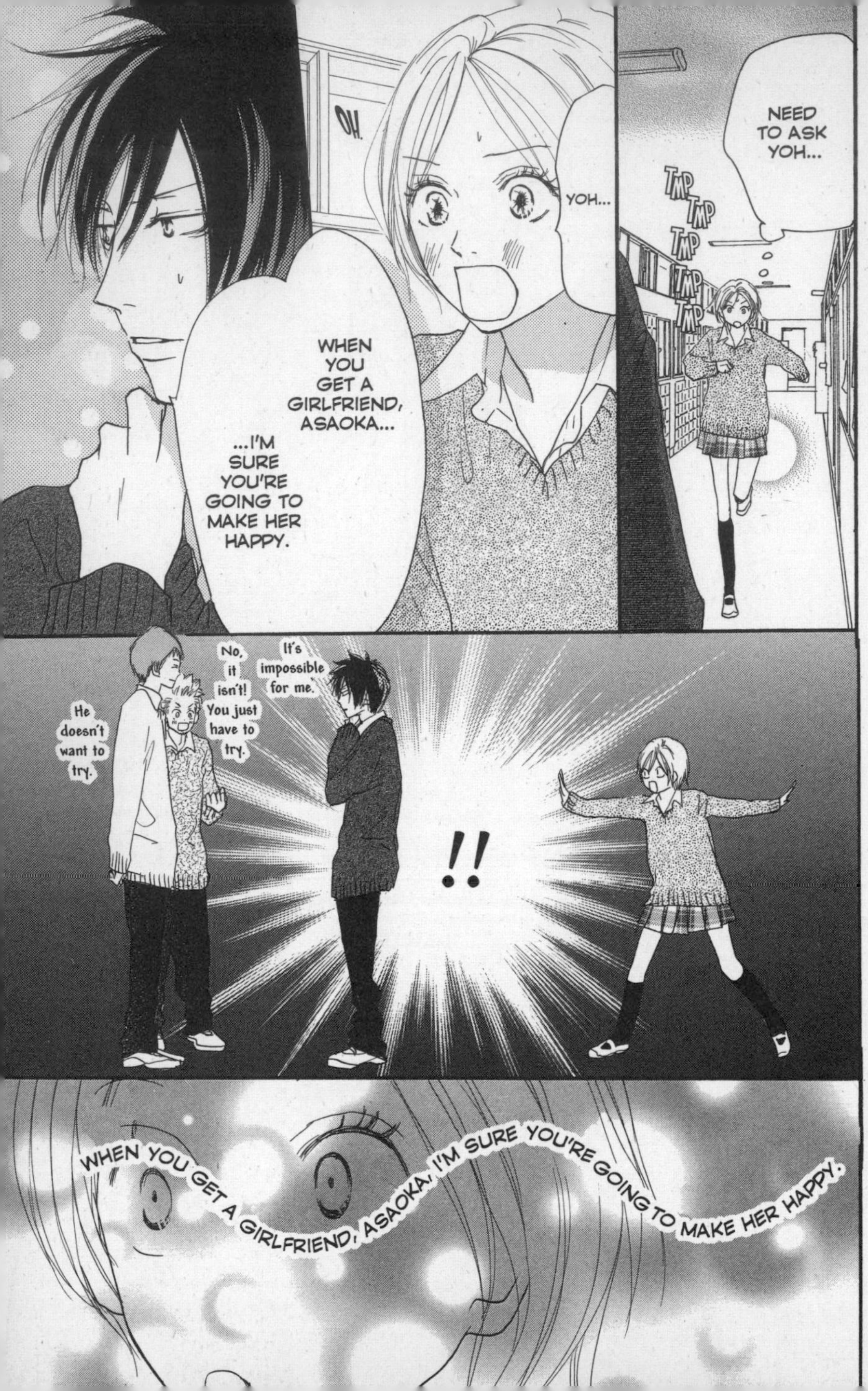
NEED TO ASK YOH...
TMP TMP TMP TMP TMP TMP
YOH...
OH.
WHEN YOU GET A GIRLFRIEND, ASAOKA...
...I'M SURE YOU'RE GOING TO MAKE HER HAPPY.
!!
It's impossible for me.
No, it isn't! You just have to try.
He doesn't want to try.
WHEN YOU GET A GIRLFRIEND, ASAOKA, I'M SURE YOU'RE GOING TO MAKE HER HAPPY.

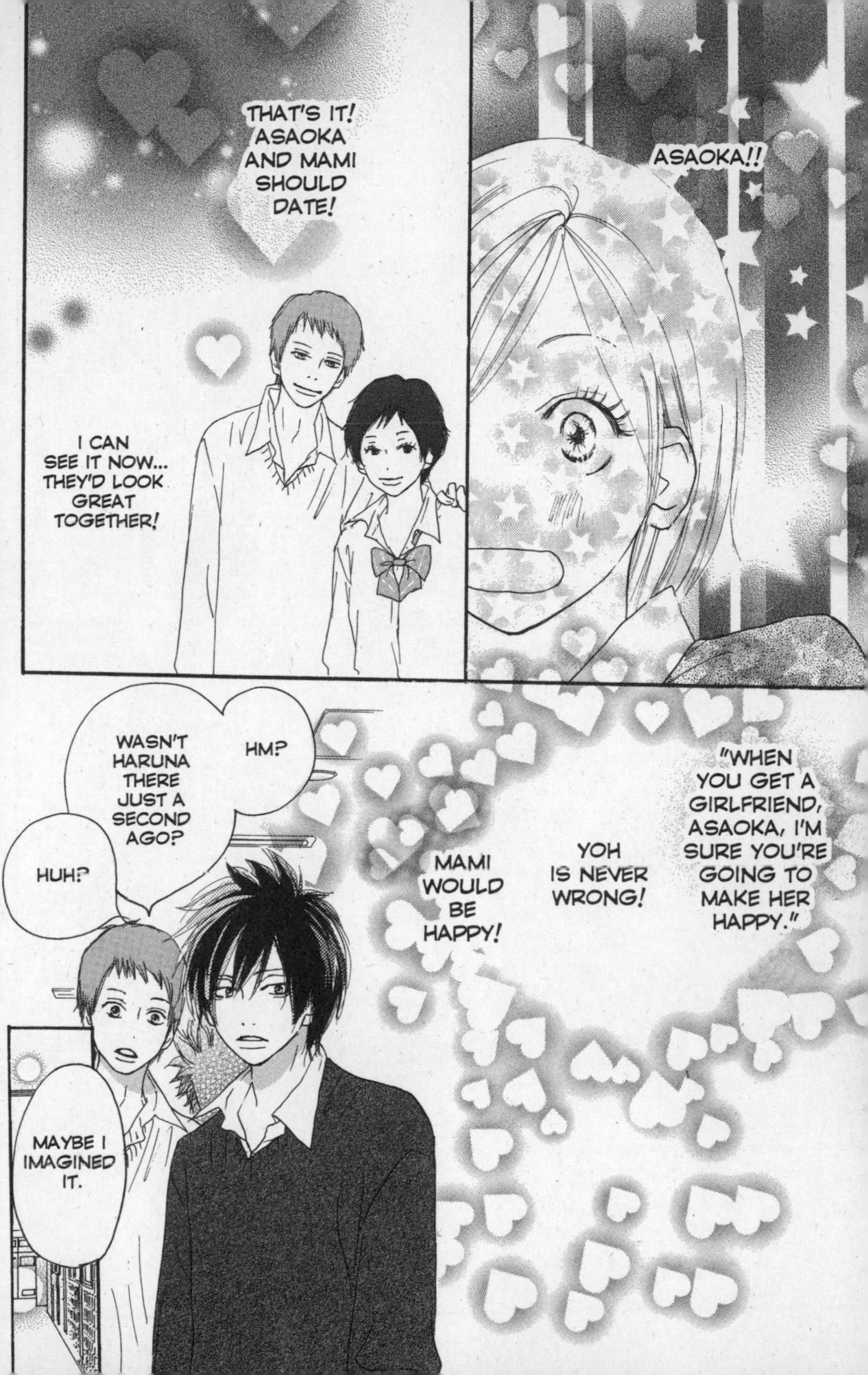
ASAOKA!!
THAT'S IT! ASAOKA AND MAMI SHOULD DATE!
I CAN SEE IT NOW... THEY'D LOOK GREAT TOGETHER!
"WHEN YOU GET A GIRLFRIEND, ASAOKA, I'M SURE YOU'RE GOING TO MAKE HER HAPPY."
YOH IS NEVER WRONG!
MAMI WOULD BE HAPPY!
HM?
WASN'T HARUNA THERE JUST A SECOND AGO?
HUH?
MAYBE I IMAGINED IT.

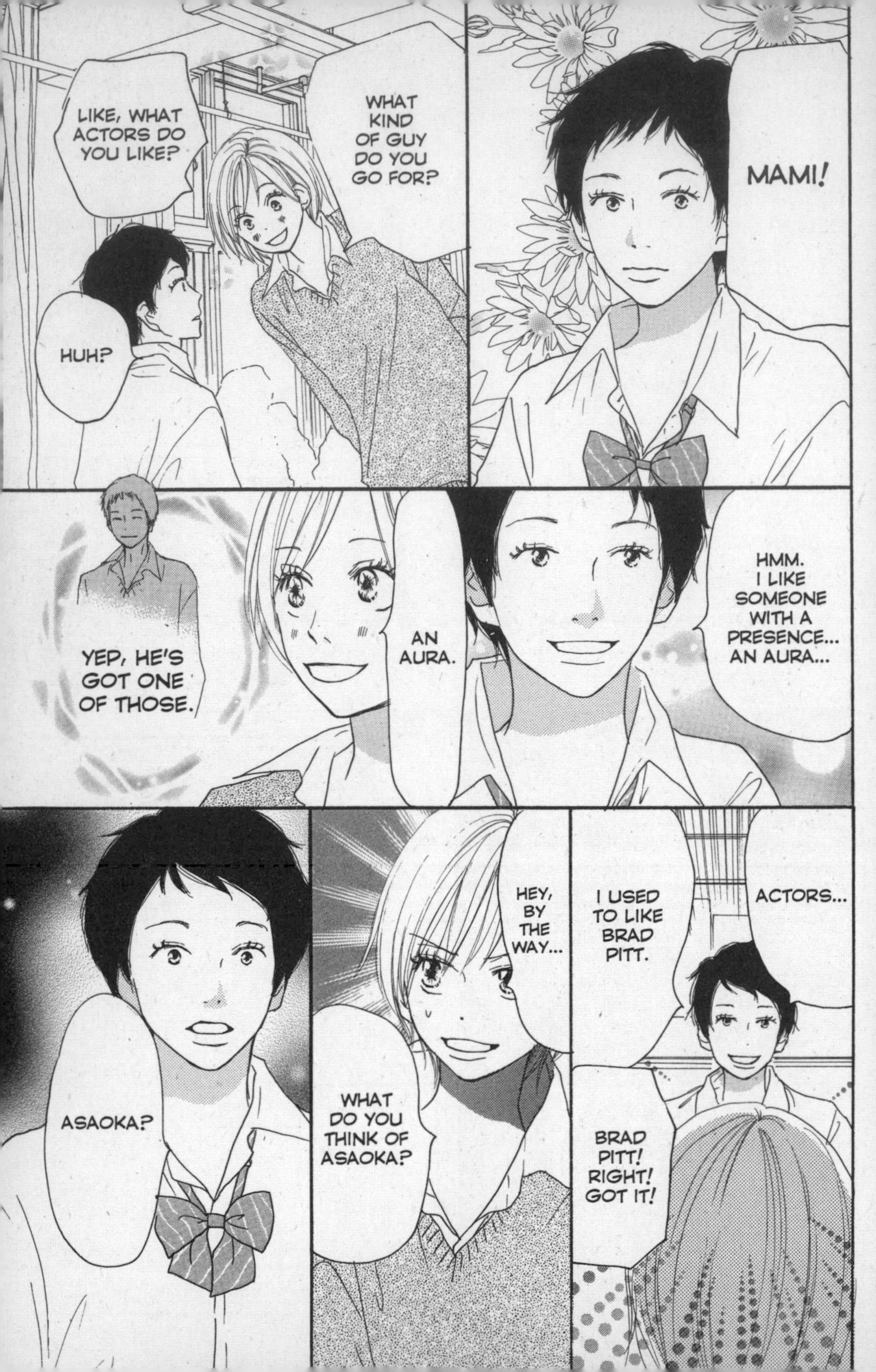
MAMI!
WHAT KIND OF GUY DO YOU GO FOR?
LIKE, WHAT ACTORS DO YOU LIKE?
HUH?
HMM. I LIKE SOMEONE WITH A PRESENCE... AN AURA...
AN AURA.
YEP, HE'S GOT ONE OF THOSE.
ACTORS...
I USED TO LIKE BRAD PITT.
BRAD PITT! RIGHT! GOT IT!
HEY, BY THE WAY...
WHAT DO YOU THINK OF ASAOKA?
ASAOKA?

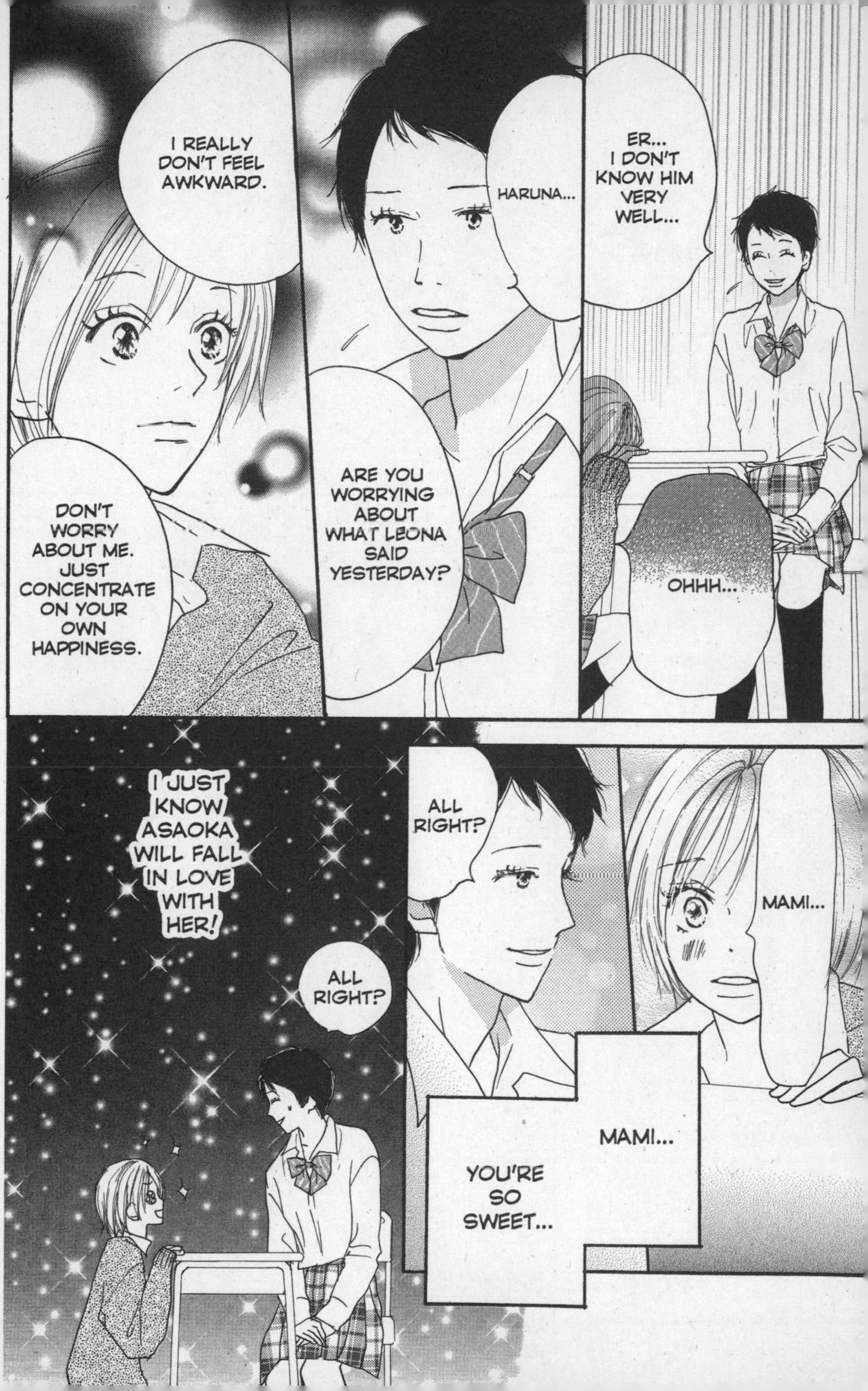
ER... I DON'T KNOW HIM VERY WELL...
OHHH...
HARUNA...
ARE YOU WORRYING ABOUT WHAT LEONA SAID YESTERDAY?
I REALLY DON'T FEEL AWKWARD.
DON'T WORRY ABOUT ME. JUST CONCENTRATE ON YOUR OWN HAPPINESS.
MAMI...
ALL RIGHT?
MAMI...
YOU'RE SO SWEET...
I JUST KNOW ASAOKA WILL FALL IN LOVE WITH HER!
ALL RIGHT?

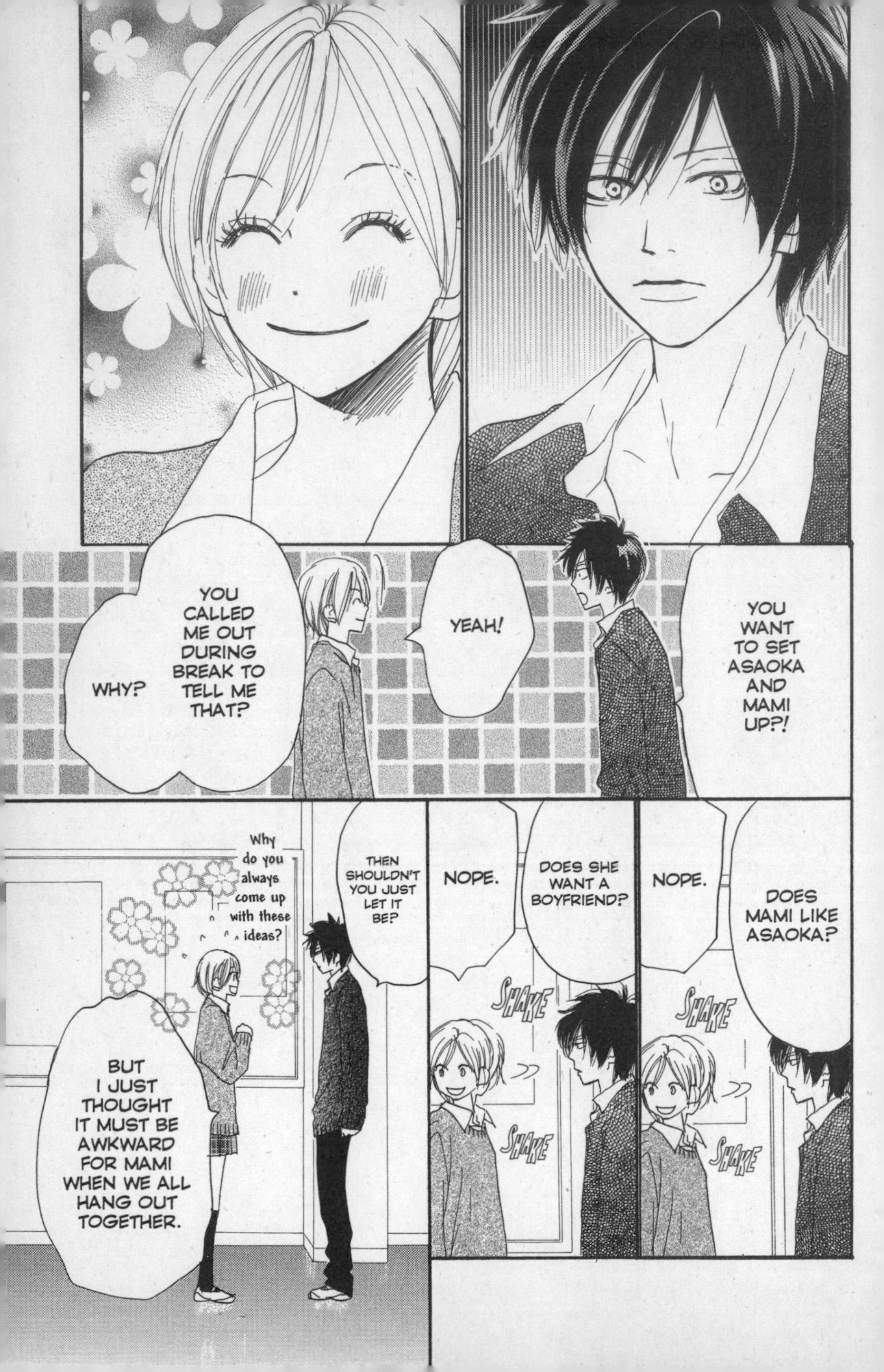
YOU WANT TO SET ASAOKA AND MAMI UP?!
YEAH!
YOU CALLED ME OUT DURING BREAK TO TELL ME THAT?
WHY?
DOES MAMI LIKE ASAOKA?
NOPE.
SHAKE
SHAKE
DOES SHE WANT A BOYFRIEND?
NOPE.
SHAKE
SHAKE
THEN SHOULDN'T YOU JUST LET IT BE?
Why do you always come up with these ideas?
BUT I JUST THOUGHT IT MUST BE AWKWARD FOR MAMI WHEN WE ALL HANG OUT TOGETHER.

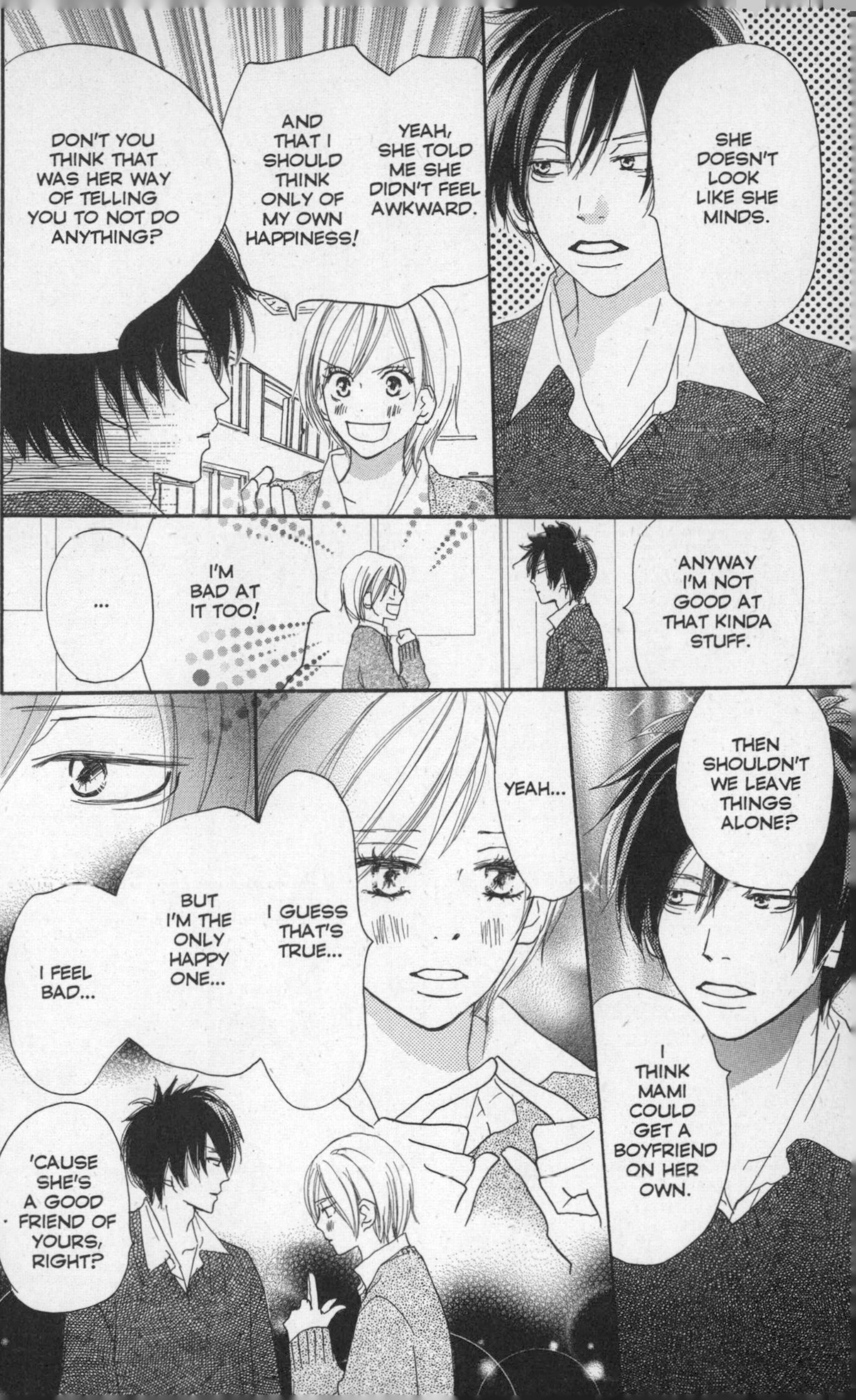
SHE DOESN'T LOOK LIKE SHE MINDS.
YEAH, SHE TOLD ME SHE DIDN'T FEEL AWKWARD.
AND THAT I SHOULD THINK ONLY OF MY OWN HAPPINESS!
DON'T YOU THINK THAT WAS HER WAY OF TELLING YOU TO NOT DO ANYTHING?
ANYWAY I'M NOT GOOD AT THAT KINDA STUFF.
I'M BAD AT IT TOO!
...
THEN SHOULDN'T WE LEAVE THINGS ALONE?
I THINK MAMI COULD GET A BOYFRIEND ON HER OWN.
YEAH...
I GUESS THAT'S TRUE...
BUT I'M THE ONLY HAPPY ONE...
I FEEL BAD...
'CAUSE SHE'S A GOOD FRIEND OF YOURS, RIGHT?

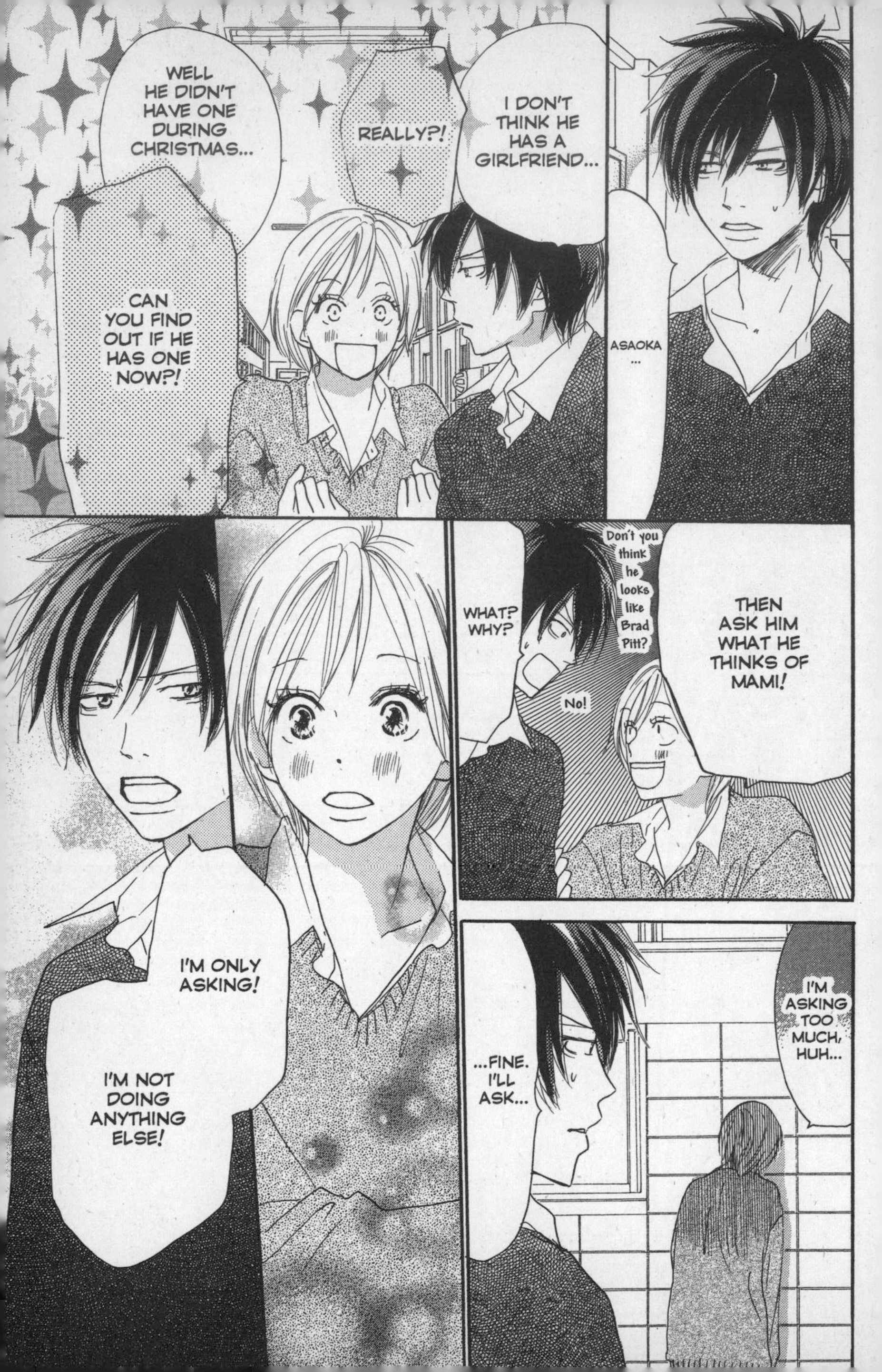
ASAOKA ...
I DON'T THINK HE HAS A GIRLFRIEND...
REALLY?!
WELL HE DIDN'T HAVE ONE DURING CHRISTMAS...
CAN YOU FIND OUT IF HE HAS ONE NOW?!
THEN ASK HIM WHAT HE THINKS OF MAMI!
Don't you think he looks like Brad Pitt?
WHAT? WHY?
No!
I'M ASKING TOO MUCH, HUH...
...FINE. I'LL ASK...
I'M ONLY ASKING!
I'M NOT DOING ANYTHING ELSE!

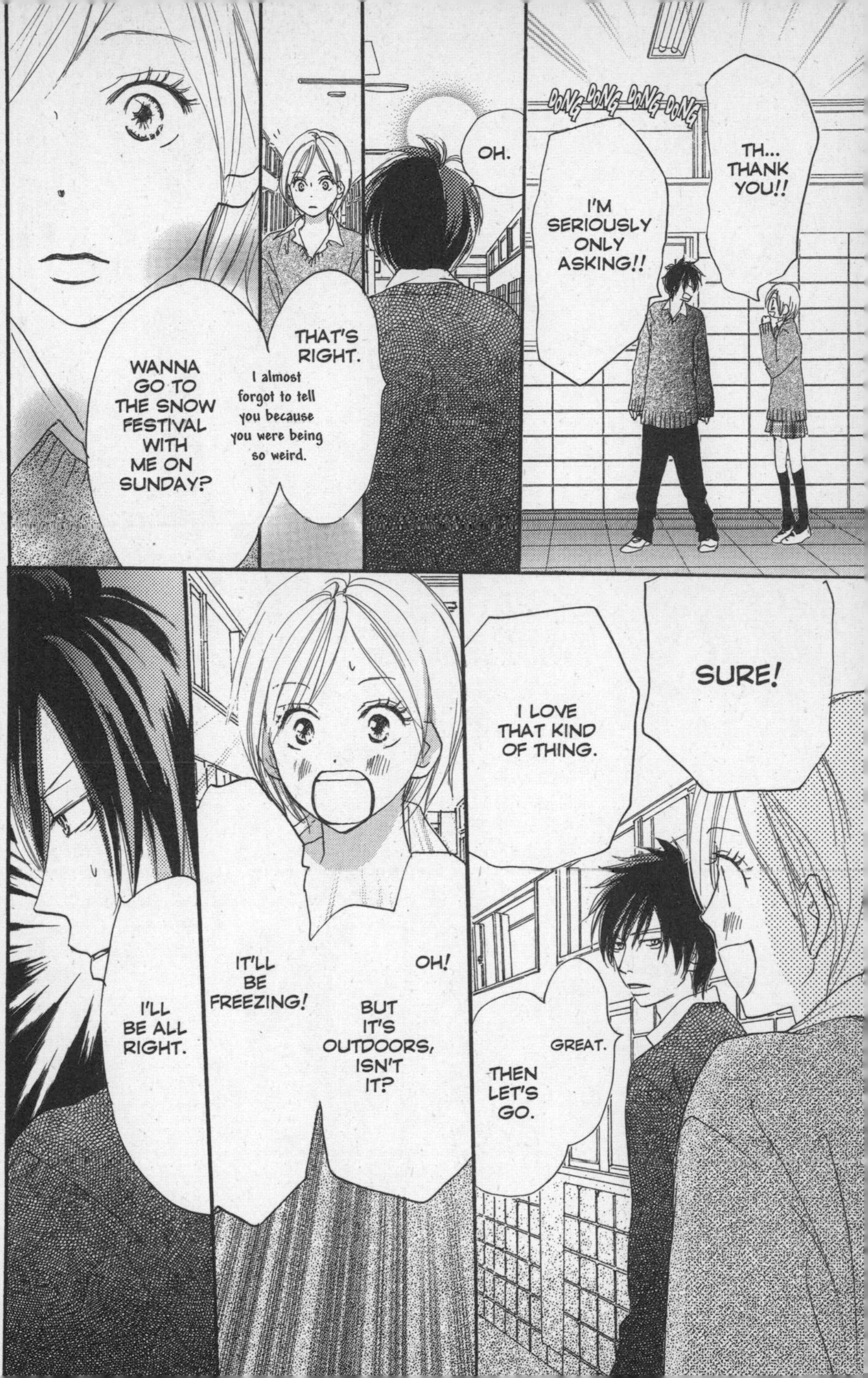
TH... THANK YOU!!
DONG DONG DONG DONG
I'M SERIOUSLY ONLY ASKING!!
OH.
THAT'S RIGHT.
I almost forgot to tell you because you were being so weird.
WANNA GO TO THE SNOW FESTIVAL WITH ME ON SUNDAY?
SURE!
I LOVE THAT KIND OF THING.
GREAT.
THEN LET'S GO.
OH!
BUT IT'S OUTDOORS, ISN'T IT?
IT'LL BE FREEZING!
I'LL BE ALL RIGHT.

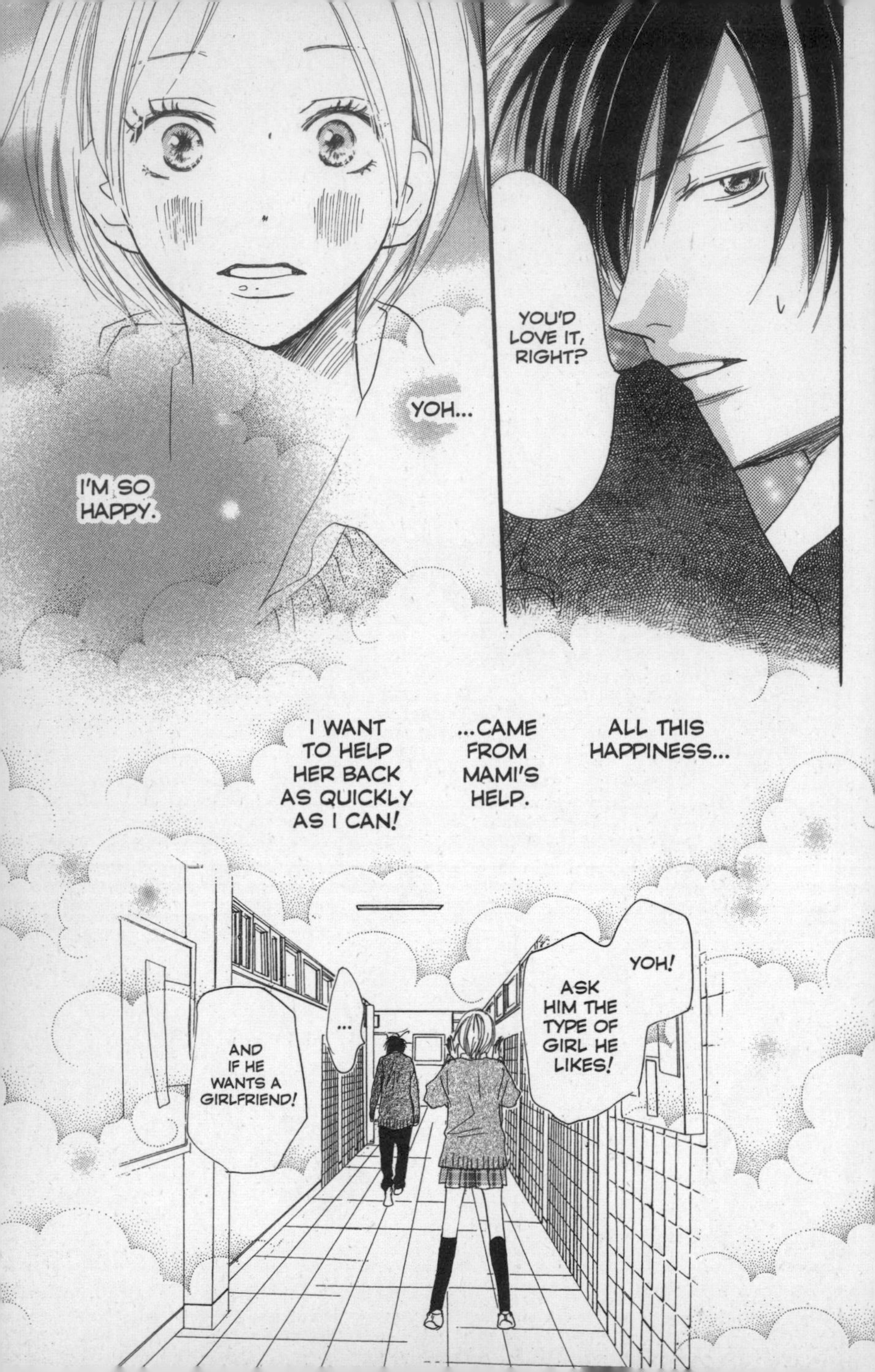
YOU'D LOVE IT, RIGHT?
YOH...
I'M SO HAPPY.
ALL THIS HAPPINESS...
...CAME FROM MAMI'S HELP.
I WANT TO HELP HER BACK AS QUICKLY AS I CAN!
YOH! ASK HIM THE TYPE OF GIRL HE LIKES!
...
AND IF HE WANTS A GIRLFRIEND!

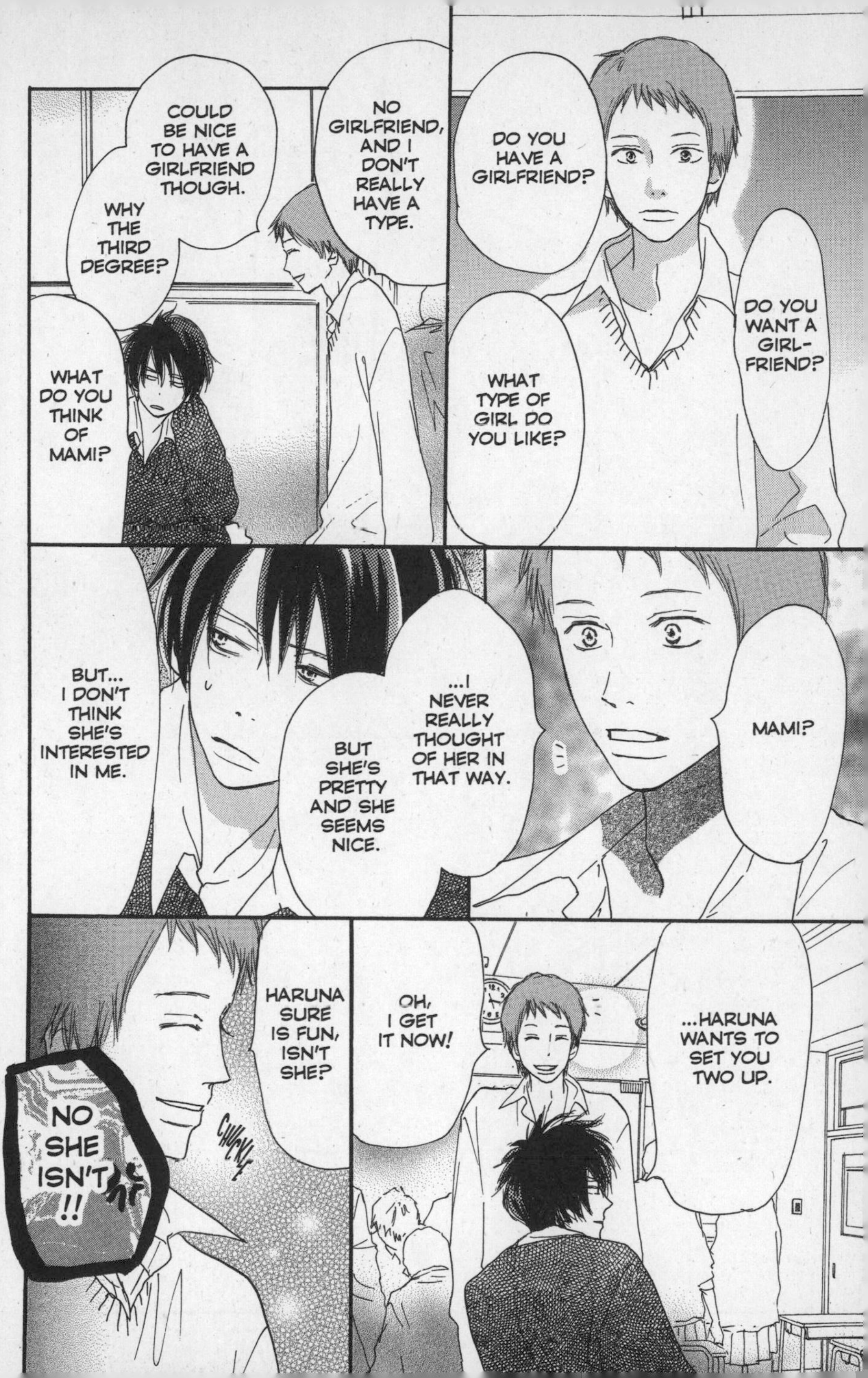
DO YOU HAVE A GIRLFRIEND?
DO YOU WANT A GIRL-FRIEND?
WHAT TYPE OF GIRL DO YOU LIKE?
NO GIRLFRIEND, AND I DON'T REALLY HAVE A TYPE.
COULD BE NICE TO HAVE A GIRLFRIEND THOUGH.
WHY THE THIRD DEGREE?
WHAT DO YOU THINK OF MAMI?
MAMI?
...I NEVER REALLY THOUGHT OF HER IN THAT WAY.
BUT SHE'S PRETTY AND SHE SEEMS NICE.
BUT... I DON'T THINK SHE'S INTERESTED IN ME.
...HARUNA WANTS TO SET YOU TWO UP.
OH, I GET IT NOW!
HARUNA SURE IS FUN, ISN'T SHE?
CHUCKLE
NO SHE ISN'T!!

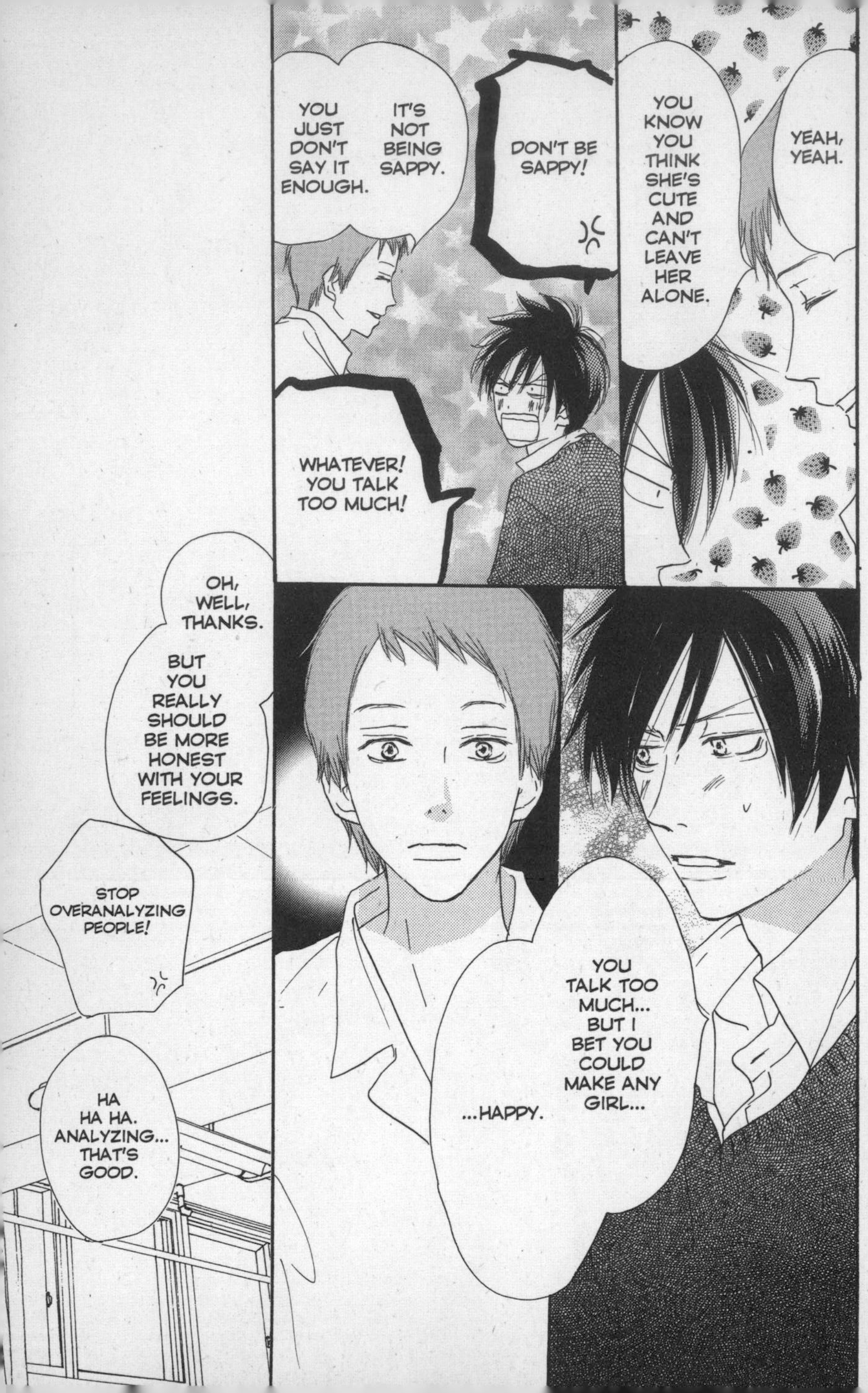
YEAH, YEAH.
YOU KNOW YOU THINK SHE'S CUTE AND CAN'T LEAVE HER ALONE.
DON'T BE SAPPY!
IT'S NOT BEING SAPPY.
YOU JUST DON'T SAY IT ENOUGH.
WHATEVER! YOU TALK TOO MUCH!
YOU TALK TOO MUCH... BUT I BET YOU COULD MAKE ANY GIRL...
...HAPPY.
OH, WELL, THANKS.
BUT YOU REALLY SHOULD BE MORE HONEST WITH YOUR FEELINGS.
STOP OVERANALYZING PEOPLE!
HA HA HA. ANALYZING... THAT'S GOOD.

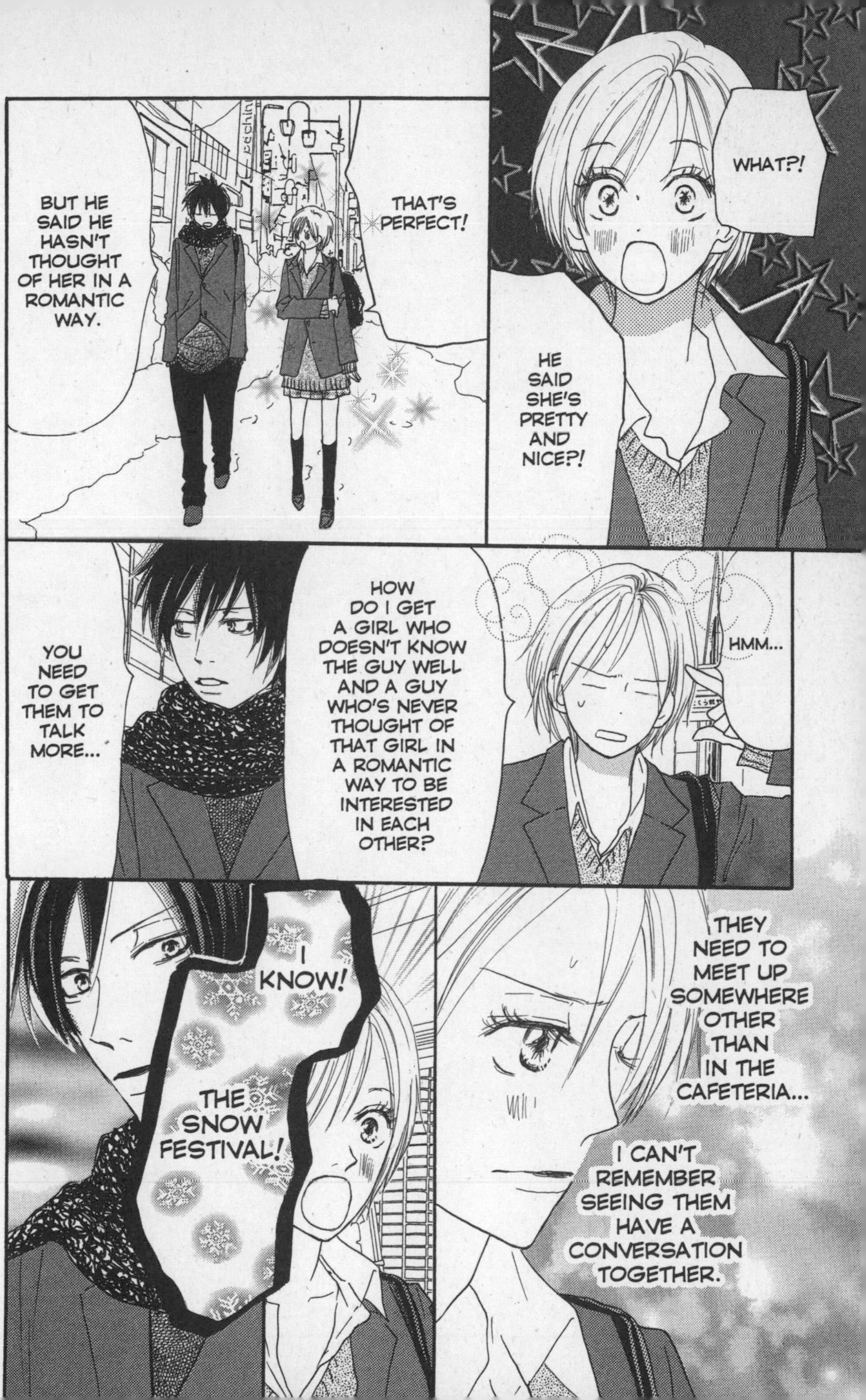
WHAT?!
HE SAID SHE'S PRETTY AND NICE?!
THAT'S PERFECT!
BUT HE SAID HE HASN'T THOUGHT OF HER IN A ROMANTIC WAY.
HMM...
HOW DO I GET A GIRL WHO DOESN'T KNOW THE GUY WELL AND A GUY WHO'S NEVER THOUGHT OF THAT GIRL IN A ROMANTIC WAY TO BE INTERESTED IN EACH OTHER?
YOU NEED TO GET THEM TO TALK MORE...
THEY NEED TO MEET UP SOMEWHERE OTHER THAN IN THE CAFETERIA...
I CAN'T REMEMBER SEEING THEM HAVE A CONVERSATION TOGETHER.
I KNOW!
THE SNOW FESTIVAL!

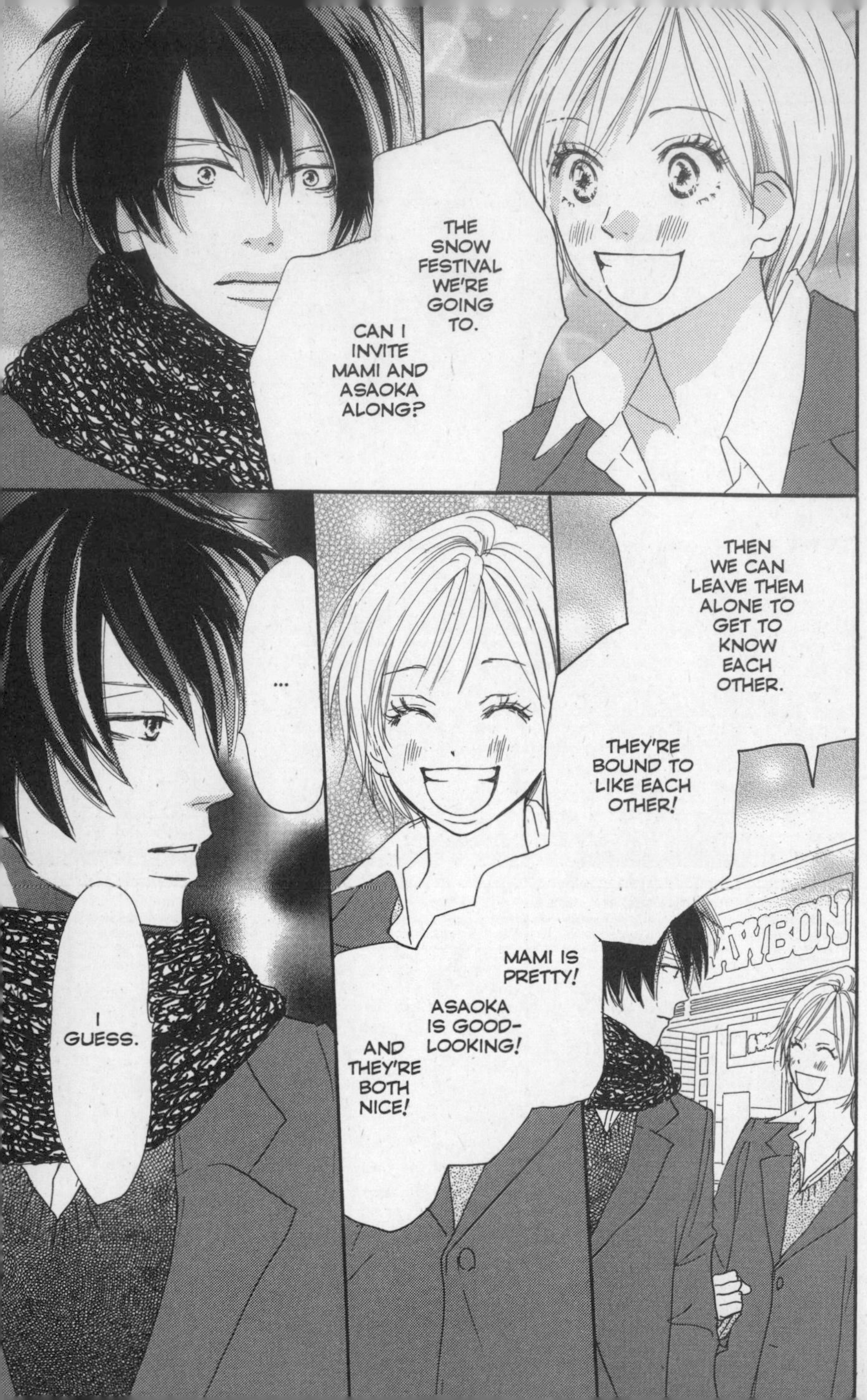
THE SNOW FESTIVAL WE'RE GOING TO.
CAN I INVITE MAMI AND ASAOKA ALONG?
THEN WE CAN LEAVE THEM ALONE TO GET TO KNOW EACH OTHER.
THEY'RE BOUND TO LIKE EACH OTHER!
MAMI IS PRETTY!
ASAOKA IS GOOD-LOOKING!
AND THEY'RE BOTH NICE!
...
I GUESS.

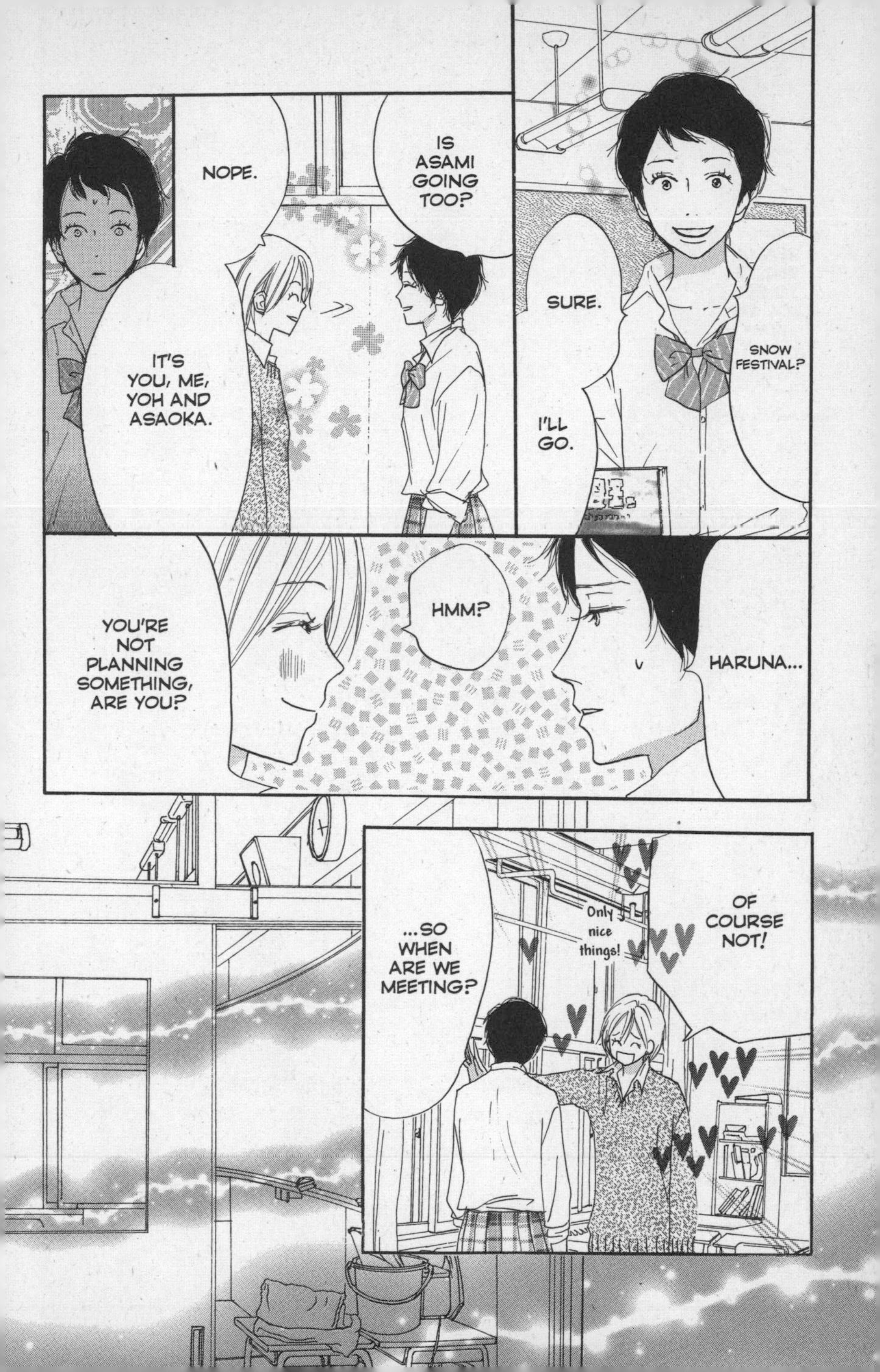
SNOW FESTIVAL?
SURE.
I'LL GO.
IS ASAMI GOING TOO?
NOPE.
IT'S YOU, ME, YOH AND ASAOKA.
HARUNA...
HMM?
YOU'RE NOT PLANNING SOMETHING, ARE YOU?
OF COURSE NOT!
Only nice things!
...SO WHEN ARE WE MEETING?

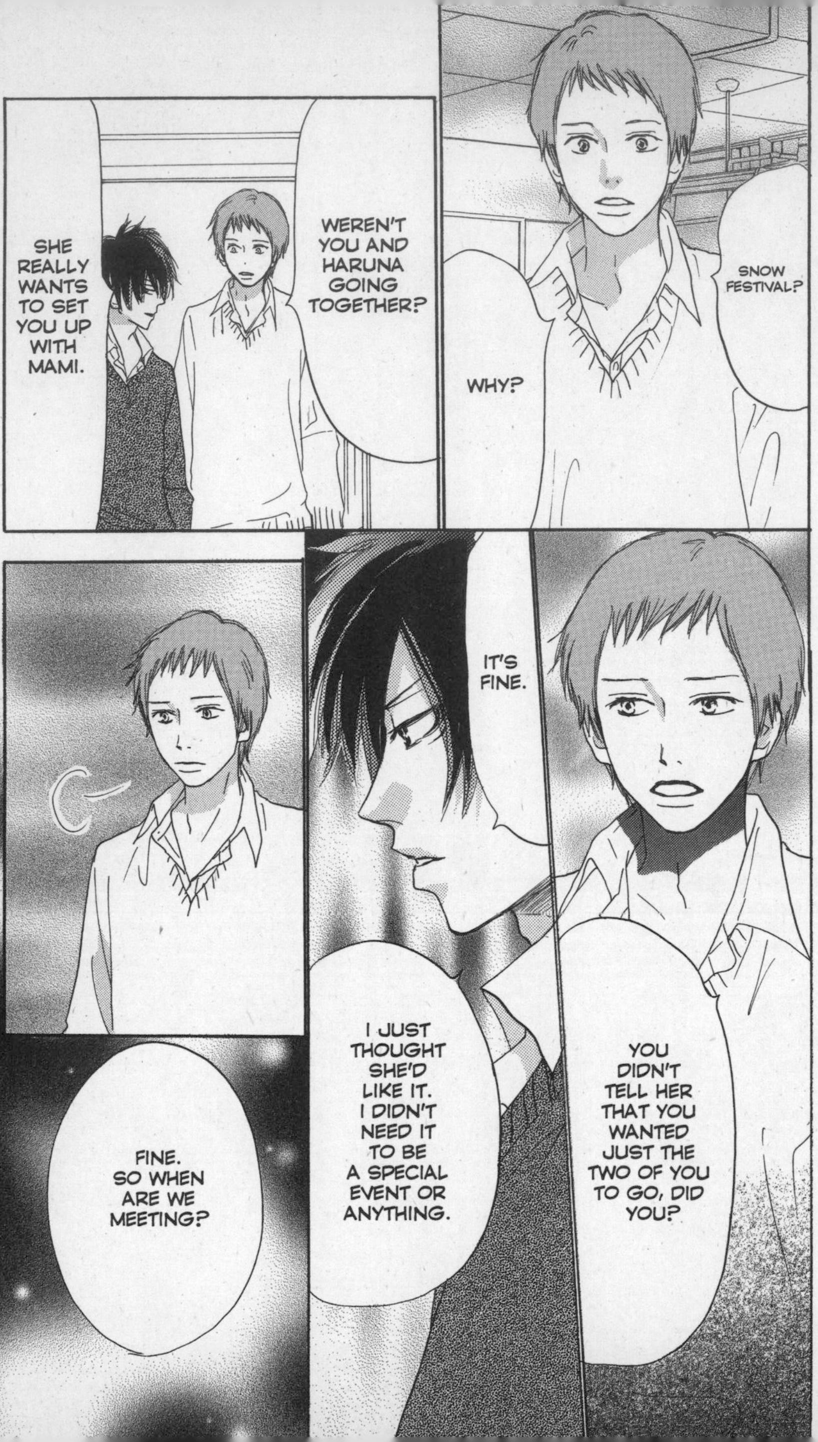
SNOW FESTIVAL?
WHY?
WEREN'T YOU AND HARUNA GOING TOGETHER?
SHE REALLY WANTS TO SET YOU UP WITH MAMI.
YOU DIDN'T TELL HER THAT YOU WANTED JUST THE TWO OF YOU TO GO, DID YOU?
IT'S FINE.
I JUST THOUGHT SHE'D LIKE IT. I DIDN'T NEED IT TO BE A SPECIAL EVENT OR ANYTHING.
FINE. SO WHEN ARE WE MEETING?

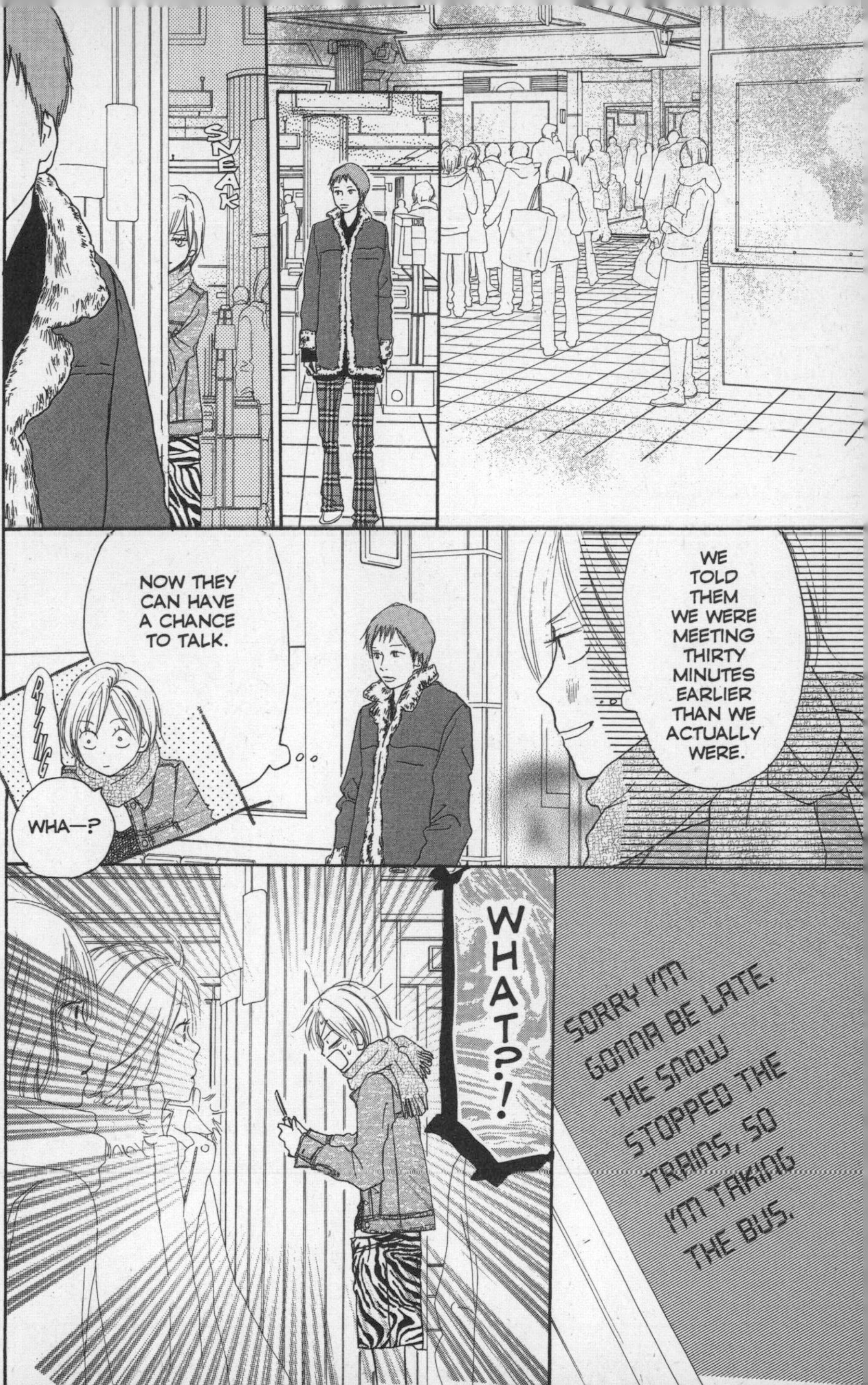
SNEAK
WE TOLD THEM WE WERE MEETING THIRTY MINUTES EARLIER THAN WE ACTUALLY WERE.
NOW THEY CAN HAVE A CHANCE TO TALK.
RIIING
WHA—?
SORRY I'M GONNA BE LATE. THE SNOW STOPPED THE TRAINS, SO I'M TAKING THE BUS.
WHAT?!

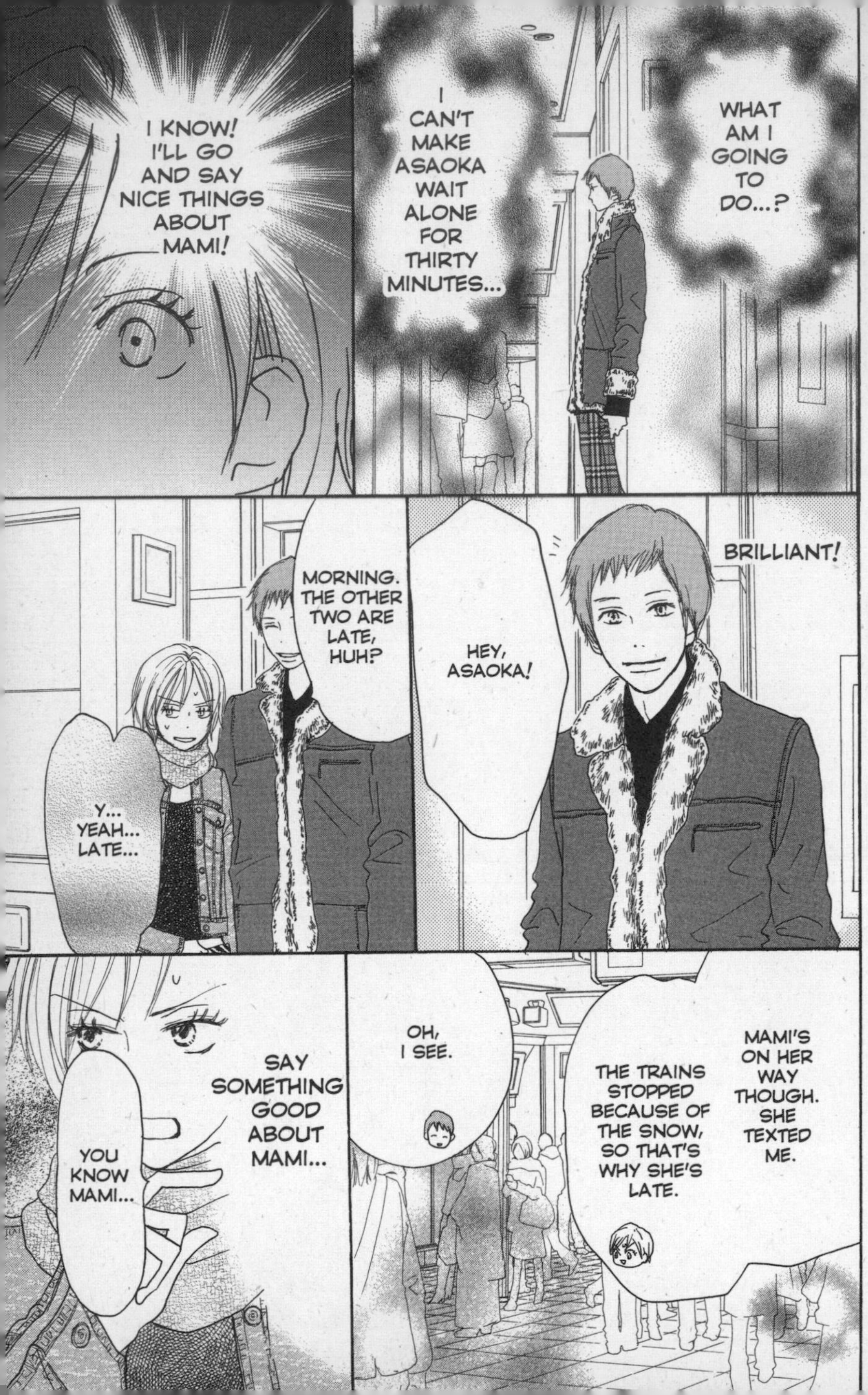
WHAT AM I GOING TO DO...?
I CAN'T MAKE ASAOKA WAIT ALONE FOR THIRTY MINUTES...
I KNOW! I'LL GO AND SAY NICE THINGS ABOUT MAMI!
BRILLIANT!
HEY, ASAOKA!
MORNING. THE OTHER TWO ARE LATE, HUH?
Y... YEAH... LATE...
MAMI'S ON HER WAY THOUGH. SHE TEXTED ME.
THE TRAINS STOPPED BECAUSE OF THE SNOW, SO THAT'S WHY SHE'S LATE.
OH, I SEE.
SAY SOMETHING GOOD ABOUT MAMI...
YOU KNOW MAMI...

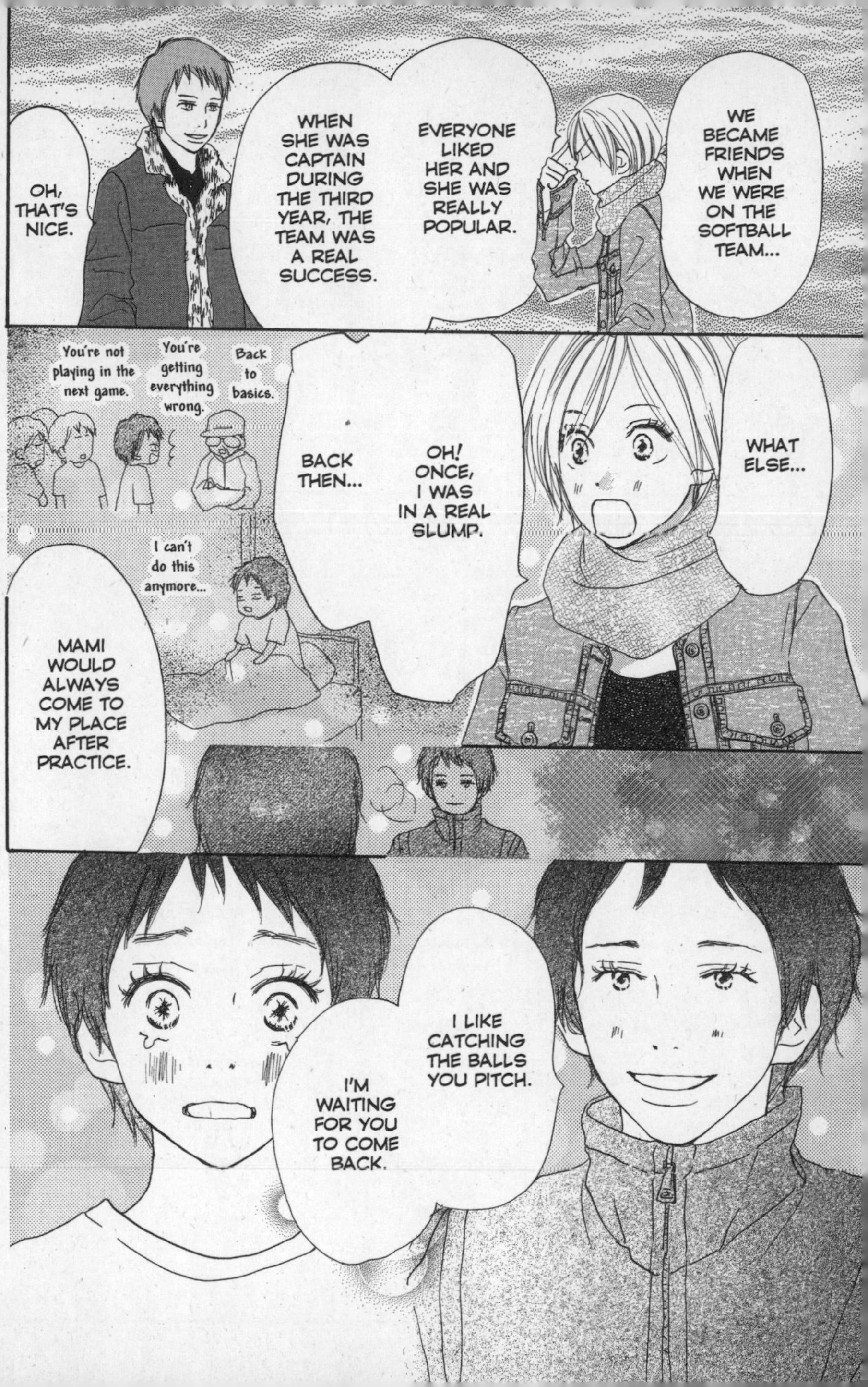
WE BECAME FRIENDS WHEN WE WERE ON THE SOFTBALL TEAM...
EVERYONE LIKED HER AND SHE WAS REALLY POPULAR.
WHEN SHE WAS CAPTAIN DURING THE THIRD YEAR, THE TEAM WAS A REAL SUCCESS.
OH, THAT'S NICE.
WHAT ELSE...
OH! ONCE, I WAS IN A REAL SLUMP.
BACK THEN...
Back to basics.
You're getting everything wrong.
You're not playing in the next game.
I can't do this anymore...
MAMI WOULD ALWAYS COME TO MY PLACE AFTER PRACTICE.
I LIKE CATCHING THE BALLS YOU PITCH.
I'M WAITING FOR YOU TO COME BACK.

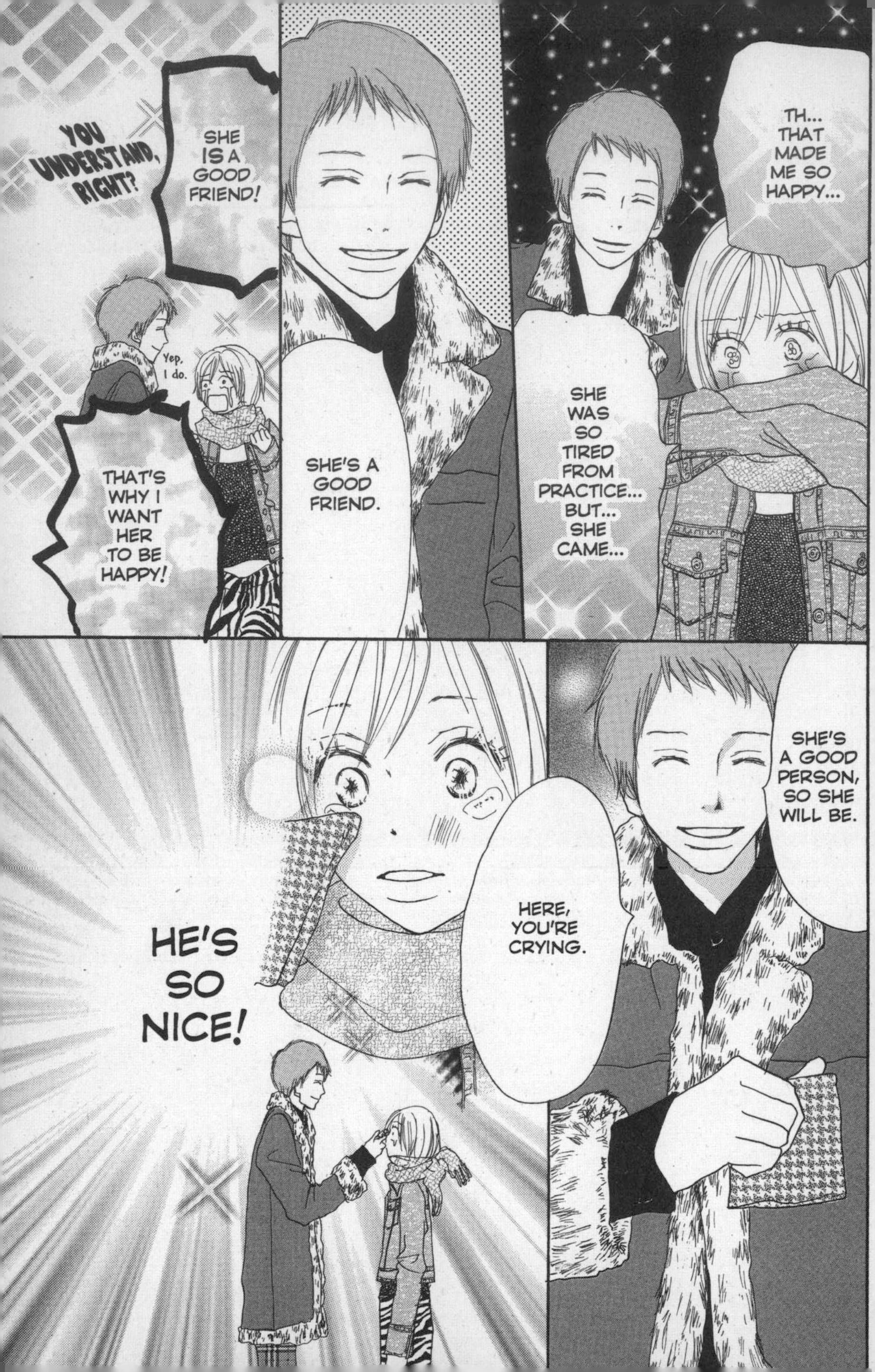
TH... THAT MADE ME SO HAPPY...
SHE WAS SO TIRED FROM PRACTICE... BUT... SHE CAME...
SHE'S A GOOD FRIEND.
SHE IS A GOOD FRIEND!
YOU UNDERSTAND, RIGHT?
Yep, I do.
THAT'S WHY I WANT HER TO BE HAPPY!
SHE'S A GOOD PERSON, SO SHE WILL BE.
HERE, YOU'RE CRYING.
HE'S SO NICE!

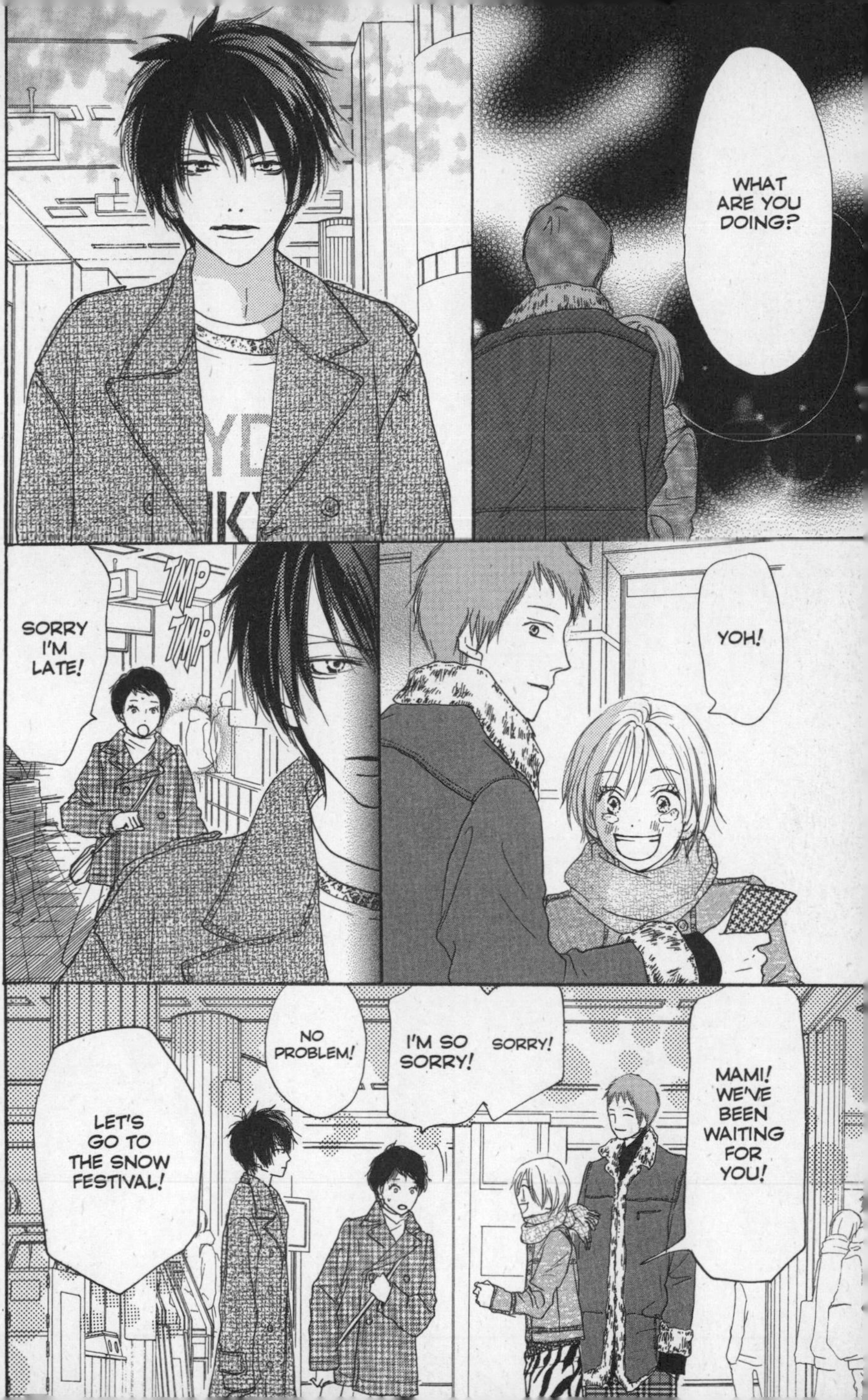
WHAT ARE YOU DOING?
YOH!
SORRY I'M LATE!
TMP TMP
MAMI! WE'VE BEEN WAITING FOR YOU!
SORRY!
I'M SO SORRY!
NO PROBLEM!
LET'S GO TO THE SNOW FESTIVAL!

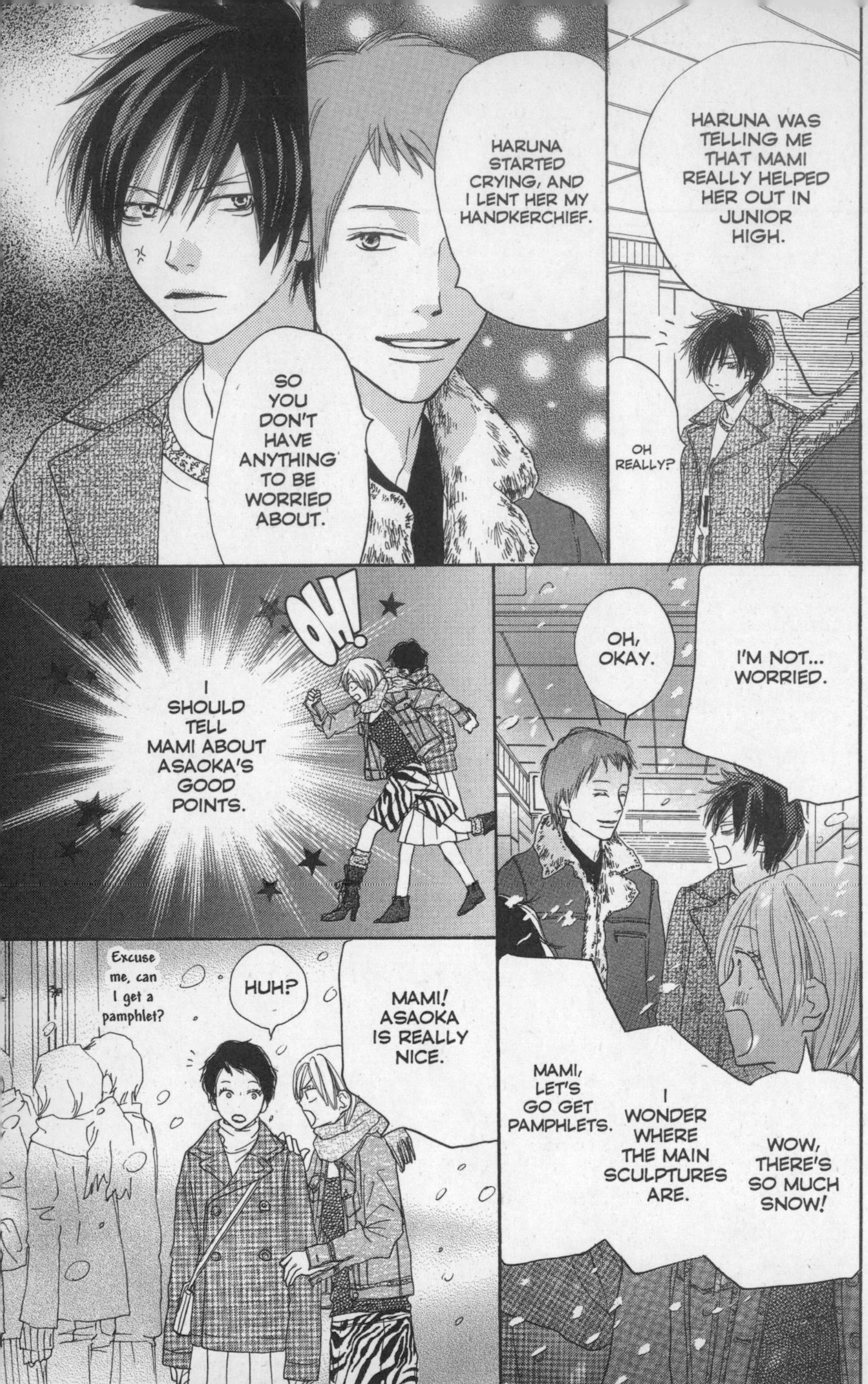
HARUNA WAS TELLING ME THAT MAMI REALLY HELPED HER OUT IN JUNIOR HIGH.
OH REALLY?
HARUNA STARTED CRYING, AND I LENT HER MY HANDKERCHIEF.
SO YOU DON'T HAVE ANYTHING TO BE WORRIED ABOUT.
I'M NOT... WORRIED.
OH, OKAY.
OH!
I SHOULD TELL MAMI ABOUT ASAOKA'S GOOD POINTS.
WOW, THERE'S SO MUCH SNOW!
I WONDER WHERE THE MAIN SCULPTURES ARE.
MAMI, LET'S GO GET PAMPHLETS.
MAMI! ASAOKA IS REALLY NICE.
HUH?
Excuse me, can I get a pamphlet?

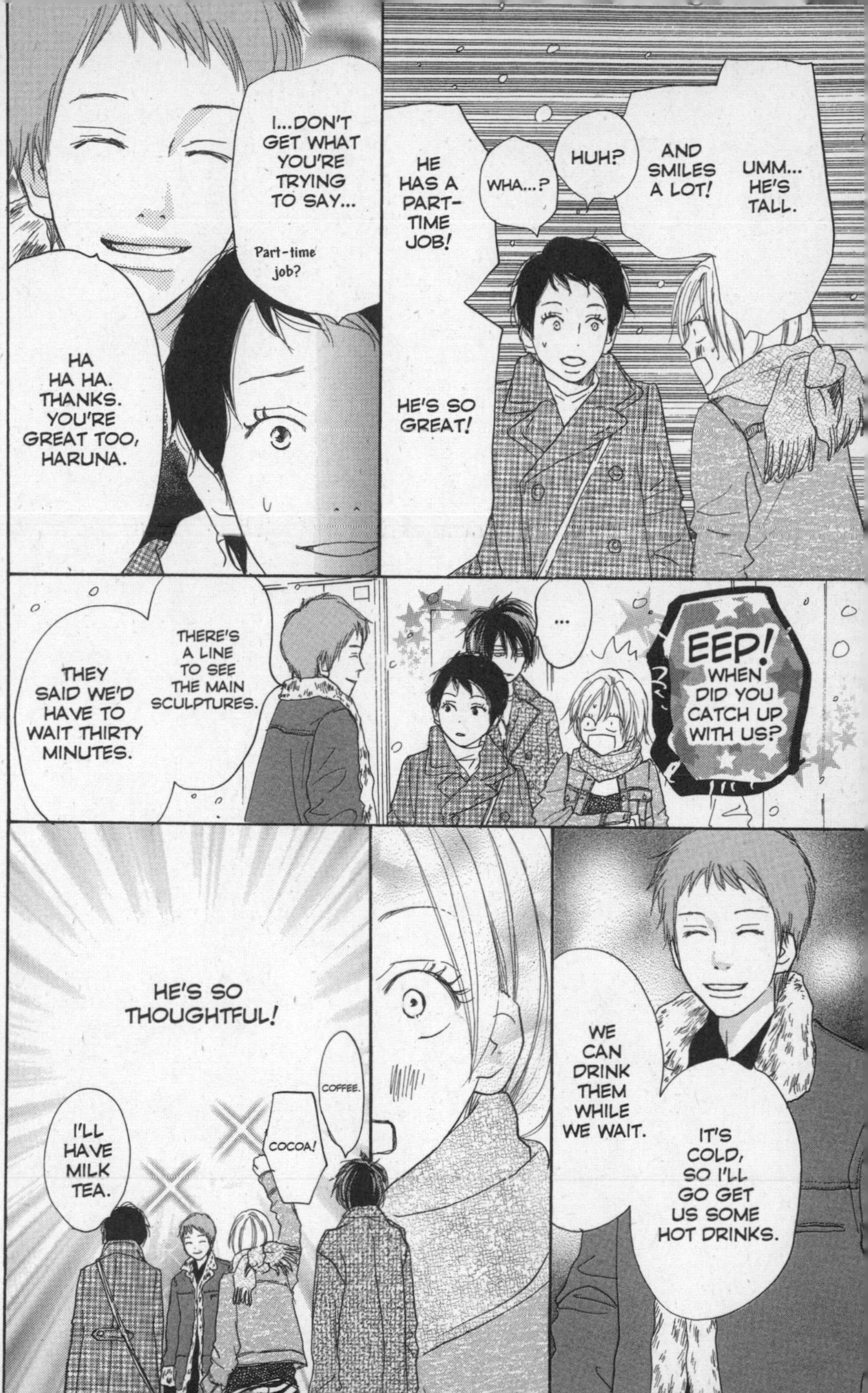
UMM... HE'S TALL.
AND SMILES A LOT!
HUH?
WHA...?
HE HAS A PART-TIME JOB!
HE'S SO GREAT!
I...DON'T GET WHAT YOU'RE TRYING TO SAY...
Part-time job?
HA HA HA. THANKS. YOU'RE GREAT TOO, HARUNA.
EEP! WHEN DID YOU CATCH UP WITH US?
...
THERE'S A LINE TO SEE THE MAIN SCULPTURES.
THEY SAID WE'D HAVE TO WAIT THIRTY MINUTES.
IT'S COLD, SO I'LL GO GET US SOME HOT DRINKS.
WE CAN DRINK THEM WHILE WE WAIT.
HE'S SO THOUGHTFUL!
COFFEE.
COCOA!
I'LL HAVE MILK TEA.

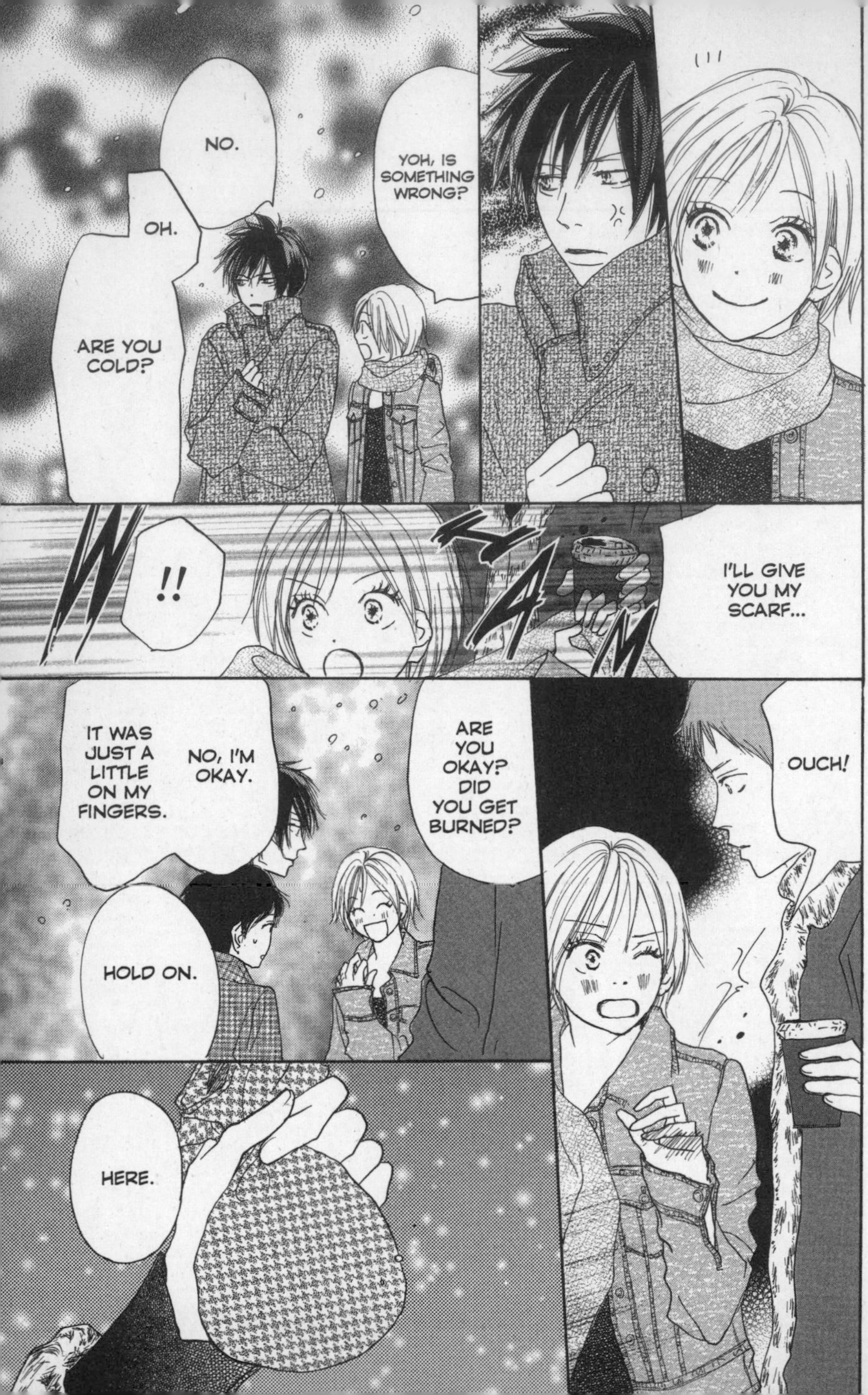
YOH, IS SOMETHING WRONG?
NO.
OH.
ARE YOU COLD?
I'LL GIVE YOU MY SCARF...
WHAM
!!
OUCH!
ARE YOU OKAY? DID YOU GET BURNED?
NO, I'M OKAY.
IT WAS JUST A LITTLE ON MY FINGERS.
HOLD ON.
HERE.

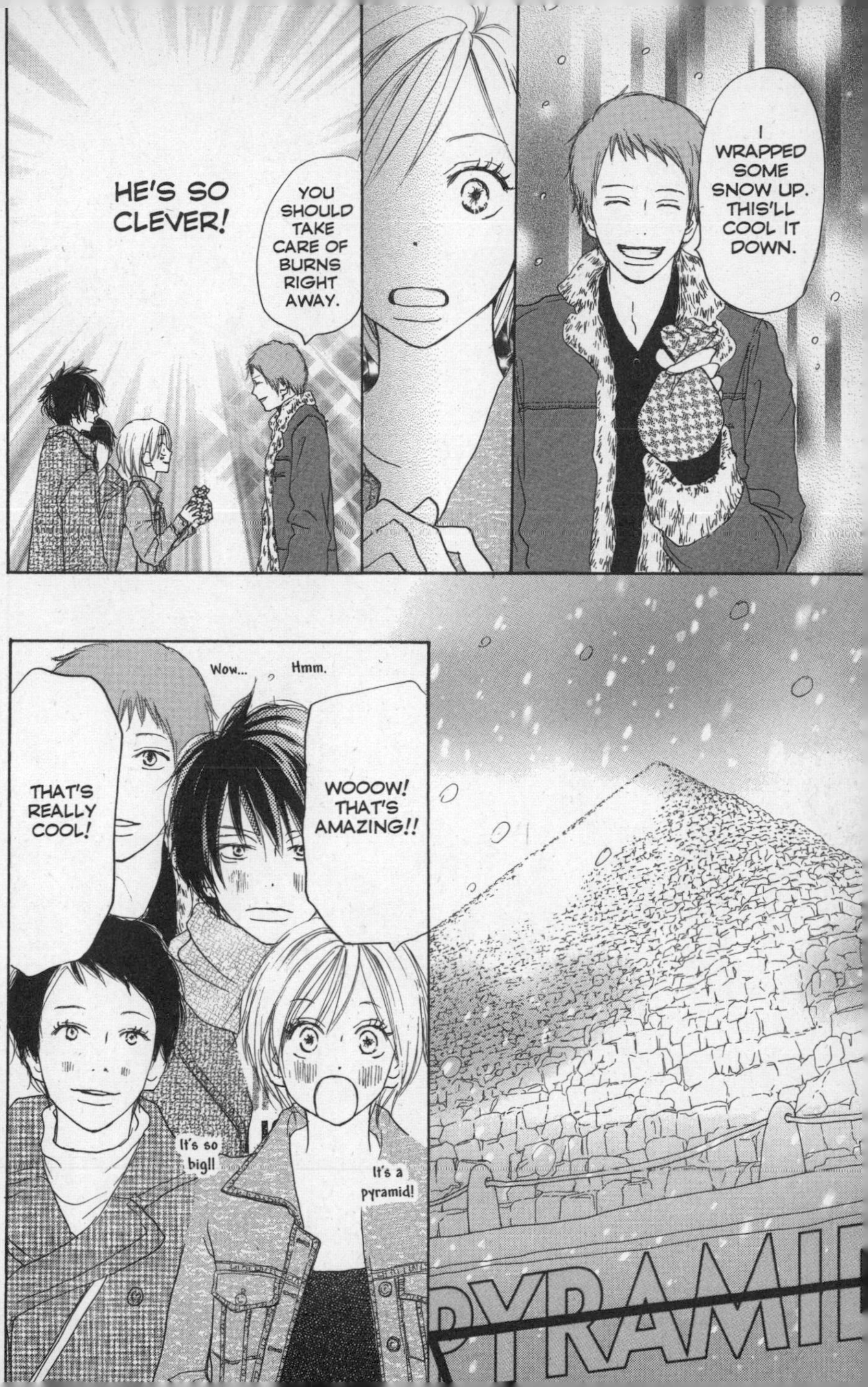
I WRAPPED SOME SNOW UP. THIS'LL COOL IT DOWN.
YOU SHOULD TAKE CARE OF BURNS RIGHT AWAY.
HE'S SO CLEVER!
PYRAMI
WOOOW! THAT'S AMAZING!!
Hmm.
Wow...
THAT'S REALLY COOL!
It's a pyramid!
It's so big!!

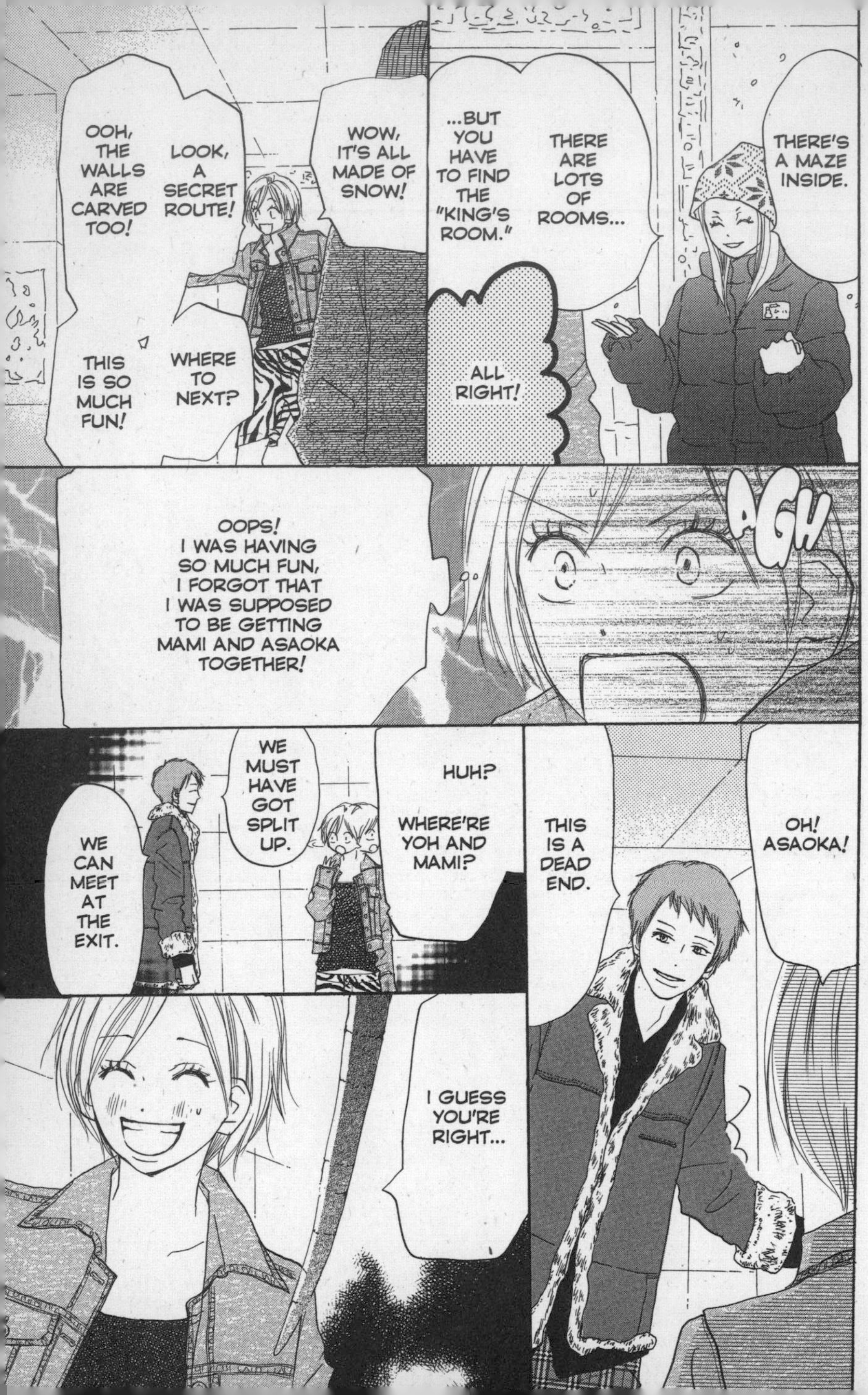
THERE'S A MAZE INSIDE.
THERE ARE LOTS OF ROOMS...
...BUT YOU HAVE TO FIND THE "KING'S ROOM."
ALL RIGHT!
WOW, IT'S ALL MADE OF SNOW!
LOOK, A SECRET ROUTE!
OOH, THE WALLS ARE CARVED TOO!
WHERE TO NEXT?
THIS IS SO MUCH FUN!
AGH
OOPS! I WAS HAVING SO MUCH FUN, I FORGOT THAT I WAS SUPPOSED TO BE GETTING MAMI AND ASAOKA TOGETHER!
OH! ASAOKA!
THIS IS A DEAD END.
HUH?
WHERE'RE YOH AND MAMI?
WE MUST HAVE GOT SPLIT UP.
WE CAN MEET AT THE EXIT.
I GUESS YOU'RE RIGHT...

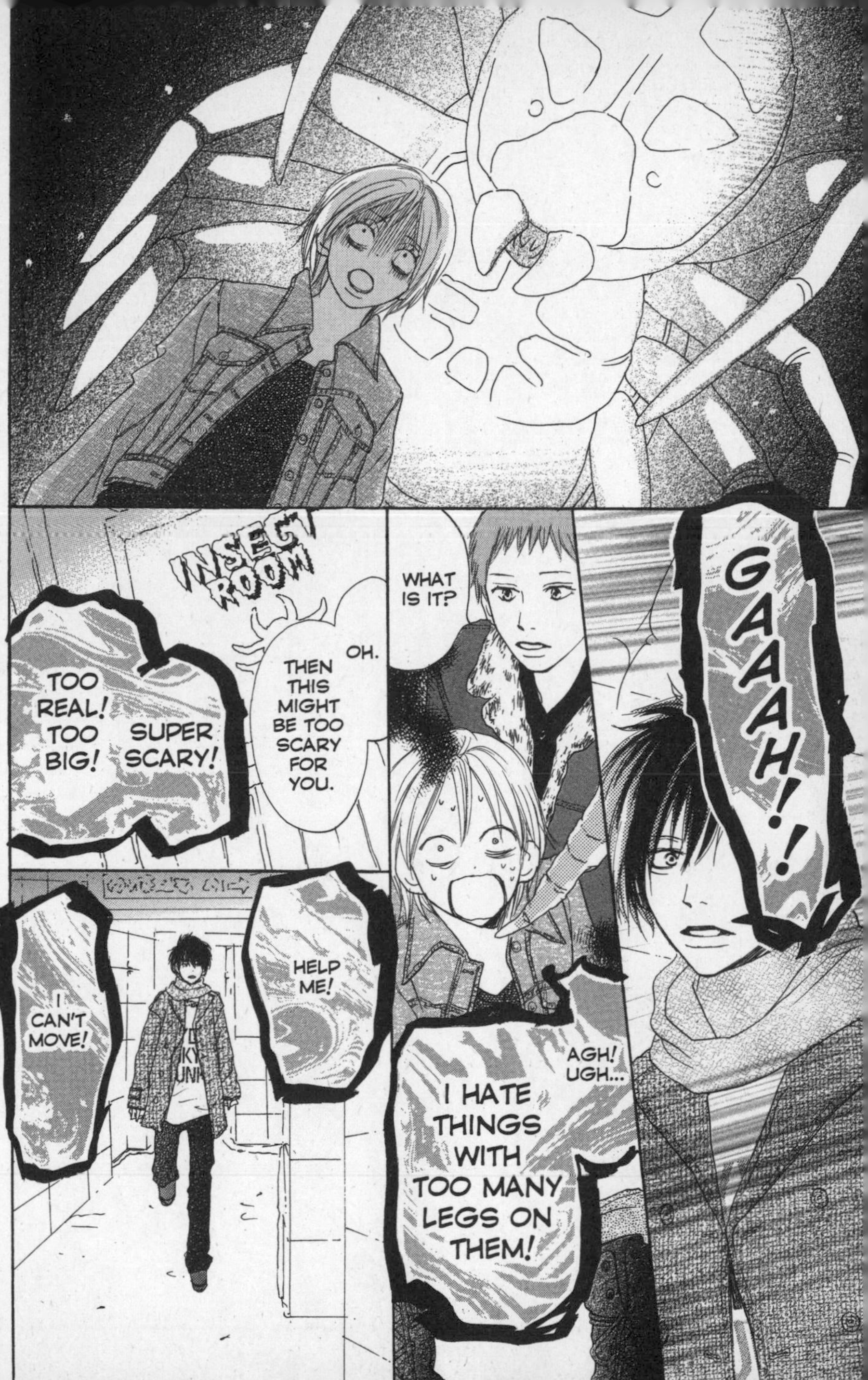
GAAAH!!
WHAT IS IT?
OH. THEN THIS MIGHT BE TOO SCARY FOR YOU.
INSECT ROOM
SUPER SCARY!
TOO REAL! TOO BIG!
AGH! UGH...
I HATE THINGS WITH TOO MANY LEGS ON THEM!
HELP ME!
I CAN'T MOVE!

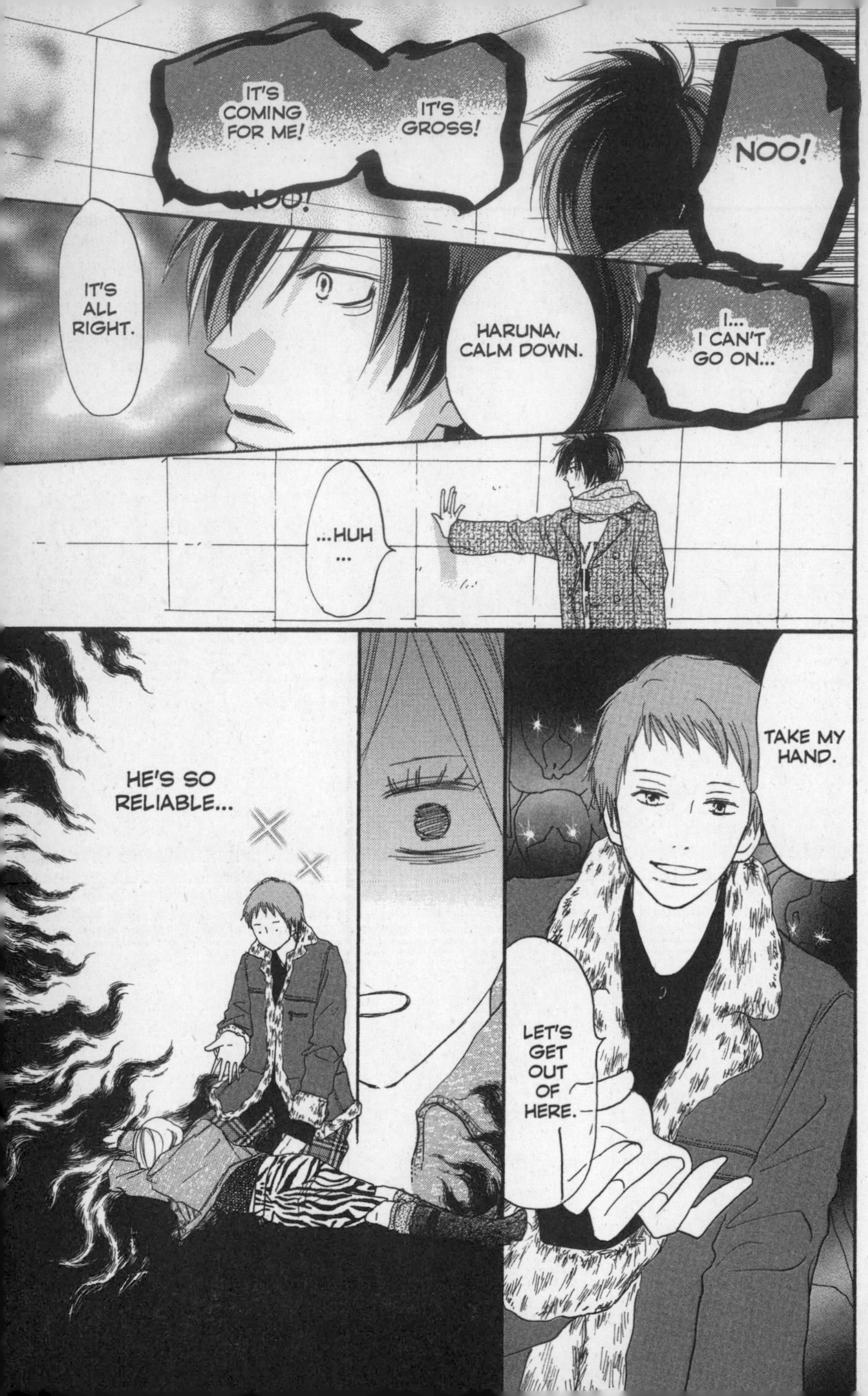
NOO!
IT'S GROSS!
IT'S COMING FOR ME!
I... I CAN'T GO ON...
HARUNA, CALM DOWN.
IT'S ALL RIGHT.
...HUH ...
TAKE MY HAND.
LET'S GET OUT OF HERE.
HE'S SO RELIABLE...

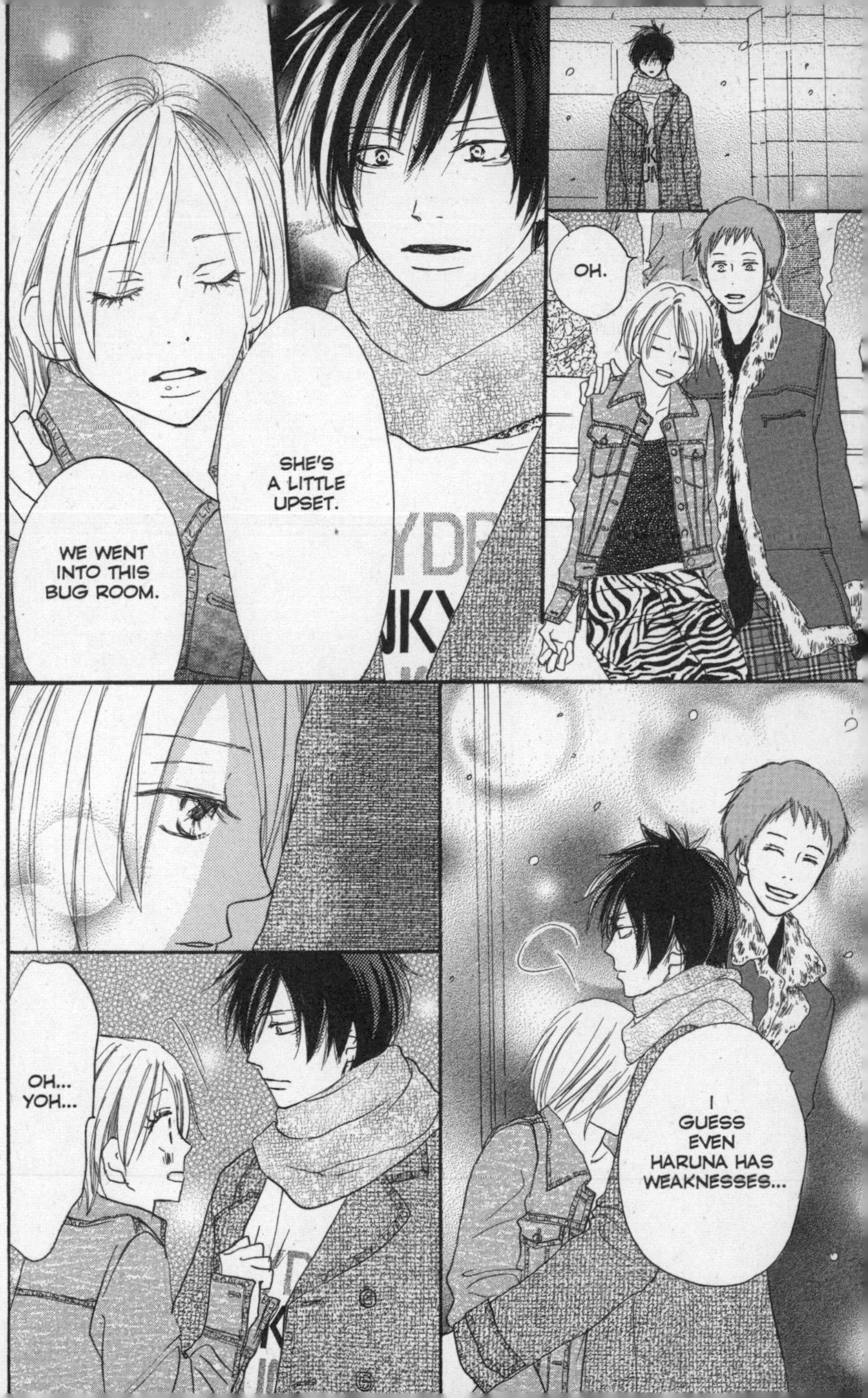
OH.
SHE'S A LITTLE UPSET.
WE WENT INTO THIS BUG ROOM.
I GUESS EVEN HARUNA HAS WEAKNESSES...
OH... YOH...

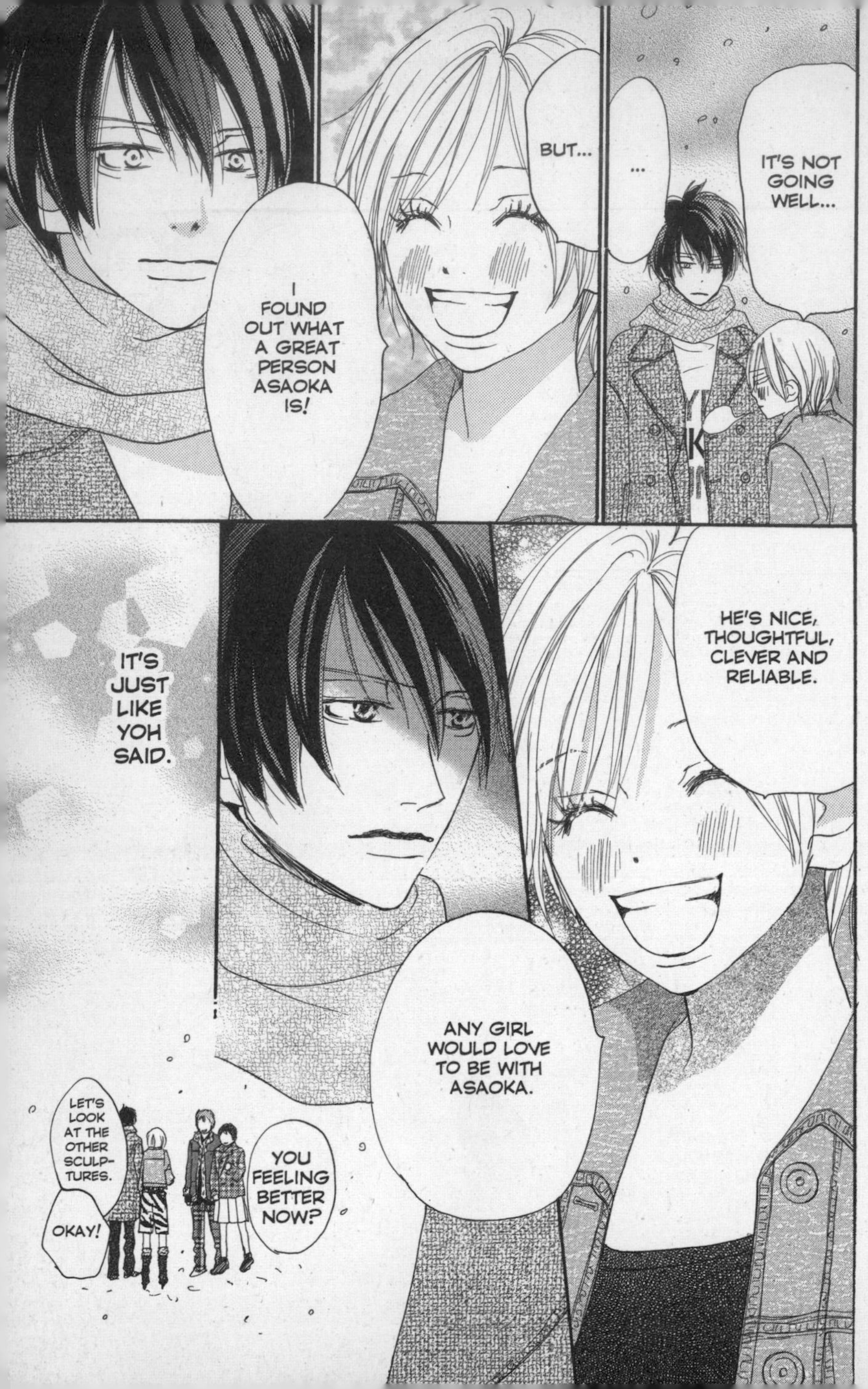
IT'S NOT GOING WELL...
...
BUT...
I FOUND OUT WHAT A GREAT PERSON ASAOKA IS!
HE'S NICE, THOUGHTFUL, CLEVER AND RELIABLE.
ANY GIRL WOULD LOVE TO BE WITH ASAOKA.
IT'S JUST LIKE YOH SAID.
YOU FEELING BETTER NOW?
LET'S LOOK AT THE OTHER SCULP-TURES.
OKAY!

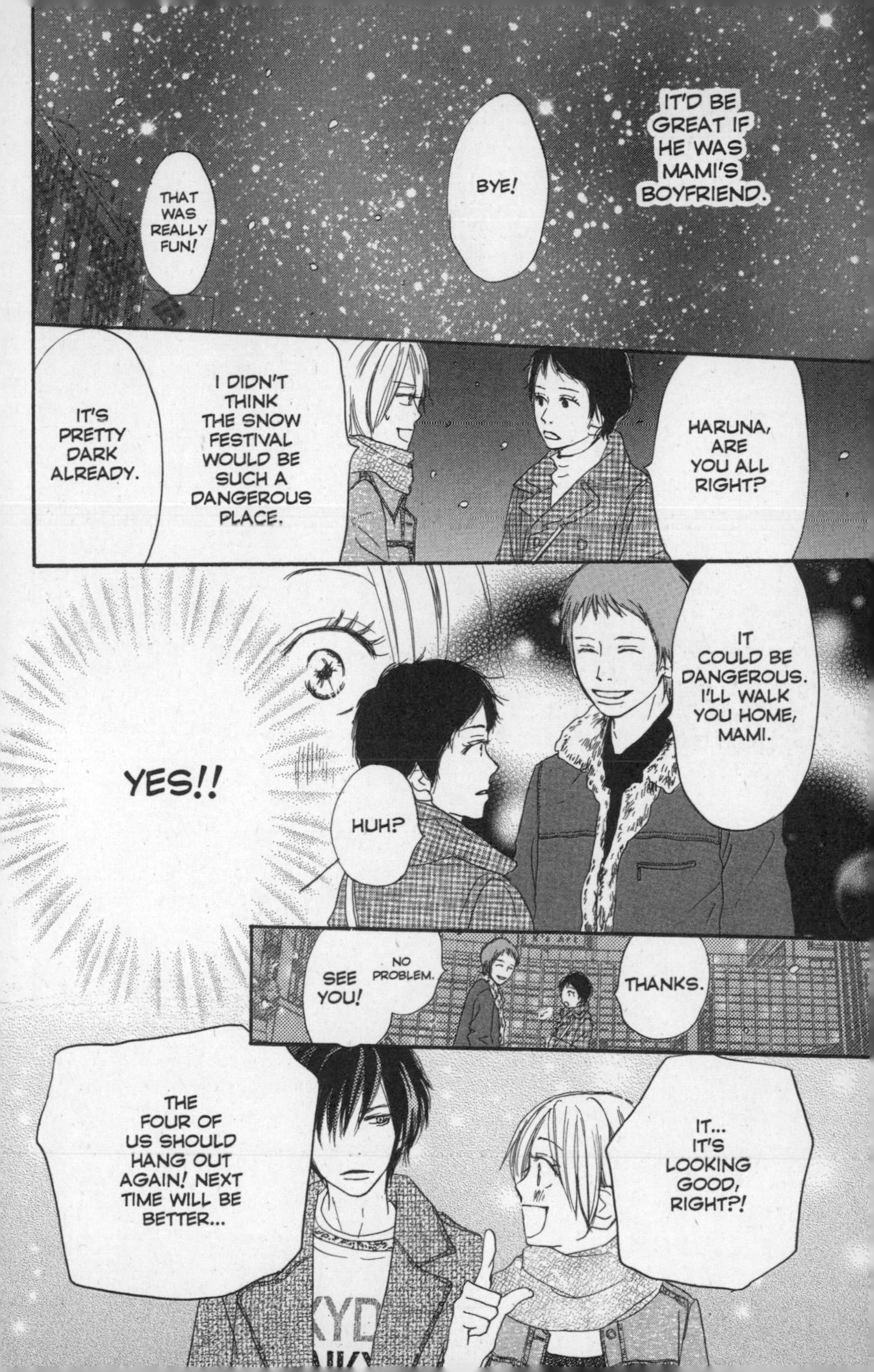
IT'D BE GREAT IF HE WAS MAMI'S BOYFRIEND.
BYE!
THAT WAS REALLY FUN!
HARUNA, ARE YOU ALL RIGHT?
I DIDN'T THINK THE SNOW FESTIVAL WOULD BE SUCH A DANGEROUS PLACE.
IT'S PRETTY DARK ALREADY.
IT COULD BE DANGEROUS. I'LL WALK YOU HOME, MAMI.
HUH?
YES!!
THANKS.
NO PROBLEM.
SEE YOU!
IT... IT'S LOOKING GOOD, RIGHT?!
THE FOUR OF US SHOULD HANG OUT AGAIN! NEXT TIME WILL BE BETTER...

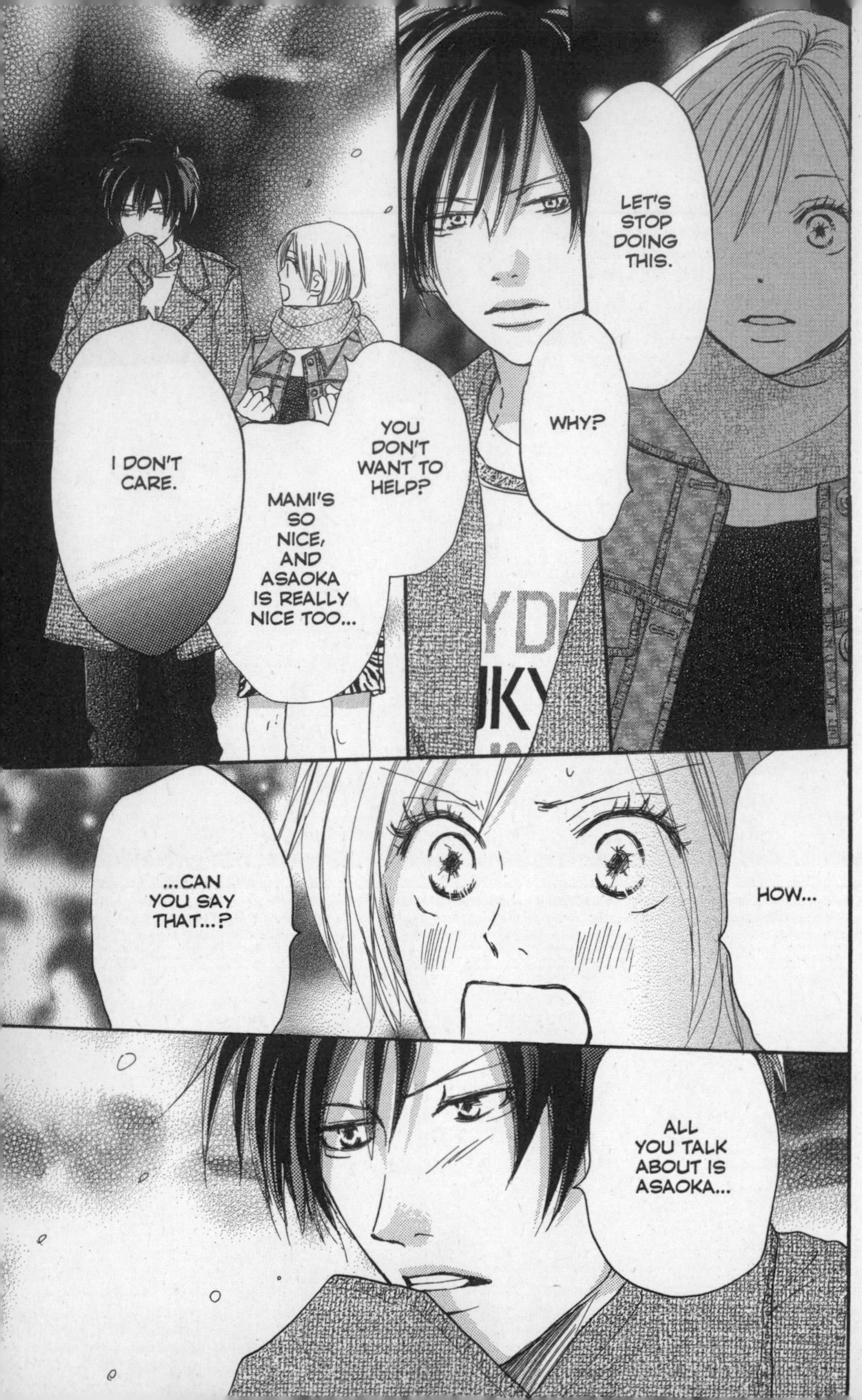
LET'S STOP DOING THIS.
WHY?
YOU DON'T WANT TO HELP?
MAMI'S SO NICE, AND ASAOKA IS REALLY NICE TOO...
I DON'T CARE.
HOW...
...CAN YOU SAY THAT...?
ALL YOU TALK ABOUT IS ASAOKA...

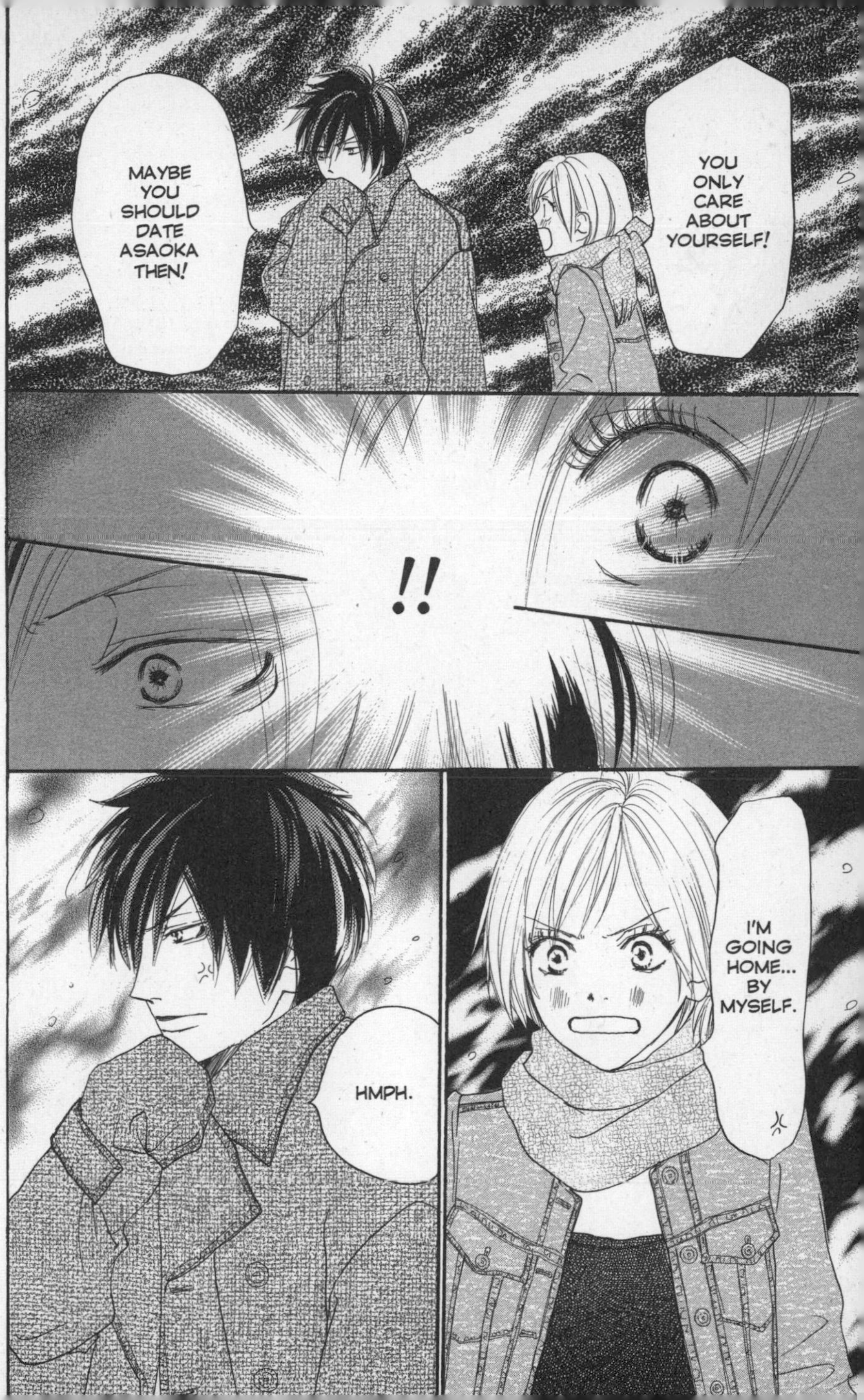
YOU ONLY CARE ABOUT YOURSELF!
MAYBE YOU SHOULD DATE ASAOKA THEN!
!!
I'M GOING HOME... BY MYSELF.
HMPH.

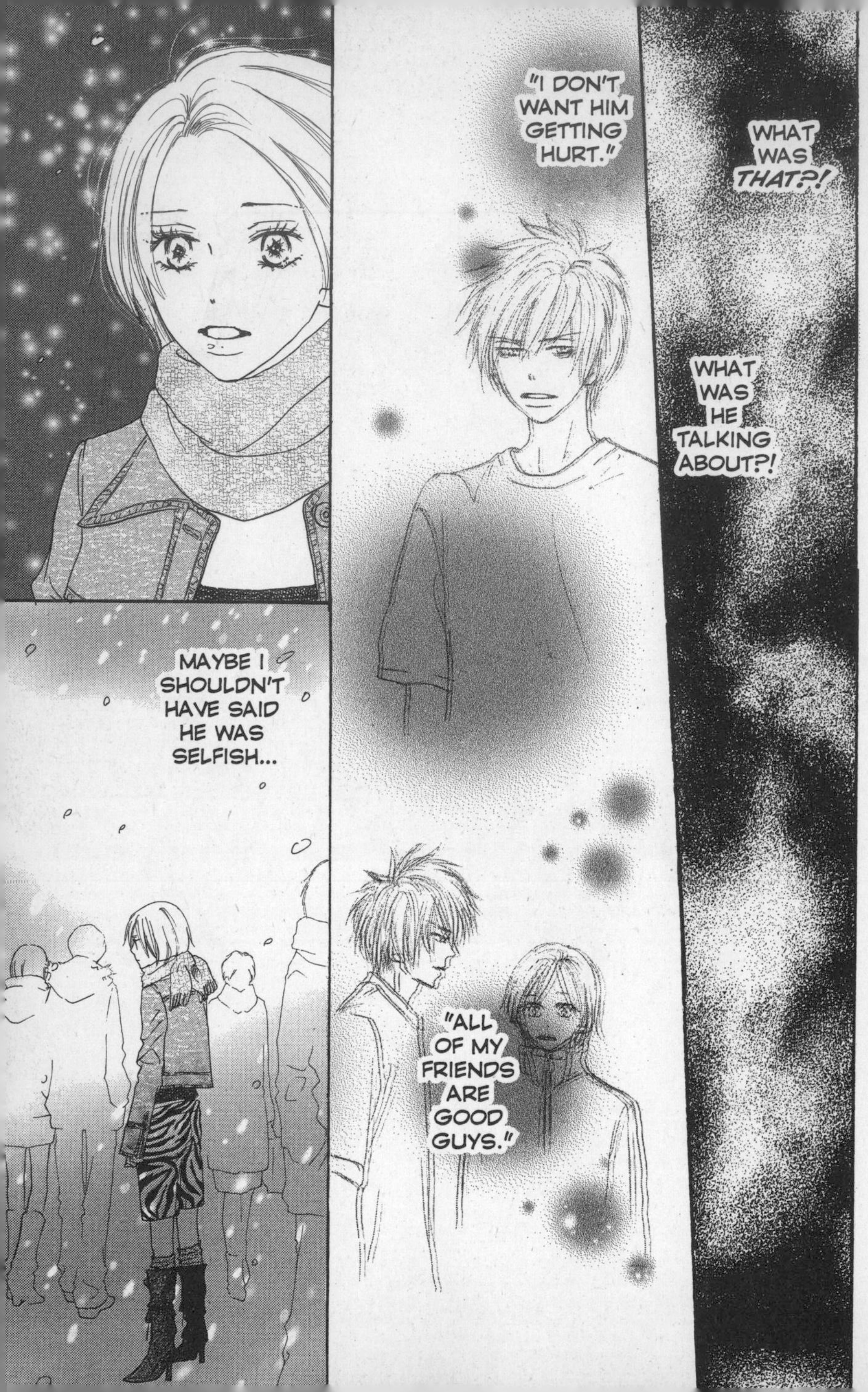
WHAT WAS *THAT?!*
WHAT WAS HE TALKING ABOUT?!
"I DON'T WANT HIM GETTING HURT."
"ALL OF MY FRIENDS ARE GOOD GUYS."
MAYBE I SHOULDN'T HAVE SAID HE WAS SELFISH...

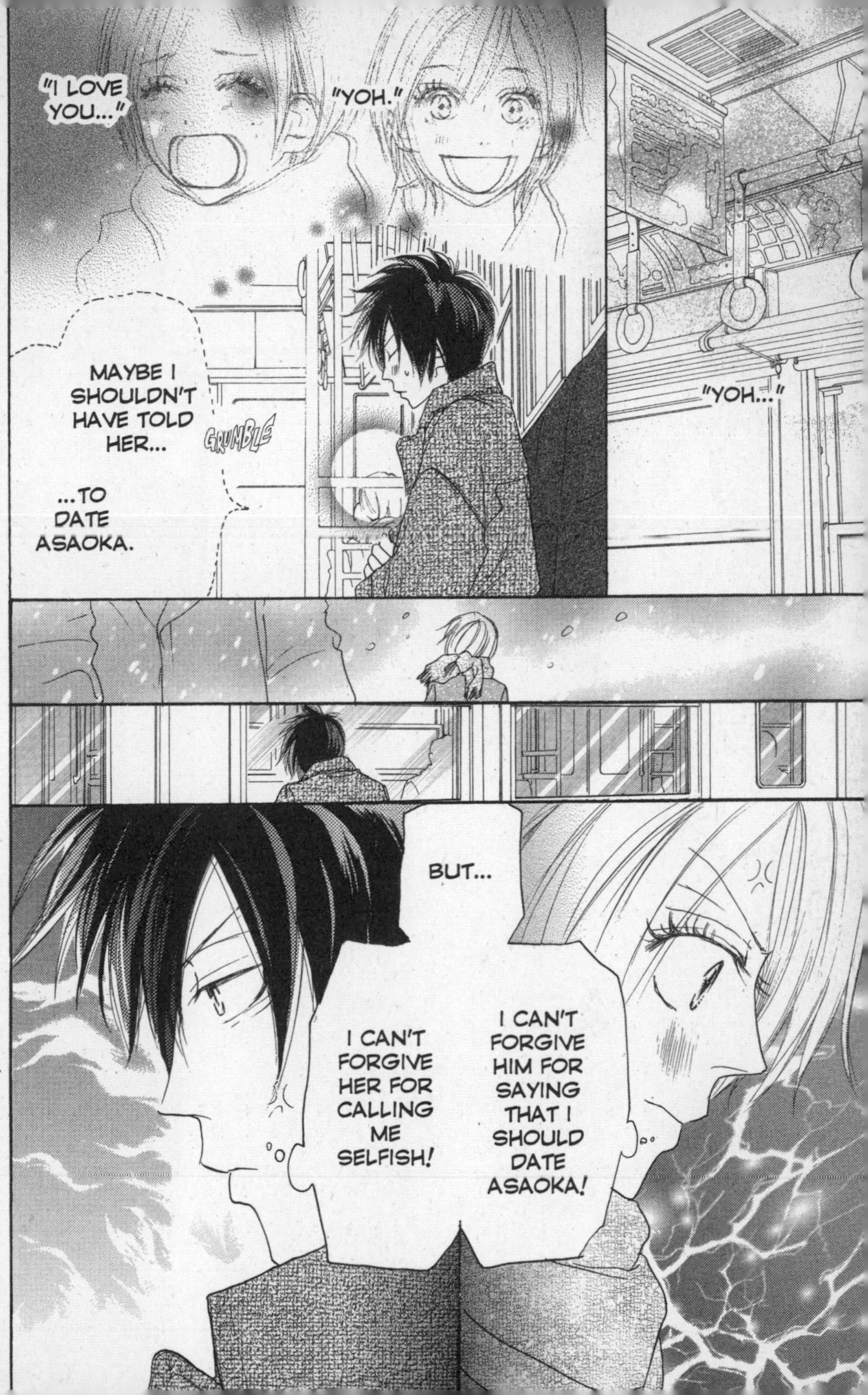
"YOH..."
"YOH."
"I LOVE YOU..."
MAYBE I SHOULDN'T HAVE TOLD HER...
GRUMBLE
...TO DATE ASAOKA.
BUT...
I CAN'T FORGIVE HIM FOR SAYING THAT I SHOULD DATE ASAOKA!
I CAN'T FORGIVE HER FOR CALLING ME SELFISH!

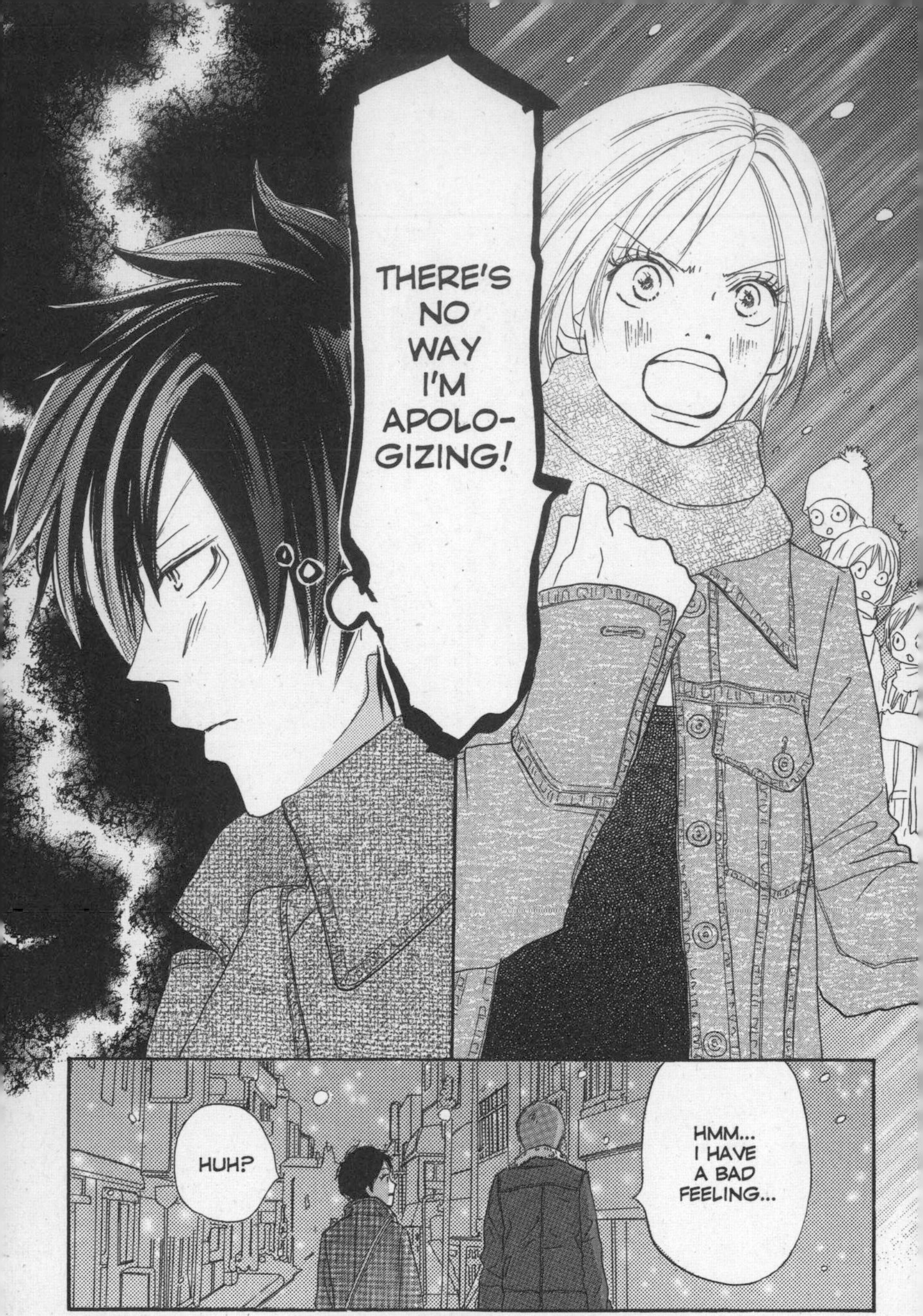
THERE'S NO WAY I'M APOLO-GIZING!
HMM... I HAVE A BAD FEELING...
HUH?

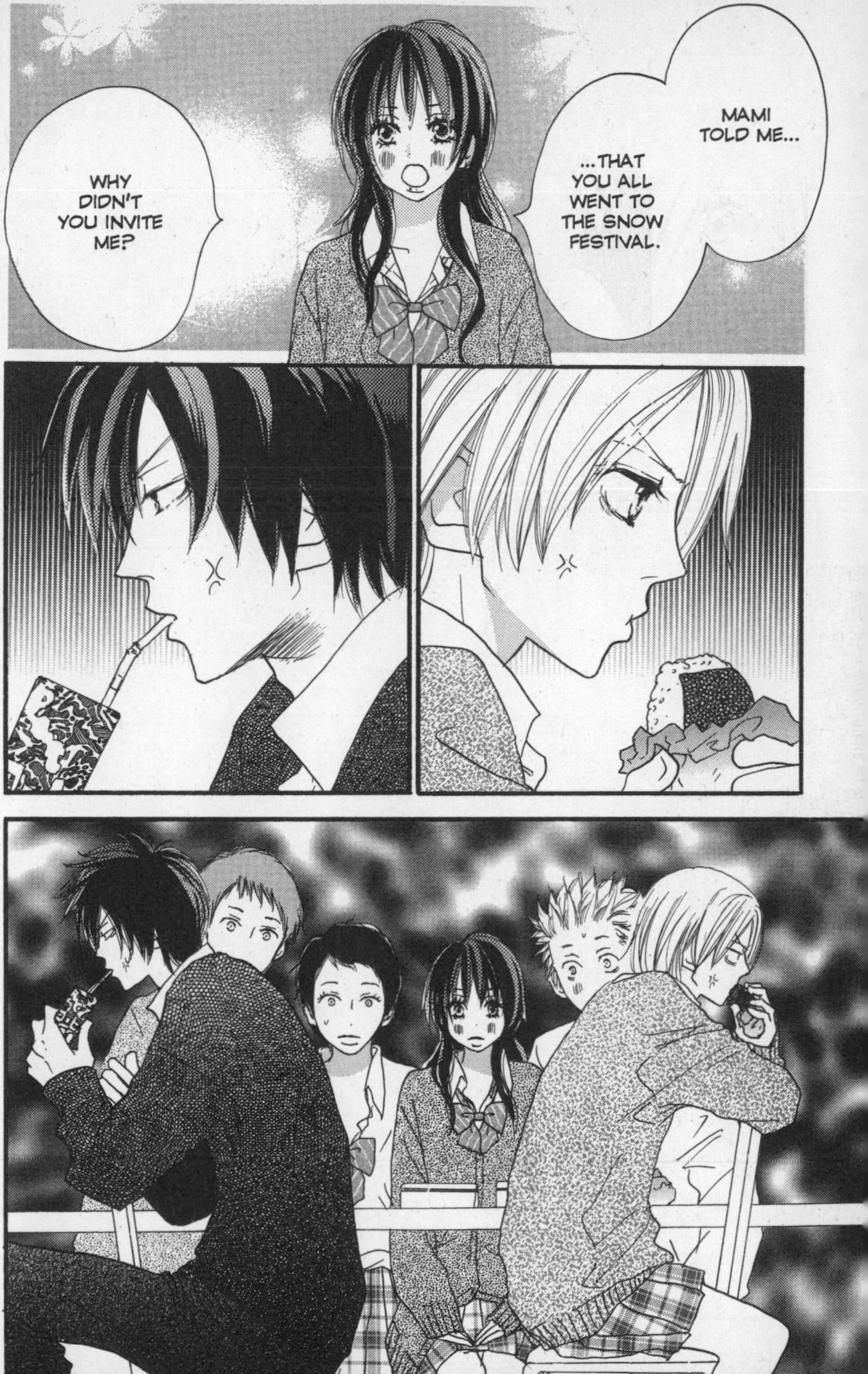
MAMI TOLD ME...
...THAT YOU ALL WENT TO THE SNOW FESTIVAL.
WHY DIDN'T YOU INVITE ME?

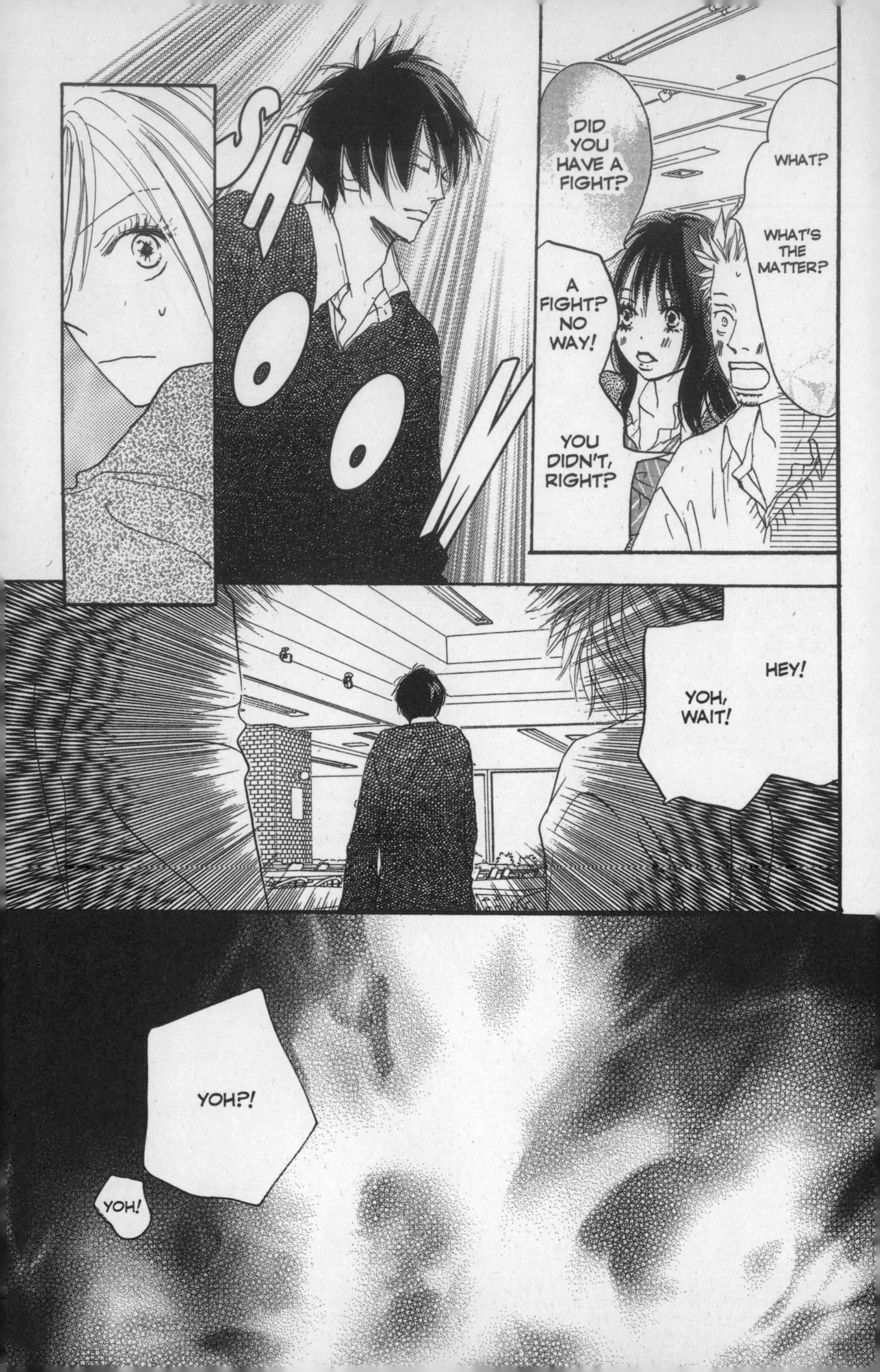
WHAT?
DID YOU HAVE A FIGHT?
WHAT'S THE MATTER?
A FIGHT? NO WAY!
YOU DIDN'T, RIGHT?
HEY!
YOH, WAIT!
YOH?!
YOH!

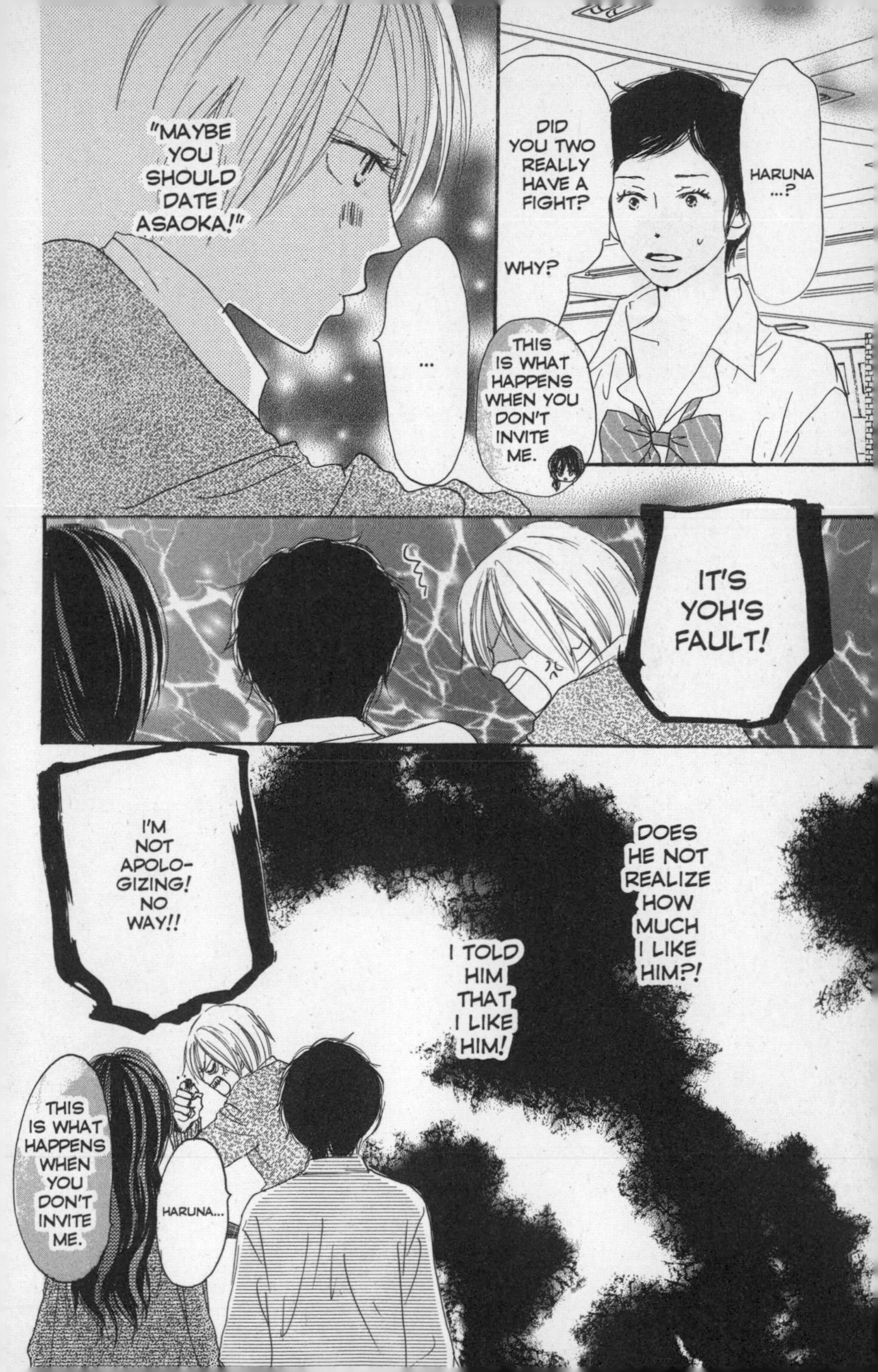
HARUNA ...?
DID YOU TWO REALLY HAVE A FIGHT?
WHY?
THIS IS WHAT HAPPENS WHEN YOU DON'T INVITE ME.
"MAYBE YOU SHOULD DATE ASAOKA!"
...
IT'S YOH'S FAULT!
DOES HE NOT REALIZE HOW MUCH I LIKE HIM?!
I TOLD HIM THAT I LIKE HIM!
I'M NOT APOLO-GIZING! NO WAY!!
HARUNA...
THIS IS WHAT HAPPENS WHEN YOU DON'T INVITE ME.

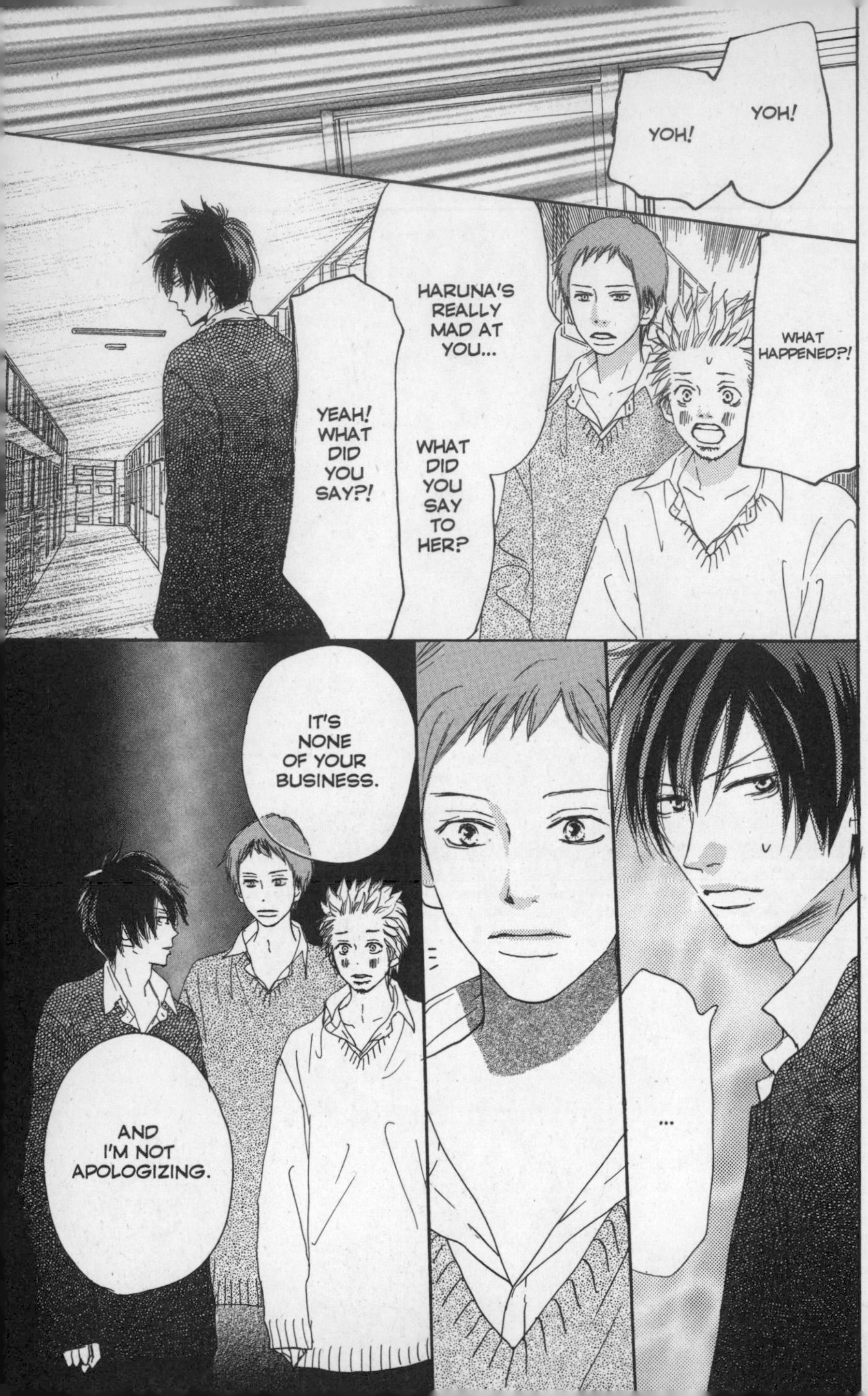
YOH!
YOH!
WHAT HAPPENED?!
HARUNA'S REALLY MAD AT YOU...
WHAT DID YOU SAY TO HER?
YEAH! WHAT DID YOU SAY?!
...
IT'S NONE OF YOUR BUSINESS.
AND I'M NOT APOLOGIZING.

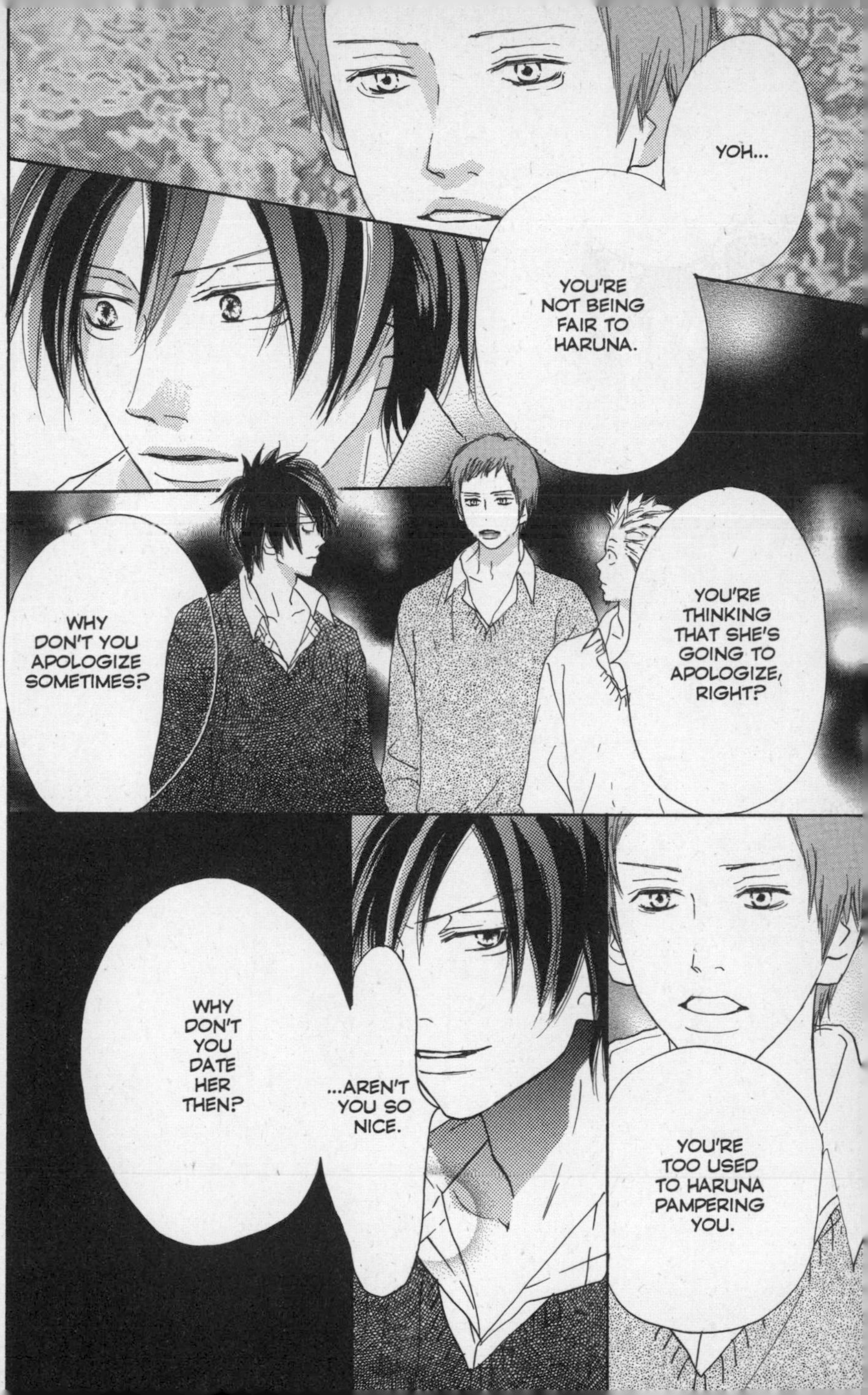
YOH...
YOU'RE NOT BEING FAIR TO HARUNA.
YOU'RE THINKING THAT SHE'S GOING TO APOLOGIZE, RIGHT?
WHY DON'T YOU APOLOGIZE SOMETIMES?
YOU'RE TOO USED TO HARUNA PAMPERING YOU.
...AREN'T YOU SO NICE.
WHY DON'T YOU DATE HER THEN?

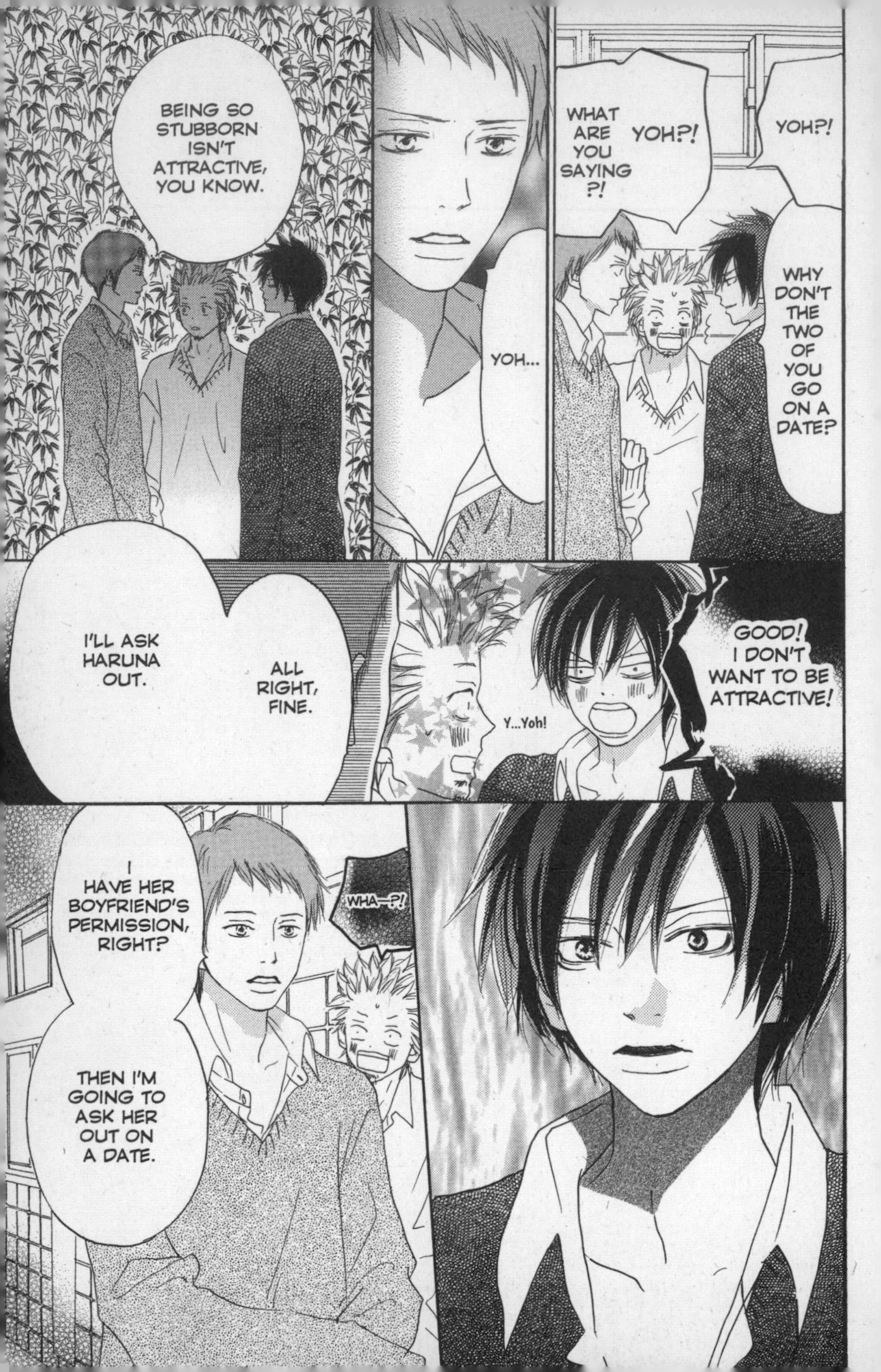
YOH?!
WHAT ARE YOU SAYING?! YOH?!
WHY DON'T THE TWO OF YOU GO ON A DATE?
YOH...
BEING SO STUBBORN ISN'T ATTRACTIVE, YOU KNOW.
GOOD! I DON'T WANT TO BE ATTRACTIVE!
Y...Yoh!
ALL RIGHT, FINE.
I'LL ASK HARUNA OUT.
I HAVE HER BOYFRIEND'S PERMISSION, RIGHT?
WHA—?!
THEN I'M GOING TO ASK HER OUT ON A DATE.

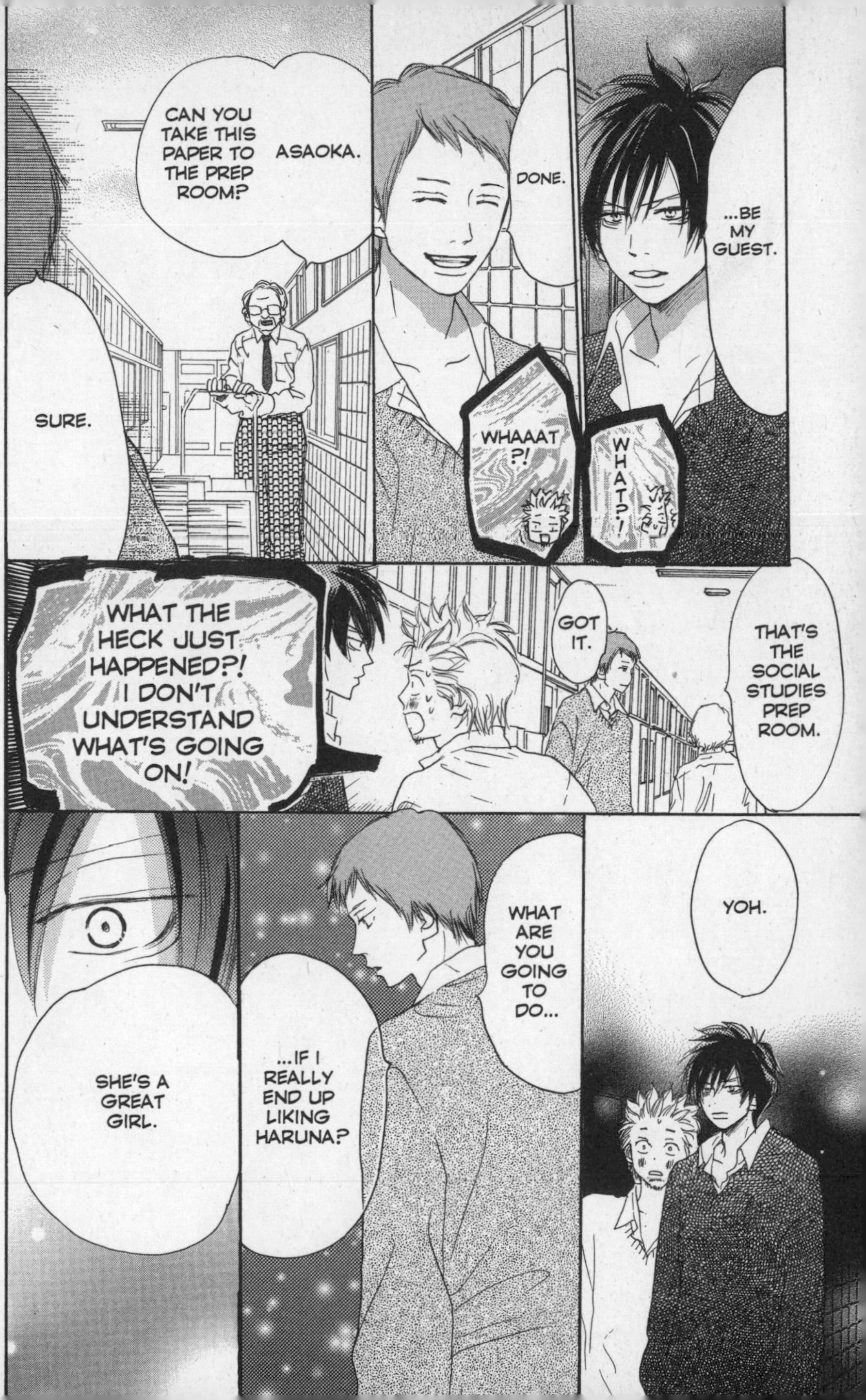
...BE MY GUEST.
WHAT?!
DONE.
WHAAAT?!
ASAOKA.
CAN YOU TAKE THIS PAPER TO THE PREP ROOM?
SURE.
THAT'S THE SOCIAL STUDIES PREP ROOM.
GOT IT.
WHAT THE HECK JUST HAPPENED?! I DON'T UNDERSTAND WHAT'S GOING ON!
YOH.
WHAT ARE YOU GOING TO DO...
...IF I REALLY END UP LIKING HARUNA?
SHE'S A GREAT GIRL.

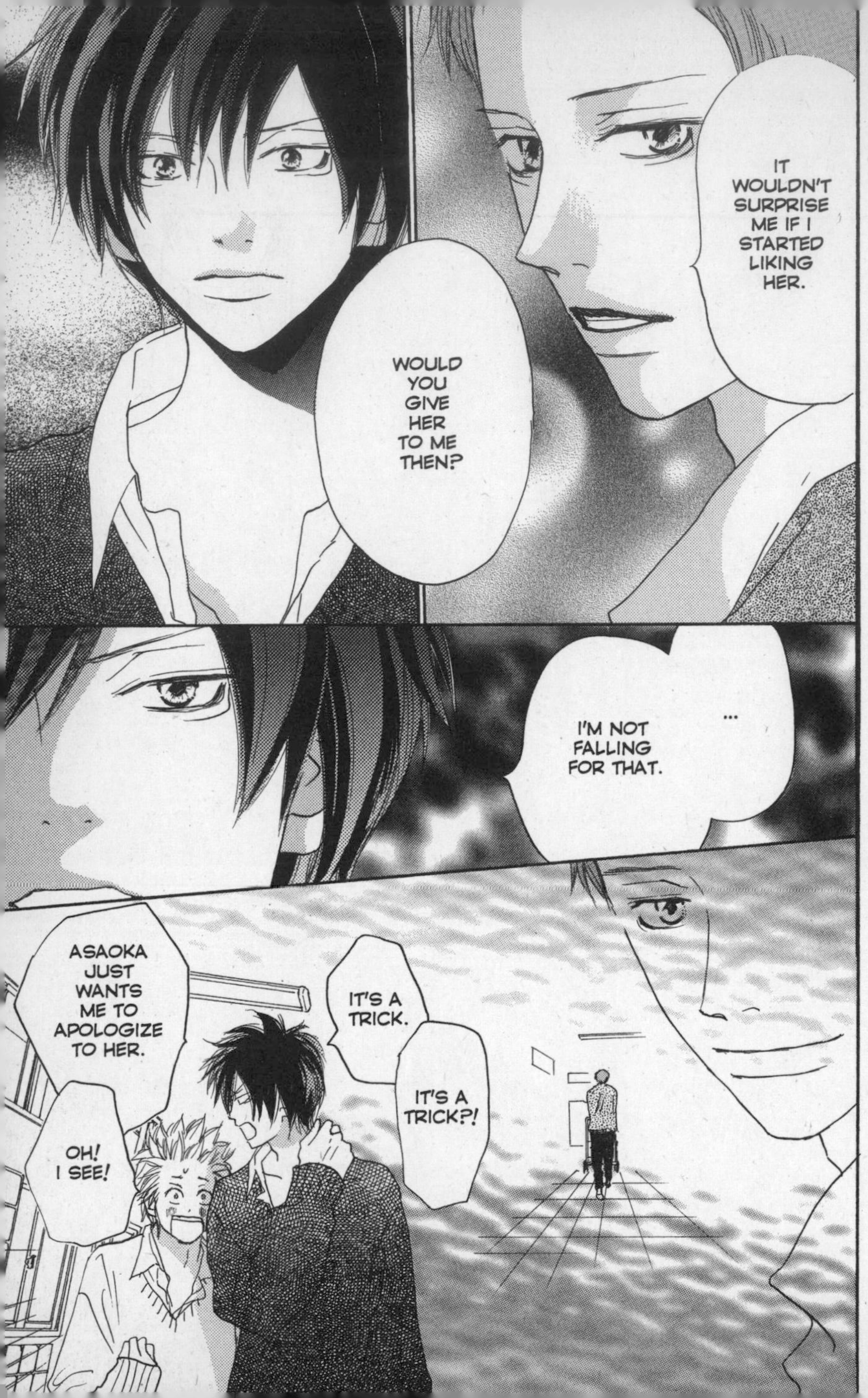
IT WOULDN'T SURPRISE ME IF I STARTED LIKING HER.
WOULD YOU GIVE HER TO ME THEN?
...
I'M NOT FALLING FOR THAT.
IT'S A TRICK.
IT'S A TRICK?!
ASAOKA JUST WANTS ME TO APOLOGIZE TO HER.
OH! I SEE!

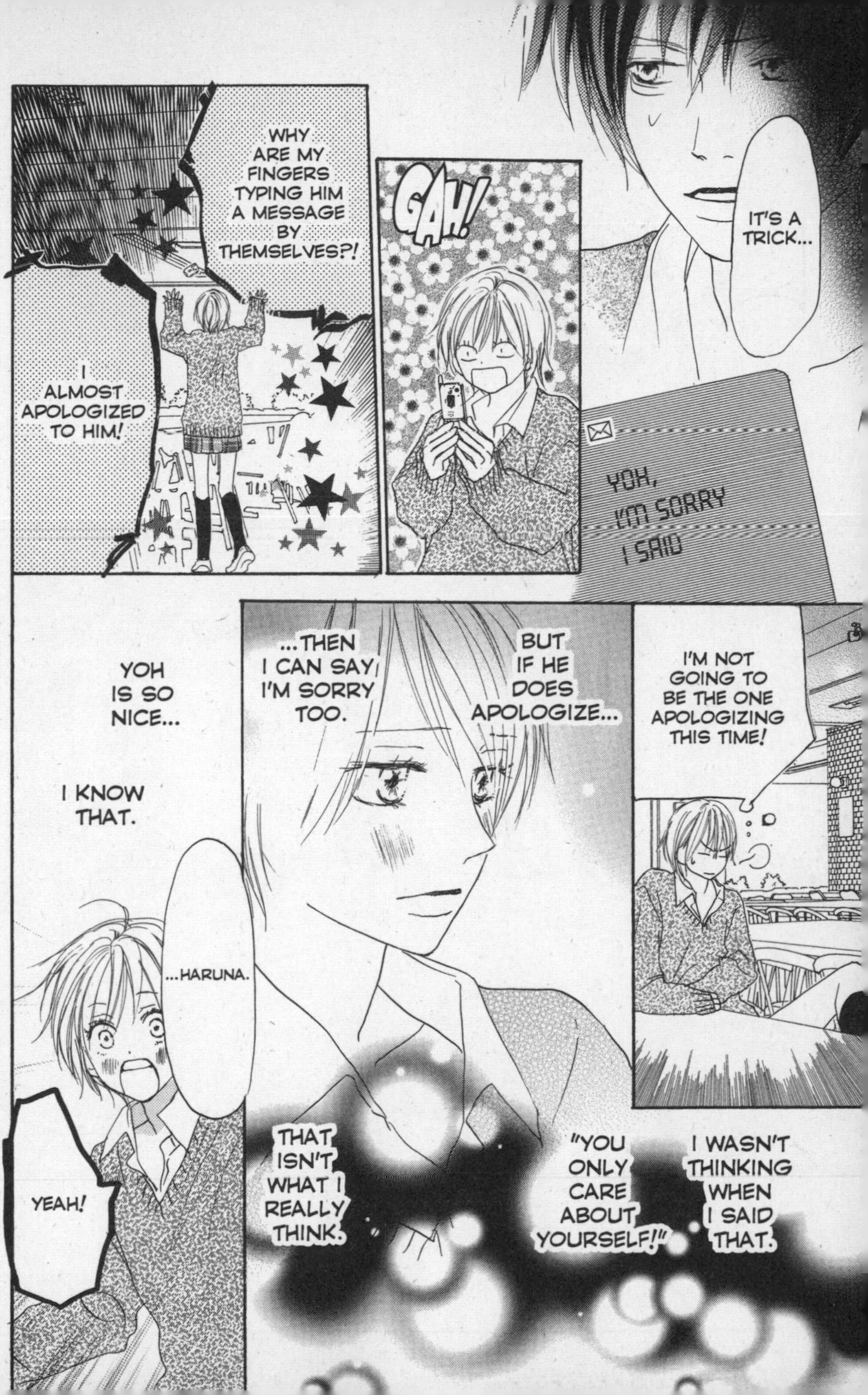
IT'S A TRICK...
YOH, I'M SORRY I SAID
GAH!
WHY ARE MY FINGERS TYPING HIM A MESSAGE BY THEMSELVES?!
I ALMOST APOLOGIZED TO HIM!
I'M NOT GOING TO BE THE ONE APOLOGIZING THIS TIME!
BUT IF HE DOES APOLOGIZE...
...THEN I CAN SAY I'M SORRY TOO.
I WASN'T THINKING WHEN I SAID THAT.
"YOU ONLY CARE ABOUT YOURSELF!"
THAT ISN'T WHAT I REALLY THINK.
YOH IS SO NICE...
I KNOW THAT.
...HARUNA.
YEAH!

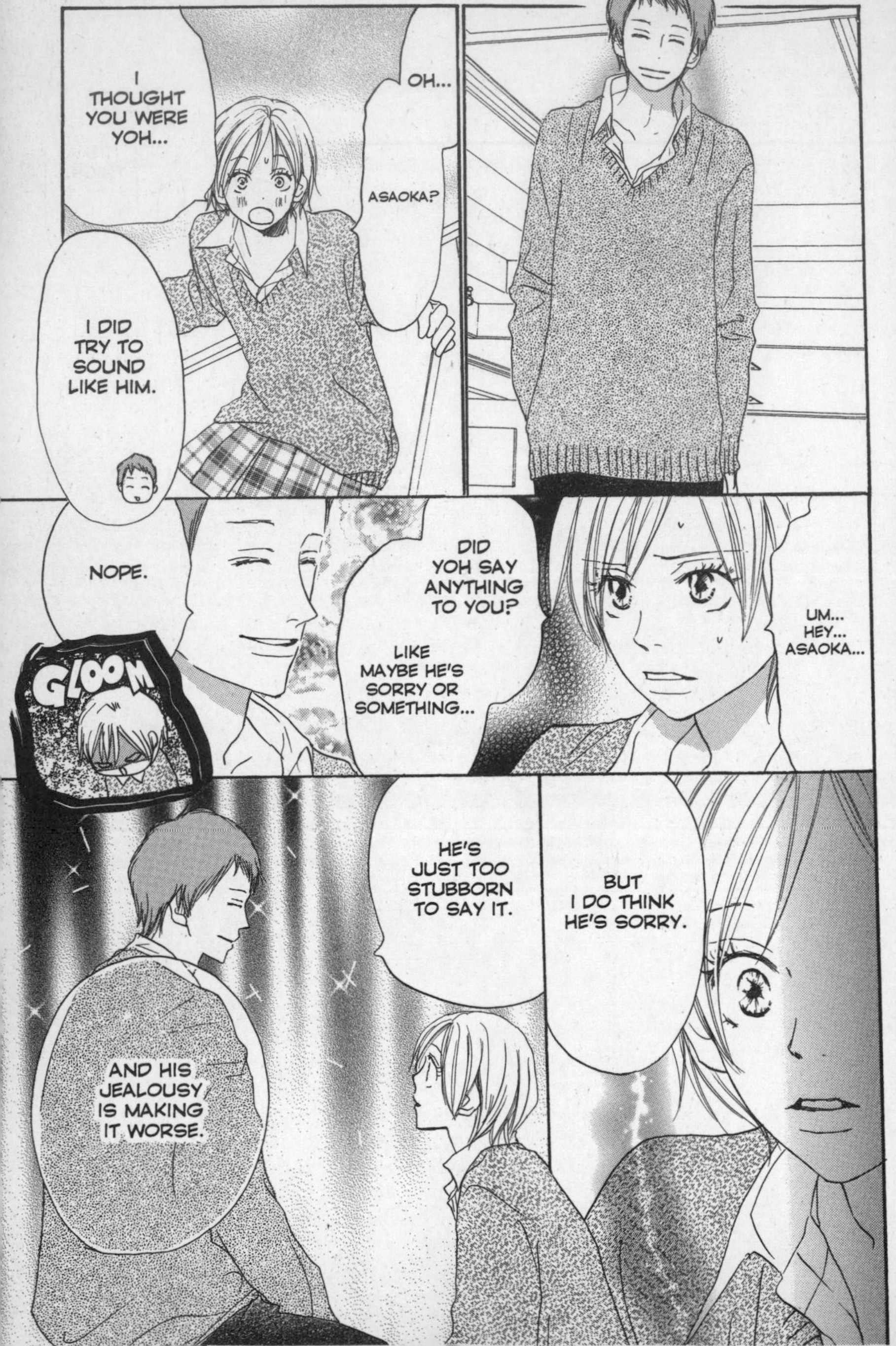
OH... ASAOKA?
I THOUGHT YOU WERE YOH...
I DID TRY TO SOUND LIKE HIM.
UM... HEY... ASAOKA...
DID YOH SAY ANYTHING TO YOU?
LIKE MAYBE HE'S SORRY OR SOMETHING...
NOPE.
GLOOM
BUT I DO THINK HE'S SORRY.
HE'S JUST TOO STUBBORN TO SAY IT.
AND HIS JEALOUSY IS MAKING IT WORSE.

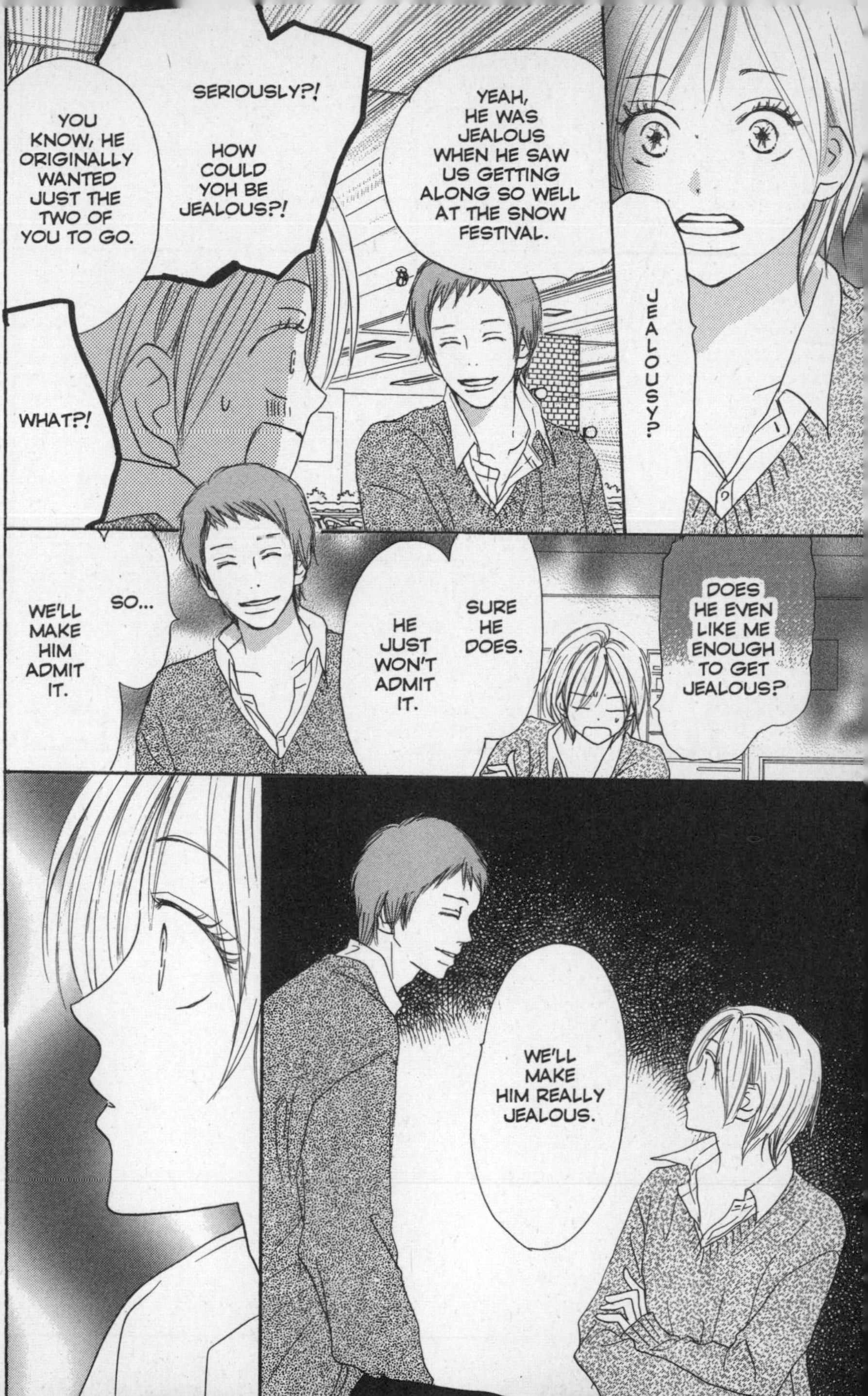
JEALOUSY?
YEAH, HE WAS JEALOUS WHEN HE SAW US GETTING ALONG SO WELL AT THE SNOW FESTIVAL.
SERIOUSLY?!
HOW COULD YOH BE JEALOUS?!
YOU KNOW, HE ORIGINALLY WANTED JUST THE TWO OF YOU TO GO.
WHAT?!
DOES HE EVEN LIKE ME ENOUGH TO GET JEALOUS?
SURE HE DOES.
HE JUST WON'T ADMIT IT.
SO...
WE'LL MAKE HIM ADMIT IT.
WE'LL MAKE HIM REALLY JEALOUS.

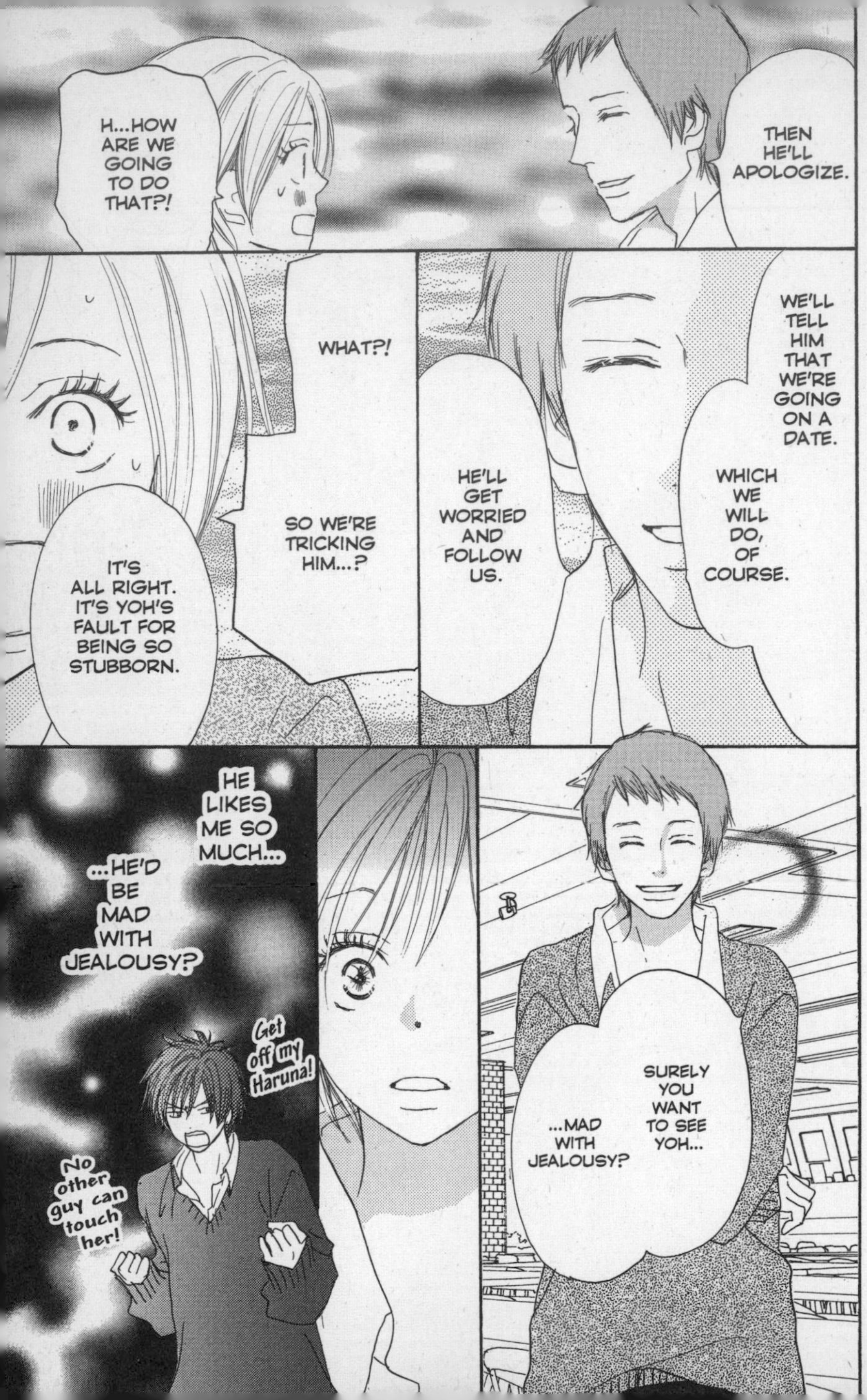
THEN HE'LL APOLOGIZE.
H...HOW ARE WE GOING TO DO THAT?!
WE'LL TELL HIM THAT WE'RE GOING ON A DATE.
WHICH WE WILL DO, OF COURSE.
HE'LL GET WORRIED AND FOLLOW US.
WHAT?!
SO WE'RE TRICKING HIM...?
IT'S ALL RIGHT. IT'S YOH'S FAULT FOR BEING SO STUBBORN.
SURELY YOU WANT TO SEE YOH...
...MAD WITH JEALOUSY?
HE LIKES ME SO MUCH...
...HE'D BE MAD WITH JEALOUSY?
Get off my Haruna!
No other guy can touch her!

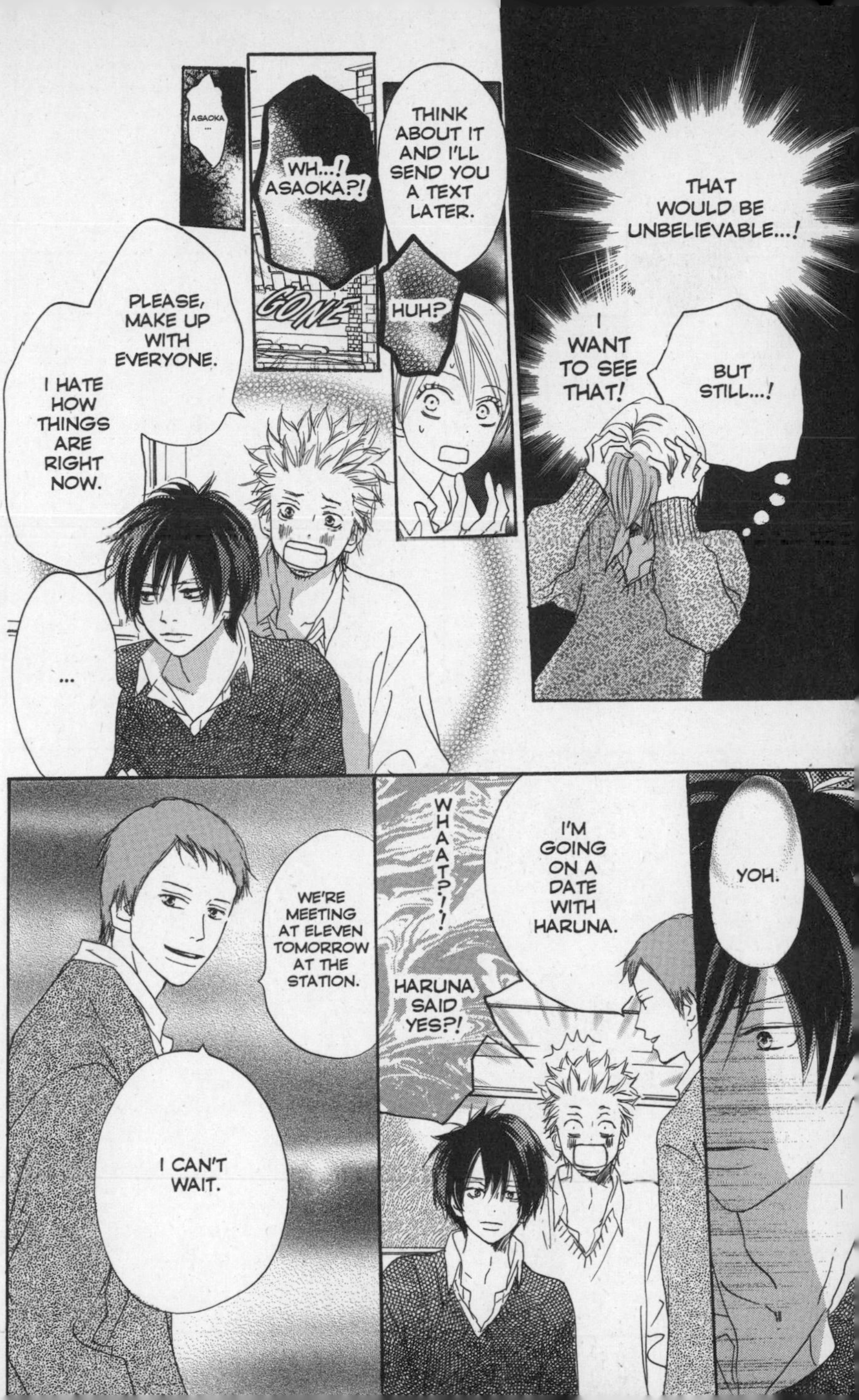
THAT WOULD BE UNBELIEVABLE...!
BUT STILL...!
I WANT TO SEE THAT!
THINK ABOUT IT AND I'LL SEND YOU A TEXT LATER.
HUH?
WH...! ASAOKA?!
GONE
ASAOKA ...
PLEASE, MAKE UP WITH EVERYONE.
I HATE HOW THINGS ARE RIGHT NOW.
...
YOH.
I'M GOING ON A DATE WITH HARUNA.
WHAAT?!!
HARUNA SAID YES?!
WE'RE MEETING AT ELEVEN TOMORROW AT THE STATION.
I CAN'T WAIT.

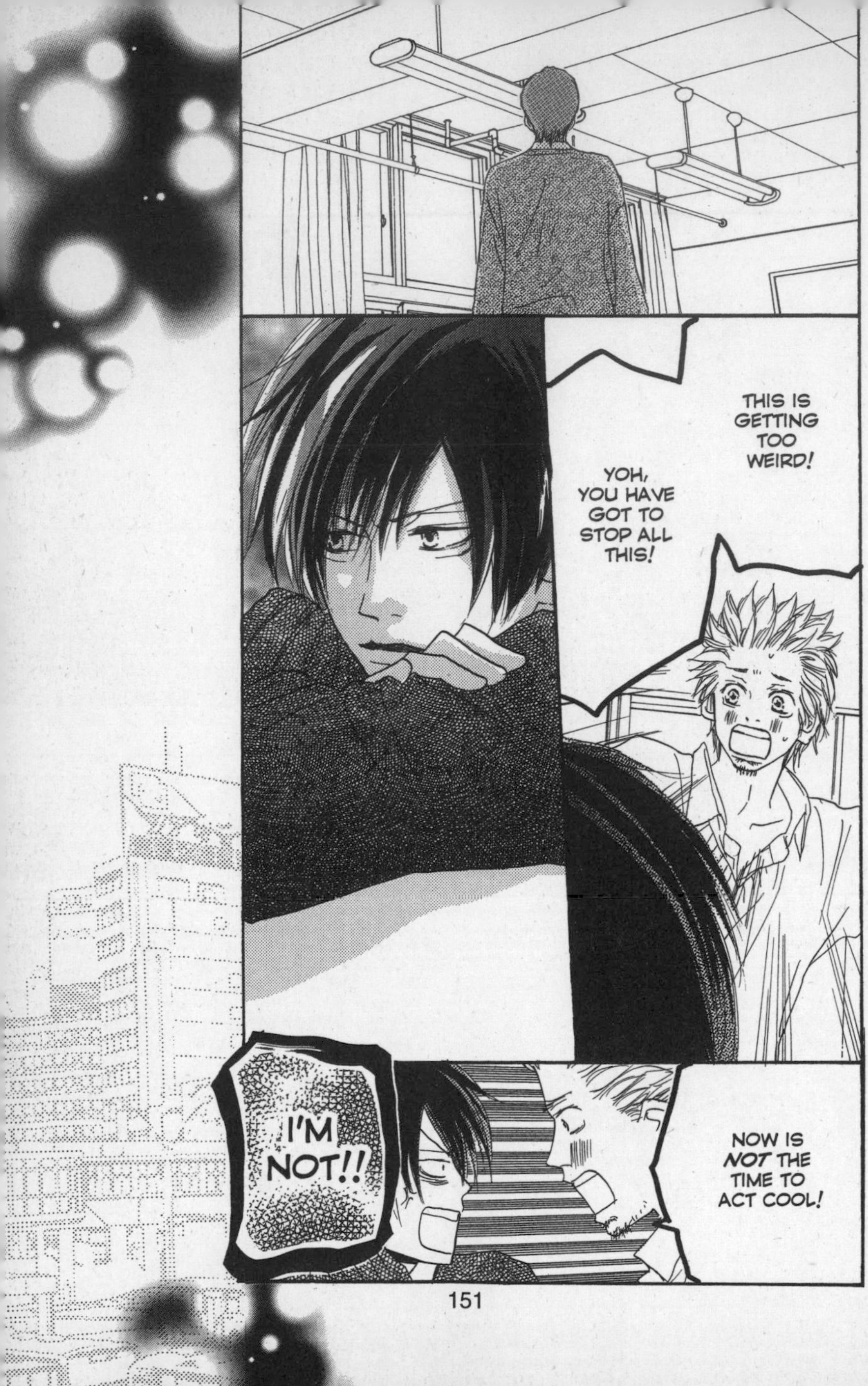
THIS IS GETTING TOO WEIRD!
YOH, YOU HAVE GOT TO STOP ALL THIS!
NOW IS *NOT* THE TIME TO ACT COOL!
I'M NOT!!

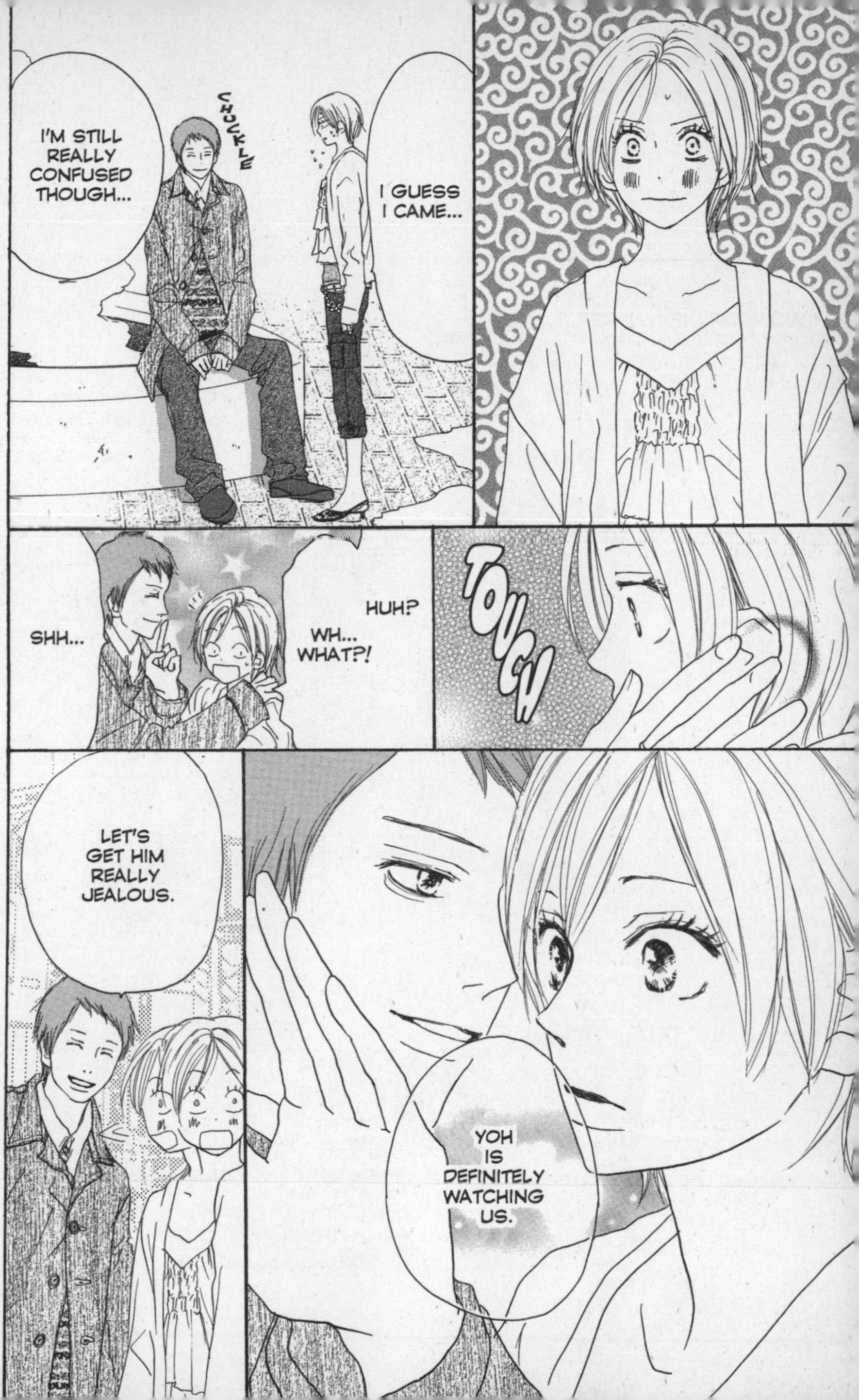
I GUESS I CAME...
CHUCKLE
I'M STILL REALLY CONFUSED THOUGH...
TOUCH
HUH?
WH... WHAT?!
SHH...
YOH IS DEFINITELY WATCHING US.
LET'S GET HIM REALLY JEALOUS.

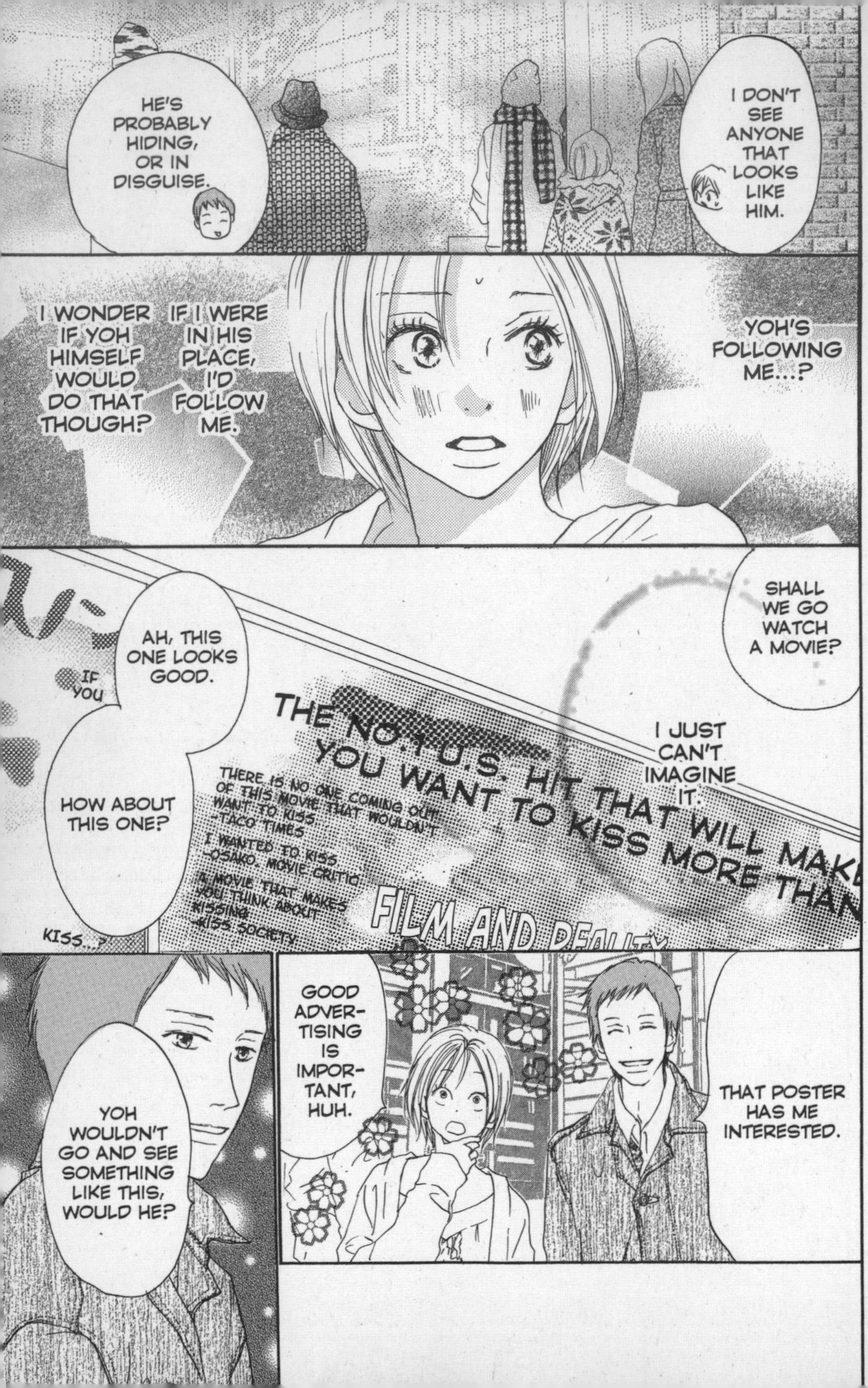
I DON'T SEE ANYONE THAT LOOKS LIKE HIM.
HE'S PROBABLY HIDING, OR IN DISGUISE.
YOH'S FOLLOWING ME...?
IF I WERE IN HIS PLACE, I'D FOLLOW ME.
I WONDER IF YOH HIMSELF WOULD DO THAT THOUGH?
SHALL WE GO WATCH A MOVIE?
I JUST CAN'T IMAGINE IT.
THE NO.1 U.S. HIT THAT WILL MAKE YOU WANT TO KISS MORE THAN
THERE IS NO ONE COMING OUT OF THIS MOVIE THAT WOULDN'T WANT TO KISS -TACO TIMES
I WANTED TO KISS -OSAKO, MOVIE CRITIC
A MOVIE THAT MAKES YOU THINK ABOUT KISSING -KISS SOCIETY
FILM AND
AH, THIS ONE LOOKS GOOD.
IF YOU
HOW ABOUT THIS ONE?
KISS...?
THAT POSTER HAS ME INTERESTED.
GOOD ADVERTISING IS IMPORTANT, HUH.
YOH WOULDN'T GO AND SEE SOMETHING LIKE THIS, WOULD HE?

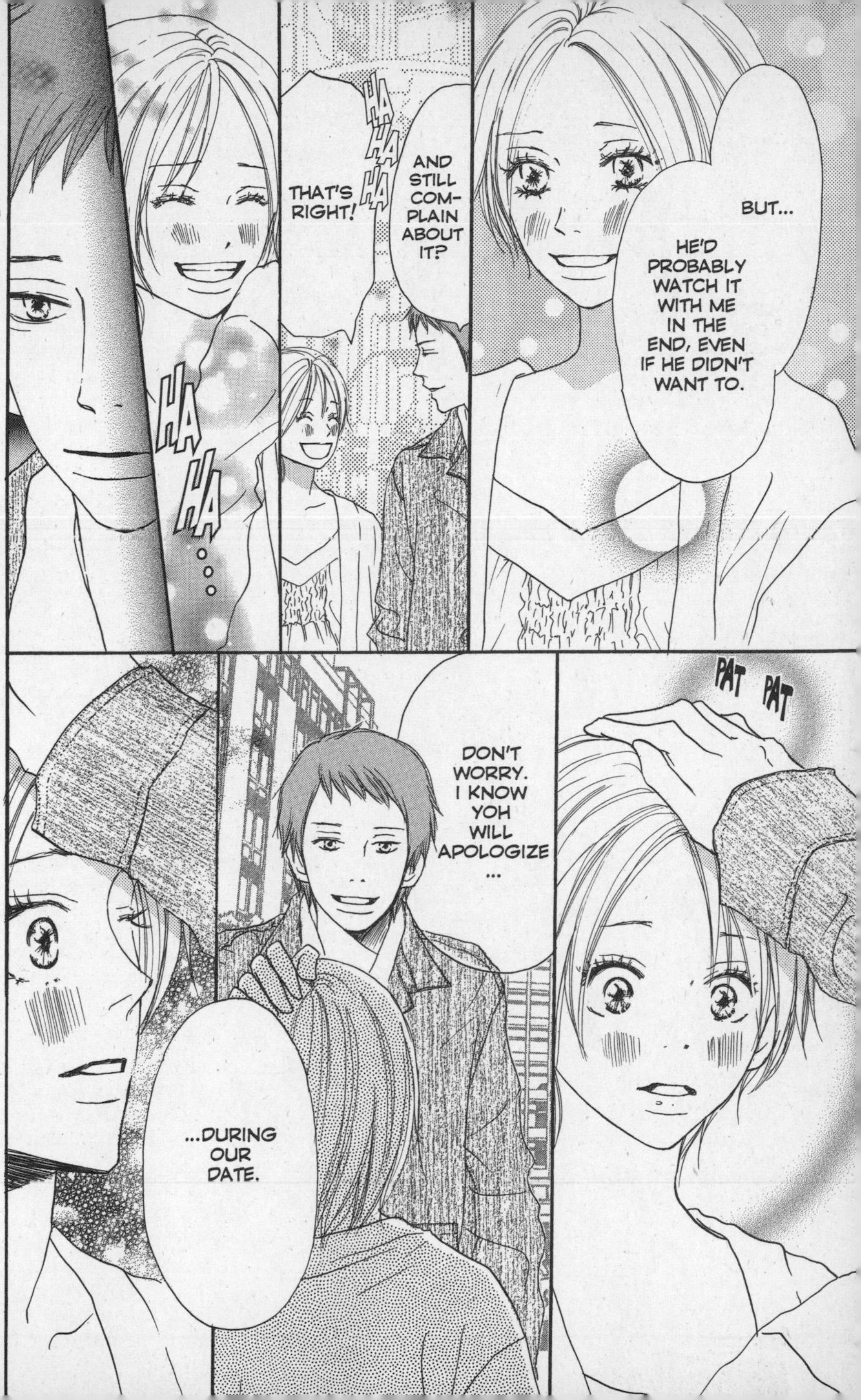
BUT...
HE'D PROBABLY WATCH IT WITH ME IN THE END, EVEN IF HE DIDN'T WANT TO.
AND STILL COM-PLAIN ABOUT IT?
HA HA HA
THAT'S RIGHT!
HA HA HA...
PAT PAT
DON'T WORRY. I KNOW YOH WILL APOLOGIZE...
...DURING OUR DATE.

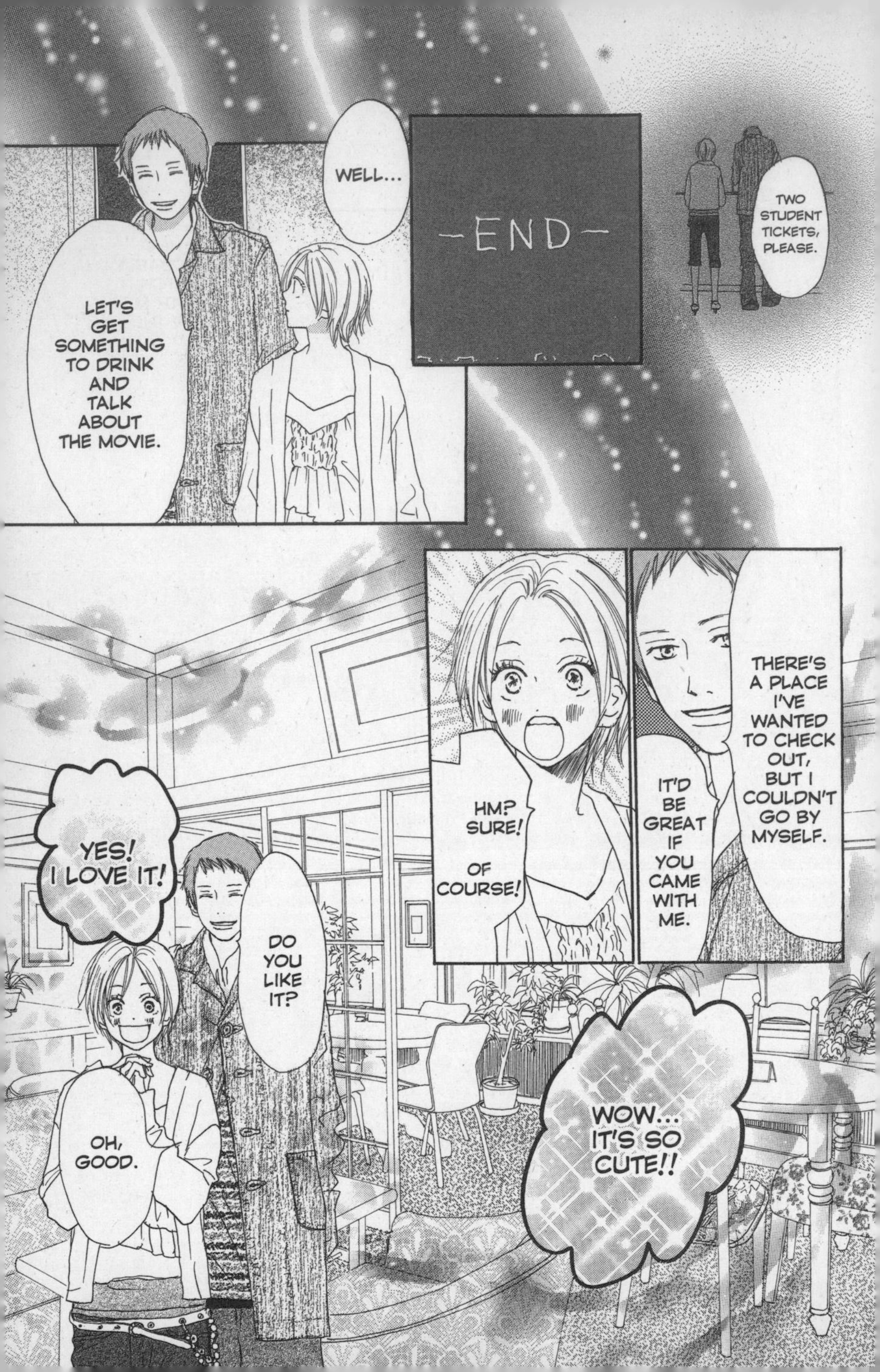
TWO STUDENT TICKETS, PLEASE.
-END-
WELL...
LET'S GET SOMETHING TO DRINK AND TALK ABOUT THE MOVIE.
THERE'S A PLACE I'VE WANTED TO CHECK OUT, BUT I COULDN'T GO BY MYSELF.
IT'D BE GREAT IF YOU CAME WITH ME.
HM? SURE!
OF COURSE!
WOW... IT'S SO CUTE!!
DO YOU LIKE IT?
YES! I LOVE IT!
OH, GOOD.

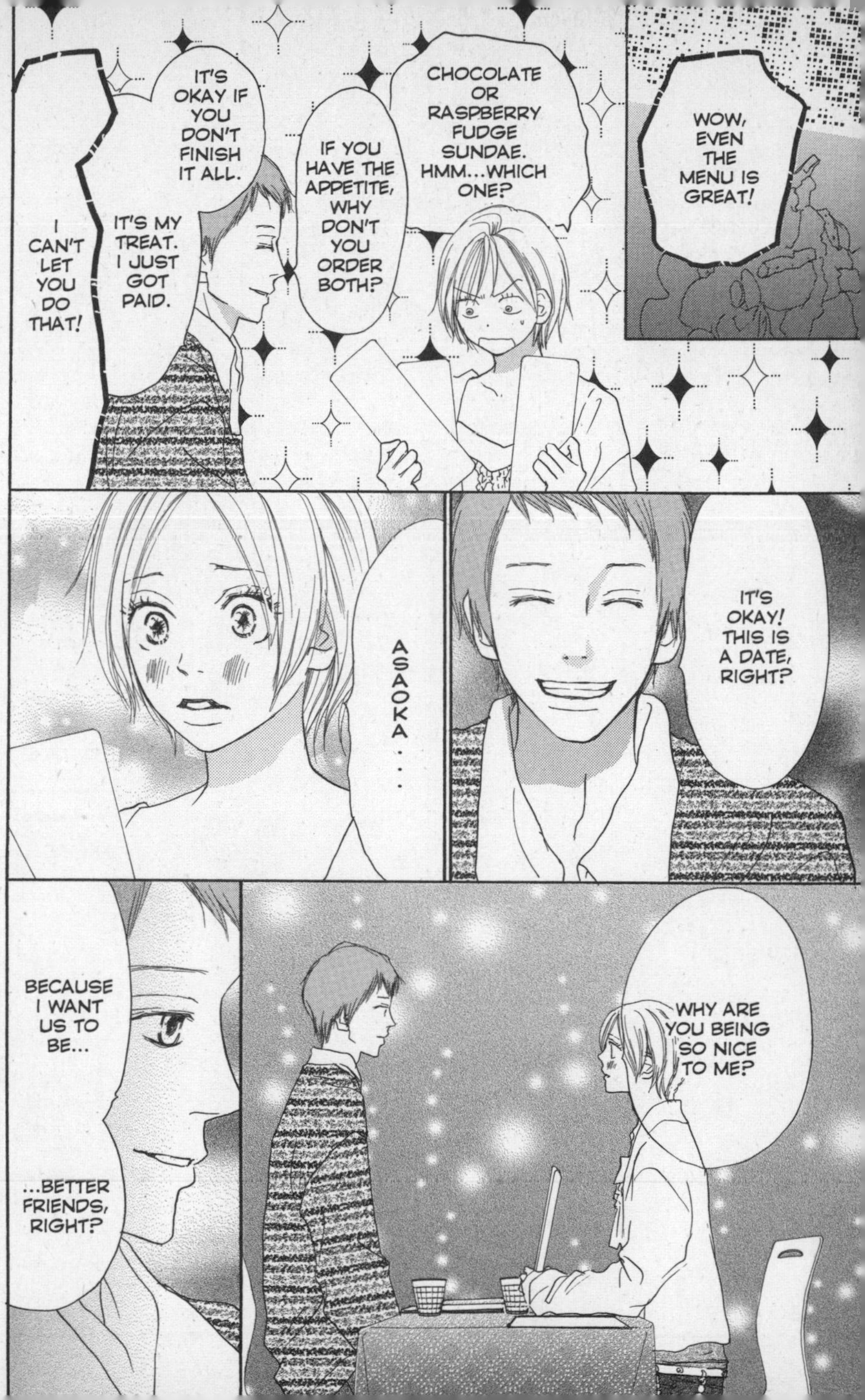
WOW, EVEN THE MENU IS GREAT!
CHOCOLATE OR RASPBERRY FUDGE SUNDAE. HMM...WHICH ONE?
IF YOU HAVE THE APPETITE, WHY DON'T YOU ORDER BOTH?
IT'S OKAY IF YOU DON'T FINISH IT ALL.
IT'S MY TREAT. I JUST GOT PAID.
I CAN'T LET YOU DO THAT!
IT'S OKAY! THIS IS A DATE, RIGHT?
ASAOKA...
WHY ARE YOU BEING SO NICE TO ME?
BECAUSE I WANT US TO BE...
...BETTER FRIENDS, RIGHT?

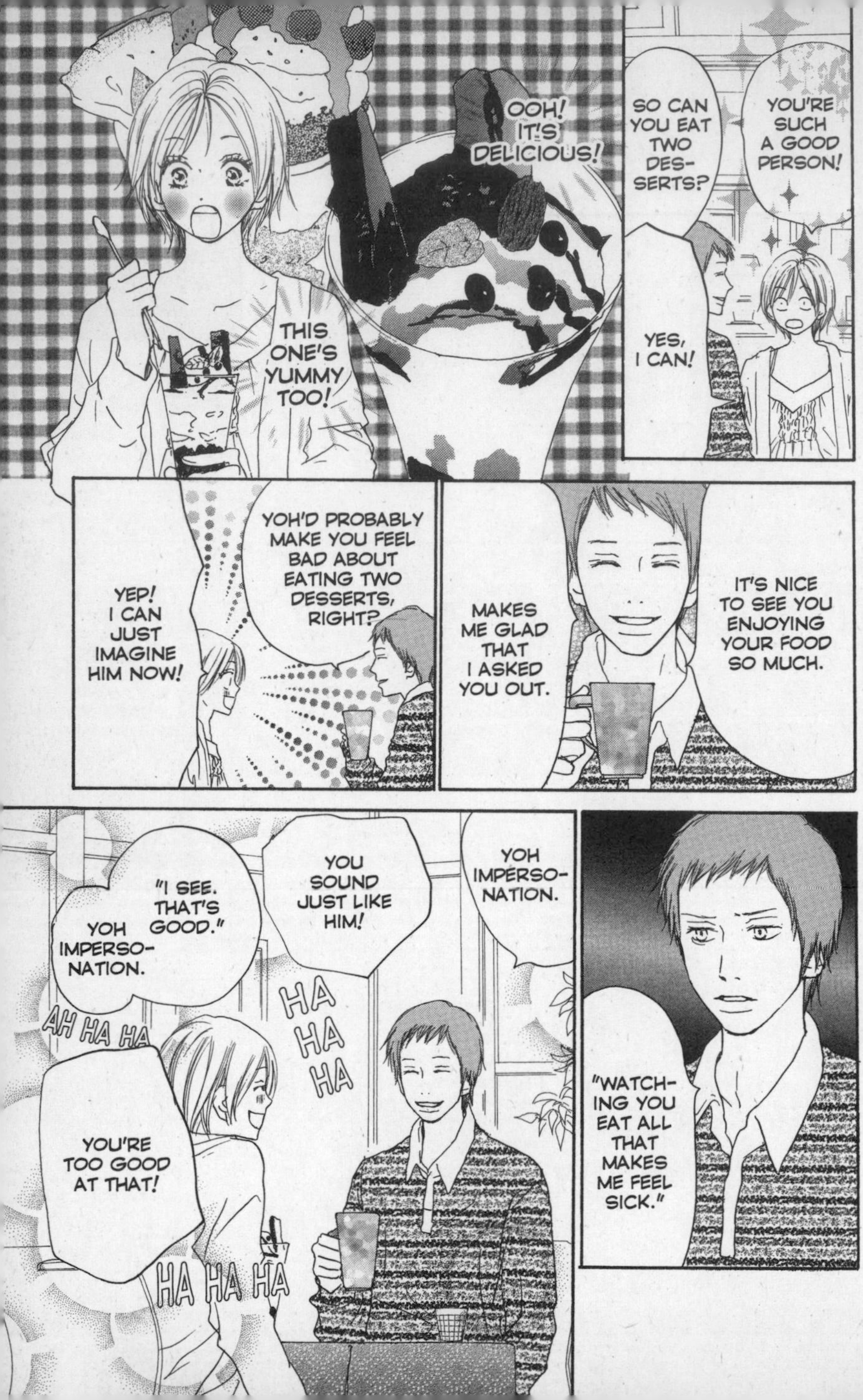
YOU'RE SUCH A GOOD PERSON!
SO CAN YOU EAT TWO DES-SERTS?
YES, I CAN!
OOH! IT'S DELICIOUS!
THIS ONE'S YUMMY TOO!
IT'S NICE TO SEE YOU ENJOYING YOUR FOOD SO MUCH.
MAKES ME GLAD THAT I ASKED YOU OUT.
YOH'D PROBABLY MAKE YOU FEEL BAD ABOUT EATING TWO DESSERTS, RIGHT?
YEP! I CAN JUST IMAGINE HIM NOW!
"WATCH-ING YOU EAT ALL THAT MAKES ME FEEL SICK."
YOH IMPERSO-NATION.
YOU SOUND JUST LIKE HIM!
"I SEE. THAT'S GOOD."
YOH IMPERSO-NATION.
HA HA HA
AH HA HA
YOU'RE TOO GOOD AT THAT!
HA HA HA

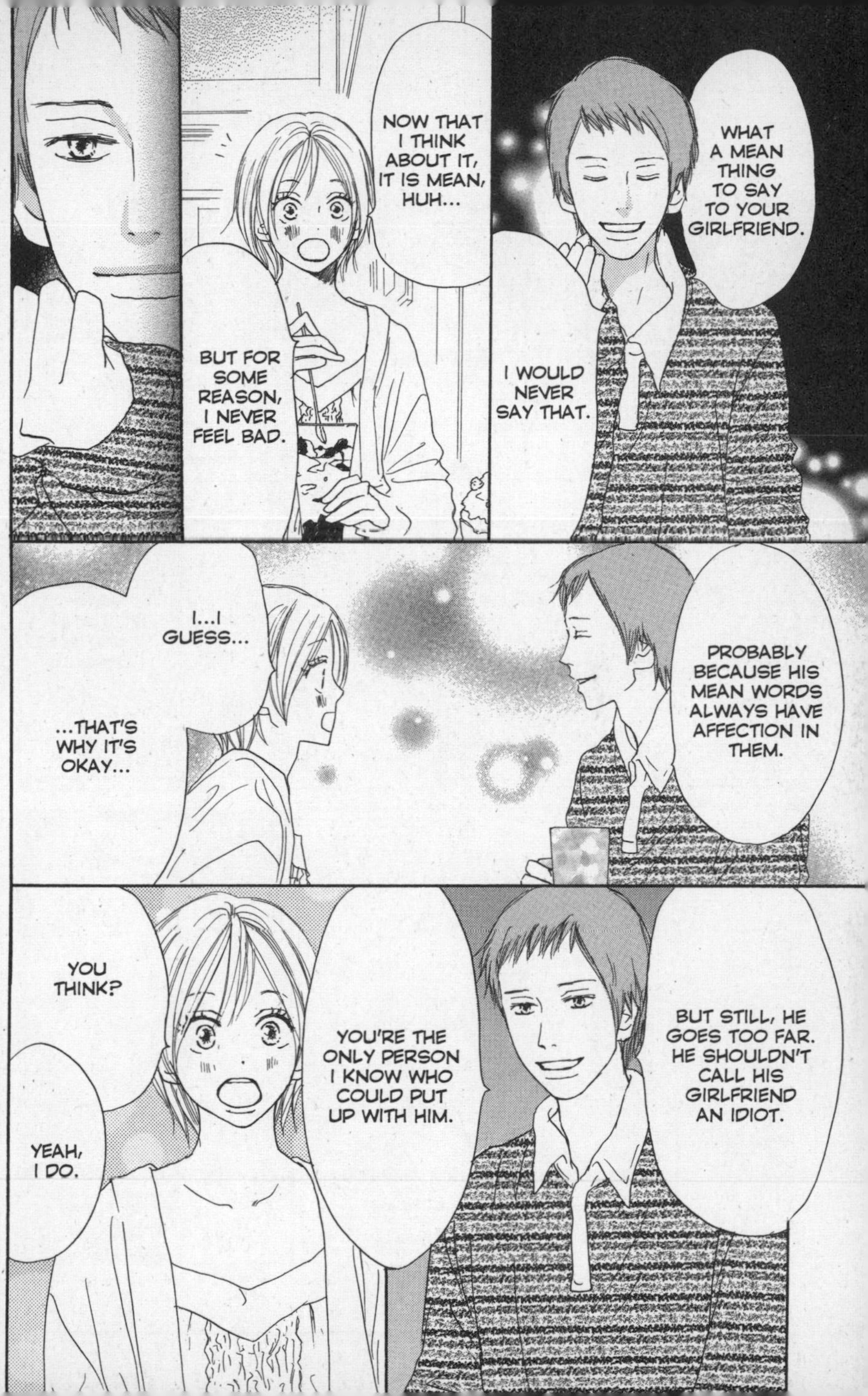
WHAT A MEAN THING TO SAY TO YOUR GIRLFRIEND.
I WOULD NEVER SAY THAT.
NOW THAT I THINK ABOUT IT, IT IS MEAN, HUH...
BUT FOR SOME REASON, I NEVER FEEL BAD.
PROBABLY BECAUSE HIS MEAN WORDS ALWAYS HAVE AFFECTION IN THEM.
I...I GUESS...
...THAT'S WHY IT'S OKAY...
BUT STILL, HE GOES TOO FAR. HE SHOULDN'T CALL HIS GIRLFRIEND AN IDIOT.
YOU'RE THE ONLY PERSON I KNOW WHO COULD PUT UP WITH HIM.
YOU THINK?
YEAH, I DO.

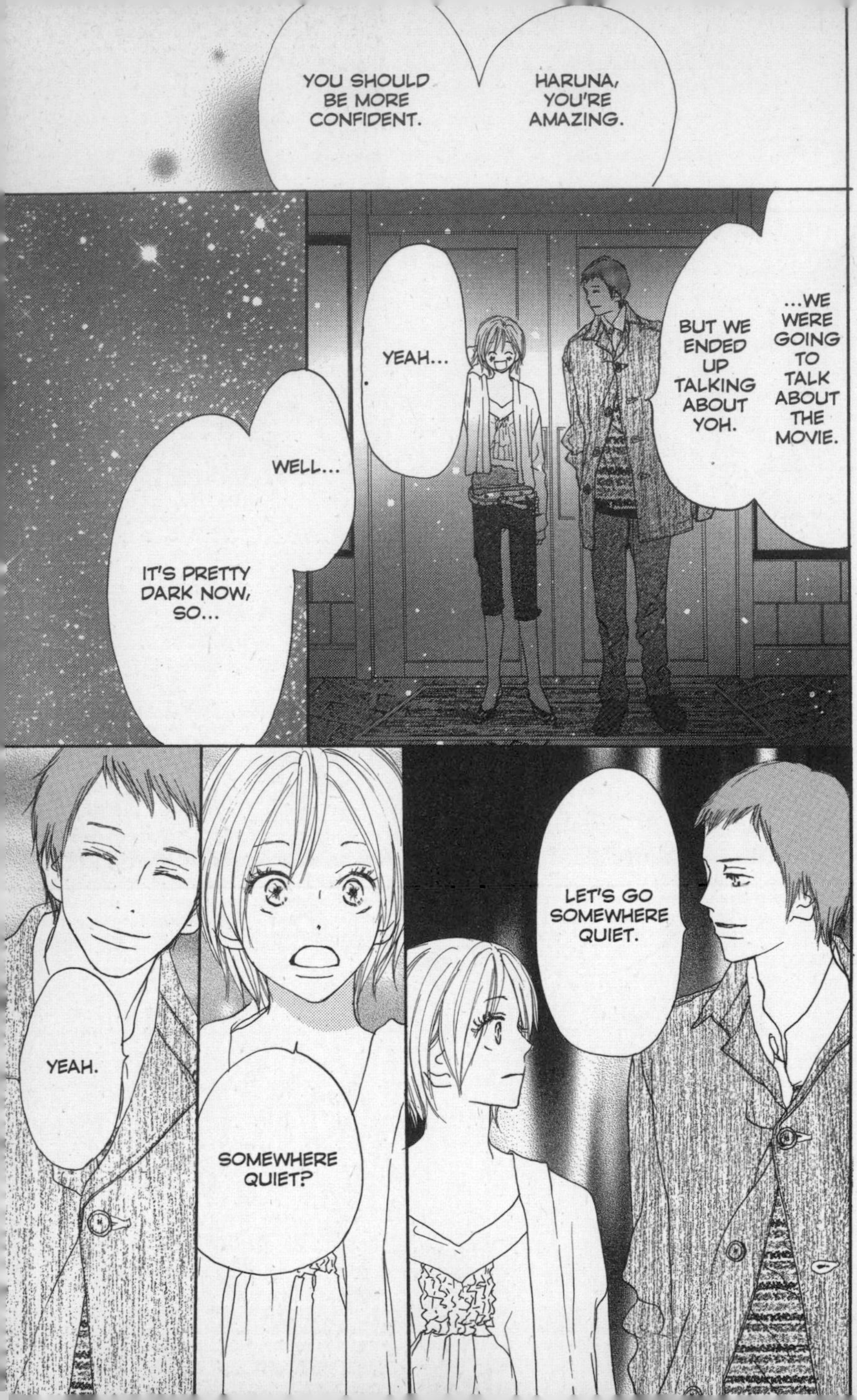
HARUNA, YOU'RE AMAZING.
YOU SHOULD BE MORE CONFIDENT.
...WE WERE GOING TO TALK ABOUT THE MOVIE.
BUT WE ENDED UP TALKING ABOUT YOH.
YEAH...
WELL...
IT'S PRETTY DARK NOW, SO...
LET'S GO SOMEWHERE QUIET.
SOMEWHERE QUIET?
YEAH.

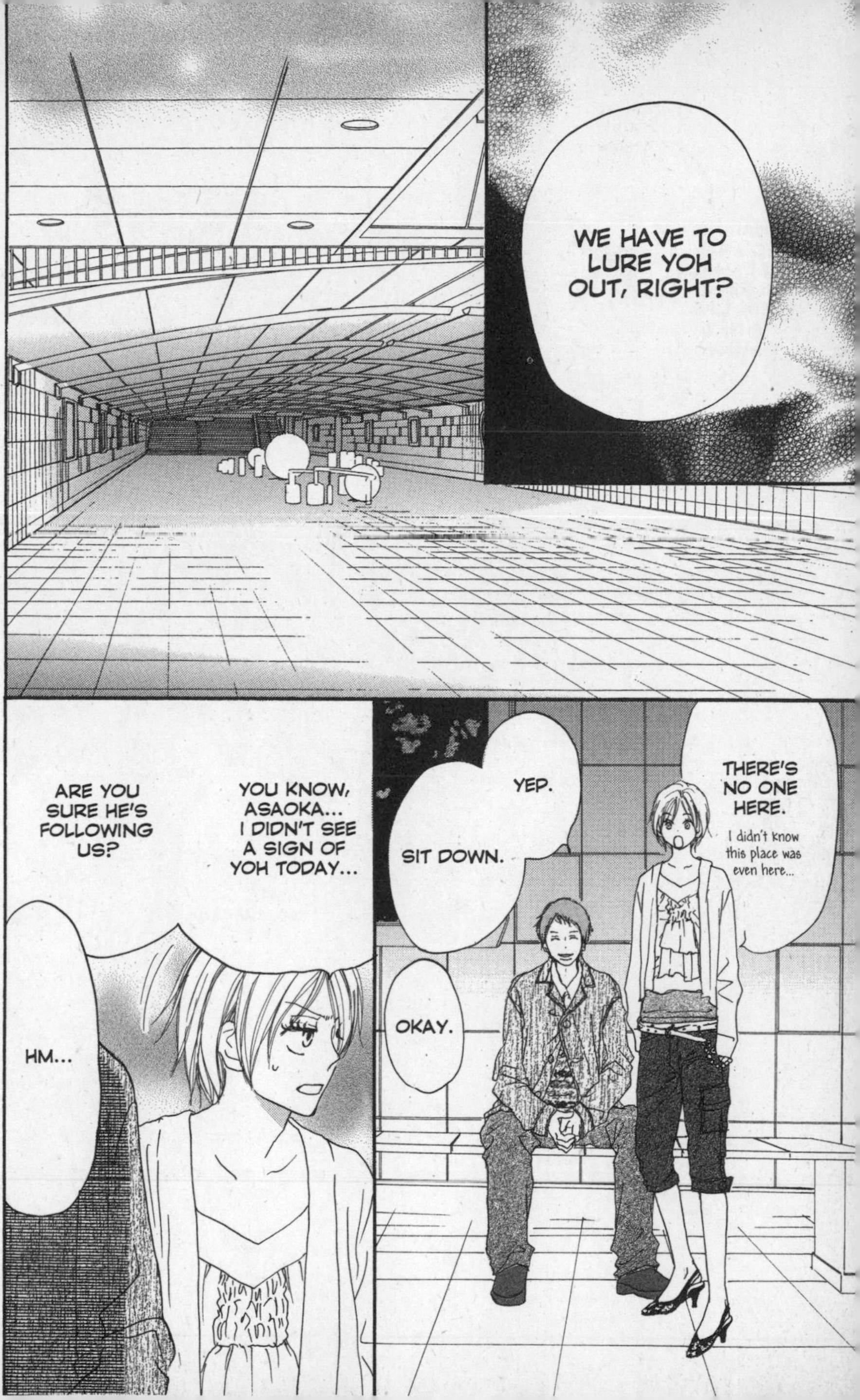
WE HAVE TO LURE YOH OUT, RIGHT?
THERE'S NO ONE HERE.
I didn't know this place was even here...
YEP.
SIT DOWN.
OKAY.
YOU KNOW, ASAOKA... I DIDN'T SEE A SIGN OF YOH TODAY...
ARE YOU SURE HE'S FOLLOWING US?
HM...

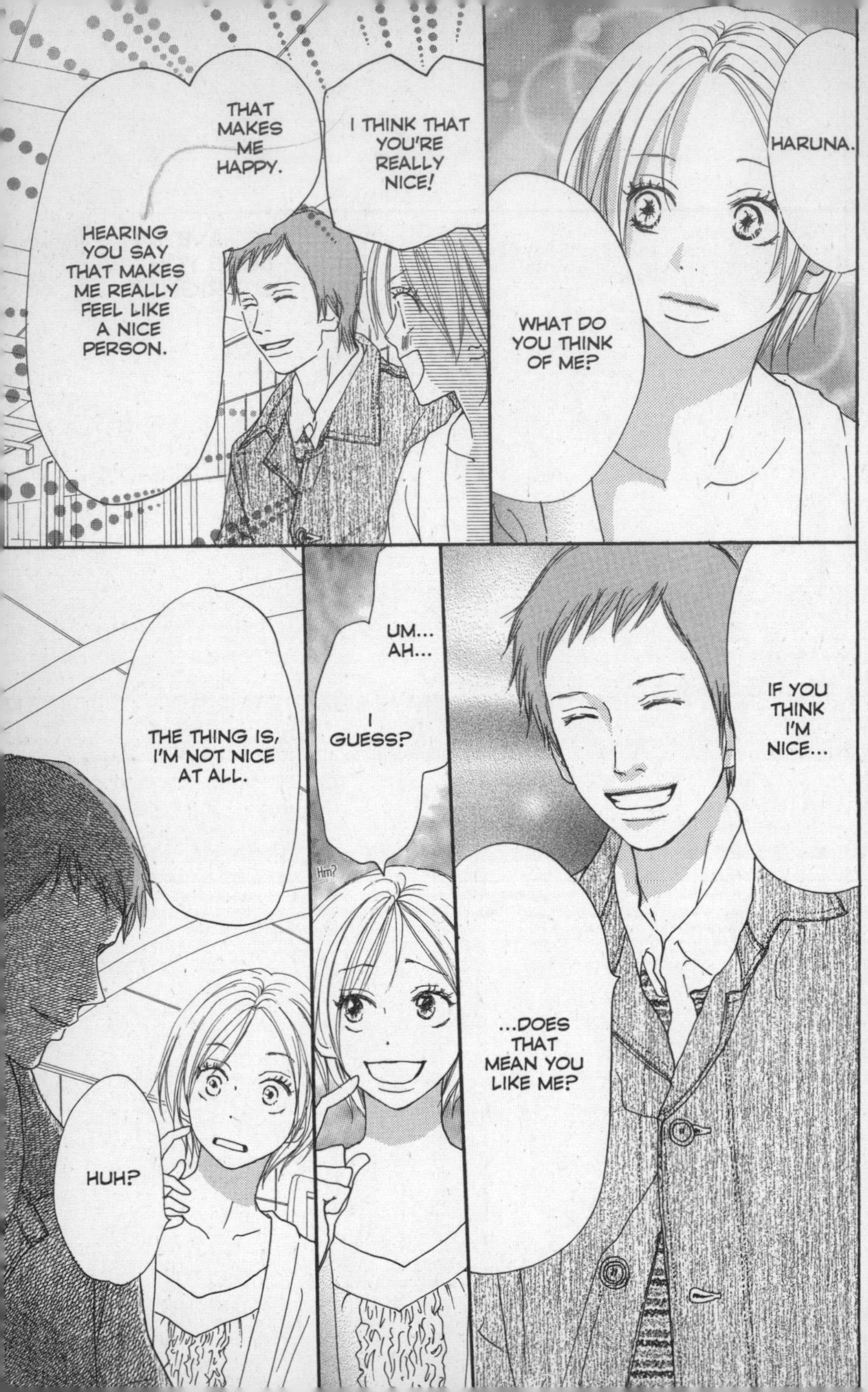
HARUNA.
WHAT DO YOU THINK OF ME?
I THINK THAT YOU'RE REALLY NICE!
THAT MAKES ME HAPPY.
HEARING YOU SAY THAT MAKES ME REALLY FEEL LIKE A NICE PERSON.
IF YOU THINK I'M NICE...
...DOES THAT MEAN YOU LIKE ME?
UM... AH...
I GUESS?
Hm?
THE THING IS, I'M NOT NICE AT ALL.
HUH?

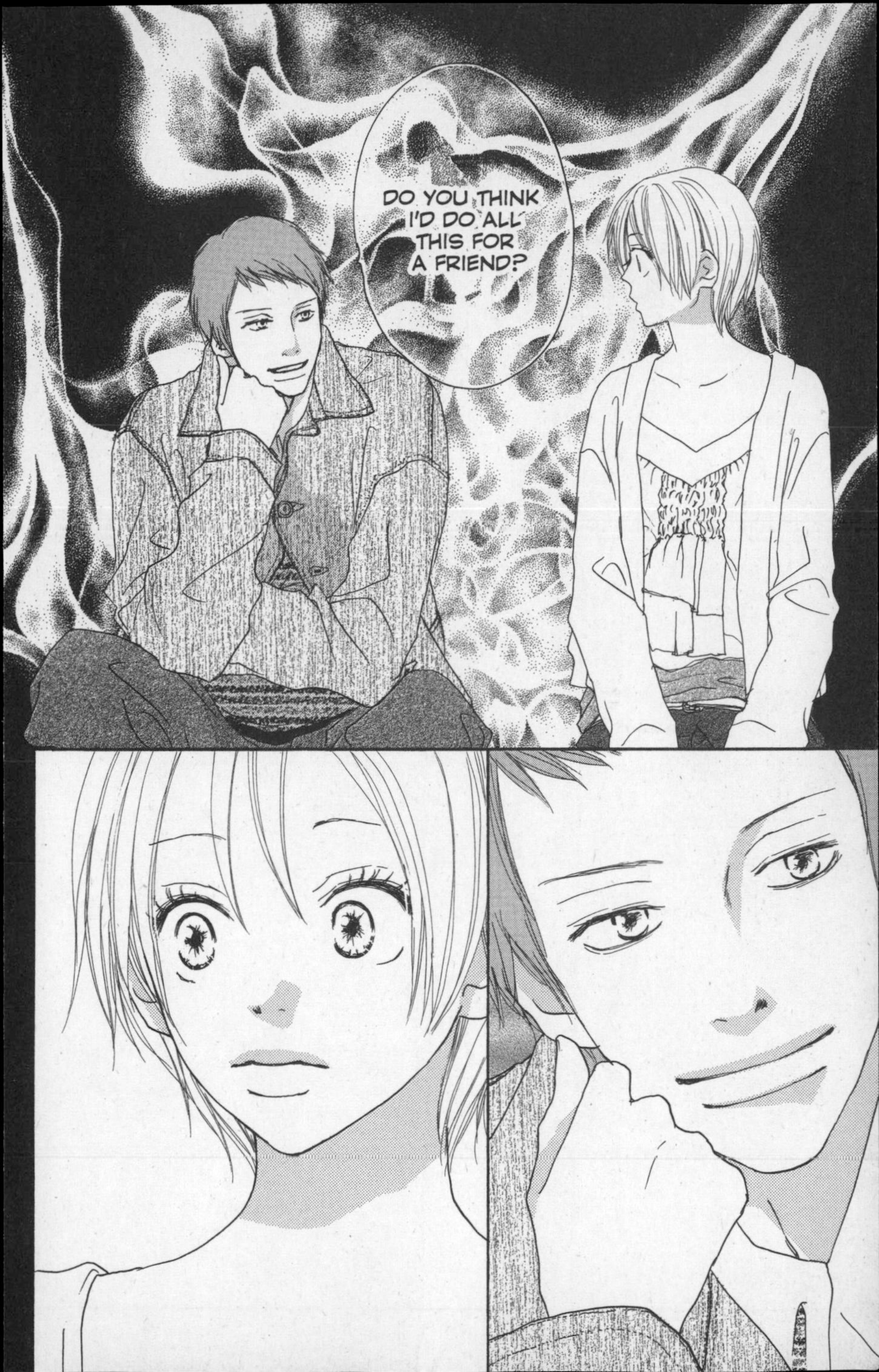
DO YOU THINK
I'D DO ALL
THIS FOR
A FRIEND?

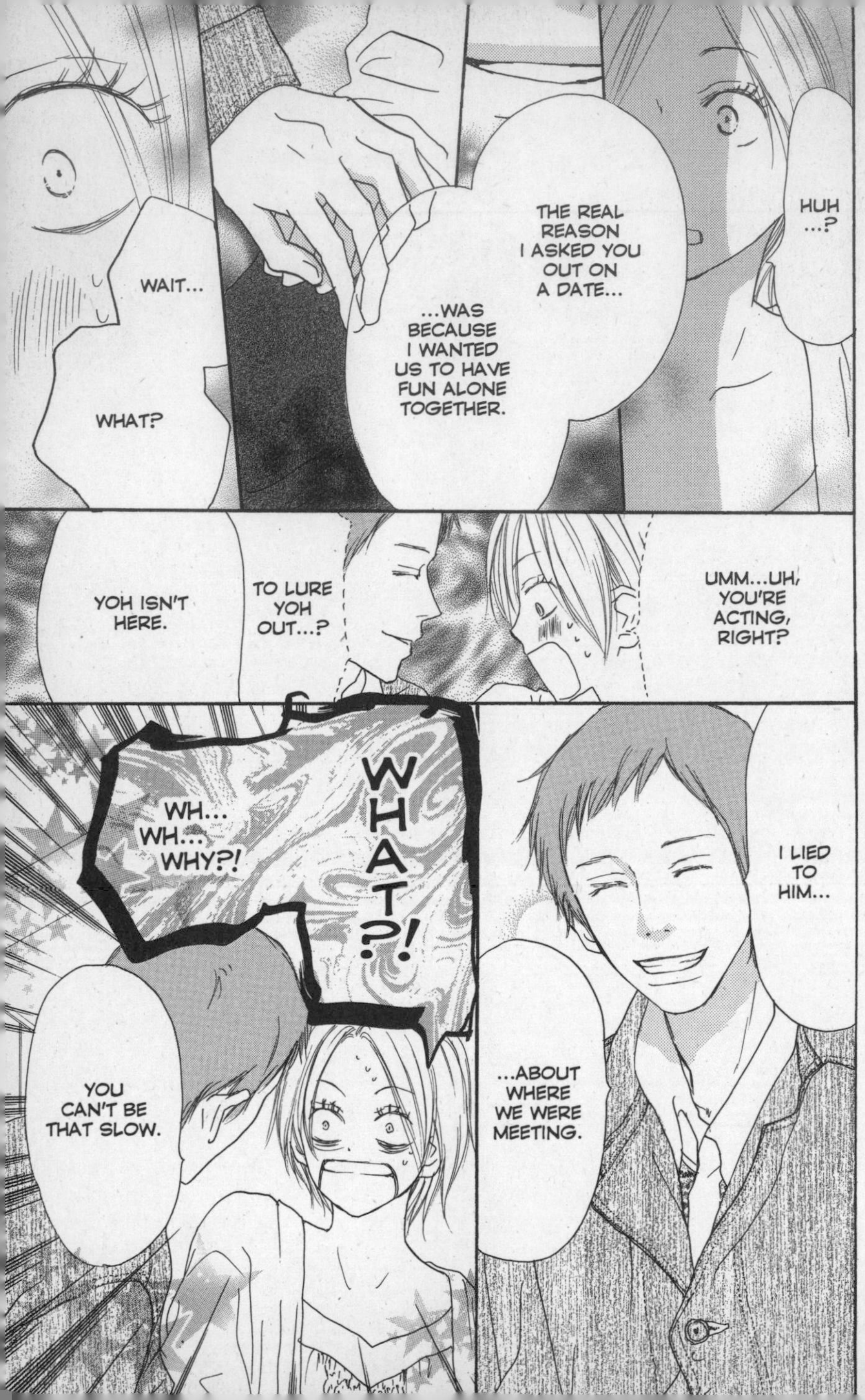
HUH ...?
THE REAL REASON I ASKED YOU OUT ON A DATE...
...WAS BECAUSE I WANTED US TO HAVE FUN ALONE TOGETHER.
WAIT...
WHAT?
UMM...UH, YOU'RE ACTING, RIGHT?
TO LURE YOH OUT...?
YOH ISN'T HERE.
I LIED TO HIM...
...ABOUT WHERE WE WERE MEETING.
WHAT?!
WH... WH... WHY?!
YOU CAN'T BE THAT SLOW.

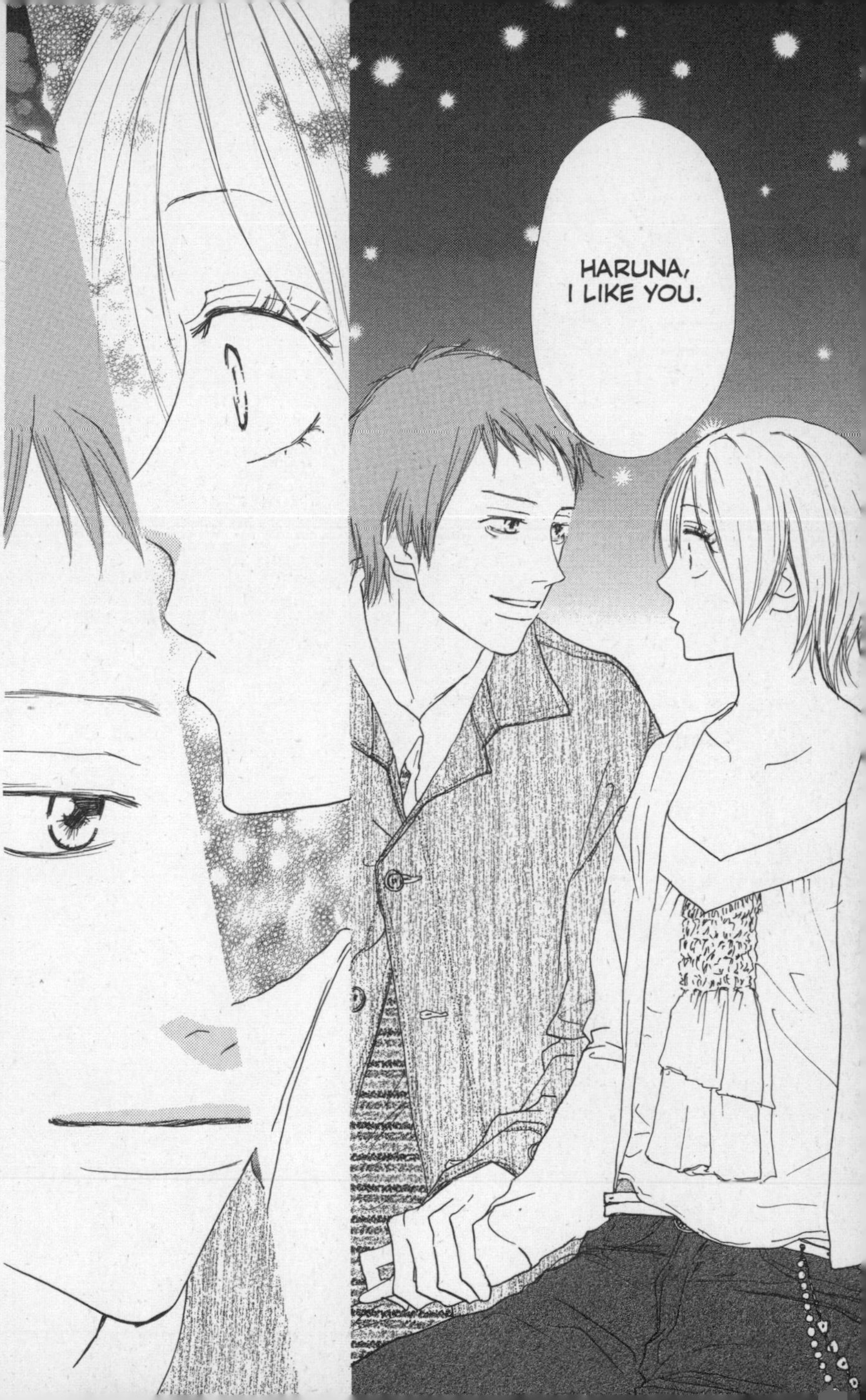
HARUNA,
I LIKE YOU.

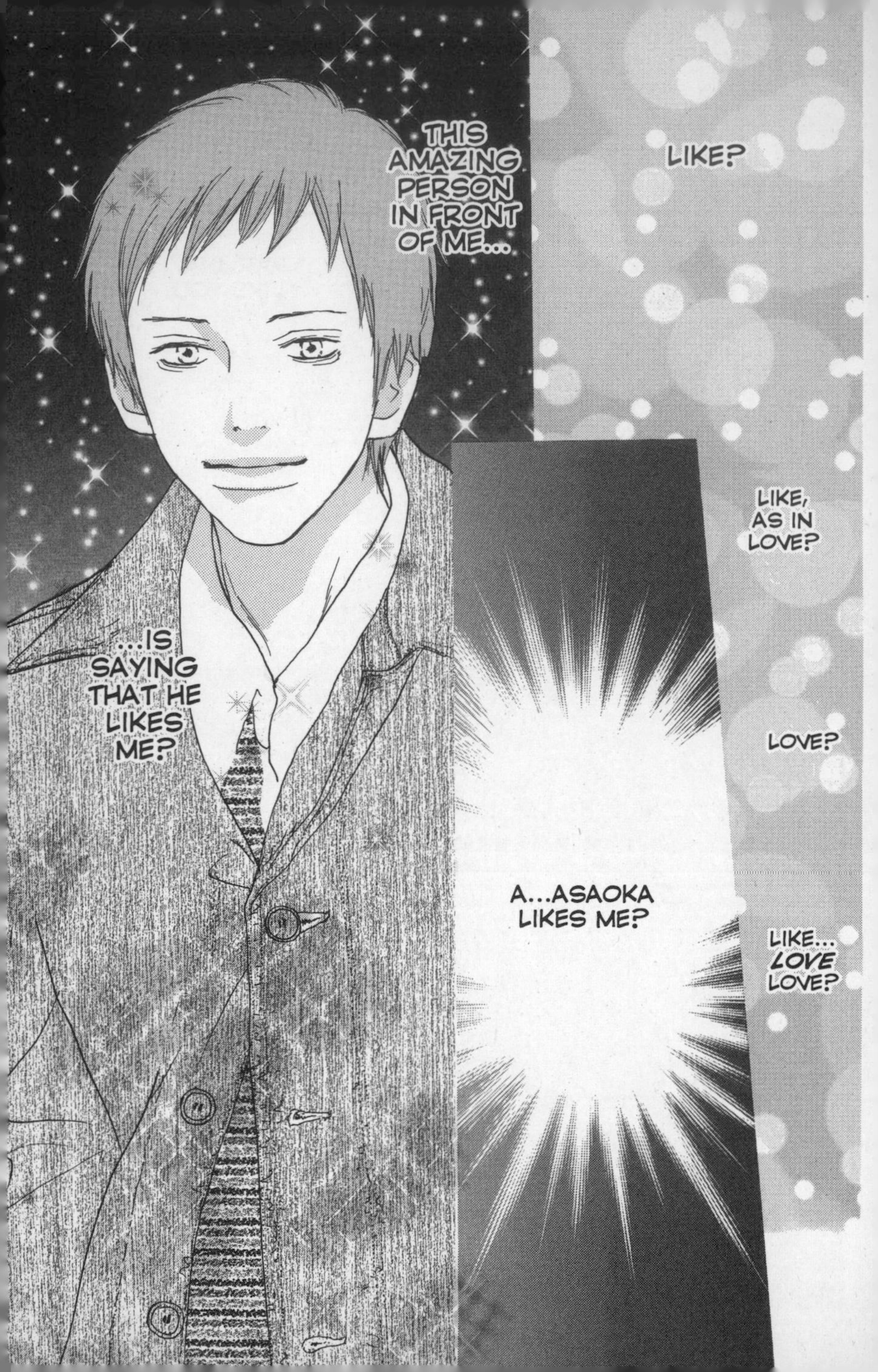
THIS AMAZING PERSON IN FRONT OF ME...
...IS SAYING THAT HE LIKES ME?
A...ASAOKA LIKES ME?
LIKE?
LIKE, AS IN LOVE?
LOVE?
LIKE... LOVE LOVE?

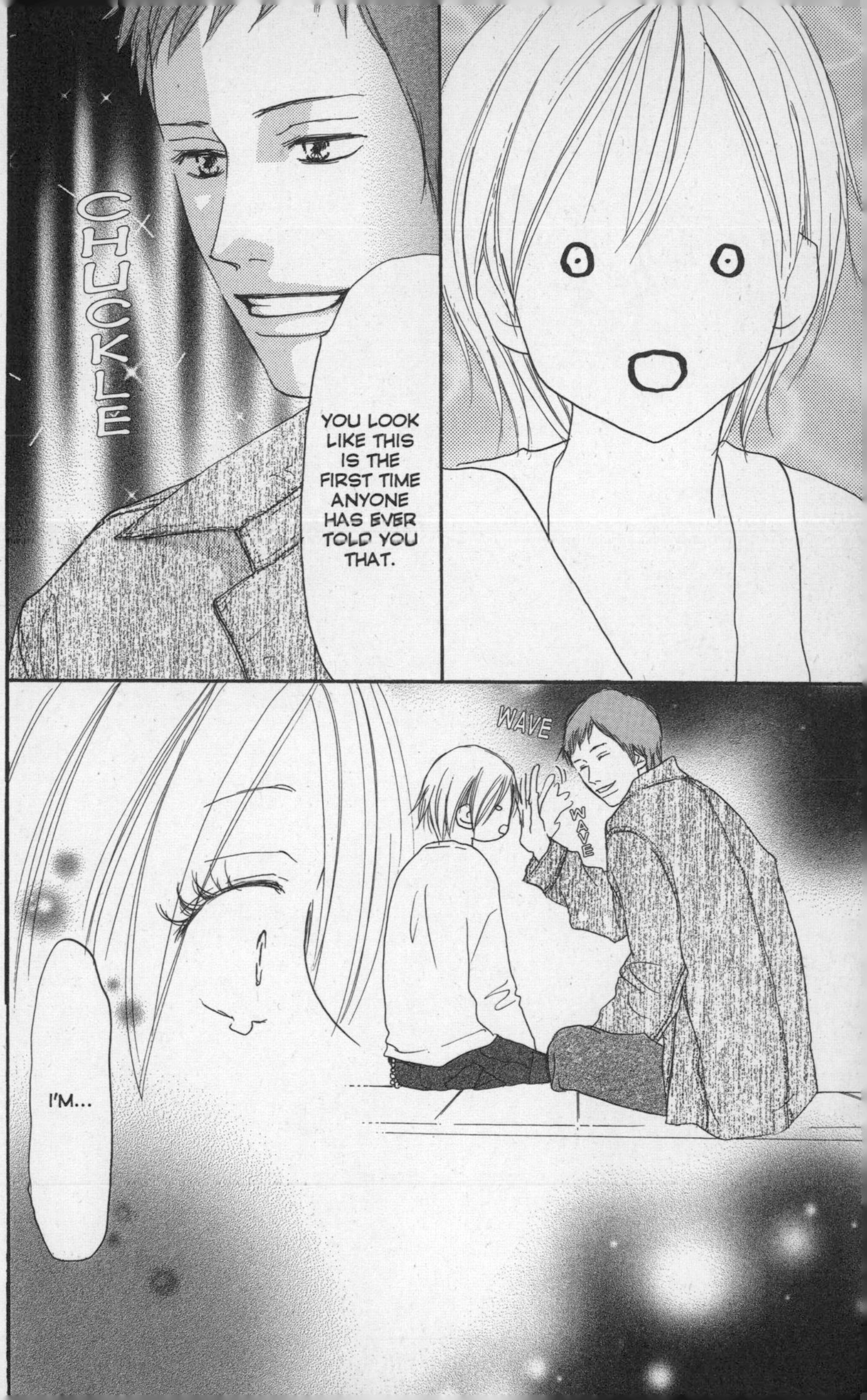
YOU LOOK LIKE THIS IS THE FIRST TIME ANYONE HAS EVER TOLD YOU THAT.
CHUCKLE
WAVE
WAVE
I'M...

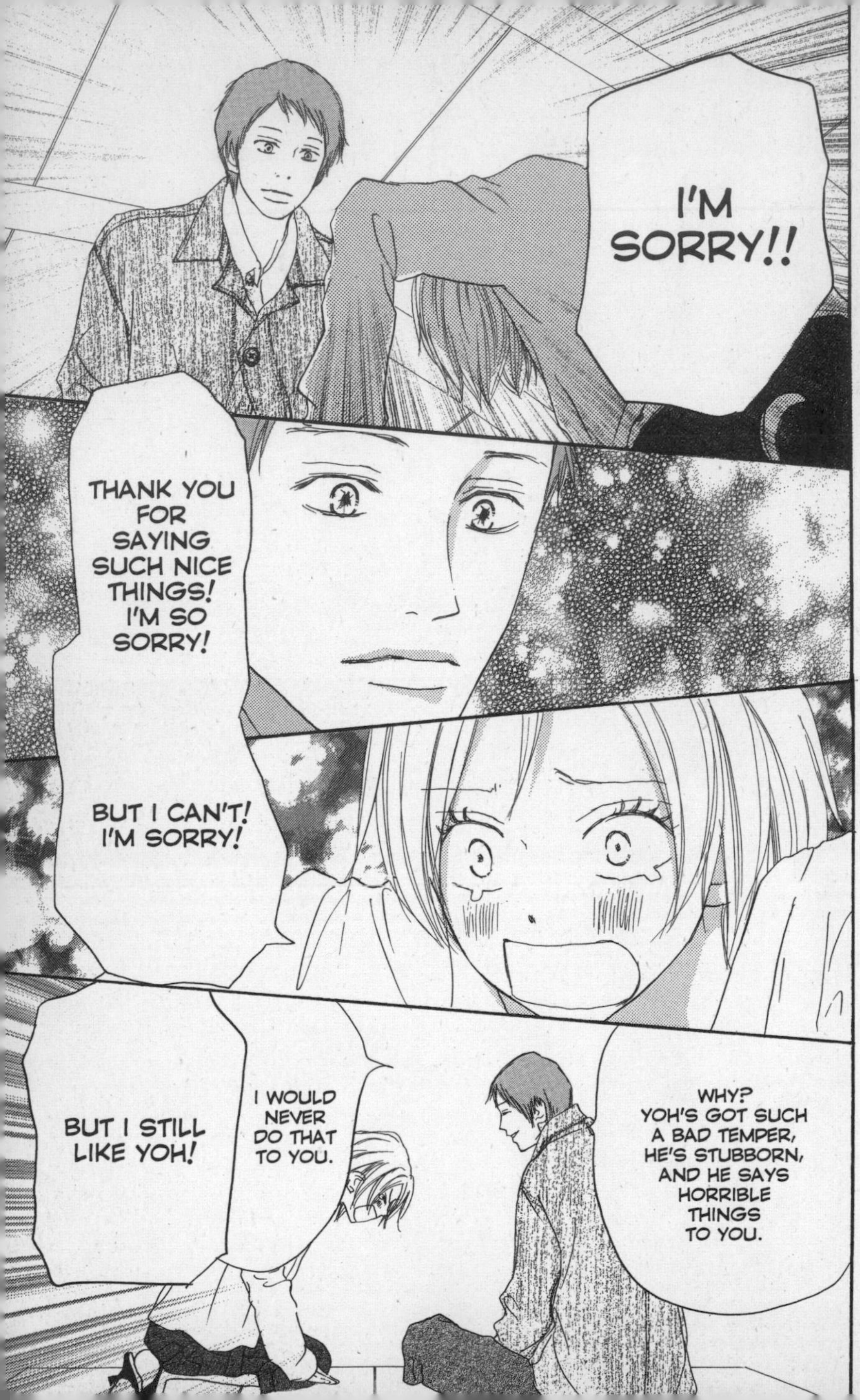
I'M SORRY!!
THANK YOU FOR SAYING SUCH NICE THINGS! I'M SO SORRY!
BUT I CAN'T! I'M SORRY!
WHY? YOH'S GOT SUCH A BAD TEMPER, HE'S STUBBORN, AND HE SAYS HORRIBLE THINGS TO YOU.
I WOULD NEVER DO THAT TO YOU.
BUT I STILL LIKE YOH!

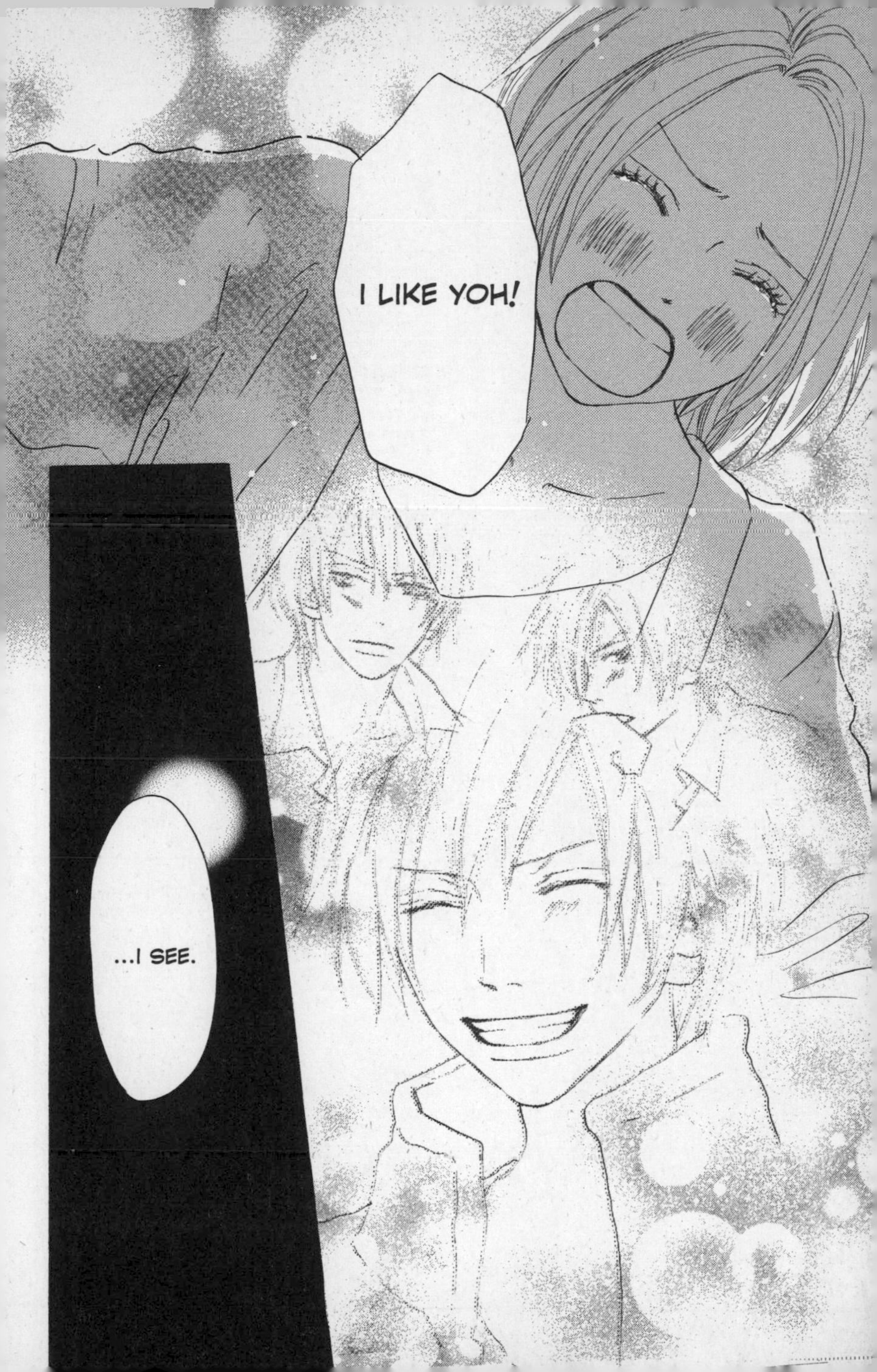
I LIKE YOH!
...I SEE.

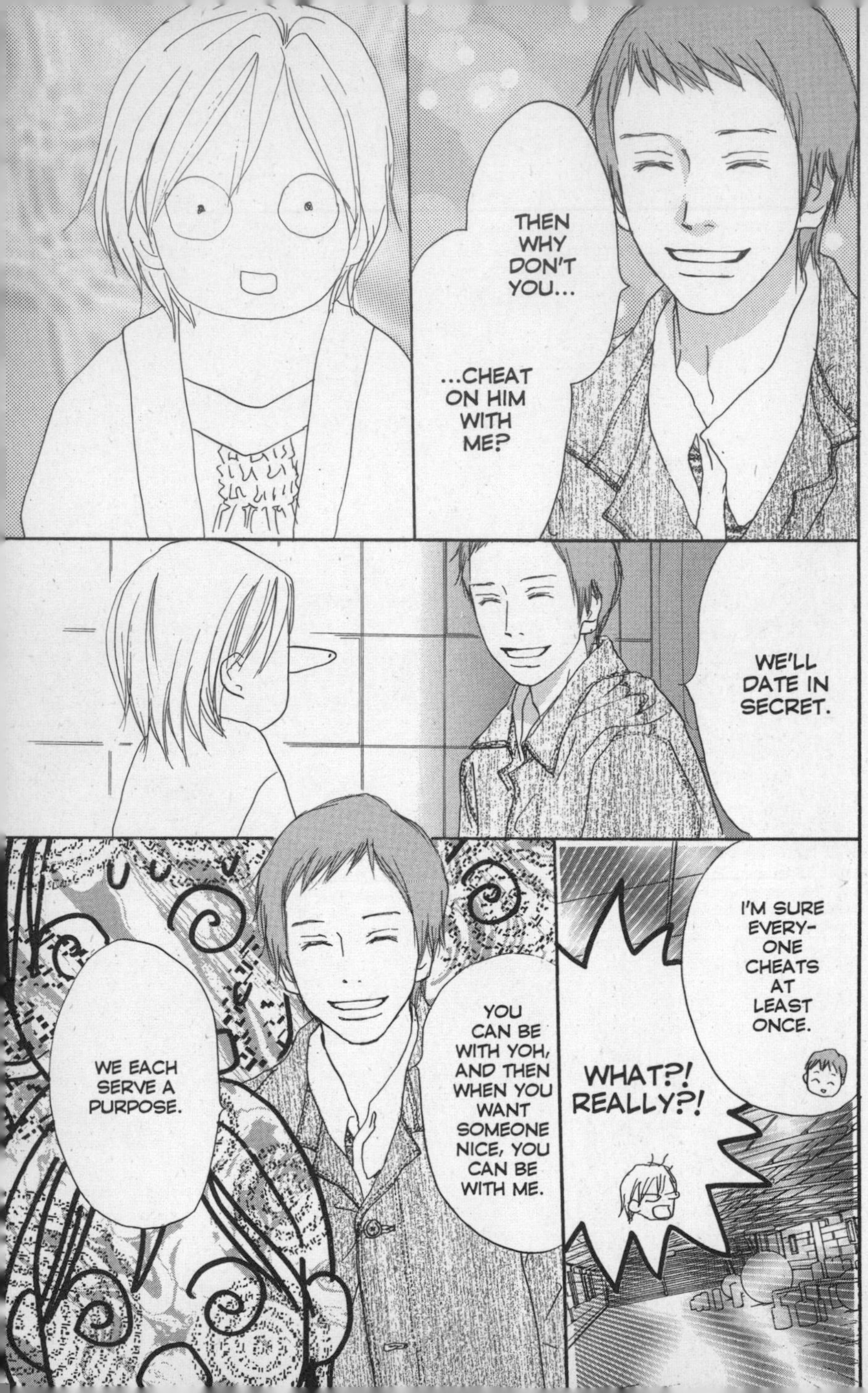
THEN WHY DON'T YOU...
...CHEAT ON HIM WITH ME?
WE'LL DATE IN SECRET.
I'M SURE EVERY-ONE CHEATS AT LEAST ONCE.
WHAT?! REALLY?!
YOU CAN BE WITH YOH, AND THEN WHEN YOU WANT SOMEONE NICE, YOU CAN BE WITH ME.
WE EACH SERVE A PURPOSE.

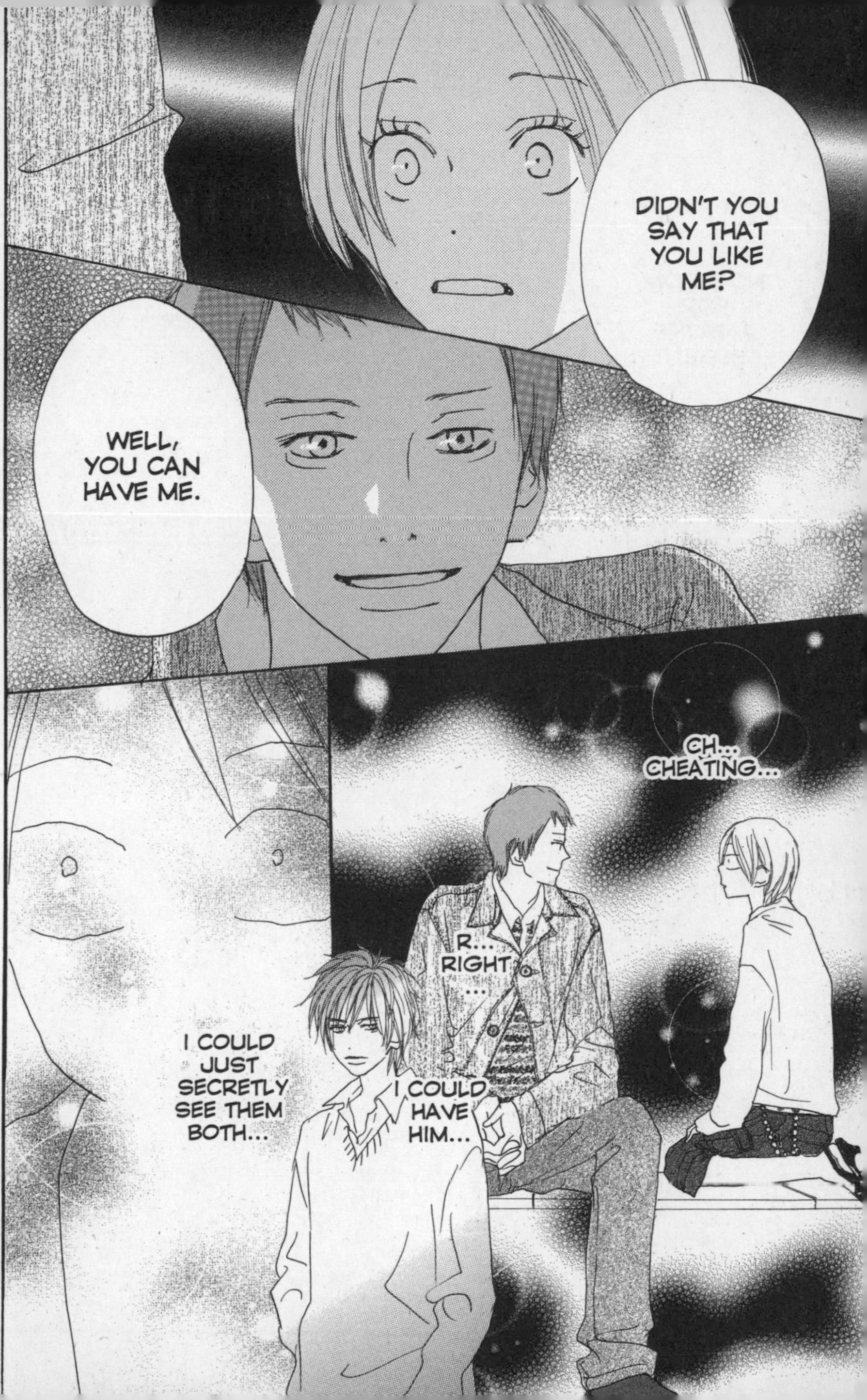
DIDN'T YOU SAY THAT YOU LIKE ME?
WELL, YOU CAN HAVE ME.
CH... CHEATING...
R... RIGHT...
I COULD HAVE HIM...
I COULD JUST SECRETLY SEE THEM BOTH...

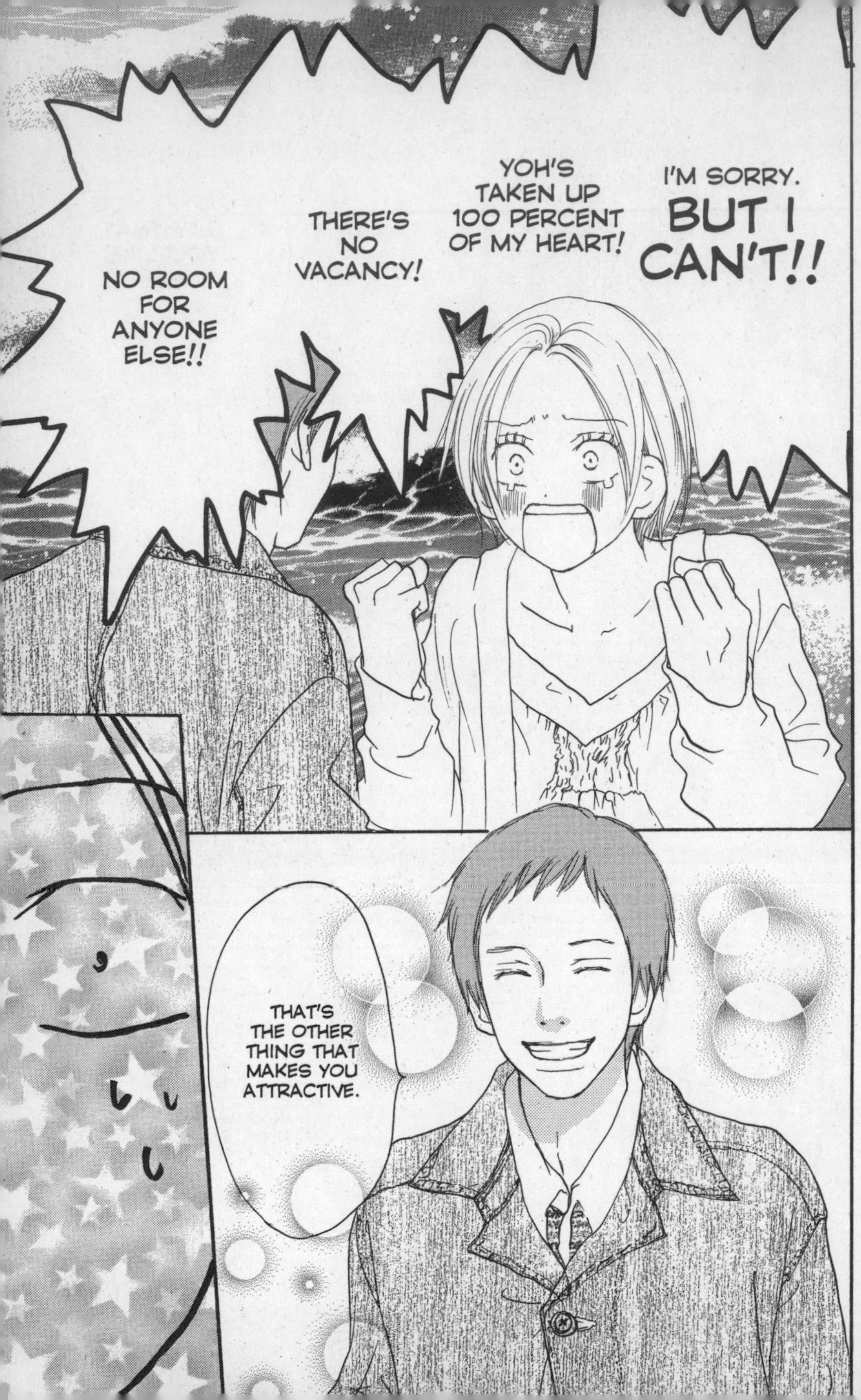
I'M SORRY. BUT I CAN'T!!
YOH'S TAKEN UP 100 PERCENT OF MY HEART!
THERE'S NO VACANCY!
NO ROOM FOR ANYONE ELSE!!
THAT'S THE OTHER THING THAT MAKES YOU ATTRACTIVE.

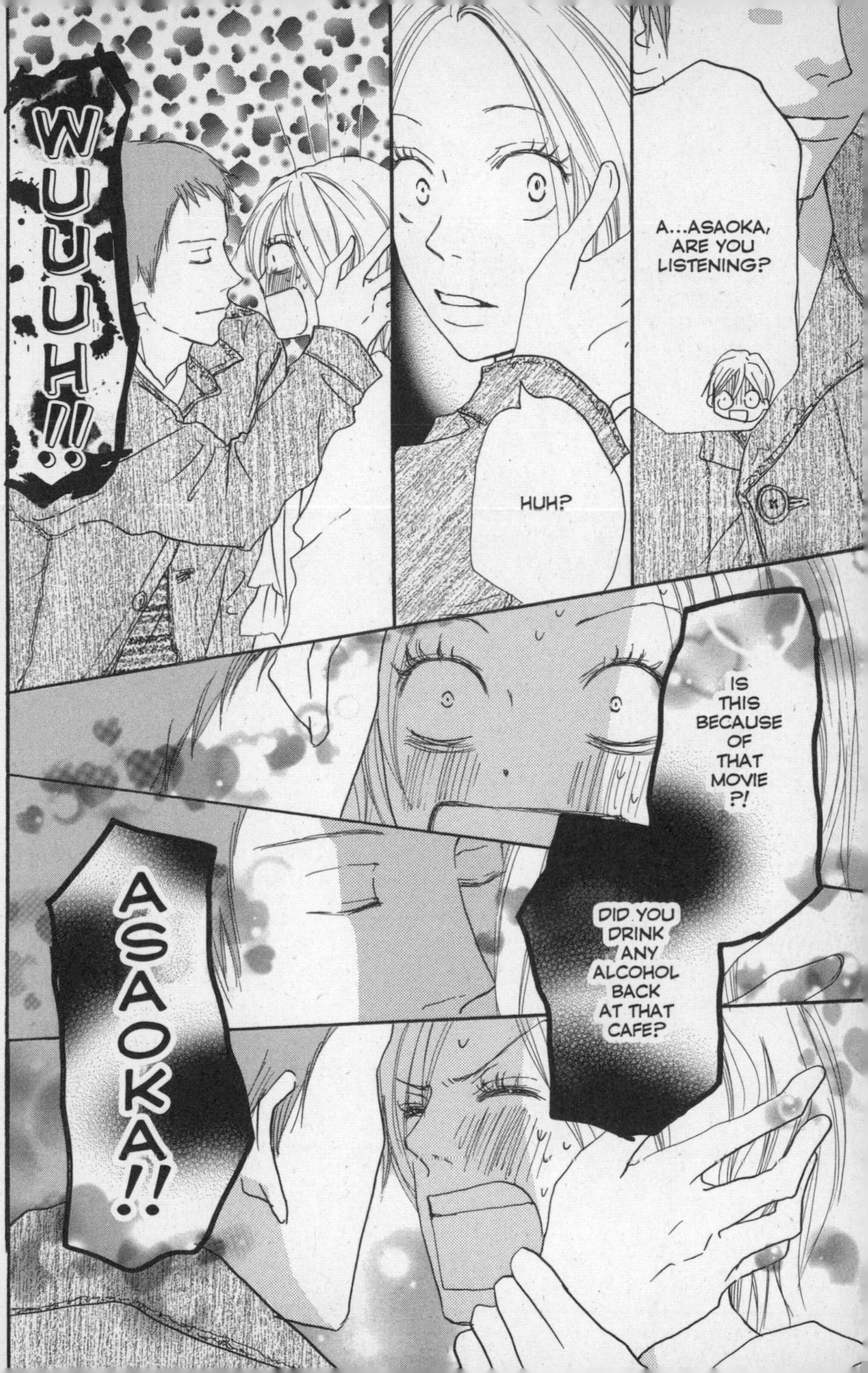
A...ASAOKA, ARE YOU LISTENING?
HUH?
WUUUH!!
IS THIS BECAUSE OF THAT MOVIE?!
DID YOU DRINK ANY ALCOHOL BACK AT THAT CAFE?
ASAOKA!!

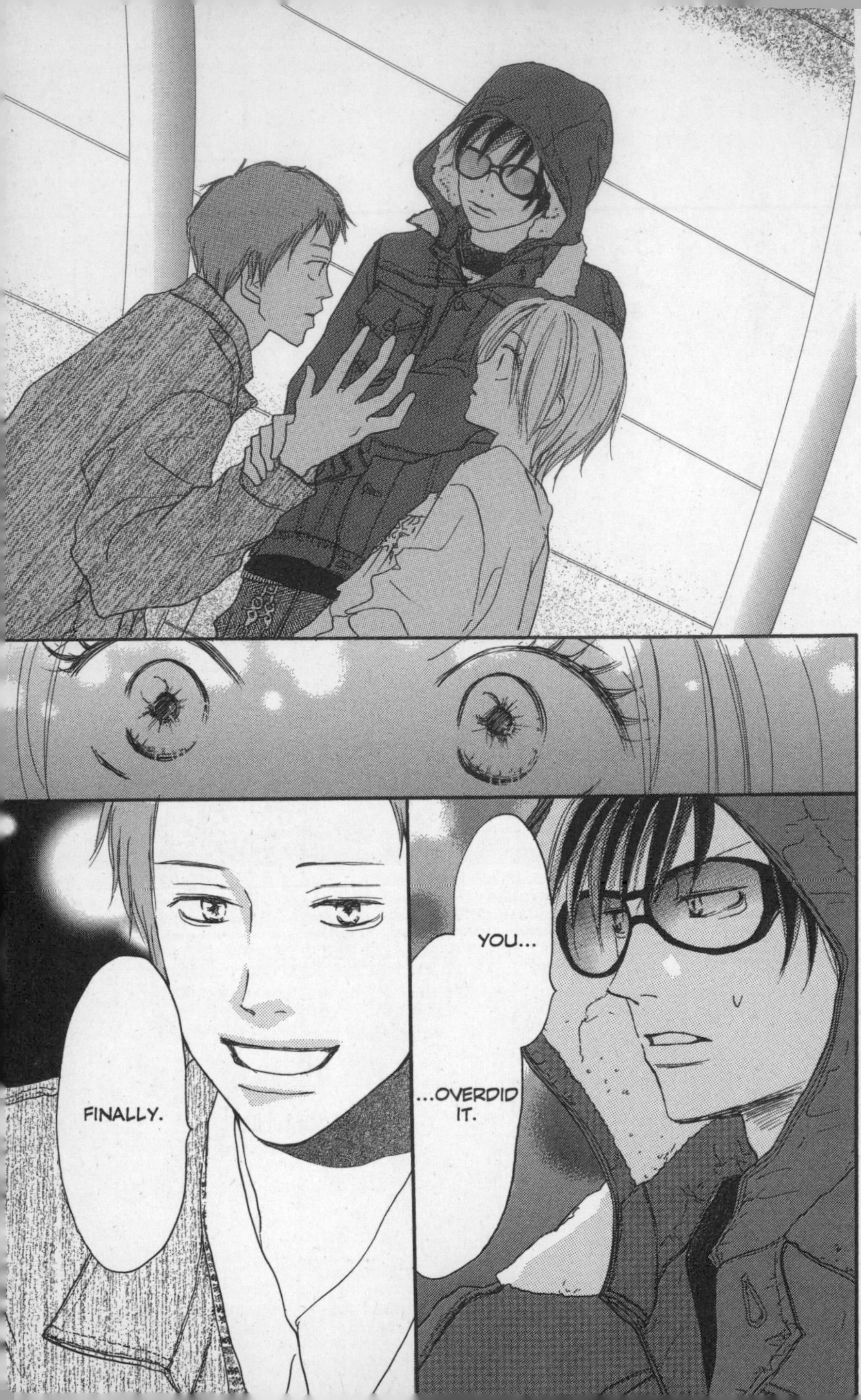
YOU...
...OVERDID IT.
FINALLY.

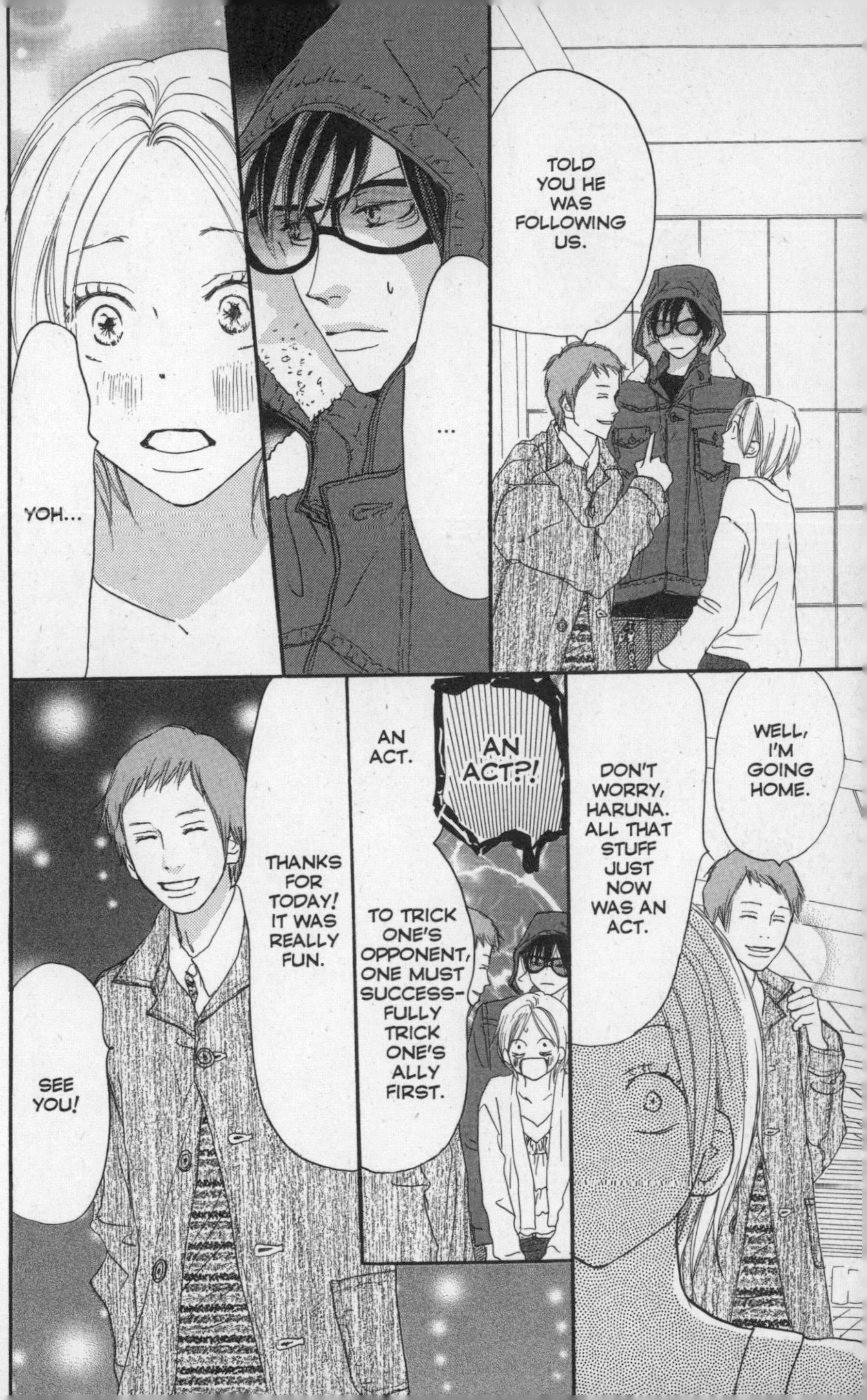
TOLD YOU HE WAS FOLLOWING US.
...
YOH...
WELL, I'M GOING HOME.
DON'T WORRY, HARUNA. ALL THAT STUFF JUST NOW WAS AN ACT.
AN ACT?!
AN ACT.
TO TRICK ONE'S OPPONENT, ONE MUST SUCCESSFULLY TRICK ONE'S ALLY FIRST.
THANKS FOR TODAY! IT WAS REALLY FUN.
SEE YOU!

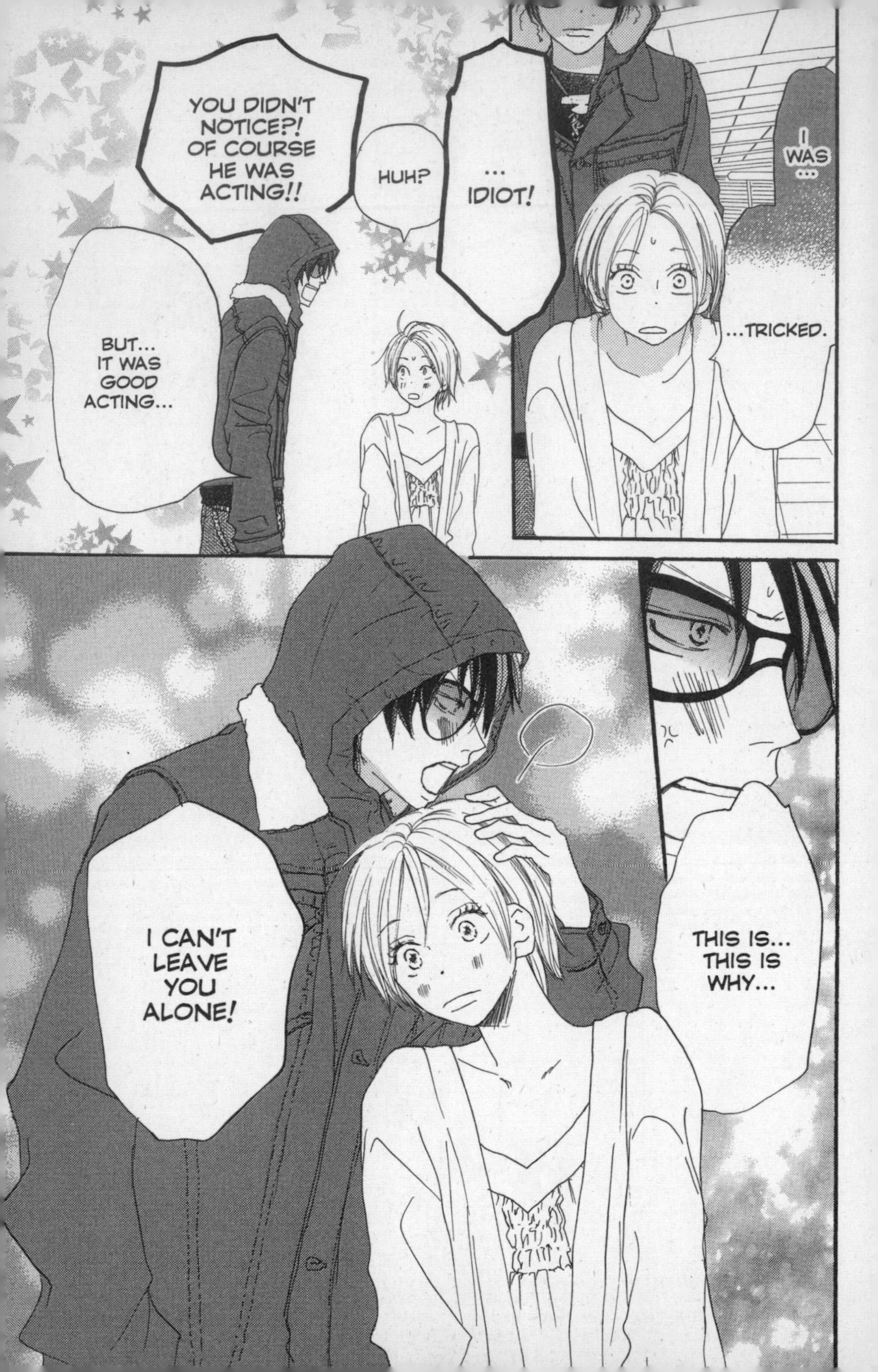
I WAS...
...TRICKED.
...IDIOT!
HUH?
YOU DIDN'T NOTICE?! OF COURSE HE WAS ACTING!!
BUT... IT WAS GOOD ACTING...
THIS IS... THIS IS WHY...
I CAN'T LEAVE YOU ALONE!

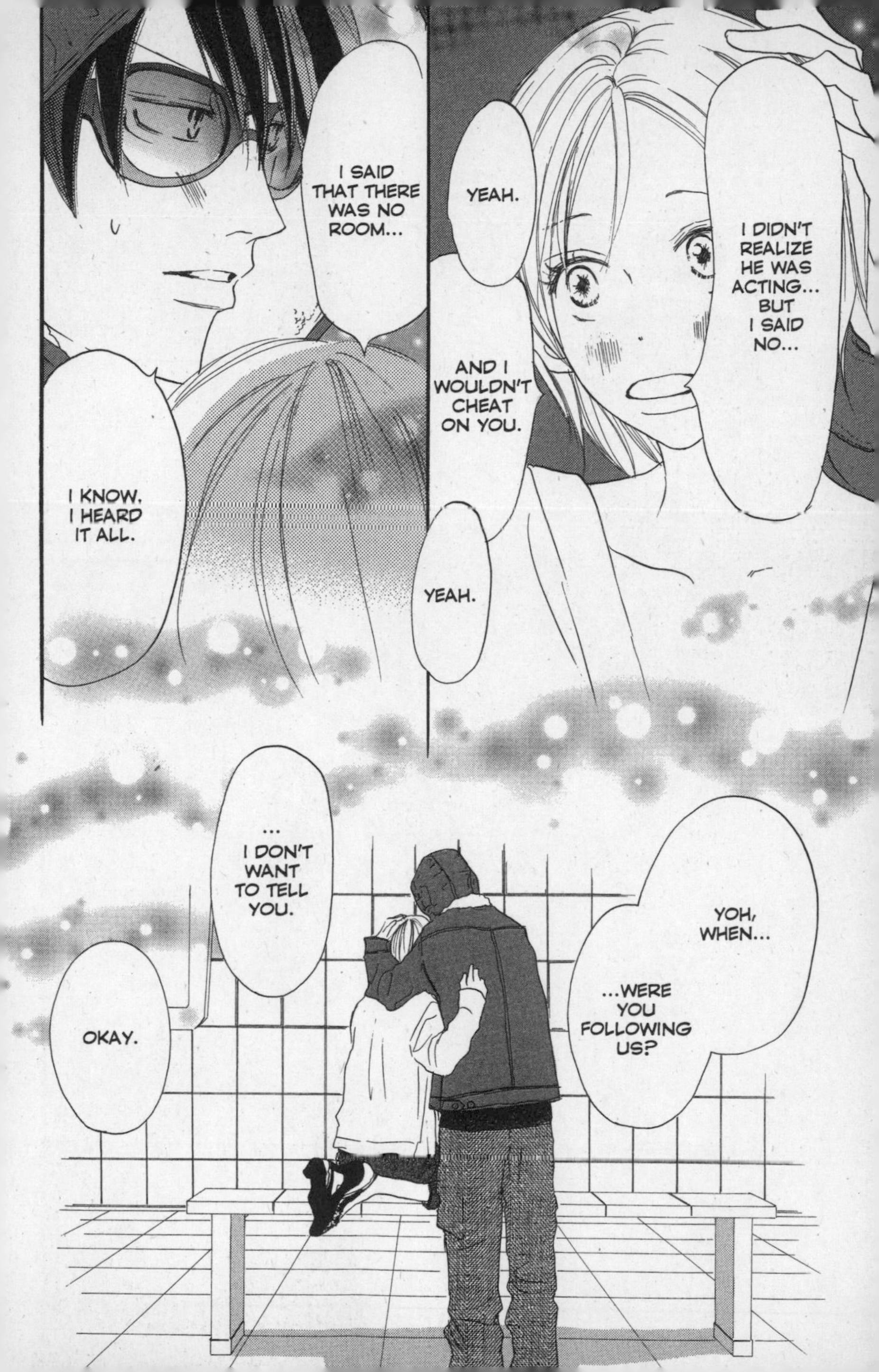
I DIDN'T REALIZE HE WAS ACTING... BUT I SAID NO...
YEAH.
AND I WOULDN'T CHEAT ON YOU.
YEAH.
I SAID THAT THERE WAS NO ROOM...
I KNOW, I HEARD IT ALL.
YOH, WHEN...
...WERE YOU FOLLOWING US?
... I DON'T WANT TO TELL YOU.
OKAY.

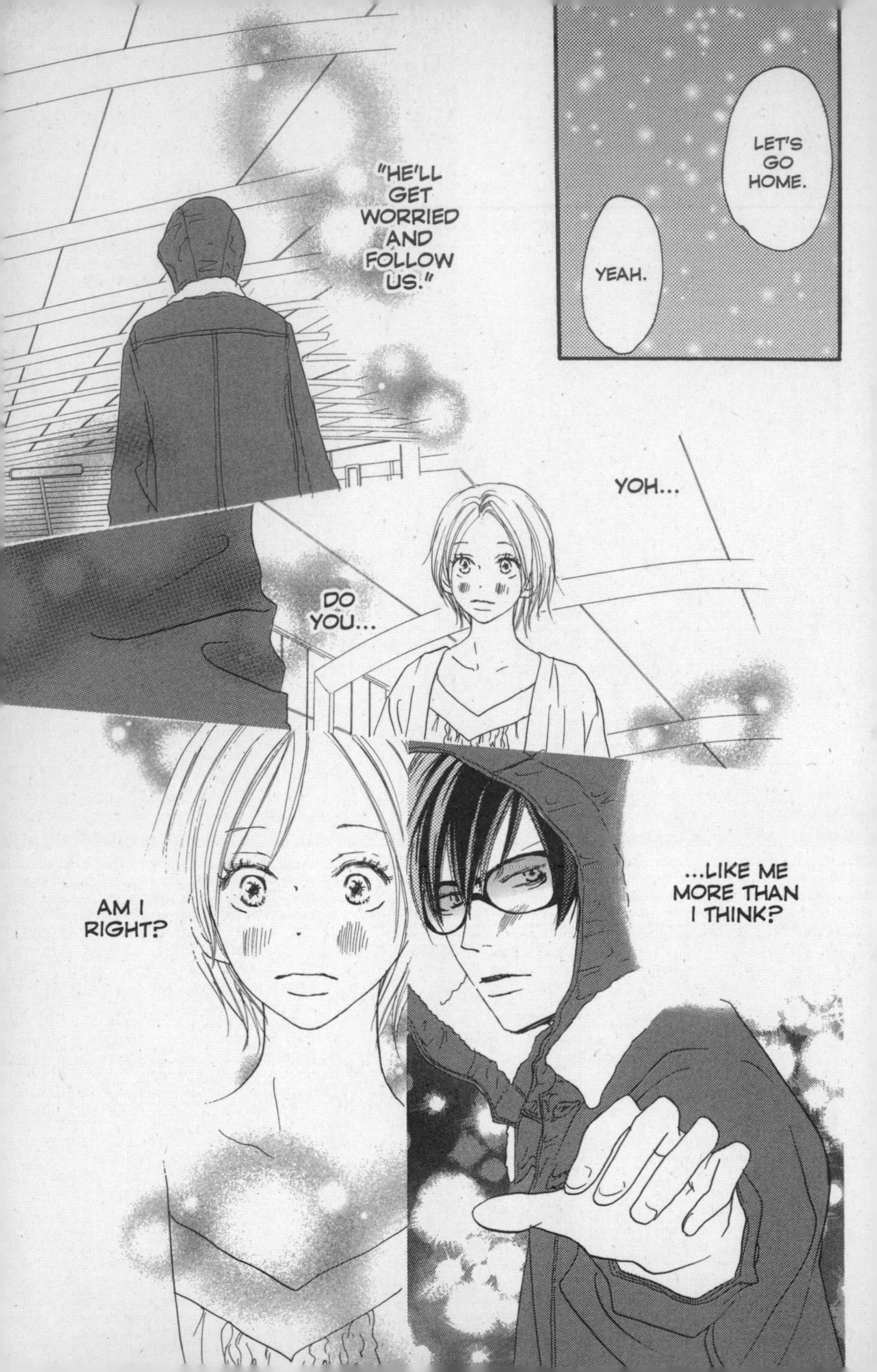
LET'S GO HOME.
YEAH.
"HE'LL GET WORRIED AND FOLLOW US."
YOH...
DO YOU...
...LIKE ME MORE THAN I THINK?
AM I RIGHT?

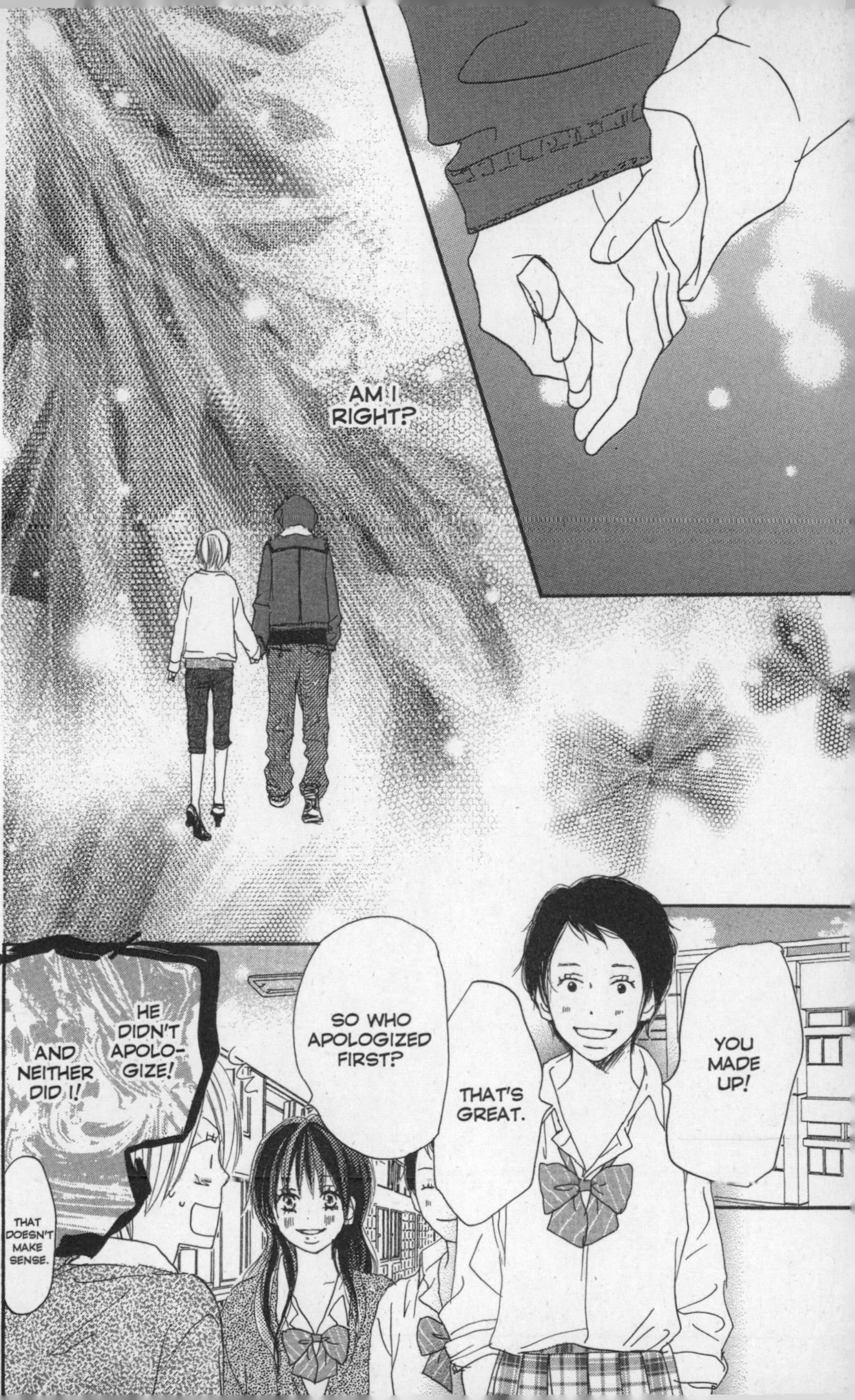
AM I RIGHT?
YOU MADE UP!
THAT'S GREAT.
SO WHO APOLOGIZED FIRST?
HE DIDN'T APOLO-GIZE!
AND NEITHER DID I!
THAT DOESN'T MAKE SENSE.

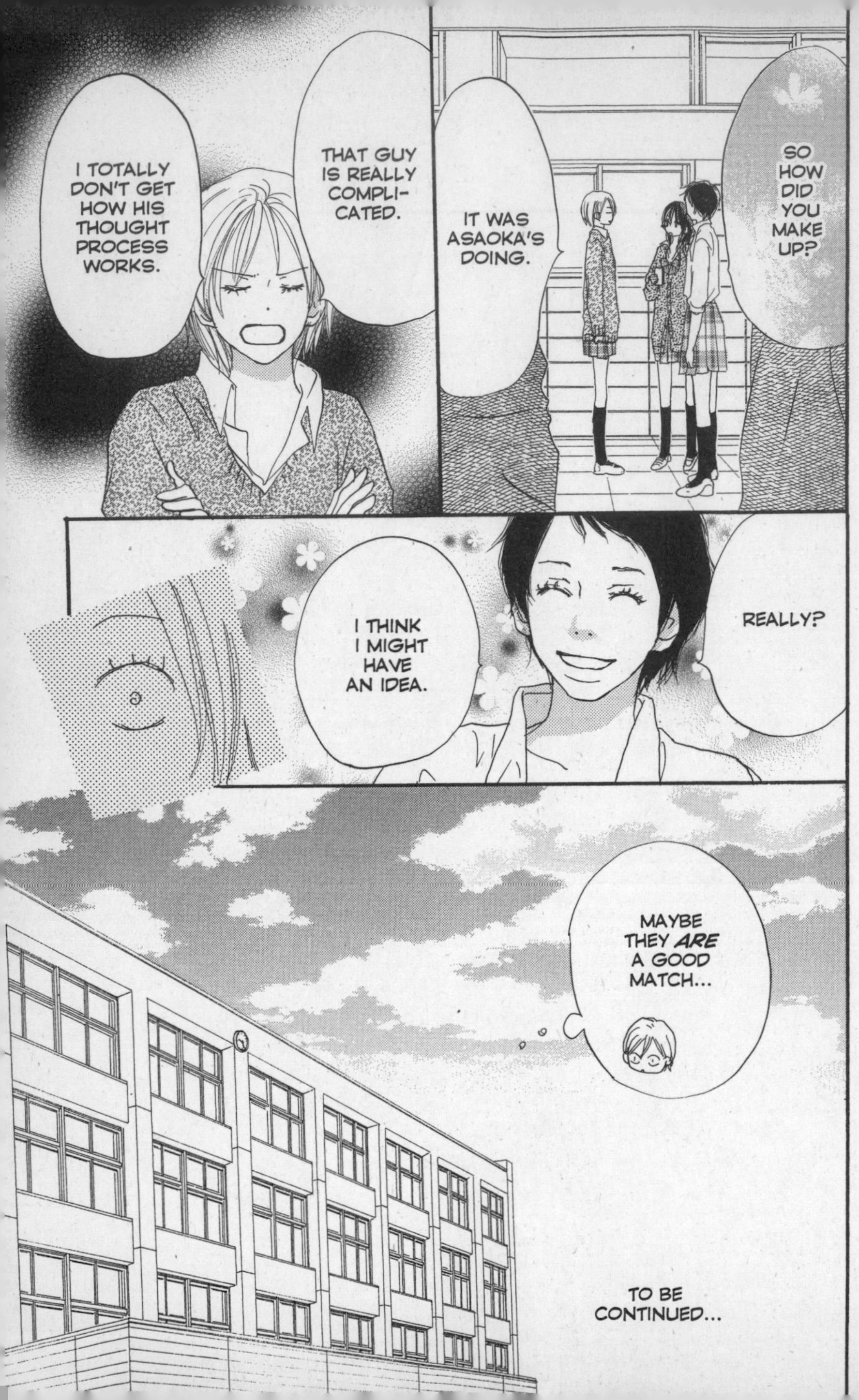
SO HOW DID YOU MAKE UP?
IT WAS ASAOKA'S DOING.
THAT GUY IS REALLY COMPLI-CATED.
I TOTALLY DON'T GET HOW HIS THOUGHT PROCESS WORKS.
REALLY?
I THINK I MIGHT HAVE AN IDEA.
MAYBE THEY *ARE* A GOOD MATCH...
TO BE CONTINUED...

My cell phone charger is broken, so I have to
go to the store... I entered my cell PIN wrong
three times, so I have to go to the store... That's
what I've been telling myself for a year now!
I'm used to not having a cell phone, but it is
inconvenient.

– Kazune Kawahara

Kazune Kawahara is from Hokkaido prefecture
and was born on March 11th (a Pisces!). She
made her manga debut at age 18 with *Kare no
Ichiban Sukina Hito* (His Most Favorite Person).
Her other works include *Sensei!*, serialized in
Bessatsu Margaret magazine. Her hobby is
interior redecorating.

HIGH SCHOOL DEBUT
VOL. 5
Shojo Beat Edition

STORY & ART BY
KAZUNE KAWAHARA

Translation & Adaptation/Gemma Collinge
Touch-up Art & Lettering/Mark Griffin, HudsonYards
Design/Izumi Hirayama
Editor/Amy Yu

VP, Production/Alvin Lu
VP, Sales & Product Marketing/Gonzalo Ferreyra
VP, Creative/Linda Espinosa
Publisher/Hyoe Narita

KOKO DEBUT © 2003 by Kazune Kawahara
All rights reserved.
First published in Japan in 2003 by SHUEISHA Inc., Tokyo.
English translation rights arranged by SHUEISHA Inc.

Printed in Canada

Published by VIZ Media, LLC
P.O. Box 77010
San Francisco, CA 94107

10 9 8 7 6 5 4 3 2
First printing, September 2008
Second printing, April 2010

www.viz.com   www.shojobeat.com

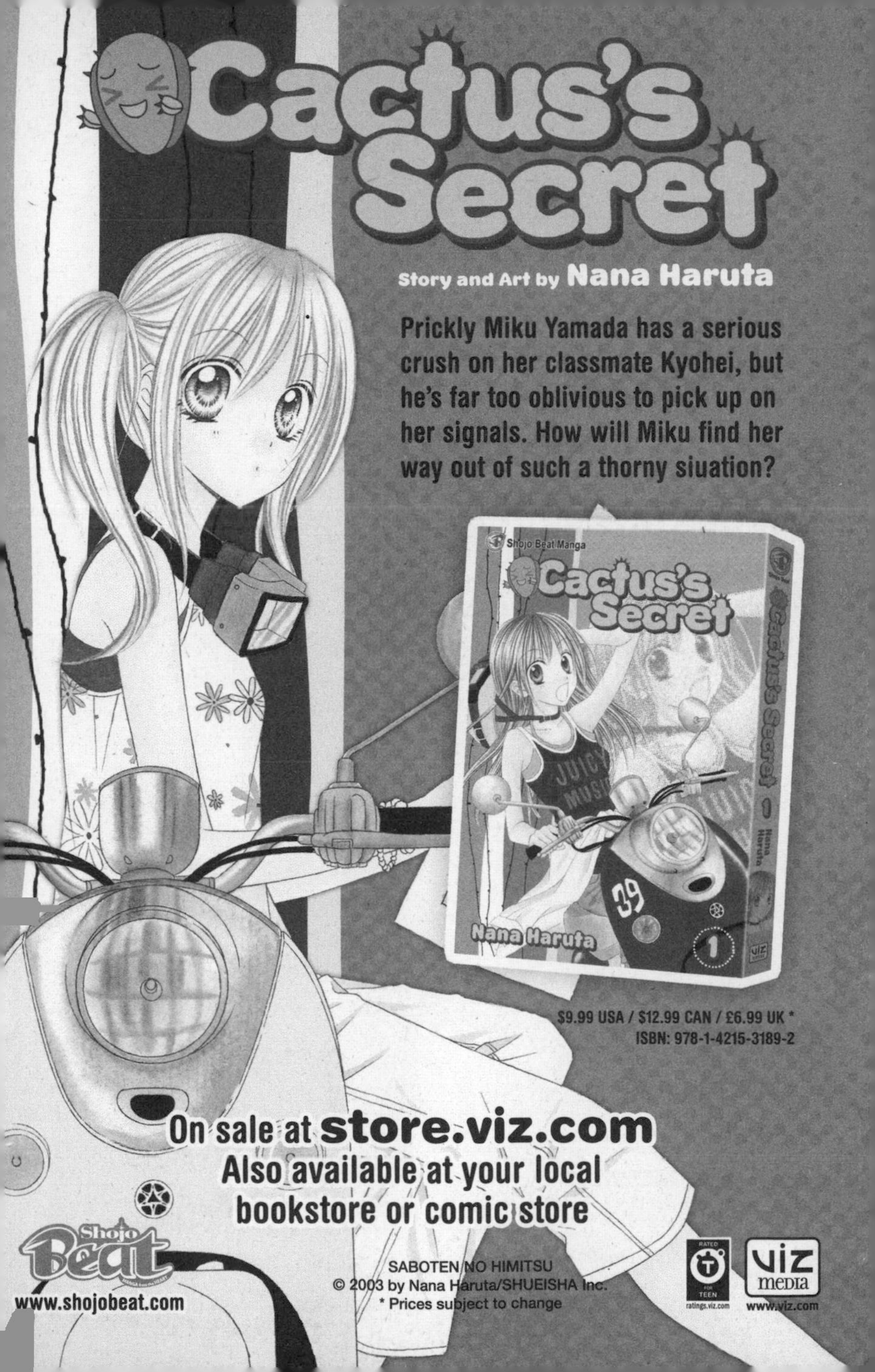
Cactus's Secret
Story and Art by Nana Haruta
Prickly Miku Yamada has a serious crush on her classmate Kyohei, but he's far too oblivious to pick up on her signals. How will Miku find her way out of such a thorny siuation?
Shojo Beat Manga
Cactus's Secret
Nana Haruta
1
$9.99 USA / $12.99 CAN / £6.99 UK *
ISBN: 978-1-4215-3189-2
On sale at store.viz.com
Also available at your local bookstore or comic store
Shojo Beat
www.shojobeat.com
SABOTEN NO HIMITSU
© 2003 by Nana Haruta/SHUEISHA Inc.
* Prices subject to change
RATED T FOR TEEN
ratings.viz.com
VIZ media
www.viz.com

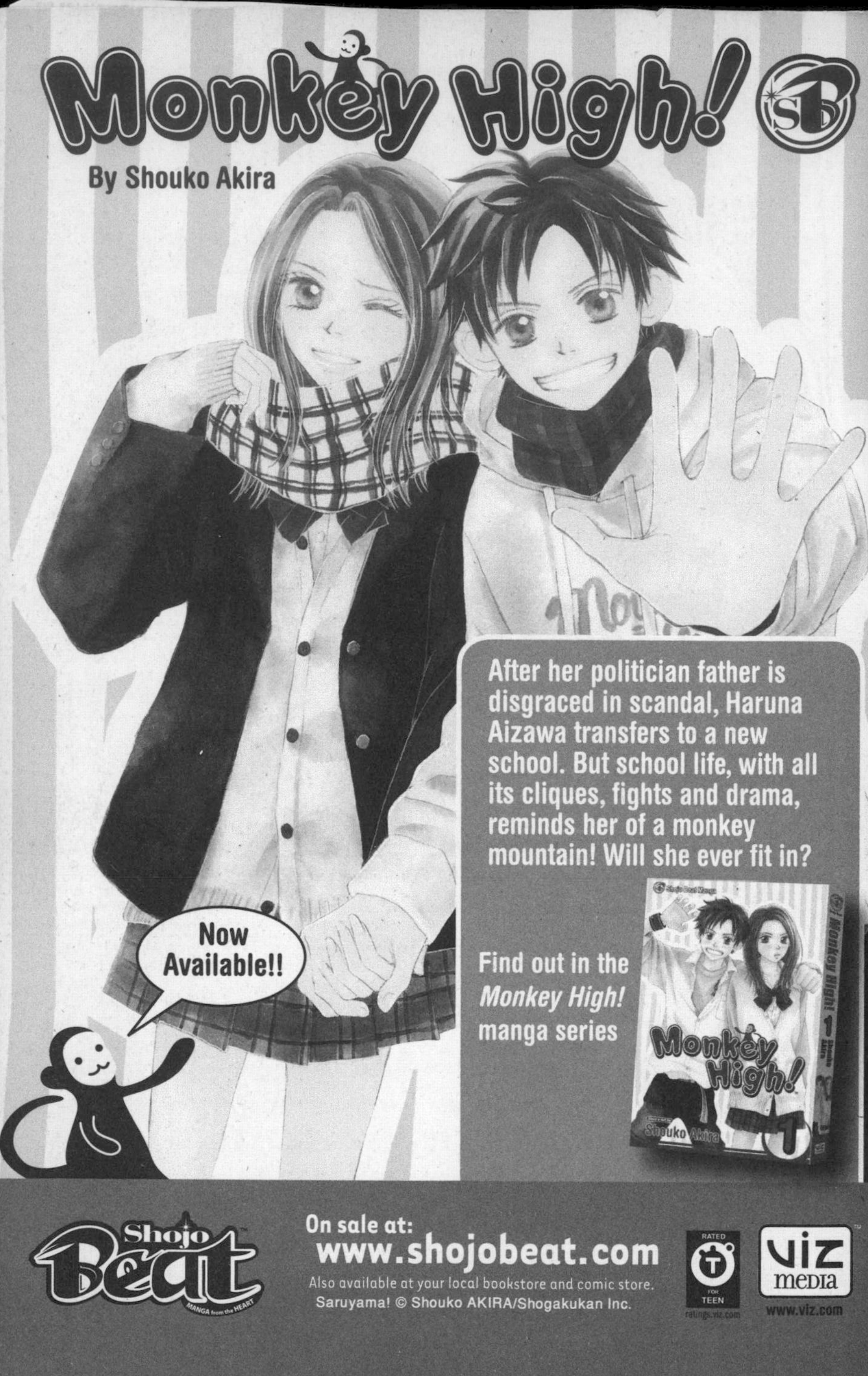
Monkey High!
By Shouko Akira
After her politician father is disgraced in scandal, Haruna Aizawa transfers to a new school. But school life, with all its cliques, fights and drama, reminds her of a monkey mountain! Will she ever fit in?
Find out in the *Monkey High!* manga series
Now Available!!
Monkey High!
Shouko Akira
1
Shojo Beat
MANGA from the HEART
On sale at:
www.shojobeat.com
Also available at your local bookstore and comic store.
Saruyama! © Shouko AKIRA/Shogakukan Inc.
RATED
T
FOR TEEN
ratings.viz.com
VIZ media
www.viz.com